PATHS OF ACCOMMODATION

Western African Studies

Willing Migrants
Soninke Labor Diasporas, 1848–1960
FRANÇOIS MANCHUELLE

El Dorado in West Africa
The Gold-Mining Frontier, African Labor, and
Colonial Capitalism in the Gold Coast, 1875–1900
RAYMOND E. DUMETT

Nkrumah & the Chiefs
The Politics of Chieftaincy in Ghana, 1951–60
RICHARD RATHBONE

Ghanaian Popular Fiction
'Thrilling Discoveries of Conjugal Life'
& Other Tales
STEPHANIE NEWELL

Paths of Accommodation
Muslim Societies and French Colonial Authorities in
Senegal and Mauritania, 1880–1920
DAVID ROBINSON

From Slavery to Free Labour in Rural Ghana*
Labour, Land & Capital in Asante, 1807–1956
GARETH M. AUSTIN

Between the Sea & the Lagoon*
An Eco-social History of the Anlo of Southeastern Ghana,
c.1850 to Recent Times
EMMANUEL AKYEAMPONG

'Civil Disorder is the Disease of Ibadan'*
Chieftaincy and Civil Culture in a Colonial City
RUTH WATSON

*forthcoming

Paths of Accommodation

*Muslim Societies and French Colonial Authorities in
Senegal and Mauritania, 1880–1920*

DAVID ROBINSON

Ohio University Press
ATHENS

James Currey
OXFORD

Ohio University Press
Scott Quadrangle
Athens, Ohio 45701

James Currey
73 Botley Road
Oxford OX2 0BS

British Library Cataloguing in Publication Data is available
ISBN 0-85255-457-5 (James Currey, paper)
ISBN 0-85255-458-3 (James Currey, cloth)

Library of Congress Cataloging-in-Publication Data
Robinson, David, 1938–
    Paths of accommodation : Muslim societies and French colonial authorities in
Senegal and Mauritania, 1880–1920 / David Robinson.
    p.   cm. — (Western African studies)
    Includes bibliographical references and index.
    ISBN 0-8214-1353-8 (alk. paper) — ISBN 0-8214-1354-6 (pbk. : alk. paper)
    1. Africa, French-speaking West—History—To 1884. 2. Africa, French-
speaking West—History—1884-1960. 3. Muslims—Africa, French-speaking
West—History. 4. France—Colonies—Africa—History. I. Title. II. Series.

DT541.65 .R63 2000
966.1'01—dc21   00-044614

Contents

Illustrations

Preface

IT IS DIFFICULT TO CONSTRUCT an appropriate preface for something so long in the making. This project began in 1984–85, with a Fulbright research fellowship to Senegal. At that time I began to collect information at archives in Dakar and Saint-Louis, and from informants in a number of locations, on the processes of accommodation of Muslim societies and French colonial authorities. I have continued the collecting, sifting, and writing process over the years since then, thanks in great part to grants from the National Endowment for the Humanities, the Social Science Research Council, the American Council of Learned Societies, and Michigan State University. At Michigan State I particularly appreciated the encouragement of Gordon Stewart, the department chair, and John Eadie, the college dean, and the opportunity to work with an able and collegial group of graduate students. The process of composition has involved numerous trips to Senegal, Mauritania, and France, and a long and fruitful collaboration with Jean-Louis Triaud, professor of history at the University of Provence. I have particularly benefited from working in various parts of the colonial archives at the Centre des Archives d'Outre-Mer in Aix-en-Provence. The richest archival source for this work remains, however, the Archives Nationales of Senegal in Dakar.

I would like to express my appreciation to the directors of those archival sources, and particularly to Saliou Mbaye, conservateur-en-chef of the Archives Nationales in Dakar, Jean-François Maurel, formerly conservateur-en-chef at the archives in Aix, and Abdoul Aïdara, director of the Centre de Recherche et Documentation du Sénégal in Saint-Louis, for their generous assistance on many occasions.

I have been fortunate to have numerous attentive readers of this manuscript, or portions of it. I would like to thank, for discussions and written feedback, Hilary Jones, Mohamed Mbodj, Abdel Wedoud Ould Cheikh, Ibrahima Abou Sall, Ibrahima Thioub, and my dear departed friend Mohammed Moustapha

Kane. I have benefited greatly from the close reading of Cheikh Babou, Louis Brenner, Tim Carmichael, Martin Klein, Ghislaine Lydon, Harold Marcus, and Richard Roberts. All of these colleagues have saved me from numerous errors and provided rich insight along the way. Responsibility for errors of fact and interpretation obviously do not lie with any of them. But the quality of the work has been significantly improved by the interventions of my principal editors at Ohio University Press, Gill Berchowitz, Nancy Basmajian, and Beth Pratt, copy editor Dennis Marshall, and my cartographer at Michigan State, Ellen White.

I wish finally to thank my muse during the composition and revision process, Glenfiddich—constant companion, patient puppy, sympathetic with a long-anticipated goal.

Acknowledgments

THE AUTHOR WISHES TO THANK the publishers of the following articles, which in revised form appear as chapters of this work.

"France as a 'Muslim Power,'" *Africa Today* (Indiana University) 46 (1999) (as chapter 4)

"Sa'd Buh, the Fadiliyya and French Colonial Authorities," *Islam et Sociétés au Sud du Sahara* 11 (1997) (as chapter 8)

"Shaikh Sidiyya Baba: Co-architect of Colonial Mauritania," *Islam et Sociétés au Sud du Sahara* 13 (1999) (as chapter 9)

"Malik Sy, Teacher in the New Colonial Order," in Triaud and Robinson, eds., *L'ascension d'une confrérie musulmane* (as chapter 10)

"The Murids: Surveillance *and* Accommodation," *Journal of African History* 40 (1999) (as chapter 11)

Note on Orthography

A BOOK OF THIS SORT REQUIRES working across a number of languages, cultures, and kinds of source material. I have used a simplified system for transcribing words in Arabic, Pular, Wolof, and French. For Arabic, Pular, and Wolof expressions I usually omit all diacritics, with the exception of an occasional 'ain (ʿ) or hamza ('). I have kept some French and Arabic expressions in italics throughout, while I have put others in italics only for the first citation. For the names of persons I have followed an anglicized form of the standard French version or transliteration, except for persons living in the last four decades. For place-names, I have followed the standardized names on French maps.

Abbreviations

ACLS	American Council of Learned Societies
AFPO	Affaires Politiques
ANM	Archives Nationales du Mali
ANS	Archives Nationales du Sénégal
ASSR	Archives des Sciences Sociales des Religions
BIFAN	*Bulletin de l'Institut Français (Fondamental) d'Afrique Noire*
BCAF/RC	*Bulletin du Comité d'Afrique Française, Renseignements Coloniaux*
BSOAS	*Bulletin of the School of Oriental and African Studies*, London
CAOM	Centre des Archives d'Outre-Mer, Aix-en-Provence, France
CEA	*Cahiers d'Etudes Africaines*, Paris
CEHSAOF	Comité des Etudes Historiques et Scientifiques de l'Afrique Occidental Française
CHEAM	Centre des Hautes Etudes Administratives sur l'Afrique et l'Asie Modernes, Paris
CNRS	Centre National de la Recherche Scientifique, Paris
CRDS	Centre de Recherche et Documentation du Sénégal, Saint-Louis
DSL	Dakar–Saint-Louis railway
EHESS	Ecole des Hautes Etudes en Sciences Sociales, Paris
FOSD	Feuille Officiel du Sénégal et Dépendancies
GG	Gouvernement-général or Gouverneur-général
IFAN	Institut Français (Fondemental) d'Afrique Noire
IJAHS	*International Journal of African Historical Studies*, Boston
ISASS	*Islam et sociétés du sud du Sahara*, Paris

JAH	*Journal of African History,* London
JCSL	"Journal de la Congrégation de Saint-Louis"
JO	Journal Officiel
MAE	Ministère des Affaires Etrangères, Paris
MC	Ministère des Colonies, Paris
MMC	Ministère de la Marine et des Colonies, Paris
MSD	*Moniteur du Sénégal et Dépendancies*
MSH	Maison des Sciences de l'Homme, Paris
ORSTOM	Office de la Recherche Scientifique et Technologique d'Outre-Mer
REMMM	*Revue du Monde Musulman et de la Méditerranée,* Aix
RHCF	*Revue de l'Histoire des Colonies Françaises,* Paris
RIM	République Islamique de la Mauritanie
RMM	*Revue du Monde Musulman,* Paris

Introduction

Samuel Huntington has suggested that the next great conflicts, in the aftermath of the cold war, will come between the West and "the rest."[1] Within "the rest" he places special emphasis on the threat from Islam, which he understands as a single civilization. His formulation, as well as the popular association of Islam and terrorism, does violence to the variety and complexity of Islamic practice, across all the continents. This book is about practice in one part of the Islamic world—the far western edge of the African Sahel, a region that I call the Senegalo-Mauritanian zone.

Islam and islamization have a long history in this region, but it is only in the last century that Muslim Sufi orders became closely linked to the cash-crop economy and the colonial regime. I am looking at the four principal orders, their leadership during the genesis of these links (from ca. 1880 to ca. 1920), and their "paths of accommodation" with the French colonial authorities. I am also interested in the "path of accommodation" pursued by the French with these Muslim communities. I use a wide variety of French, Arabic, and oral documentation, as well as frameworks adapted from social scientists such as Pierre Bourdieu and Antonio Gramsci.

In the four decades between 1880 and 1920, a remarkable development occurred in the southern portions of Mauritania and the northern and central parts of Senegal. Muslim Sufi orders, a venerable North and West African institution, became pillars of the colonial economy. Their leaders negotiated relations of accommodation with the Federation of French West Africa. In these relations, they preserved considerable autonomy within the religious, social, and economic realms, while abandoning the political sphere to their non-Muslim rulers. This was a striking development because the local inhabitants had a strong conscious-ness of belonging to the Dar al-Islam, the "world of Islam" in which Muslims ruled themselves.

The conditions for the overall development are complex, and they consume the first half of this book. In part 1, "The Framework," I set the stage with the decline of the anciens régimes in the nineteenth century and the emergence of a stronger colonial order (chapter 1). Part 2, "Bases of Accommodation," begins with a treatment of sources, discourses, and knowledge, concentrating on the frameworks, actors, and their use of that knowledge (chapter 2). I then look at how the French went about conquest and establishing colonial rule (chapter 3) and the ways in which they created a "practice" of relating to Muslim societies (chapter 4). I consider how the institutions of civil society (chapter 5) and the presence of a francophile Muslim community (chapter 6) helped prepare the ways of accommodation. Chapters 5 and 6 focus on Saint-Louis (called Ndar in Wolof and Hassaniyya), the town that served as the base for French expansion and became the capital of the territories of both Senegal and Mauritania.

In the process of developing these interrelated strands of explanation, I bring together three historiographies that emerged along separate lines. One is the precolonial story of the independent regimes of the Senegalo-Mauritanian zone, both those that might be called traditional aristocracies and those that claimed the mantle of Islamic states (see chapter 1). All were in various stages of decline in the nineteenth century. This narrative usually ends with resistance to conquest and capitulation to colonial rule.[2] Another sequence deals with the citizens of France: the French; the mulatto, or *métis*, population; and African in-habitants of the four communes of coastal Senegal, and how they practiced a certain form of Republican democracy amid the command structure of imperi-alism (see chapter 5). Their story is usually portrayed as preparation for the election of Blaise Diagne as the first African deputy of Senegal in 1914. The final sequence deals with the Muslim orders themselves, and particularly their marabout founders, as portrayed by disciples and later generations of admiring interpreters (see chapters 7–11). This material does not speak to the decline of the old regimes, much less the emerging colonial polity of which the orders were a vital part. I contend that one cannot understand these histories in isola-tion, and that all of them are necessary to explain the endurance of the paths of accommodation.

In part 3, "Patterns of Accommodation," I look at the most important Muslim configurations in the Senegalo-Mauritanian zone. The first group serves as an example of non-accommodation. The inheritors of the mantle of Al-Hajj Umar were too fragmented and captive of an ideology of resistance to establish a pattern of cooperation during this early period (chapter 7). I then try to do justice to the similarities and differences in the trajectories of four movements that were able to follow what I have called "paths of accommodation." These groups are placed in a certain chronological sequence and in an arc stretching from north to south. Saad Buh and the Fadiliyya (chapter 8) were the first to establish working and workable relations with the colonial regime and economy, out of a base in southwestern Mauritania. Sidiyya Baba and his network (chapter 9) fashioned a more spectacular collaboration at the end of the century in the same zone. Malik Sy and his Tijaniyya disciples (chapter 10) moved more steadily into the colonial orbit in the older peanut basin at the turn of century.[3] At about that time, the Muridiyya (chapter 11) were working their way into the economy of the newer peanut basin, even as Amadu Bamba was living in a French-imposed exile.

By the end of World War I and the death of the four marabout founders (*grands marabouts,* in colonial parlance), the new colonial order was in place.[4] It included the very hierarchical French structure and the maraboutic orders linked to the peanut economy, and even a spokesman for the Umarian network, in the person of Seydu Nuru Tal.[5] The administrators relied heavily on their Muslim collaborators, even though they had no official roles within the regime. This reliance was consistent with the evolution of the relationship, and very different from the experience of most African subjects under the command system that was French West Africa. It would not be too much to call this change, however gradual and fitful, a revolution in colonial rule and Muslim practice.

In preparing this work I have paid close attention to the particular cultures, developments, and sources of the region. While I have not conducted the research or analysis with a specific theory in mind, I have used themes and frameworks that have explanatory power across the chapters. I introduce them here and return to them in the conclusion.

The first theme is the close relationship between *knowledge and power,* and between presumed knowledge and presumed power. The main documentation in this case deals with the French. They accumulated a growing array of letters and reports, commissioned new missions and studies, and established enduring interpretations and priorities about their situation and alliances. These commentaries were often communicated orally, or became unwritten assumptions, making them difficult to trace. As this body of written material and oral commentary accumulated, as forms were created for the regular collection of information on chiefs and marabouts, the French gained more confidence in their ability to explain, predict, and control. By the time Paul Marty, the Islamicist who worked in the government-general of Dakar from 1912 to 1921, published his volumes on Islam, that confidence had reached an all-time high. The systems and stereotypes called *Islam noir* and *Islam maure* were securely in place.[6]

But it is important to qualify this knowledge and this power. The French interest in knowing was very practical. It was focused on finding enduring alliances, maintaining order, and securing support for the colonial economy. If they obtained information that led obviously to disaster, they would reevaluate it along with the informants and methods of accumulation.[7] But most of the time, the data and perspectives approximated their expectations. African informants, the mediators and disseminators of information, were crucial at every juncture. It was not easy for the French to verify what they were saying, and the informants learned to manipulate the system.[8] They knew what kind of information was sought, needed, and believed, and how to integrate their own interests with that information.

The chiefs, marabouts, and other actors at the top of the social pyramid learned the same lessons. They had their own informants, produced their own propaganda, and came to know the French in their own ways. Indeed, all sides of the action worked with partial knowledge and revised it, within the parameters of their assumptions, stereotypes, and experience. All of this presents the historian with a particular problem: sorting through the layers of knowledge, not so much to find the "real" core at the bottom but to understand each formulation, its purpose and audience, discern the interactions, and interpret the results.

All of this is to stress the importance of human agency. The social and political structures determined much of the course of events and conditioned knowledge and action. But the individual actors, be they informants, chiefs, governors, merchants, or marabouts, played critical roles as well. The most effective agents were those who recognized the close relations of knowledge and power, the forms in which to present knowledge, and the limitations and possibilities for their own action. The most visible were always men, and what is most acutely missing from the sources and the narrative are women and their agency.

A related theme is the *construction of identities*. Individuals established genealogies, narratives, and images of themselves that helped them pursue their goals. This is particularly evident with the African and European "agents" introduced in the chapters that follow. Ruling classes, commercial elites, and ethnic collectivities were also constructing identities, often in opposition or distinction from their neighbors, allies, and enemies. Typically, the image makers assigned some sort of superiority or distinction to themselves.

The French, as relative newcomers to the region, accepted many images mediated by others. They often took terms and identities from the inhabitants of Saint-Louis and the Wolof of Walo and Cayor. For example, they used *Tokolor* for the Futanke of the middle valley of the Senegal River and labeled them "fanatic" Muslims. These images usually concealed as much as they revealed. In fact, the French had a kind of religious and political ethnography (chapter 4) that served as a road map for much of their action in the nineteenth century. It yielded slowly and grudgingly to contrary evidence.

Many of their assumptions related to the main "nationalities" or ethnic groups featured in this story: the Moors, Fulbe, Futanke, and Wolof. Others related to race. The French placed great store in their own superiority, based on color, European identity, and national culture.[9] Conditioned by their own racism, they were prone to accept the racial distinctions that were expressed in the Senegalo-Mauritanian zone. The most telling example was the attitude of superiority that the Moors felt toward the black inhabitants: the Moors were *bidan,* "whites," not *sudan,* "blacks"; they were "Arabs," who were "natural" Muslims, not "recent" converts to the faith. When French and Moorish racial attitudes were joined, in the conquest of Mauritania and its incorporation into French West Africa, the consequences were enormous.

The third theme is *capital,* designating the accumulation of values of different kinds.[10] It is possible to distinguish, for my purposes, economic, social, and symbolic forms. Economic capital consists of the material possessions or production of an individual, family, or group. These possessions might be expressed in animals, food crops, gum or peanuts, slaves, farm land, oases, or urban real estate. Social capital refers to networks of relationships and skills that could be mobilized for particular needs and constituencies. Its most important manifestations during my period were the ability to cross cultural frontiers and to navigate the emerging colonial bureaucracy. Social capital had its roots in economic or symbolic capital, or both.

I use the term *symbolic capital* to denote the accumulation of prestige and power within a group marked by language, custom, kinship, or religion. It refers to the traditional and Islamic aristocracies of the interior (chapter 1), but also to the French administration to the extent that it developed a reputation for working with Muslim societies (chapter 4) and the Muslim traders who became emissaries for the compatibility of their faith with European rule (chapter 6).

Symbolic capital also refers to the qualities by which certain Muslim "professionals" were able to gain and exercise authority. This form could be vested in credentials of learning, Sufi achievement, the performance of miracles, genealogical descent, or important works—such as making the pilgrimage or leading the "jihad of the sword" (holy war). For each marabout and his following, several of these distinct but mutually reinforcing credentials were involved. I prefer *symbolic capital* to the term charisma, which bears too heavy a burden from its Weberian past and does not capture the complexity of repertory, reputation, and constituency of these marabouts.[11]

A critical dimension of these different forms of capital is their convertibility, indeed their constant conversion, and the ways in which one form enhanced the other. The most spectacular conversion was undoubtedly from symbolic to economic capital. One need only look at the recent decades of literature on the Muridiyya to see the fascination of scholars with this linkage.[12] But I maintain also that social capital, including the ability of marabouts to help their followers find their way in the new order, could generate the other forms, and that the "traditional" symbolic capital of the old ruling classes survived well into the colonial era—often with effective translation in the new economic order.

The various forms of convertible capital, responding to changing values within the changing local societies, provided considerable insulation from accusations of collaboration with the colonial authorities. Amadu Bamba's conflicts with the administration enhanced his value, and this capital in turn gave protection to the members of his inner circle who worked closely with the French. Saad Buh might be called *marabout chrétien,* but the charge rarely stuck for the critical mass of followers. Baba's intimate involvement in conquest might pose problems for subsequent generations of Sidiyya, but no significant embarrassment during the marabout's lifetime.

The symbolic capital that the French developed as a regime capable of working with Muslim societies (chapter 4) mitigated the need for the constant application of force. This mitigation suggests a final theme, of *hegemony and civil society.* The relationship of the colonial authorities with the prestigious Muslims of Saint-Louis, and then with leading figures of the interior, provided a certain invitation to accommodation. By the twentieth century, the French thought of themselves as a "Muslim power," a European imperial nation that knew how to relate to Muslim subjects and to respect their institutions of civil society. The most important institutions were the Sufi orders and Islamic law, as it was practiced through the courts and arbitration proceedings.[13] This "practice" was the companion of conquest and colonial rule and it played a significant role in the extension of French hegemony.

One might be tempted here to introduce the Gramscian notion of an "organic intellectual."[14] I would certainly argue that the four *grands marabouts* who successfully pursued paths of accommodation forged their careers amid the emerging colonial order. They developed social capital for their constituencies by the ability to solve problems and interpret solutions in terms of a continuing Dar al-Islam. But they were also careful to develop and protect a symbolic capital that was quite autonomous from the colonial regime and that the regime in turn came to accept.[15]

I also use *civil society* in a different sense. The Third Republic implemented part of the heritage of the French Revolution in the form of electoral institutions in the four communes. These institutions, and the citizens who competed to control them, created a political and commercial regime of their own—especially in Saint-Louis. That regime was not generally opposed to French conquest and colonial rule, but it sought participation in the process plus protection and benefit for its own economic and social capital—including its allies in the interior. The ancien régime of Saint-Louis, or some of its members, were thus often in conflict with the colonial regime (chapter 5). The effect was to create confusion but also opportunity for Muslims of the interior societies to negotiate relations of accommodation in the emerging colonial order. This "pluralism" of the French presence was a significant dimension of colonial hegemony.[16]

One might be tempted to introduce the concept of the "colonial state" as developed by Bruce Berman and John Lonsdale.[17] The administration of British Kenya, confronted by the conflicting demands of European settlers, European missionaries, and African farmers and pastoralists, assumed—however badly—the role of arbiter. It was caught between the requirements of developing capitalism and maintaining social order, and this could mean imposing restraint on some of its constituencies. But the French administration of Senegal and Mauritania played a very different role. While seeking to develop capitalism and maintain order, it was also the chief advocate of the consolidation and intensification of colonial rule. It was often arrayed against not only traditional and Islamic ruling classes, but also certain local Republican interests who advocated different forms of French suzerainty. Arbitration, to the extent that it existed, came from the heights of the French imperial and Republican regime in Paris, or from the system of rights and citizenship that stretched across metropole and empire. My story deals with the administration's consolidation, but through a "path of accommodation" in which colonial authorities were forced to face the pluralism of power and develop new ways to exercise hegemony.

─PART I─

The Framework

~I~

Space, Time, and Structure

BOTH THE SPACE AND THE PERIOD that I propose in this book fly in the face of conventional definitions. The name Senegalo-Mauritanian zone seems an anomaly. It ignores the obvious geographical boundary, the Senegal River, which became the political boundary erected between the territories and nation-states of Mauritania and Senegal. It flies in the face of the racial, color, and cultural distinctions that many Mauritanians and Senegalese have long held. Mauritania is dominated demographically and politically by the *bidan* (the whites). The *bidan* define themselves as Arab and as superior to the *sudan* (the blacks), whether they are referring to black Mauritanians in the southern part of the country or those living across the river in Senegal. Senegal has been dominated for centuries by blacks, who define themselves in many ways. Those definitions become racial when they look to the north and remember the intervention of the *bidan* in their lives. In general, that intervention is invoked negatively: as raids, kidnaping, and enslavement, on the one hand, or pretensions to superiority in Islamic learning and practice, on the other. The pogroms and expulsions of 1989 have intensified these distinctions of geography, nation-state, race, color, and culture.

So why persist in an expression such as the Senegalo-Mauritanian zone? Because it corresponds to a sphere of commercial and cultural relations that have existed for several centuries and well into the twentieth; because it corresponds to the hinterland of the French colonial center of Saint-Louis, which remained the capital of both countries, Mauritania and Senegal, into the 1950s;[1] and

11

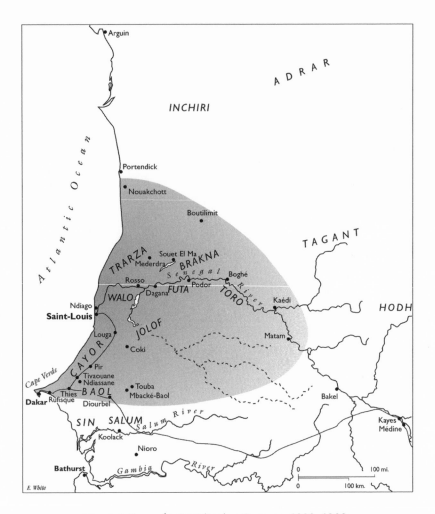

Map 1.1. Senegalo-Mauritanian Zone, ca. 1880–1920

because it corresponds to the reach of the seventeenth-century Islamic reform movement called Sharr Bubba, which defines much of the pattern of islamization down to the present. In this movement, Nasir al-Din mobilized his forces against "Arab" pillagers in southern Mauritania, but he briefly extended his influence through the river valley and the Wolof states to the south, thanks to indigenous Muslim reformers of the same mold.

The most important reason for this definition of space is that it frames "the paths of accommodation." From Saint-Louis, the French developed an Islamic practice built around their relations with their neighbors: Moors, Fulbe, Futanke, and Wolof. The Muslim clerics and merchants of the town symbolized the compatibility of European rule and Islamic practice across the nineteenth century. As the French demonstrated their determination to transform influence into control, these Muslims helped to secure the acquiescence if not the outright support of the marabouts and disciples who form the subject of the second half of this book. Even when colonial operations were centralized in Dakar in the early twentieth century, the experience of Islamic practice that the governor-general used was the one developed over many decades out of Saint-Louis. The literature of the Muslim "brotherhoods," so often equated with *Islam noir* and the French West African Federation, is really a product of the Senegalo-Mauritanian zone.[2]

The region did not have sharp boundaries, but rather a set of peripheries: Sin and Salum in the south, the Ferlo, the Upper Senegal valley, and Tagant-Hodh in the east, and the desert proper in the north. In general, the core expanded and created an ever-widening periphery. At a given moment, one part of the region might be subject to more intense occupation and exploitation; the north bank of the Senegal, for example, was the base of operations for the conquest of Mauritania for the decade before World War I.[3]

Then what is one to make of a period that extends from 1880 to 1920? The period straddles the end of precolonial and the beginning of colonial times. It brings together very different chronologies for the territories of Senegal and Mauritania. The conquest of Senegal was complete by the 1890s. The conquest of Mauritania took considerably longer, until the interwar period and the campaigns in the north, near the Spanish Sahara; it was only then that Mauritania acquired a civilian lieutenant governor in place of a military commander.

But my period makes sense if one looks at the processes of conquest, consolidation, resistance, and accommodation as gradual. The French proceeded in fits and starts, experimented, sought and changed coalitions, and accommodated to local realities. Their Senegalo-Mauritanian allies informed them, or tried to inform, counsel, cajole, and embarrass them; they had some significant sway in the process. The erstwhile opponents of the French fell by the wayside, or lost their constituencies, or kept those constituencies by finding a way of accommodation.

And for my region, the period makes particular sense. I am not focusing in this book on central or northern Mauritania, the upper valley of the river, or the southern portions of Senegal. The Senegalo-Mauritanian zone undergoes a dramatic transformation between 1880 and 1920, and each portion of the zone has a significant influence on the whole. The desert and the Sahel were "descending" to the south, ultimately to the peanut basin of Wolof Senegal. Muslim leaders ambitious for wealth, security, and the extension of the faith, both for themselves and their followers, had to find a connection to the peanut economy.

THE OLD ORDER

The social structures of the Senegalo-Mauritanian zone were remarkably similar, despite boundaries and variations of race, color, language, and ethnicity.[4] On the one hand, the political elites lived by providing security to their constituents in return for taxation and other forms of extraction. This function was expressed in codes of honor on which they were raised and remembered.[5] On the other hand, they survived by waging war, raiding, and confiscating the property of others—near and far. The confiscation included enslavement. Newly enslaved people moved into the local societies or the principal slave trades within West Africa, across the Sahara or across the Atlantic.[6] While the internal and transsaharan slave trades continued throughout the nineteenth and into the twentieth century, the transatlantic trade wound down by the mid 1800s.[7]

The pattern of security and extraction is usually attributed to the ruling classes of the states that have dominated the river valley and the Wolof regions since about 1500. The pattern of raiding and confiscation is more often assigned to the warrior classes of the southern desert, which operated in shifting confederations and a pattern of *siba* (institutionalized dissidence). In fact, most political classes of the Senegalo-Mauritanian zone operated in both ways. Their key constituents depended on some minimum of security and booty, and some primacy of access to weapons. When the elites were not able to provide this threshold of support, they were killed, overthrown, or driven into exile, where they would await another opportunity to seize power.

Commercial elites shared the space at the top of the social pyramid. Typically they were practicing Muslims. Many were also Muslim "professionals," persons learned in law and other forms of Islamic authority. Their knowledge strengthened their ability to operate across state, ethnic, and ecological boundaries and to deal with conflicts across the whole spectrum of society. But they often depended upon the warrior elites for protection. Indeed, some of them spent considerable time at the courts advising the rulers and arbitrating disputes.[8]

A large class of commoners, in many instances a majority, operated below the dominant elites. They were usually the main producers and thus the principal base for taxation. They provided grain, animals, and other goods for local consumption or export. Through their elders, these commoners might have some voice in the councils of power. The ruling elites had their origins among the commoners, and often they had complex networks of kinship and alliance down the social ladder.

Many of these commoner producers were Muslim. Through their piety, learning, and desire for security, some of them succeeded in creating autono-mous space at some distance from the courts. If this autonomy were threatened by the extraction or raiding of the political elites, these Muslims might resist on the basis of their faith and seek to create an Islamic state.[9] This was an impor-tant motif in the movement of Sharr Bubba, discussed below.

The next level of the social pyramid consisted of artisan classes or castes. They were a relatively small percentage of the population, but performed very critical skills in working metals, wood, leather, and other products.[10] Several branches of this category specialized in the transmission of knowledge to musical accompaniment. Called *griots* in the local French, these people were of-ten attached to and supported by the dominant classes. They learned by ap-prenticeship and then passed down chronicles, genealogies, and ethnographies that have framed much of the culture of the region. They were mediators and disseminators of knowledge par excellence, and their versions of events were rebroadcast by royal elites, the French, and Western-educated Africans through-out the nineteenth century.

The last category of the social pyramid consisted of slaves. The conventional distinction between those newly enslaved and those born into slavery operated across the whole zone, at least in theory and rhetoric, but this difference should not obscure the constantly changing cast of slavery. Some individuals and fami-lies got "out" through emancipation, escape, and migration, or by assimilating and reconstructing their identities. Others came "in"—commoners, royals, even occasional members of the artisan castes.[11] These "recruits" were obtained through wars, raids, and purchase, and were brought in to perform agricultural, pastoral, or domestic labor. Their owners included the political and commercial elites, commoners, some artisans, and the wealthier inhabitants of Saint-Louis. The Saint-Louisians used their slaves as boat crews, skilled tradesmen, militia, and in a variety of other ways. Some slaves—the crown slaves and personal bodyguards of the political and commercial elites—exercised considerable power through their patrons.[12] These *ceddo,* the name in Wolof and Pular, had a fearsome reputation for raiding, disorder, and the consumption of alcohol; they had the antithesis of the image of the pious and productive Muslim. On occasion they might even transform their weapons and fighting ability into the exercise of power in their own name.[13] Slavery remained a fundamental institution of Senegalo-Mauritanian societies through the nineteenth and into the twentieth centuries, and the internal slave trade continued to recruit new labor for the work to be done. The French made some inroads into the trading and raiding process, but their commitment to the abolition process was neither strong nor consistent.

Across the whole spectrum of classes lay patterns of individual and group clientship. The weaker or less prestigious needed patrons; the patrons in turn needed followers. Political and commercial elites formed coalitions to maintain their position and were constantly challenged by rivals or rival coalitions. They had to deal with threats of secession and movements of revolt, whether from Muslim producer communities or crown slaves. Successful challenges were more likely to yield change in personnel rather than structure, but some of them contained a sharp critique of the establishment. Occasionally these critiques produced ambitious replacements of the status quo.

THE PRACTICE OF ISLAM

The only viable religious practice in the Senegalo-Mauritanian zone for several centuries was Islam.[14] The integrity of the older religions, primarily ethnically based, had disintegrated. Masks, shrines, and priesthoods had virtually disappeared, even though many of their rituals and functions were adopted by marabouts. The political, commercial, and religious elites considered themselves Muslim and their lands part of the Dar al-Islam. From this vantage point they called the Europeans *Nasrani,* "Christians" and People of the Book, who should function as *dhimmi,* "protected" but tributary communities whose appropriate activity was trade, not war.[15]

If Islam was the dominant practice, it was manifested in a multiplicity of forms. Despite a growing sense of belonging to the Dar al-Islam, Muslim communities recognized no common political or religious authority. They had their marabouts, who were sometimes distinguished teachers and writers with significant reputations in the wider region. Many of the marabouts had credentials in the two main institutions of Muslim civil society set out in the introduction: Islamic law and Sufi orders. They arbitrated disputes, ran schools and initiation practices, received *ziyara,* or visits on special occasions, and organized tours to the home areas of their constituents. Some of their constituents were the political authorities of the various states.

It is difficult to generalize about the orientations of these marabouts to the political arena, but it is possible to distinguish three main positions. The first was maintaining distance from the centers of power while maximizing the autonomy of one's own Muslim community. The second was participation at the courts of the ruling classes, as counselors, judges, and imams. The third was the determination to change the system through the jihad of the sword—what I call in the section below the impulse of Islamic reform.

These positions were not mutually exclusive. Those who maintained their distance often found it necessary to intervene at court, if only to defend their constituents. Sometimes the first and the third options went together. Reformers would gain a following and sharpen a critique by their distance from the courts; then, if the situation permitted, they would attack the citadels of power and establish regimes that would be "Islamic"—by which they meant the application of the *shari'a,* divinely revealed Islamic law. It was the failure of the regimes that had been established by the third option, as well as decisive French intervention, that pushed the maraboutic generation featured in this book to find "paths of accommodation" with a new kind of political authority.

In the nineteenth century, the three positions and a considerable portion of Muslim identity were transmitted through Sufi affiliation. The older allegiance, initially restricted to a small elite, was called the Qadiriyya. The significant spread began in the late eighteenth century under the impetus of the Kunta family, and especially Sidi al-Mukhtar (1729–1811), who attracted disciples from a large region to his base north of Timbuktu.[16] One of his disciples was Sidiyya al-Kabir, the founder of the Sidiyya lineage featured in chapter 9 of this book. The Kunta and Sidiyya Qadiriyya expressed strong reservations about the exercise of power, but they developed commercial interests and social capital that made it impossible to ignore the political realm. Because of their learning and prestige, they were often called upon to intervene at the capitals, and even to settle succession disputes. Many of the leading Qadiriyya rejected the reform option, or at least its manifestation in jihad, out of their self-interest, their pessimism about changing the status quo, and their location in nomadic societies of the Sahara and Sahelian fringe. They were not opposed, however, to ties with the successful regimes created by Islamic reform movements in Futa Toro, Futa Jalon, Masina, and Hausaland.

Most of the leading Qadiriyya were *bidan* or Tuareg, and they often had a strong sense of racial and religious superiority to the *sudan,* the "black" Muslims.[17] For all of these reasons—the sense of superiority, the rejection of jihad, and the reputation for learning and Sufi prestige—the French sought out relationships with Qadiriyya communities in the nineteenth century. When the Qadiriyya saint and scholar Ma El Ainin led the resistance against their conquest of Mauritania, the French had to revise their assumptions about this Sufi order.

The rival Sufi affiliation in the nineteenth century was the Tijaniyya, which began in Algeria and Morocco in the late eighteenth and spread through Mauritania in the nineteenth century. In West Africa it became closely associated with reform and the jihad of the sword under the influence of Al-Hajj Umar in the 1850s (see below). The founder, Ahmad al-Tijani, claimed special revelations from the Prophet and from God that provided a more direct access to spiritual power, and this orientation was used by the emerging Tijaniyya leaders in West Africa to challenge the Qadiriyya establishment. It also led to intensive debate about the legitimacy of the Tijani claims to proximity to the sources of the faith.[18] The French, just as they linked the Qadiriyya with the anti-jihad impulse, associated the West African Tijaniyya with militant reform. They used this assumption to justify a number of military campaigns at the end of the nineteenth century.

Many of the debates within Senegalo-Mauritanian societies revolved around these affiliations and options about the appropriate Muslim relationship to power. It is possible to identify two main perspectives and protagonists: members of the political elite and their spokesmen, on the one hand, and clerics inspired by the reform impulse, on the other. The ruling elites and their supporters put the priority on honor and the arts of politics and war: they accepted the rituals of Islam but combined them with alcohol consumption, luxurious display, and the presence of women with men in public settings. Some marabouts supported this tradition or tried to change it from within. Accustomed to the vicissitudes of power, mindful of the difficulty of implementing Islamic law in a complex setting, they became defenders of the status quo. They bore the brunt of the sharpest criticism of the advocates of change.[19]

The reformers considered these combinations to be exploitative and syncretistic, if not "pagan." When they gained the attention of a wider audience, they attempted to establish an Islamic state.[20] In several sequences they did succeed in taking power. Success depended on a combination of the inspiration of previous reforms, good leadership, and a deterioration in material conditions—the convergence of extraction, violence, epidemics, and insecurity. Reformers were particularly outraged by one dimension of insecurity—the enslavement of Muslims for one of the operative slave trades—and they used it to mobilize support.[21]

The social pyramid described in the preceding section was shaken by a reform movement of the seventeenth century that framed the pattern of islamization and social relations for the next two hundred years.[22] Sharr Bubba was occasioned by the spread into the far western Sahara, from the fourteenth century on, of Arab nomadic groups, called the Banu Hassan. These groups made their way south, as far as the Senegal River, spread their version of spoken Ar-

abic *(hassaniyya)*, and established increasing domination over the indigenous inhabitants, who spoke a Berber language.

By the 1670s, Nasir al-Din, a scholar and warrior from the southwestern
part of today's Mauritania, rebelled against this domination and fashioned a coalition largely around the indigenous inhabitants. For a few years he established
an embryonic Islamic state and put the *hassan* on the defensive, portraying them
as "bandits" who did not practice the faith. His entourage of clerics, or *zwaya*,
recruited disciples in Futa Toro and the Wolof regions of Senegal, and these
followers were successful in exploiting local grievances and overthrowing—
however briefly—their ruling dynasties.

The traditional political elites regained power quickly, with some support
from the French trading interests based in Saint-Louis.[23] North of the river, the
hassan not only reasserted their domination but established emirates, confederations of tribes dominated by one "warrior" lineage.[24] The dominant division of
the *bidan* ruling classes has its origins, or at least its codification, in the final
victory of the warrior elite. In this arrangement the *hassan* dominated the political and military spheres, while the *zwaya* controlled religious instruction, adjudication, commerce, and agriculture. Both enjoyed the support of tributaries
and slaves.

South of the river, some of the disciples survived and transmitted their
visions of an Islamic society to future generations. They constituted a kind of
international reform network in the region.[25] Like their counterparts in other
parts of the West African savanna, they operated in autonomous spheres or at
the frontiers of states. They used their distance from the courts to organize and
train followers. Over time, those communities of disciples might threaten the
established political elites. They played a significant role in casting Islam as a
potential ideology of resistance to the abuse of power.

The impact of Sharr Bubba lasted well beyond the seventeenth century,
thanks especially to its interpreters. The *zwaya* writers themselves, beginning
with a scholar of the mid eighteenth century named Muhammad al-Yadali,
kept the tradition alive.[26] In so doing they emphasized their piety, learning,
and commitment to a Muslim society. It provided a framework for understanding the *bidan* and their division into ruling classes, commercial elites, and tributaries. Sidiyya Baba and his contemporaries of the late nineteenth century
offered this interpretation to the colonial authorities, who were in the process
of building colonial Mauritania around selected *zwaya* lineages. The fit between African perspective and European need was perfect, or at least so it
seemed for several decades.

LATER MOVEMENTS OF ISLAMIC REFORM

Several reform movements had some success after Sharr Bubba. The most influential effort at the level of state and society came in the middle valley of the Senegal in the late eighteenth century. The almamate, as the regime came to be known, had a strong impact on the Islamic culture of Futa Toro. In the nineteenth century, the Futanke were associated with strong traditions of piety and learning.[27] Some of them migrated to the west and south and became active agents of islamization in Saint-Louis and the Wolof areas, where a claim to Futanke origin was highly prized.

The "Islamic revolution" of Futa Toro had a close relationship with Nasir al-Din and his Wolof and Fulbe disciples.[28] The reformers, called *torobbe* (seekers), emerged as a group in the mid eighteenth century. They were closely related by marriages contracted in their grandparents' generation—almost certainly the product of participation in the earlier reform movement. They studied and traveled throughout the region where Sharr Bubba had had its strongest partisans.[29] By the 1760s, they were complaining about the corruption of the court and the inability of the local Denyanke regime to maintain stability and security, especially against the raids of *hassan* warriors and their Moroccan allies.[30]

A cleric named Sulaiman Bal led the first phase of the reform movement. He criticized the failures of the Denyanke and led a number of campaigns against the court and the *bidan* raiders. When he died in battle, the torobbe swore allegiance to Abdul Kader Kane as their first imam, or almamy, the head of their new Islamic state.[31] Abdul Kader was a kinsman and graduate of Pir, the school in Saniokhor where a number of the torobbe had studied. He had traveled and taught across southern Mauritania and northern Senegal. After his inauguration in the late 1770s, he established mosques, schools, and courts in the villages to encourage literacy and the practice of the faith. These institutions of Muslim civil society deepened the Islamic culture of the Futanke and made them leaders in the processes of islamization in the wider region. Abdul also founded settlements at the key river fords, to provide protection; his policy was to stop the *hassan* raids at the river, rather than actively to encourage settlement on the north bank.[32] Finally, he signed treaties with the French that prohibited the enslavement of Muslims and spelled out the "customs" the French should pay for the right to trade in the river valley.[33]

Almamy Abdul maintained a strict and personalized control over events and relations in Futa. Over time, he came into conflict with his allies of the first hour, powerful regional lords from Fulbe families who were close to older traditions of pastoralism and autonomy. They did not share the commitment to islamization, and by the early 1800s they were ready to revolt.[34] On the external front, Abdul enjoyed initial success. He engineered a successful campaign against the *hassan* leader Eli Kowri, head of the Trarza Confederation and ally of Moroccan forces in the Sahara. Then he resumed the mission of Sharr Bubba: as the patron of militant Muslim minorities in the Wolof areas, he imposed his will on the ruling dynasties.[35]

The momentum shifted abruptly. In 1797, the king of Cayor defeated Abdul's army, destroyed the local reform communities, and took Abdul prisoner for several months.[36] A short time later, the almamy tried to impose his will in the other direction, against the Fulbe regime of Bundu. He incurred the wrath of the dominant power of the upper valley, the Bamana of Karta, and lost the support of some of his most respected Muslim contemporaries. Mukhtar wuld Buna, a *zwaya* scholar who had praised the victory over Eli Kowri, had this to say:

> As for me, I was disgusted with the religion of the Moors and came among the Blacks to learn their religion and abandoned the thinking of people who don't believe at all. But you [Almamy Abdul], you have convoked this man [the almamy of Bundu] in the name of Islam [and sentenced him without hearing his testimony and then killed him]. Why have you acted in this way?[37]

The almamy's brittle personality and advancing age, the growing internal opposition, and the desire of Karta for revenge brought Abdul down in 1807.[38] His death was treated as a martyrdom, at the hands of "pagans" and "apostates." It marked the end of strong central government and the beginning of domination by regional lords. But the effect of the fundamental reforms did survive. Futanke preserved a strong sense of Islamic identity, education, and commitment to jihad, and maintained ties with militant Muslim communities across the Senegalo-Mauritanian zone.[39]

If the torobbe and Almamy Abdul produced the most fundamental islamization in the Senegalo-Mauritanian zone, another citizen of Futa produced the most controversial Muslim movement two generations later. Umar Tal was born at the end of the eighteenth century. Using the pilgrimage and affiliation to the Tijaniyya Sufi order, he built a following in the mid nineteenth century. He channeled that following into a jihad against "paganism," incarnated in the Bamana states of Segu and Karta.[40] The military campaigns required massive recruitment, which Umar conducted with particular intensity in his homeland.

Three dimensions of the Umarian jihad are critical for this study. The first

was the imposition of an Umarian and exclusivist interpretation on the Tijaniyya order in West Africa. Umar made the pilgrimage for three successive seasons (1828–30). One of his principal motivations was to spend time with
Muhammad al-Ghali, a North African appointed by Ahmad al-Tijani to be his
khalifa (deputy) in the Hijaz. Ghali imparted the secrets of the order to Umar,
including a license to serve in turn as the khalifa for West Africa, use all the
rituals and recitations, and appoint his own *muqaddam* (agents). Upon his return,
Umar wrote up this experience, took charge of spreading the order at the expense of the older affiliation of the Qadiriyya, and linked it to the jihad. Like
the founder, he considered the Tijaniyya to be the last and greatest of the Sufi
orders, incompatible with other affiliations.[41]

The second dimension was maintaining social distance from European authorities and translating that distance into controlled forms of resistance. Umar
and his men had several tense encounters with the regime of Governor Léon
Faidherbe during the 1850s. Most of them were skirmishes, but two merit mention here. The first sequence occurred in 1855, after the French imposed an embargo on arms sales in the Upper Senegal, as a way to protect their local allies
from the Umarian jihad. The Futanke reformer retaliated with the confiscation
of French merchandise. When some Muslim traders complained, Umar wrote the
"sons of Ndar" to warn them against association with Europeans who rejected
tributary status and sought to dominate Muslim societies.[42]

The other confrontation occurred in 1857, when Umar attacked the fort of
Medine, which cut into his lines of supply and recruitment in the Upper Senegal.
The jihadists laid siege to the fort at the height of the dry season in April 1857,
but Faidherbe lifted the blockade in July, when he was able to get gunboats to
the upper river. Faidherbe became the hero and "founder" of Senegal and the
prototypical governor for his successors. Umar became the incarnation of Islamic
resistance to European intrusion. From this moment on, his recruitment was
framed as *hijra* (emigration) from polluted areas of European influence.[43] *Tijaniyya* became synonymous in the French lexicon with *fanatic* and *Tokolor,* the
name the French gave to the Futanke, or inhabitants of the middle valley of the
Senegal River. I discuss the implications of these images of Faidherbe, Umar, and
Tokolor in chapters 2, 4, 6, and 7.

The third dimension of the Umarian jihad relates to its last years (1862–
64). Al-Hajj Umar turned his wrath against another Muslim Fulbe state,
Masina, because of its support for the bamana of Segu. When letters and ulti-
matums failed, Umar invaded and ruled over the area for about a year. Then a
surging revolt, supported by the Kunta network, brought his downfall and

death. The campaign, revolt, and subsequent struggles produced destruction throughout the Middle Delta of the Niger. The Masina operation was questioned by many observers, in ways that the campaigns against "paganism" never were. It has gone down in many annals as an example of *fitna,* "civil strife" within the Islamic community.[44] The Masina debacle also forced Umar's oldest son, Amadu Sheku, into reigning over the vast unstructured conquests with very little preparation. This "Tokolor Empire," as the French were wont to call it, survived until Archinard's conquests of the early 1890s, but its reputation was forever tarnished by the Masina campaign and the struggles that Amadu waged against his brothers and other rivals.[45]

The three Islamic movements described thus far have no peer: Sharr Bubba as a symbol of a social charter; Futa Toro in terms of creating a civic culture; and the Umarian commitment to destroy "paganism" and resist European expansion. But two later efforts provoked even sharper conflicts, military and ideological, among those bidding for control of the peanut basin—the heart of what was becoming the colonial political economy in the late nineteenth century.

Ma Ba Diakhu posed a direct challenge to his contemporaries and the colonial authorities in the 1860s.[46] Drawing on Futanke and Umarian connections, Ma Ba crystallized the grievances of many Muslims about the oppression and raiding practiced by the courts of Mandinka, Serer, and Wolof states between the Gambia and Senegal Rivers. He waged a series of successful campaigns against his enemies for several years, arousing the concern of the French about the security of the peanut basin. In the process, he had a significant impact on two important Wolof royals, Lat Dior Diop and Albury Ndiaye, and on two religious leaders of the next generation, Amadu Bamba and Malik Sy.[47] But Ma Ba did not succeed in establishing a new social order; he died in 1867 in a battle against the ruler of Sin, and much of his potential impact was lost.

A third Tijaniyya movement had a more negative impact on the commitment to a Muslim state and society. The Madiyanke, sons of a self-proclaimed Mahdi from Toro, mobilized a large following in the wake of the cholera epidemic of 1867–68.[48] From a base in Jolof, they moved freely through western and central Futa Toro, Ndiambur, and Cayor. They threatened the eastern flow of Muslims recruited by Amadu Sheku for his campaigns against his brothers,[49] producing the first public fissures within the Tijaniyya order in the region. They threatened a good portion of the peanut basin, creating considerable anxiety in the colonial and commercial milieus of Saint-Louis.[50] Where Ma Ba began to forge an alliance between marabout and younger aristocracy, the Madiyanke tended to drive traditional chiefs into the arms of the administration.

Lat Dior and Albury Ndiaye, the erstwhile clients of Ma Ba, now joined forces with the colonial regiments. At the battle of Samba Sadio in 1875, the coalition defeated the militants and destroyed most of its leadership. The impact of the defeat resonated through northwestern Senegal. In Cayor, two Muslim clerics debated the legitimacy of confiscating the booty of the Madiyanke, and by implication the proper relationship of Muslims to power. The senior figure was Ma Diakhate Kala, *qadi* at the court of Lat Dior; he held that by claiming to be a prophet, the principal Madiyanke leader had forfeited his Islamic identity. His young protagonist was Amadu Bamba, who maintained that the Madiyanke were Muslims who had been misunderstood.[51] Their quarrel echoed the debate about the legitimacy of the Umarian attack on Hamdullahi.

The Muslim reform efforts articulated well the failures of the old order, but they failed to put anything better in its place. Sharr Bubba was a memory and an inspiration. The Umarians were alive, but they waged jihad against pagans to the east and gave little attention to the transformation of society. Ma Ba put little of his vision into practice; his successors operated as petty chiefs, indistinguishable from the other ruling lineages. The almamate of Futa Toro was weakened by internal dissension and the effort to impose its will on other states. The Madiyanke mounted the most ambitious attack on chieftaincy and the colonial order, but they were literally eliminated from contention in 1875.[52] The symbolic capital of Islamic reform movements had virtually disappeared by the late nineteenth century.[53]

Islam was the actively practiced religion of the great majority in the late nineteenth century, and there was no rival rallying cry. But Islam meant different things to different people. Court clerics such as Ma Diakhite might be compromised, but reformers had not been able to deliver on more just or secure regimes. They were just as likely to create dynasties as their traditional counterparts, and in the second generation to engage in infighting and exploitation. After the mid nineteenth century, they also ran the risk of brutal opposition if they threatened vital French interests.

Futa Toro ceased to be a model for other areas after the martyrdom of Almamy Abdul and the massive exodus of young recruits with Shaikh Umar.[54] The Umarian call to jihad against "paganism" and hijra from European pollution resonated in the Senegalo-Mauritanian zone, but it was not a very viable option for most people.[55] The Tijaniyya was no solution. The Umarians asserted their right to control of the Sufi order, but the Madiyanke and *bidan* practitioners contested their claim.[56] Muslim royals, such as Lat Dior and Albury, were sensitive to the faith in ways that perhaps their ancestors were not, but they could not deliver on demands for rectitude and social justice.

In short, the traditional aristocracies and the Islamic movements that were designed to change them were difficult to distinguish in the nineteenth century, and it is appropriate to call all of them *anciens régimes*.[57] The way was open to explore new forms of Islamic symbolic capital, including links between corporate Sufism and the peanut economy and between Islamic practice and European overrule.

ANCIENS RÉGIMES IN THE LATE NINETEENTH CENTURY

The relevant experience for the marabouts and orders featured in the second half of this work is that of the late nineteenth century. During those decades, the traditional and Islamic states were still recognizable. Most of the dynasties were in their conventional capitals, with their retainers, boundaries, and configurations of identity. Subjects still looked to the ruling lineages to resolve issues of security and prosperity. Merchants of all stripes visited the courts, paid tribute, and worked the markets. Marabouts were present, sometimes in official capacities as judges, sometimes as informal counselors. They defended their own interests, participated in discussions about public responsibility, and intervened to end strife and insecurity for their constituents. Saad Buh, Sidiyya Baba, Malik Sy, and Amadu Bamba were certainly involved in such discussions, even while keeping a certain distance from the exercise of power.[58]

But in fact little remained of the power and grandeur of an earlier day. The slave trades had taken their toll of the population and its loyalty. The people found that the court could be as dangerous as the external invader. The French had effective control of the waterways and could mount significant short campaigns on land, even during the "pause" between the expansion led by Governor Faidherbe (1854–61, 1863–65) and the resumption under Governor Brière de l'Isle (1876–81). French control of the export-import economy was even more compelling.

Trarza lay at the northwestern end of the Senegalo-Mauritanian zone. The Awlad Ahmad min Daman had developed significant power in the eighteenth century, with some help from the Moroccan sultanate.[59] Muhammad Lhabib replicated that pattern in the nineteenth century (1827–60); he married the leader of one of the two principal matrilineages of Walo and laid the basis for control of the Wolof province. But intense civil war, strong French opposition, and a campaign led by Faidherbe put an end to overt Trarza claims. The assassination of Lhabib began a long series of struggles among his sons and grandsons in which the French, the *zwaya,* and other groups inevitably became involved. Each *hassan* faction sought to accumulate enough wealth through trade goods and raiding to win the turban of power, but this produced more competition, violence, and insecurity.[60] Well before Xavier Coppolani began his campaign of "pacification" in 1902, the French administration was seeking a solution to chronic Trarza instability.

Brakna, the confederation just to the east, was also badly divided. Contenders in the ruling lineages found support in stronger neighbors: the Trarza *hassan* to the west, the Idawaish confederation to the east, and the French interests along the river, expressed particularly through the fort and commandant of Podor.[61] The Sidiyya lineage of eastern Trarza had considerable sway in the Brakna arena; Sidiyya al-Kabir, grandfather of Sidiyya Baba, is remembered for significant intervention in favor of *bidan* unity, against the interests of Saint-Louis and its candidate for the emirate.[62] The administration did exercise more effective authority among the Brakna than they could mount in the Trarza sphere, particularly during the reign of Sidi Eli (1858–93).

Futa Toro had no effective central leadership after the death of Almamy Abdul and the recruitment of Shaikh Umar. The French added to the problem by a policy of "dismemberment" in which they established protectorates under provincial dynasties. They were most effective in the west, around Dagana and Podor, the two market towns that could be reached by boat during the entire year.[63] Only in central Futa, where Abdul Bokar Kane built his domain as a regional elector and warlord (see chapter 6), was it possible to maintain some of the independence and pride of the almamate.[64] Abdul accumulated a host of enemies over his long period of domination (ca. 1860–90), and these people actively collaborated with the French to eliminate him and establish colonial protectorates in 1891.

Walo, the northernmost Wolof state, was under a French protectorate from the time of Faidherbe, but it also remained subject to heavy pressures from Trarza to the north and Jolof and Cayor to the south. It was not a particularly rich agricultural area, because of the salt deposits in the soil, and consequently was never very densely populated. But it had a strategic location. It constituted the outskirts of Saint-Louis, the lower valley of the river, the meeting point of caravans moving north and south, and a place of refuge for *bidan* communities fleeing from strife in Mauritania. Walo was also the setting for Yamar Mbodj, the most effective colonial chief in the last decades of the nineteenth century. He combined training in French with traditional legitimacy; he was able to satisfy both subjects and colonial overlords.[65]

In Cayor, fast becoming the heart of the peanut basin, the French had an even stronger interest than in Futa Toro and Walo. Faidherbe intervened very actively in the 1850s and 1860s, establishing protectorates over the northern and southern provinces and a coastal telegraph line. In the 1870s, his successors established a workable compromise with Lat Dior, after the damel returned from his tutelage with Ma Ba.[66] In the 1880s, the administration and French commercial interests built the Dakar–Saint-Louis (DSL) railway to speed the development of peanut production and take advantage of the superior port facilities of Dakar. The project, completed in 1885, ran through the heart of Cayor and spelled the end of autonomy of the ancien regime. Lat Dior recognized this, after initially signing on to the plan, and died in a skirmish with French forces in 1886. This last act, as distinguished from the numerous compromises of his earlier career, has been elevated to the level of national resistance by Senegalese historians.[67]

Jolof and Baol were more peripheral zones for the French in the 1880s. Albury Ndiaye, the other royal apprentice of Ma Ba, was able to take the Jolof throne with French support after the defeat of the Madiyanke in 1875. Thereafter, he struggled to balance the interests and independence of his subjects against the growing encroachments of the French. In 1890, the administration was ready to move against this pocket of autonomy, driving Albury into exile in the form of a hijra.[68] At the same time, the colonial authorities established a protectorate over Baol, a Wolof province that had often been under the jurisdiction of Cayor. They selected a member of the royal family to serve as the chief but assigned no official to supervise his stewardship.[69] By the mid 1890s, the French had created a network of chiefs across Jolof, Baol, and Cayor, linking up with the system in Walo, of which Yamar Mbodj was a part. They were then in position to expand peanut production in a major way and to consider extending rail links in new directions.

Many people lived at the margins of these declining states or in areas that were under no governmental control. Foremost among them were the pastoral and semipastoral Fulbe. They provided for their own security. Their economy was based principally on cattle, but they raised other animals and often engaged in some farming. They exchanged meat and dairy products with the sedentary agricultural population and worked out means of resolving conflicts when they moved their herds through farming areas. Many of these Fulbe, especially those living in Walo, supplied meat and dairy products to the population of Saint-Louis (see chapter 5). *Bidan* pastoralists also moved across the region, or took refuge south of the river during periods of conflict in Trarza and Brakna. Other *bidan* settled permanently in Senegal, as teachers, farmers, and traders who took on some dimensions of Wolof identity.[70]

THE EMERGING POLITICAL ECONOMY IN THE SENEGALO-MAURITANIAN ZONE

The indigenous economy of the savanna and the sahel was rooted in agricultural and pastoral production and associated artisan skills. Enslavement and slavery were increasingly tied to production in two principal ways. On the one hand, slave labor played an increasing role in production. On the other, the process of enslavement, through war, raids, or kidnaping, disrupted the productive process. The newly enslaved could be traded into the internal, transsaharan and transatlantic trades, as outlined above. In the nineteenth century, the slave trades, and especially the transatlantic traffic, was labeled illegitimate (i.e., compared with the "legitimate" trade in nonhuman products in the region and in Africa as a whole). But the abolitionist ideology was applied inconsistently, and rarely against the institution of slavery itself. Consequently, owners used their slaves to produce "legitimate" goods—gum and peanuts in the case of Senegalo-Mauritanian zone—throughout the nineteenth century.[71]

When the French returned to their West African installations after the Napoleonic wars, they were interested in the "legitimate" product of gum, found in the acacia "forests" close to the river valley.[72] Gum had a number of industrial and medicinal uses in the developing European economies. French and African merchants, operating out of Saint-Louis, encouraged local producers to supply gum to trade fairs at particular sites, called *escales,* along the river. In exchange, they furnished arms, other manufactures, and *guinées,* a blue cloth that served as currency and clothing in the zone. The principal local beneficiaries of the gum trade were the *bidan:* the *zwaya* organized the production through their slaves and clients, while the *hassan* provided protection for the caravans en route to the escales. Most of the best gum was brought from Trarza and Brakna trees to markets in the Dagana and Podor areas.[73] Much of the economy of Saint-Louis, as well as that of Trarza, Brakna, Futa, and Walo, was linked to the gum trade in the first half of the nineteenth century. Production remained significant until about 1900, when the Kordofanian gum of the Sudan became dominant.

The interest in gum was compatible with the metaphor that the indigenous

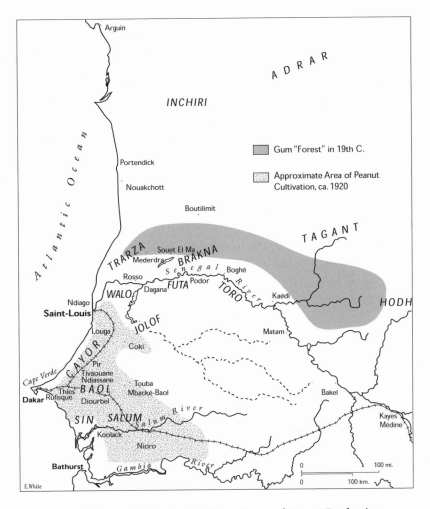

Map 1.2. Senegalo-Mauritanian Zone: Gum and Peanut Production

inhabitants used to describe Europeans during much of the nineteenth century. The Nasrani ("Christians") were "masters of the water," but not of the land. They could control the rivers and the sea, they were good at trade, but they did not know how to fight. Gaspard Mollien, a Frenchman who explored the areas south of the river in 1818, recorded a typical version of this perspective:

> These Negroes believed that Europeans live exclusively upon the water; that they have neither land, houses nor cattle; they added that the rivers and great waters belong to us, in the same manner as all the earth is their patrimony. I therefore concluded that this was the reason why white men alone were

forced to pay imposts to Negro kings, who regard them as their tributaries;
They had not a high opinion of our courage, affirming that we did not even
know how to fire a musket.[74]

This image began to change in the mid nineteenth century, when Governor
Faidherbe, with significantly increased resources, demonstrated the French capacity to fight and become "masters of the land." The people of Cayor, who
bore the brunt of several offensives, called him the "great warrior," in tribute to
this prowess.[75]

The main reason for the Cayorian offensives was a new economic interest.
In the 1840s the French began to encourage the production of peanuts.[76] The
peanut had an even wider range of industrial and pharmaceutical uses than
gum and could be grown in the sandy soils near the coast and the ports of
Saint-Louis, Rufisque, and Dakar. By the 1860s the total value of exports exceeded that of gum; it was evident that the economic future lay in the peanut
basin. Groups from all over the Senegalo-Mauritanian zone began to converge
on the production and marketing process.

One of the most signal growers was Bu Kunta, a *bidan* and descendant of
the famous Kunta lineage. His father had settled in southern Cayor, at Ndiassane in the traditionally Muslim province of Saniokhor. Bu Kunta, using his genealogical credentials instead of Islamic learning to develop symbolic capital,
acquired a considerable number of disciples and fields; he set the first to working the second. His combination of Muslim identity, Sufi community, and insertion into the peanut economy set the stage for the maraboutic orders of the
early twentieth century.[77]

Another important investment came in the form of beasts of burden supplied by pastoralists for the harvesting season. To get the unshelled nuts from
farms to markets and ports, a large number of animals were needed. The favored beast, at least in northern Cayor, was the camel, and *bidan* pastoralists began coming in with their herds on an annual basis in the late nineteenth
century.[78] This practice continued well after the introduction of the DSL railway, at which point the animals took the crops to the nearest depot, which was
called a rail escale by analogy with the river markets for gum.

The rail itself produced a dramatic rise in the production of peanuts and in
profits for the French commercial houses. It made the administration more eager to control and protect the Wolof zones against the slightest provocation.
The governors and governors-general also began to plan around the superior

port facilities of Dakar, in contrast to the bar and silting problems near Saint-Louis. The new orientation led them to consider expansion directly to the east of Dakar and Rufisque, into the areas of Baol and Salum. In the early twentieth century, this shift was translated into a second railway, the one that extended east from Thies to Bamako in the Soudan.[79]

SAINT-LOUIS AS COMMERCIAL CAPITAL

The headquarters for the commerce of gum and peanuts in the nineteenth century was Saint-Louis. At the same time, it was the headquarters for the French colonial administration and armed forces. In the 1850s, Ndar (to use the Wolof and *hassaniyya* name) was a town of about fifteen thousand inhabitants divided into a mixture of racial, cultural, and functional categories (see table 1.1).[80]

Table 1.1. Population of Saint-Louis in the Mid Nineteenth Century

French merchants and dependents:	about 200
French administrative and military personnel:	about 800
Métis—merchants, traders, administrators, and dependents, largely Christian and French in culture:	about 1,000
Africans, largely Wolof and Muslim and connected to trade:	about 6,000
Recently freed Africans, of diverse origins:	about 7,000

The population grew to about twenty thousand by 1900, and the distinction between free and recently freed Africans was increasingly blurred. None of these figures reflect the expansion into the suburbs (Sor) across the river to the east, nor some individuals who stayed at their posts throughout the year.

The principal livelihood for the population was gum and peanut production. Both trades were structured according to a hierarchy of functions and fees. The wholesalers and semiwholesalers, under the titles *négociant* and *marchand,* stood at the top and handled the export-import business; they were overwhelmingly French and primarily from Bordeaux. *Traitants* (traders) handled the exchanges between Saint-Louis and escales in the interior, where they spent several months each year. Most were African and Muslim, but some were métis and Christian. Many traitants became quite prosperous in the great days of gum in the 1830s and 1840s.[81] Each traitant might have one or more *sous-traitants* at

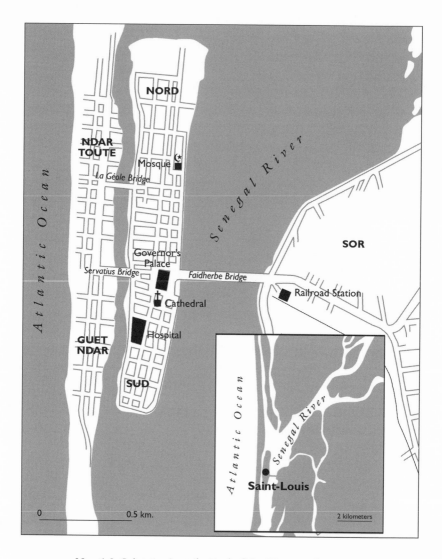

Map 1.3. Saint-Louis at the End of the Nineteenth Century

his disposal, sending them out in the countryside or to the smaller river ports. All of these Saint-Louisians knew the main language spoken at the escale, but they used interpreters, *maîtres de langues,* to negotiate with important caravan leaders to bring their wares to their stores. The interpreters functioned particularly in relation to the gum trade and the *bidan* who controlled it. They were the first commercial brokers along the river and supplied the model for the interpreter role within the administration.[82]

At mid century, the French changed the structure to permit the Bordeaux houses to trade directly with the producers of gum and peanuts. This innovation, coupled with the loss of slaves in the emancipation decree of 1848, drove many of the traitants, especially in the métis community, to ruin. Some became employees of the European houses, some tried new factories along the Guinea coast, and some went into administrative and military roles. African Muslim traitants — the group I discuss in chapter 6 — remained active in the river valley and peanut basin, but mostly as agents of the French merchants.

Many Saint-Louisians were former slaves of the métis and free African population, or refugees from the interior. For them, Saint-Louis was a place of opportunity, offering jobs as domestics, boat hands, messengers, and soldiers. In time they might become sous-traitants, or, if they acquired French, a position as clerk or interpreter. They also learned Wolof and adopted Islam as part of their upward mobility.[83] Saint-Louis attached the same stigma to slave status as the other Senegalese societies, but its inhabitants frequently crossed the lines, refurbished their identities, and acquired economic and social capital.

Saint-Louis was one of the four communes along the Senegal coast that benefited from the Republican and revolutionary heritage of France. White, métis, and black inhabitants of these towns petitioned Paris in 1789, in 1848, and then again after the establishment of the Third Republic for their full rights as French citizens. The practice of these rights, especially through the electoral institutions created by the Third Republic, is the subject of chapter 5.

The oldest companion to Saint-Louis was Gorée, a small island off the Cape Verde peninsula. Easily defensible, it served as a center for the collection and reexport of slaves into the Atlantic trade until the nineteenth century.[84] Then it became a convenient base for the French navy and the administration of commercial interests to the south. In the second half of the century, it lost its preeminence to Rufisque and Dakar.

Rufisque developed on the mainland as an export center for peanuts. Some Saint-Louisians moved there, along with representatives of the main French commercial houses. In contrast to Gorée, it maintained its demographic and commercial importance into the twentieth century, when it was rapidly surpassed by Dakar, the port and administrative center on the Cape Verde peninsula. With the relocation of the government general and the investments in headquarters by the main commercial houses, Dakar became the dominant city in Senegal and French West Africa. By 1920, when this study ends, it had surpassed Saint-Louis in terms of population and administrative and commercial infrastructure, and rivaled it in educational facilities. Métis and African citizens were not able to dominate the public life of Dakar, or Rufisque, in the ways they developed in Saint-Louis.

—— ——

THE SENEGALO-MAURITANIAN ZONE outlined here had considerable commercial and cultural cohesion in the period under study. Traditional aristocracies and so-called Islamic regimes shared similar social structures and they all failed to provide conditions of protection, prosperity, and identity for their subjects. Their failures and struggles were the context in which the four marabouts featured in this work grew up.

At the same time, the French presence was growing. Peanut production rose steadily. Metropolitan firms increasingly dominated the trade and put pressure on the administration to protect their growers, transport systems, and warehouse facilities. By 1900, when gum production declined precipitously, it was obvious that the economic center of gravity of the Senegalo-Mauritanian zone lay to the south. Communities throughout the zone would need strong connections to the peanut basin.

Some of those communities were corporate Muslim networks, headed by marabouts born in the mid nineteenth century. The two led by Malik Sy and Amadu Bamba were centered in the peanut basin itself; Malik Sy settled in the older area of Cayor, while Bamba concentrated on the newer zone of Baol. The two networks led by the *bidan* clerics Saad Buh and Sidiyya Baba established their connection through discipleship and clientship. That connection was manifested by collection tours at every harvest season — tours that were approved by the colonial administration as part of doing business and keeping order.

But the paths into the colonial economy and regular relations with the administration were not simple. What was required was a transition from a world where people assumed that they were part of the Dar al-Islam to one in which Islamic identity could be maintained underneath, or in spite of, European overrule. The next five chapters describe dimensions that allowed the accommodation to occur. The first need was for mutual comprehension. A major part of this was information that would give the French a familiarity and confidence about the Muslim societies of the Senegalo-Mauritanian zone. It was this knowledge, or presumed knowledge, that enabled the administration to chart its own path of accommodation. This is the subject of the next chapter.

PART 2

Bases of Accommodation

—2—

Sources, Discourses, and Mediators of Knowledge

THE SOURCES USED IN DOCUMENTING this book were generated under the very special conditions of French conquest, colonial rule, and the successor states of Senegal and Mauritania. The French, like other Europeans, relied heavily on local informants—often their key allies—for information. They acquired greater knowledge of the indigenous societies, or at least thought they did, and this in turn gave them greater confidence in the solidity of colonial rule. They framed the acquisition and the knowledge in certain forms or discourses. Since they were dealing with Muslim societies, the frameworks were strongly influenced by the "orientalism" of the "occident"—the French experience in the Maghrib. To understand and write the history of this period, it is vital to understand these sources, discourses, and the mediators of both.

The same analysis is critical for understanding materials generated outside of the colonial framework, particularly the sources created by Muslim leaders and followers, in Arabic, Pular, Wolof, or French. Across roughly two generations, these Senegalese and Mauritanians were forced to acknowledge the growing intensity and apparent permanence of European rule. The leading marabouts adjusted their conceptions of what it meant to be a Muslim society, a part of the Dar al-Islam. They sustained the old patterns of study and composition; apart from declarations for or against the jihad of the sword, one might not immediately recognize the new imperial fact in their writing. But the concentration on devotional literature, Sufi affiliation, and the meaning of the good Muslim life are indications of a shift in emphasis, a reordering of priorities.[1]

This chapter looks at the different forms and mediators of knowledge, the discourses in which they are contained, and the audiences and purposes that they served. It is an integral part of the "paths of accommodation." I start in the "middle," the formative period for French control in the early twentieth century when much of the structure of knowledge was framed. I then move to the "end," the Senegalese and Mauritanian literatures produced in the last four decades, showing that much of the framing is still in place. Finally, I go back to the "beginning" and a consideration of the primary materials produced contemporaneously with the events and relations under study.

THE FRAMEWORK OF FRENCH COLONIAL RULE

French orientalism and ethnography played a large role in framing the study of West Africa at the turn of the century. The first tradition originated in Algeria, the colonial laboratory for studies of Islam. As France began to develop its occupation of Muslim-dominated areas of West Africa, it looked to the Algerian experience and "experts" for assistance. Jules Cambon, governor-general of Algeria from 1891 to 1897, intensified many of these linkages (see chapter 4). Ethnographic studies developed in the late nineteenth century and became instrumental in the construction of the empire in sub-Saharan Africa, Asia, and the Pacific. Over time, the ethnographic dimension dominated the orientalist perspective in "black Africa," but the two traditions melded in the study of the Sahelian and Saharan regions of West Africa.[2] This was particularly true in the journal *Revue du Monde Musulman,* started by the Islamicist and sociologist Alfred Le Châtelier at the turn of the century. While it featured the Muslim societies of the Mediterranean, it devoted considerable attention to the Sahelian area of West Africa.[3]

The orientalist and ethnographic dimensions converged in French West Africa, the federation organized out of Dakar from 1902 until 1960.[4] The governor-general exercised direct authority over a series of lieutenant governors in the territorial capitals. The colonial staff at both the federal and territorial levels generated a considerable body of letters, reports, and syntheses that formed the basis for communication to the Ministry of Colonies in Paris and for research of many kinds. Much of that inquiry was conducted by departments of the government-general or the research enterprises that it created in Dakar.

The Dakar structure was a more elaborate successor to what the French had been doing out of Saint-Louis in the nineteenth century.[5] From this base, the governor of Senegal oversaw operations in the peanut basin, which became the heart of the political economy of Senegal, and the river valley, which formed the axis of advance into the Soudan and the base for the conquest of Mauritania.[6] Over the course of the century, the Saint-Louis administration established the main categories and traditions of reporting and accountability that passed on to Dakar.[7] The system created layers of material of great importance, especially for the Senegalo-Mauritanian sphere. The material itself fed the growing confidence that the French manifested about their control.

The first governor-general in the new Dakar setting was Ernest Roume, a man of considerable talent. He had wide experience, but none of it had been in West Africa.[8] He had worked principally at the Ministries of Colonies and Commerce in Paris and he brought the confidence and resources of the metropole to bear upon the task of establishing the Federation of French West Africa. Six years at the helm (1902–8) enabled Roume to make significant changes. He organized the educational and medical-assistance systems. He invested considerable energy and money in port, river, telegraph, and rail facilities. He provided the critical support to Xavier Coppolani's plan for the "pacification" of Mauritania, and remained a partisan of French expansion in the Sahara after Coppolani's assassination in 1905.

From the perspective of research and documentation, Roume made two notable contributions. He organized the Muslim Affairs service in 1905–6 and gave responsibility for it to Robert Arnaud, an Algerian Islamicist who had accompanied Coppolani to Soudan and Mauritania. Arnaud, influenced by North African models, established the basic procedures of the bureau, including the *fiches de renseignements* by which French officials tracked the Muslim teachers, scholars, and mystics who had now come under their control. He laid the foundations for the work of his successor, Paul Marty, who published the volumes on Islam in French West Africa that have been a major souce of reference ever since.[9] Roume also, in 1907, launched the *Bulletin de la Société de Géographie de l'AOF.* Arnaud was one of its main contributors, and the inspector of education served on its editorial committee. The journal did not survive Roume's departure, but it served as an important model for things to come.

William Ponty succeeded Roume and continued to fill out the infrastructure of the federation for seven years (1908–15). He presided over Claude Faure's reorganization of the archives of the federation and the development of the educational system under Georges Hardy. Hardy founded the *Bulletin de l'Enseignement en AOF,* which later became *Education africaine.* It featured discussions of pedagogy and gave opportunity for Western-educated Africans to publish ethnographical material on local societies. Hardy gave new energy to the Ecole Normale, the teacher training school launched in Saint-Louis before its transfer to to Gorée and Sebikotane. The school, which subsequently took the name William Ponty, formed many of the Western-educated elite of the federation during the colonial period.

Hardy helped form, under Governor-general Joseph Clozel, the next major chapter of the research enterprise, the Comité d'Etudes Historiques et Scientifiques de l'AOF.[10] By 1918 this group was publishing a bulletin, which quickly became the major scholarly journal on francophone West Africa. It went considerably deeper than the publications of the metropole, such as the more propagandistic *Bulletin du Comité d'Afrique Française* and its supplement *Renseignements Coloniaux,* or more general journals like the *Revue Coloniale* or the *Revue des Deux Mondes.*[11] This work of Roume, Ponty, and their associates marked the coming of age of the federation as both a part of the empire and as an instrument of knowledge and control.

In 1938 the French transformed the comité into a more significant research enterprise, the Institut Français d'Afrique Noire (IFAN), and entrusted its development to an energetic natural scientist, Théodore Monod.[12] Over the next twenty years, Monod created a remarkable library and museum. He presided over individual and team research across the whole spectrum of the humanities and the social and natural sciences. The results emerged in two large and regular journals,[13] a series of *Mémoires,* and other publications. During the same period, the Dakar headquarters spawned regional institutes in the territorial capitals that developed their own programs and publications.[14] It would be hard to overestimate the contribution of the comité, the institut, and their publications to the knowledge and discourses about francophone West Africa.

In the 1950s the French finally created a university. The Institut des Hautes Etudes, established in 1951, became the University of Dakar in 1957. It contained faculties of letters and human sciences, natural sciences, law and economic sciences, and medicine and pharmacy. At first the academics were almost entirely French, but West Africans, and especially Senegalese, became dominant in many departments by the 1970s. In its early years, the university supported a number of publications, built a library that complemented the facilities of nearby IFAN, and provided some funding for research. Students initially came from all over the federation.

All of the territories of the federation became independent by 1960, and all established their own institutions of research and higher education. The "regional IFANs" served as the basis for the research initiative, but they did not obtain significant funding, from local or French budgets. Neither did public libraries develop. The new universities gradually Africanized their faculties, and over the same period they watched their main support, the French Cooperation Fund, diminish. Through the 1970s and 1980s, the support for higher education dwindled to derisory levels. Instruction and research suffered as teachers, students, and government confronted one another with great frequency and no resolution.[15]

In the period since independence, when most of the younger African historians have prepared doctoral theses *(troisième cycle* et *doctorat d'état)* for French professors, they have chosen accessible local subjects. The subject choices stem from interest and constraint: the interest is the commitment to create a national historiography; the constraint is the great limitation on funding, time, and reward for research. The result has been a group of theses and publications that deal with the precolonial and more recently the colonial period, based primarily on archival and other written sources. The resources to support sustained interviewing, transcription, translation, and archiving of oral data have simply not been available. Africa-based historians have watched while their better-funded counterparts from Europe and North America have conducted more extensive research in the field and archives.

The work of all of these historians, African, European, and North American, has reinforced the temporal and spatial divisions of francophone West Africa. It has sharpened the distinction between precolonial and colonial times, a distinction that is especially difficult to maintain for the Senegalo-Mauritanian zone. It has deepened the territorial divisions established during the scramble for Africa. The federation provided some legitimacy and support for larger, "transterritorial" research, largely by French academics. The balkanization of the federation created national agendas that were often read back into the colonial or precolonial past. A critical review of the relevant literature for southwestern Mauritania and northwestern Senegal requires scrutiny of these national historiographies.

The Historiography of Senegal

The Senegalese literature is older and richer than its Mauritanian counterpart. It goes back to the interaction of trading communities, chiefs, military officers, and religious authorities, European and African, in the precolonial centuries. Researchers at IFAN and the University of Dakar combed the archival record, analyzed published accounts, and formed interpretations. It would be hard to overestimate the impact of these generations of researchers, mostly French, on the literature of francophone West Africa, in particular that of Senegal.

The direction of teaching and research shifted markedly after independence. The Africanization of the History Department at the University of Dakar, as in most universities on the continent, took the form of hiring Senegalese historians who had been trained in France and who worked primarily on precolonial Senegalese subjects. In this research enterprise, they were joined by some North American historians with a similar orientation. Both groups emphasized political and a certain kind of religious history, concentrating on resistance to conquest, whether by heads of state, such as Lat Dior of Cayor and Albury Ndiaye of Jolof, or militant Islamic leaders, such as Ma Ba Diakhu.[16] These important contributions have had some less than positive effects. They have reinforced a tendency to divide Senegalese leaders and communities into two groups, resisters and collaborators, and this dichotomization has carried over into the treatments of the colonial period. They have emphasized the role played by militant Islamic leaders, and done so at the expense of many less visible currents of Islamic practice and islamization. They have reinforced the role of male leadership at the expense of the less visible but crucial roles of women.

The work of this earlier generation of historians made it possible for scholars to produce two major syntheses of precolonial Senegal. Philip Curtin prepared the first in 1975: *Economic Change in Pre-Colonial Africa: Senegambia in the Era of the Slave Trade.* Boubacar Barry published the second in 1988: *La Sénégambie du XVe au XIXe siècle: Traite négrière, Islam, conquête coloniale.*[17] Curtin and Barry defined Senegambia in roughly similar ways, and both drew the northern boundary at the Senegal River.

Historians were slower to attack the colonial period and they have as yet produced no workable syntheses. Two figures still serve as icons of colonial Senegal, and both lived well before the French gave final shape to the territory. Léon Faidherbe, governor for almost ten years at mid century, established some of the institutions and suggested the boundaries that would come to constitute Senegal. By his energy, intelligence, manipulation of information, and the military resources put at his disposal, he transformed a collection of military and trading posts into a colony.[18] His arch antagonist, or at least the one who has dominated the opposing literature, was Umar Tal, pilgrim, writer, teacher, and leader of the jihad against Mandinka and Bamana states in the Upper Senegal and Middle Niger.[19] Faidherbe and Umar clashed on several occasions in the mid nineteenth century, most notably at Medine (see chapter 1). Faidherbe won that confrontation, but Umar survived and formulated his call to emigrate from the "pollution" of European rule.

The colonial period is still prisoner of the images of Faidherbe and Umar. Faidherbe is the "founder" of Senegal. His name appeared on schools and streets and until the 1970s his statue faced the residence of the governor-general (now the presidency) in Dakar. Umar was and is the hero of Islamic resistance to French conquest, even though his main efforts were directed against African "infidels" and his main confrontation with Faidherbe occurred in today's Mali.[20] For much of the colonial period, these images were reinforced by the governor-general and Umar's grandson, Seydu Nuru Tal. Beginning in the 1920s, Seydu Nuru, who lived a few blocks away from the official residence, served as the federation's roving ambassador. He and his French counterpart appeared at countless ceremonies together, and his robe was no less decorated with medals of honor for service to the colonial cause. His prestige, and consequent value to the administration, was in proportion to the memory of his grandfather's resistance.[21]

One work free of the Faidherbean and Umarian icons came from the historian Wesley Johnson. His *Emergence of Black Politics in Senegal: The Struggle for Power in the Four Communes* appeared more than twenty-five years ago and built on the literature associated with the four towns that acquired French institutions and citizenship in the nineteenth century.[22] Johnson understandably emphasized the election in 1914 of the first black deputy of Senegal, Blaise Diagne, and the establishment of African dominance across the body politic. Diagne became the predecessor to Galandou Diouf, Lamine Gueye, and Léopold Senghor, and thus stood at the beginning of "modern" politics in Senegal.

Economic history developed somewhat later than the political story and built upon the rich archival and published literature dealing with the trade in slaves, gum, and peanuts. It has been marked by a debate between neocapitalist and dependency orientations. Philip Curtin has been the main proponent of the former. In *Economic Change,* he emphasized the trading "diasporas," the networks of African and European merchants who worked the routes from east to west, from interior to coast.[23] The power relations between African and European entrepreneurs were roughly equal, and all merchants shifted strategies to maximize profit and security. The slave trade was one of several investments, and most of the slaves exported to the Americas came from the east, not Senegambia. The societies of the region were not markedly different in 1850 from the way they had been in 1600, according to Curtin.

The dependency perspective has played a more dominant role within

Senegalese historiography. Boubacar Barry, Charles Becker and others associated with the History Department in Dakar have placed a much greater emphasis on the Atlantic slave trade and its corrupting effects on the implicit social contract between rulers and citizens in the Senegambian states.[24] They contest less the sources or number of slaves exported to the Americas and more the effect on society of mobilization for the slave trade.[25] The ruling elites made heavy demands upon their subjects, raided them with impunity, and became increasingly preoccupied with consumption and security. In the resulting conditions of instability, Muslim communities began to defend themselves against predation and to form their own governments separate from the traditional states.[26]

More recently, the debate has taken the form of Saharan and Atlantic orientations. James Webb, a student of Curtin's, takes a broad swath of the Saharan and Sahelian bands, corresponding to southern Mauritania and northern Senegal. He stresses the exchange of North African and Saharan horses for black slaves, the great influence that *bidan* traders and warriors exercised over the ruling elites of black societies, and the large *bidan* settlement in the Wolof zones. James Searing, in focusing on the Wolof zones and the communes of the precolonial period, has emphasized the provisioning trade and slave production within a system dominated by the exportation of slaves to the Americas. The two interpretations reflect different sets of documentation and different assumptions, and it is difficult to compare the arguments or reach a larger synthesis.[27]

Historians and social scientists on the arenas defined by Webb and Searing have continued to study the trading networks, and especially those centered on the Atlantic ports and dominated by French interests. They typically divide the commercial community into three, corresponding to racial and cultural categories: a small number of French, a slightly larger number of métis, and a much larger population of African traders—most of whom were in the service of the other two groups. The sources describe two "eclipses" in the trading population. They assign the eclipse of the métis merchants to the mid nineteenth century, correlating it with the loss of wealth and workforce after the emancipation decree of 1848.[28] They assign the eclipse of African traders to the end of the century, correlating it with the full French conquest, the growing dominance of the Bordeaux houses over peanuts, and the decline in the gum trade.[29]

These two simplifications correlate with the resistance theme, the dependency orientation, and the burden of the Johnson book. Precolonial traditions are abruptly ended with the defeat, death, or deportation of traditional chiefs and Muslim leaders. In a slightly less dramatic fashion, the French take over the reins of the economy from the métis and African traders, leaving little opportunity for upward mobility in the economic sphere. Talented, ambitious, and well-educated Senegalese men, often the sons of traders, now go into administrative jobs or, after Blaise Diagne's resounding success, the political machines. Political history becomes the expansion of electoral rights from communes to country, and it culminates in the independence of Senegal under the leadership of Senghor, the poet and philosopher. Economic history becomes the narrative of peanut production, identified most closely with the Murid farmers, French commercial and industrial establishments, and heavy state intervention. African entrepreneurs dominate the political system but are virtually absent from the economic one.

The recent work of Senegalese and European historians on commercial history has begun to challenge these interpretations and to suggest the important role that African Muslim merchants played in the processes of islamization and adjustment to colonial rule.[30] Even if one retains the perspective of dependency, it is important to explore conflicts between public and private sectors among the Bordeaux establishments and across the whole range of trading interests, including the African entrepreneurs. Saint-Louis was an arena of conflict and contestation. Many of its inhabitants, and the networks in the interior that supported them, knew how to work the system and gain significant advantages for their interests. Their history, of whatever color, language, and status, is compelling.

The religious history of Senegal, as well as Mauritania, is yet to be written. At this juncture, the researcher can look at several discrete bodies of material. First, we have studies of militant Islamic leaders and their jihads, written primarily by Western or Western-trained historians and focused on the immediate precolonial period. The emphasis is political and military, and the dominant interpretation is resistance, both to French intrusion and the traditional courts.[31] Second, there is a small body of literature on colonial "Islamic policy." The most important contribution is Chris Harrison's analysis of French attitudes, categories, and practices from 1860 to 1960.[32] Using the archival record and the Muslim Affairs literature in particular, he describes the fluctuations in French practices toward Muslim societies. Inevitably, he emphasizes the conflicts that produced a deeper archival record. Finally, we have descriptions of the Murid and Tijaniyya orders, their founders and places within the contemporary political economy of Senegal.

The orders have played a dominant rule in peanut production and Islamic practice in twentieth-century Senegal. Social scientists have written extensively on the Murids, but they have been primarily interested in recent developments and the influence that the order wields in contemporary Senegalese life.[33] They have paid little attention to the Tijaniyya. The other tradition of scholarship on the orders comes from Senegalese and French scholars trained in Arabic and the Islamic sciences. They have established Muslim pedagogies, identified schools, and written intellectual biographies of the founders.[34] All of this work is descriptive. Much of it is hagiographic, corresponding to the orientation of materials generated by the orders themselves, and is cast in the resistance tradition: the founders opposed French conquest and submitted reluctantly to colonial rule.

With one partial exception, neither the social scientists nor the islamologists have put the founders and the communities that grew around them in the context of the rapidly changing social order of the turn of the century. They have not shown any significant interest in the second generation of leadership. These leaders were contemporaries of Seydu Nuru Tal and they elaborated the practices of cooperation with the colonial administration. They constituted a kind of Islamic "establishment" that carried over into the independence period.[35] The great influence of the orders and the hagiographic orientation make it increasingly difficult to reconstruct the earlier periods and the webs of influence and cooperation.

The partial exception concerns the Murid order. According to the dominant interpretation of the social scientists, Wolof society was rapidly disintegrating in the late nineteenth century. The traditional courts made draconian exactions on their own people, despite the protests of Muslim communities. The following around Amadu Bamba in the 1880s and 1890s consisted of poorly educated warriors and peasants dislocated by the conquest of the Wolof states. As the French took increasing control of the peanut basin, Amadu Bamba formulated an understanding that permitted the less educated to make a living as peanut farmers and obtain the intervention and protection of a hierarchy of marabouts. At the same time, other Murid leaders, of a more practical bent, developed enduring ties with inhabitants of the communes and members of the colonial administration.[36]

This is a suggestive interpretation, which I follow in chapter 11, but it has not been accompanied by sustained analysis. Nor have Murid developments been compared with other traditions in the Senegalo-Mauritanian zone. In the current understanding, the orders, with their strong economic and pedagogical organization, emerge suddenly from a flat landscape. The ties to the reform tradition are mentioned, because they are critical to the legitimacy of the founders and the links to resistance. The connections to Islamic leaders in Mauritania and Morocco are mentioned but not analyzed. The insertion into peanut cultivation is stressed, for the Murids, but not the larger fit into the colonial economy. The ties to the Muslim merchant community of Saint-Louis, an important part of my analysis in chapter 6, are not mentioned.

THE HISTORIOGRAPHY OF MAURITANIA

Mauritanian historiography is smaller and less layered than that of Senegal. Much of the raw material lies in Senegalese and French archives, and some of it has been treated by historians and social scientists working from a Senegalese framework. The vast Arabic literature is only now being worked. The University of Nouakchott has been affected by the debate about instruction in Arabic and French, and the argument in turn has deepened the distinction between arabophone and francophone scholars, their different audiences, and the different subjects about which they write. Much more than its Senegalese counterpart, the historiography is compartmentalized into two language frameworks, where readers and writers in one language often do not have access to the other body of materials.[37] Nonetheless, indigenous and expatriate scholars have begun to debate serious issues in the last thirty years, especially around the nature of *bidan* society.[38]

The French built up close relations with some of the political elite of southern Mauritania during the gum trade of the nineteenth century. At the time, they had little relationship with the *zwaya,* or "maraboutic," groups. Conflicts with the southwestern emirate of Trarza in mid century created a great deal of material, but not a lot of understanding of the workings of *bidan* society, and little or nothing about areas in the center and north of today's Mauritania. The administration in Saint-Louis often referred to the southern tier of emirates as *la Mauritanie sénégalaise.*

This situation changed radically beginning in 1902, with the program of conquest launched by Xavier Coppolani and Governor-general Roume. The French built their penetration around an alliance with certain *zwaya* of Trarza, particularly their old ally Saad Buh and their new friend Sidiyya Baba. Through these intermediaries, with their own considerable interests in certain interpretations of Mauritanian history, the administration built up its own perspective. This view, and the discourses that it contains, became the dominant historiography and endured well beyond independence. It has only come under critical review in the last two decades. The relation between knowledge and power, and a certain kind of knowledge and certain exercise of power, could hardly be clearer.

The French perspective was built on certain assumptions dear to the hearts of their *bidan* allies. First, Mauritania's center of gravity was in the south. It was created from south to north, and in contradistinction to older Moroccan claims of control. Indeed, it is hard to explain the investment in conquering Mauritania without the French priority on containing and controlling Morocco and thus fulfilling the "mission" of dominating all of northwestern Africa (see chapter 4). The southern and anti-Moroccan orientation explains the inclusion of Mauritania within the French West African Federation, the location of government services in Saint-Louis, and the maintenance of that framework until the 1950s, when the small outpost of Nouakchott was invested as the capital of a future Islamic Republic of Mauritania.[39] During all of that time, the southwest, particularly the area of Trarza, remained the privileged zone and main source of knowledge about social relations and history.

The second strand of the French perspective was the sharp distinction between *hassan* (i.e., the political and military classes) and *zwaya* (the religious and commercial groups). The *hassan* were descendants of Arab nomads, the Banu Maqil, who had moved across the northern Sahara and filtered down into the western portion that became Mauritania. While they often claimed descent from the Prophet and his Companions, they were given to raiding, slaving, and infighting and had little training in or commitment to Islam. They were "pillagers of the road." The *zwaya,* on the other hand, were better Muslims, of Berber origin, who had lost the Islamic revolution called Sharr Bubba in the late seventeenth century. Learned in Islamic law and Sufism, these clerics mediated disputes, organized commerce, paid tribute to the political leaders, and disdained the use of force. The French found ample justification for this view in the writings of the *zwaya* scholars themselves.[40] They implicitly privileged the Sharr Bubba history, which featured the Trarza region.

The third basic foundation of the French perspective was the segmentary lineage system. Under the influence of European anthropology, much of it built around nomadic societies in Algeria and Morocco, the French accepted and reified the genealogical narratives that their *bidan* informants provided. The Moors were constantly moving, fragmenting, and fighting on the basis of old and bitter disputes within and between families. This perpetual turbulence contrasted with the permanence of the distinction between *hassan* and *zwaya*. It also provided a justification for maintaining colonial rule. The Moors were certainly not capable of ending violence or maintaining order; living in perpetual dissidence *(siba),* they needed the external authority that the French provided.

Over the last three decades, these assumptions have been called into question. Charles Stewart demonstrates the capacity for social order within nomadic societies and the fluidity of *zwaya* and *hassan* identities. He has written one of the few extended essays on an Islamic network and leader who rejected the tradition of military jihad and a Muslim state. He lays the foundation for understanding the Sidiyya lineage and the critical role that it played in the life of colonial Mauritania.[41] Abdel Wedoud Ould Cheikh casts the construction of identities and genealogies on a broader canvas, essentially all of today's Mauritania, and over a much longer timescale, back to the Almoravids of the eleventh century.[42] Other Mauritanian scholars have begun to work the considerable Arabic literature and to produce theses in Arabic. Pierre Bonte and Ann McDougall, who have sketched the dynamism of *bidan* society over the same extended time frame, have shifted the emphasis to the Adrar as the center of trade, migration, and politics.[43] More recently, a number of North American scholars — Timothy Cleaveland, Glen McLaughlin, Raymond Taylor, and James Webb — have taken fresh looks at southern Mauritania and challenged all of the assumptions of the established view.[44]

For the colonial period, the literature is still largely a chronicle of the French conquest governed by the three assumptions. It begins with Xavier Coppolani's "pacification" of the south (1902–5), skips to Henri Gouraud's conquest of the Adrar (1908–9), and concludes with operations against the nomadic tribes of the north, extending into the 1930s.[45] Coppolani is the "founder" of Mauritania in the same way that Faidherbe is for Senegal: he established the framework and the main lines of collaboration with indigenous clerics and he has attracted a similar attention from the scholarly community.[46] Social scientists have recently shown an interest in the electoral history of Mauritania, which began in 1946.[47] This has helped to make Mauritania comparable to the other former members of the French West African Federation during the decolonization and independence periods. But neither the chroniclers nor the social scientists have offered useful interpretations of the country's colonial experience.

PRIMARY SOURCES AND DISCOURSES: THE FRENCH DOCUMENTATION

It has been customary to preface studies like this with reviews of the literature and the "primary" sources. In a period that emphasizes the sociology and deconstruction of knowledge, we cannot have so much confidence in those categories or the methods that they imply. I have thus far discussed what might be called the secondary literature, in the sense that it was written after the recounted events, and by professionals with specific research interests, not by participants. My emphasis has been on the context in which this literature was generated. For the raw materials of the participants, I am again interested in the contexts in which the documentation was produced and the implications of those contexts for understanding.

The French archival record for the years extending from 1880 to 1920 is enormous. It might seem at first glance possible to work through that record, or some significant portion of it, and be in a position to write a "complete" history. But despite the enormity of the record, it is not complete. What is there must be scrutinized very closely, for its temporal context, audience, purposes, and discourse. What is absent must also be explored: Were documents written and removed? Which documents were sent to Paris, and why? Were questions and issues left unanswered, at least in writing, and for what reasons? Finally, what is the role of what might be called the "oral"—and "aural"—in the written record? What were the oral traditions passed on to successors in the various bureaux of the metropole and colonies? Were oral commands given to subordinates to countermand written instructions?[48] Were oral instructions given in certain situations to avoid written traces? Does such an oral dimension help explain the absences and silences in the record?

The most obvious fact about the French archival material is the mediation of Africans. African clerks made and kept most of the records and controlled access to the Europeans. Interpreters, chiefs, and marabouts provided a framework for understanding local situations. This framework was usually irresistible for an administrator who knew little of the culture, received no reward for learning about it, and would be posted somewhere else in short order. The mediation was especially true for the "frontiers"—areas that the French hardly knew. Southern Mauritania is the most obvious example in this study. It was only when complaints emerged from different sources, or when practices encountered resistance, that the official—or his superior—might realize the limits of the knowledge provided.

It is sometimes difficult to find the traces of these intermediaries, but the more prominent instances are inescapable. Saad Buh supplied Saint-Louis with information and perspective on the whole Senegalo-Mauritanian zone for several decades. Sidiyya Baba planned the strategy of conquest with Xavier Coppolani and Henri Gouraud and deeply influenced the perceptions of Paul Marty. Mademba Sy was the confidant of Louis Archinard during his campaigns in the Soudan, while Buna Ndiaye became a close associate of Martial Merlin, who was successively director of political affairs, secretary-general of the federation, and then governor-general.[49] At a more fundamental level, African intermediaries shaped the conceptions of the history of the region. Yoro Diaw furnished some of the basic perspective on Walo and Cayor,[50] while Saad Buh and Sidiyya Baba framed the understanding of *bidan* history. It is often impossible to distinguish the views of broker and "framer" from those of the colonial official.

The first generation of French material on West Africa consists of explorers' accounts and diplomatic and commercial reporting set well back in the precolonial period. The second generation is dominated by military and diplomatic annals, including the processes of negotiation for securing local allies and establishing treaties of submission. This literature follows the "frontier" of conquest. For the core of what became Senegal, the conquest was completed by the 1890s; for southern Mauritania, this came in the first decade of the twentieth century. Military men, accustomed to hierarchy, described in austere detail their mobilization, logistics, conquests, casualties, and affirmations of submission. They wrote for other soldiers, but they also had to consider civilian bureaucrats and politicians. They were sensitive to the need to minimize losses, camouflage embarrassments, and interpret achievements in patriotic terms.

A third generation of literature, the largest single category of archival material, came from the administration of the conquered territory that had been "taken out" of the frontier. At the base of the chain of command was the administrative officer.[51] At the time of conquest, or in the frontier period, this was usually a military man. As colonial rule was consolidated, the personnel became civilian. This did not necessarily mean a change in competence, educational level, or orientation. The civilian hierarchy was probably less flexible than its military counterpart because it had more rules to implement and less expectation of confrontation from the subject population. The establishment of control presaged a more routine administrative environment, and this often made for less interesting communications.[52] The information went to the governor or lieutenant governor, and might occasionally make its way to the level of the governor-general, but it was seldom excerpted for the consumption of the ministry in Paris.

Potentially more important material involved crises, frontier zones, and transitions between conquest and consolidation. The authors were persons on special assignment, often drawn from the governor's (or governor-general's) political affairs bureau. They were persons of confidence who would understand the sensitivities of the situation and dangers for the careers of their superiors. For this book, three individuals are particularly significant because of the way they keep appearing at critical times and places: Victor Allys, Jean-Baptiste Théveniaut, and Martial Merlin.[53] The paper trail has not been sufficiently explored to indicate who in Paris, Dakar, or Saint-Louis made the assignments and with what interests in mind. But the careers of these three men suggest continuities of policy and strategic deployment of officials to places of crisis. All three, for example, were involved in decisions concerning Amadu Bamba, who preoccupied the administration for many years. And they certainly reinforce my main contention—that the archival record must be read with careful attention to genre, audience, situation, and author.

Elements of these military, routine, and special reports went into the syntheses that governors and the governor-general prepared for their superiors. These documents were passed along on a regular schedule, often quarterly, and were organized by region and theme. Crisis points received particular attention. The official often excerpted material from special reports, or included them as appendices, and it is by the excerpts and distribution of emphasis, and comparison with lower-level reporting, that one can discern the priorities of the administration.[54]

Another genre of administrative record can be called data collection. An early example was the *monographie de cercle.* At the onset of colonial rule, administrators were charged with establishing a survey of relevant information about the local chiefs, their attitudes, competence, and influence; the economy of production and distribution; religious affiliation; land tenure and demographics. These monographs gave the French confidence that they knew, and thus controlled, the local situation. They served as a baseline for comparison with later developments. African mediators were critical to the creation of these monographs and often succeeded in having their versions of events and relations written into the record.

At the same time the administrators began using forms (the *fiches de renseignement*) to monitor important personalities, especially chiefs and marabouts.[55] In theory, these forms were updated each year, and by each new administrator, but often the old information was repeated without change. Marty drew on this material as he wrote his surveys of Islamic practice in the federation. At times he included the raw data in his appendices, and one can see the grid of the *fiche* underlying both the form and substance of his descriptions.

The federation archives contain several other bodies of information that reveal a great deal, often unintentionally, about colonial policy and practice. The education series (J) shows a range of initiatives. Education is a revealing arena because of the emphasis that the French put on their language, culture, and school system, in its metropolitan and imperial dimensions, and the close relationship that they assumed between knowledge and power. The French often said that an "educated native" could not be "fanatic," by which they meant a Muslim hostile to French imperialism.[56]

The J series concentrates upon Saint-Louis, which remained the educational capital for some time after the government-general moved to Dakar.[57] The records on "Christian" and "lay" schools reveal controversies and conflicting projects within the educational arena. The records of the School for Sons of Chiefs and Interpreters show the continuing French efforts to create a friendly and competent group of Western-educated chiefs. In the early 1890s, Political Director Martial Merlin and Governor Henri de Lamothe initiated the most successful of these efforts (see chapter 3).[58]

At the same time, in Saint-Louis, the French established the medersa, or *franco-arabe* school, to train teachers, officials of the Muslim court system, and others who would work within the colonial system. The director was French, while the instructors were often Algerian and Senegalese. Subsequently, medersas were created in Jenne, Timbuktu, and Boutilimit. Only the Boutilimit initiative survived beyond World War I.[59]

A large body of the J files concern "Muslim" education, which meant elementary or Quranic schools and the control of their teachers. At various times the colonial authorities established a process of certification of Quranic teachers, but they never implemented this because of cost and doubts about its utility. But they did collect a vast archive of *fiches de renseignement* on the educational chains of transmission and changes in Sufi affiliation.[60] The J materials are important not for what the French achieved but for what they reveal about colonial intentions.

After Governor-general Roume created the Muslim Affairs service, the French organized a special series of data on general Islamic questions.[61] The files reflect concerns about controlling and isolating the Muslim societies of West Africa, most of which were now subsumed under the designation *Islam noir*. They contain material on the general situation in the Muslim Holy Lands, the Middle East, and North Africa; the pilgrimage, both the sea voyage (which the French could control) and the land journey across Africa; travel of Muslims within West Africa; the circulation of Arabic-language newspapers; and general surveillance of the Muslim population. French anxiety, particularly high in relation to Ottoman propaganda during World War I, generated many of the files.

The judicial series (M) contains the records of the whole range of courts that functioned within the federation and its predecessors. It contains material on the Muslim tribunals, including the petitions and lobbying pressures of the Muslim inhabitants, the establishment of courts of "native law," and reports on the personnel of the various courts. The court data, which is especially rich for Saint-Louis, reveals the multiple levels of contestation that informed people could pursue. It is there, for example, that one finds much of the information about the inquiries in 1890–91 into the summary execution of alleged assassins of a French officer.[62]

Some of this judicial material emerges from what I call the civil society of Senegal, as opposed to the administration itself, and thereby helps to provide a corrective to the hierachical view. The institutions of civil society provide elements of great utility to the historian. A number of nongovernment newspapers were published during this period; most of them did not last very long, but they indicate some of the levels of contestation.[63] The minutes of the General Council provide great insight into the viewpoints of African, métis, and French interests, which were often at odds with those of the governor or governor-general.[64] The accounts of elections for the deputyship, the General Council, and the mayors and city councils of the communes provide an additional window into the local situation. The journals of the Roman Catholic community, which was critical of what they often called the "pro-Muslim" policy of the administration, provide another point of view.[65]

PRIMARY SOURCES AND DISCOURSES: ORAL AND ARABIC DOCUMENTATION

Some of the nonadministration sources provide an internal perspective on the history of the period, at least for Saint-Louis and its more influential classes. To delve further into an internal and specifically Muslim view, one needs to go to interviews and Arabic material. Several researchers have had fruitful interviews in Saint-Louis, although the historical memory is organized more around political than social and religious phenomena.[66] Moustapha Kane and Ibrahima Sall have conducted useful sessions among people from Futa Toro in a number of locations. Cheikh Anta Mbacke Babou has obtained material on the early years of the Murids, while Ghislaine Lydon has obtained information, in several languages, about the transsaharan trade.[67] One could extend the list in many directions.

These interviews were part of individual research agendas, not conducted according to any overall plan, and they are still in the possession of the scholars.

No archive of oral materials exists for this region or period. In addition, it is very difficult to obtain information that is not contaminated by the reputations that surround the main Muslim figures—specifically, the founders of the Islamic communities that came to dominate the Senegalo-Mauritanian zone at the turn of the century.

Much of the Arabic material, to the extent that it has been cataloged and worked, does not deal directly with the new colonial order and Muslim relations to it. The Umarian material is set in the immediate precolonial material. The library that Umar established in Segu, and that was taken to Paris by Archinard, contains a few letters and treatises that reveal the thinking of that Muslim community in relation to French conquest.[68] When coupled with the *correspondance indigène*, Arabic letters addressed to the colonial authorities,[69] one can document the growing Umarian awareness of hostility expressed by the French.[70] This awareness finally issues in the "exit" option in which Amadu Sheku evacuated his last capital, Bandiagara, to head to the east and lands where Muslims were still in control.[71]

The founders of the new Muslim communities of the Senegalo-Mauritanian zone wrote poetry, treatises, and advice to their constituents. Their closest disciples formulated biographies that concentrated on "Islamic" events, such as the educational cursus, the pilgrimage or a trip to Fez, and the growth of the community. The biographies are usually patterned on the sequences of the life of the Prophet and are hagiographic in tone. Research thus far has turned up virtually no comment on the colonial authorities and Muslim obligations in the new order;[72] indeed, because this was a sensitive issue, it was probably dealt with by oral means. Nonetheless, it is possible to gain some useful perspective from this material, as Amar Samb has done in his work on Senegalese Arabic literature and Ravane Mbaye in his thesis on Malik Sy.[73]

Considerable insight comes also from Shaikh Musa Kamara, the scholar of eastern Futa who wrote a number of long treatises on the Senegalo-Mauritanian zone after World War I. He developed relationships with Henri Gaden and Maurice Delafosse, French scholars and administrators trained in the orientalist and ethnographic traditions. He gave most of his production to IFAN before his death in 1945. Kamara was a careful scholar who collected oral information during his travels, made notes, and transcribed them in a very orderly manner in his works. His most useful work is an ethnohistory of Futa Toro and the wider region, the *Zuhur al-Basatin*.[74] While Kamara does not offer overall interpretations of changing Muslim perspectives on the new order, he does provide a great deal of factual material about migration, marriage, and changing career patterns.

Another invaluable resource is available to researchers: the library of the Sidiyya family in Boutilimit. Thanks to the patient efforts of Stewart, Ould Cheikh, and their collaborators, most of the material has been microfilmed, cataloged, and surveyed for its general attributes. Within the library is a huge ethnohistory, longer than the *Zuhur,* prepared by the son of Sidiyya Baba, Harun, between the 1950s and the 1970s.[75]

One of the most interesting bodies of Arabic material consists of the *fatwa* (legal decrees). The tradition of issuing decrees, with extensive theological justification, has existed since the beginning of the Islamic era. In the context of the intense debates that raged throughout the Saharan zone at the turn of the century—debates about the legitimacy of European conquest and the submission of Muslims to non-Muslim rule—scholars issued a large number of decrees and declarations. The French, based in part on their experience in Algeria, quickly recognized the importance of using these decrees to their own advantage among Muslim societies. During the conquest of southern Mauritania, they solicited and received important "endorsements" from Sidiyya Baba and Saad Buh. The fatwas favoring submission served as a counterweight to calls to jihad.[76]

Beginning in 1910, the French secured similar endorsements from the founders of the new communities in Senegal, Malik Sy and Amadu Bamba. Although the administration encouraged these endorsements, it is probably fair to say that the statements represented the real views of these men, or at least their real "public" views. By the time of the outbreak of World War I, the French let it be known that grands marabouts would be expected to make declarations of loyalty to the regime, particularly to counter anti-European propaganda emanating from Istanbul and the Axis powers.[77]

THESE DIVERGENT CATEGORIES of "internal" material supply correctives to the archival documentation, but it is useful to end this chapter with several cautions about the lacunae in the overall historical record. At the level of French colonial operations, we do not yet appreciate the differences between the Ministries of the Colonies, Interior, and Foreign Affairs, which controlled different parts of the empire, nor the distinctions among different departments, relations with the French Assembly and the private sector, and the orientations and trajectories of civilian and military careers.[78] We have no analysis of the departments of the government-general of French West Africa or their functioning, nor of how they related to the lieutenant governors and their staffs in the various territories. For Mauritania and Senegal, we have no study of the considerable interference between territorial and federation administrations.

The Arabic literature generated during this period has been worked and studied even less, and never with a view to what it indicates about the relations between Muslim and colonial authorities. Oral data is equally unanalyzed, and even more fragmented. Historians and social scientists have used it primarily as a supplement to their accounts, often in the form of "personal communications." Islamicists and biographers of the founders of the Muslim orders often make more extensive use of oral tradition, but they tend to accept the hagiography in which the testimony is enveloped.

Perhaps the most significant problem for this period, region, and study is the difficulty of relating the different categories and contexts. Let us take just one document, the 1903 fatwa from Sidiyya Baba supporting the "pacification" of Mauritania.[79] What does it represent within his family and framework in Boutilimit? What does the same decree, in French hands, represent for them? What is signified by the commentary of the French authorities in Mauritania or Senegal on the fatwa and its use in quarterly reports to the ministry in Paris? What is intended by publishing it in the *Revue du Monde Musulman*? In the chapters that follow, without providing any sustained answers, I try to keep such questions in mind.

To conclude, what do these sources, discourses, and mediators, properly analyzed and integrated, permit me to say about "paths of accommodation"? First, they reveal a great deal more about the public than the private sphere. They speak loudly about official and visible relations between Muslim societies and colonial authorities. Second, they say very little about social issues, women, and gender. The authors were entirely men and they accepted a male-dominated universe without question. Men were the voters in Saint-Louis, the officials in the colonial administration, the visible shakers and movers in the Muslim societies, and the main interpreters of the documentation in the twentieth century.

Finally, the sources say much more about leaders than constituencies—about the marabouts who actually engaged the colonial authorities over this forty-year period than about their followers. But with this caveat: these leaders represented their constituencies. They were in a real sense created by their followers in a period of dramatic change. They led their clients across a difficult transition: the decline of anciens régimes, a period of great uncertainty, the emergence of a new political order, and the growth in importance of Sufi orders. In the process, they acquired considerable social capital. The relations between these leaders and the French authorities frame the colonial period of Senegal and Mauritania.

~3~

Conquest and Colonial Rule

"RESISTANCE" LITERATURE OFTEN PORTRAYS the conquest of Africa as an ineluc-
table and increasingly frenetic process set at the end of the nineteenth century.
It paints the conquerors as monolithic, as of one mind in their efforts to secure
land, people, and resources. It divides the subject population into resistors and
collaborators, with little sensitivity to the context and nuance that most Africans faced—such as the marabouts and followers featured in this study. While
the oversimplifications of this literature have been criticized, the dichotimiza-
tion still affects research subjects, judgements, and basic interpretative texts.[1]

A more sophisticated analysis emerges from the essays written by D. Anthony Low about East Africa and India.[2] In a section on the "intensity of
power" exercised by the British in Uganda, he suggests a range of European positions extending from influence to control. He spreads these terms over time
and over different zones of Uganda. I have applied this useful framework to the
Senegalo-Mauritanian zone. But the model retains a progressive and teleologi-
cal cast, not allowing for the variation in European power in time, space, and
sector. It assumes that any given set of Europeans operated as one entity in local
and metropolitan situations.

The conquest of Senegal and Mauritania, not to speak of many other regions
of Africa, pursued a particular trajectory. The process was incremental: one conquest served as the stage for the next contiguous area. The central peanut basin
was secured before Jolof was taken. The Senegal valley was the staging area for
taking Soudan. Two decades later, in a very different international context, it was

the platform for conquering Mauritania. For the consumption of the metropole, it was important to portray each advance as defensive, a response to provocation. Even when these conditions were met, Paris often signaled caution or a pause, such as the one between Faidherbe's main expansion and the resumption of Governor Louis Brière de l'Isle (from about 1860 to 1880). The agents of conquest and the institutions in which they operated were often divided, inconsistent, and at cross-purposes, at the metropolitan as well as the local level.[3] They had their critics and opponents, as chapter 5 reveals.

In the nineteenth century, the French colony of Senegal consisted of a series of coastal and riverine posts, with small adjacent hinterlands. Governor Faidherbe extended influence and control in some areas of the coast and interior in mid century, including the north bank of the river—a part of today's Mauritania. In about 1880, the beginning of my period, the expansion resumed on a firmer but still not completely steady basis. The conquest of the area of Senegal, as we know it today, was not completed until the mid 1890s. Until that time it is often more appropriate to speak of French preponderance, not colonial rule. Even after this period, there was considerable discussion and contestation about where and when to advance, within the administration as well as the larger francophone community.

Southwestern Mauritania, defined as the north bank of the river and the *bidan* areas beyond it, was considered part of Senegal during the nineteenth century. In the twentieth century one still finds the expression "Mauritanie sénégalaise." The French regarded the area as falling within their sphere of influence, radiating from Saint-Louis. They had significant impact through commerce in gum, firearms, cloth, and other goods, but no real control of events. Here conquest came much more suddenly than in Senegal. It started with the program of Xavier Coppolani in 1902, euphemistically labeled "pacification." It resumed under Henri Gouraud in 1908. By World War I, the outlines of southern and central Mauritania were clear.[4]

Within this overall pattern of expansion, with its interruptions and variations, this chapter describes how the administration "intensified" its power over the Senegalo-Mauritanian zone between 1880 and 1920 into something that can be appropriately labeled "colonial rule."[5] The intensification can be discerned under a series of bold and empowered governors beginning in 1888. It took a significant step after 1902, when the capital of the Federation of French West Africa was transferred from Saint-Louis to Dakar under the resourceful Ernest Roume (see plate 1). It was at that time that Roume added Mauritania to the territories of the federation. The intensification forced the Muslims of Senegal and Mauritania to submit to European rule. But all along the way, the adminis-tration faced significant division and opposition, which created spaces of ac-commodation for that submission.

Empire, Colony, and Conquest

For most of the nineteenth century, the Ministry of the Navy was the overseer of activities in the Senegalo-Mauritanian zone and other areas that became part of the French colonial empire. Its main operations were military; the small colo-nies that served as bases for fleets and soldiers were also its responsibility. It was only in 1894 that a separate Ministry of the Colonies was created. Throughout all of my period, the key bureau in Paris was the Direction of Colonies. Gover-nors, lieutenant governors, and commissioners based in Senegal and Mauritania reported to members of that office, who would draw important issues to the attention of the minister. From time to time, something might require the atten-tion of another ministry, such as Foreign Affairs, or the president and parlia-ment.[6] Many of the governors and other officials in West Africa were military officers. Most of them projected their careers around short periods of service disinguished by law and order, an occasional victory in battle, and freedom from scandal, followed by promotion to more significant assignments. They re-lied heavily on lower-level officials—French, métis, and African—who had more knowledge and investment in the local situation.

After the Napoleonic period, the French reestablished their colonial capital on the island of Saint-Louis.[7] They created a second center on the island of Gorée to the south and a number of lesser installations along the coast and up the river. The governor presided over a military contingent of fewer than a thousand men, a handful of administrators, and a small court system. For most of the nineteenth century, disease and the difficulties of recruitment kept the military and civilian numbers below their projected levels.

The governor also worked with the elaborate commercial structure de-scribed in chapter 1. Indeed, his overriding purpose was the encouragement and protection of this commerce, along with provisioning of the posts and maintaining order within the French enclaves.[8] He exercised not only executive but also legislative authority, through the decrees that he issued in the name of the ministry. He had influence over the judicial system, but its head was ap-pointed by Paris.

With limited resources and knowledge, the governor relied heavily on the more permanent inhabitants of Saint-Louis and the chiefs of the interior for good relations with the producers of the gum, hides, grain, slaves, and peanuts that fueled the commercial system.[9] On rare occasions he intervened militarily, preferably along the river or the coast, where he could maximize the impact of gunboats and minimize the exposure of soldiers to climate and enemy tactics. The image of weakness changed significantly in the middle of the century, when the government of the Second Empire made significant new investments to expand the French military, administrative, and economic presence.

This change was designed to provide more stable conditions for the exploitation of gum and peanuts.[10] The government entrusted the implementation to Faidherbe. As governor of Senegal for a relatively long period (1854–61, 1863–65), Léon Louis César Faidherbe began to change the image of the European from "master of the water" to "master of the land."[11] He was an engineer familiar with logistics, a military officer familiar with the chain of command, and an administrator who knew how to manipulate information. He had become a student of Islam and Arabic during his years of service in Algeria, and he brought that experience to bear on his activities in West Africa. He was both orientalist and ethnographer.[12] Faidherbe expanded the frontiers of the colony and developed its institutions. He created the standards by which his successors would be judged, or would judge themselves, and he continued to influence French activities in West Africa until his death in 1889. For all these reasons he is often considered the "father," or "founder," of Senegal, if not French West Africa.[13]

In military terms, Faidherbe pushed the Trarza Moors back from the lower Senegal valley, countered the influence of Al-Hajj Umar in the middle and upper valley, and made serious inroads into the kingdom of Cayor.[14] Along the river and coast, he multiplied the number of posts, which served as bases for conquest at a later period, and created several small protectorates, which provided the first significant experience in using local chiefs for administration. The river installations provided some stability for the harvesting and export of gum. The inroads into Cayor provided an infrastructure for expanding peanut and food production adjacent to the four communes. Faidherbe did not encourage the participation of members of the communes in his administration. He met regularly with the *conseil d'administration,* the only statutory consultative body at the time.[15]

In institutional terms, Faidherbe also followed a plan that had been approved some years before. He put the School of Hostages, where sons of chiefs were kept, on a sounder educational footing; it became the instrument for indoctrinating future chiefs and interpreters for the protectorates. He significantly enlarged indigenous military recruitment. Most of the local recruits went into a new structure, the Tirailleurs Sénégalais, which had a better organization and esprit de corps than the old town militias—and a much lower cost than metropolitan units.[16] He established a Muslim Tribunal to deal with property and family issues, satisfying a long-stated demand of the growing Muslim community of Saint-Louis (see chapters 4 and 6).[17]

Most of all, Faidherbe transformed the local Direction of Political Affairs, which handled relations with both protectorates and independent areas, into a truly effective instrument of central control. The bureau contained his most able and ambitious assistants, personally recruited, and was located next to that of the governor's offices, providing easy access in both directions. It contained key files of correspondence and reports—the beginnings of much of the colonial archives—and provided a wealth of information on relations with chiefs, marabouts, and the societies of the interior in general. The bureau ran an intelligence service, a hospitality center for visiting dignitaries, and the Arabic translation service discussed in the next chapter.[18] Many of the key figures in French imperial history, such as Joseph Galliéni and Martial Merlin, launched their careers from this office.[19]

Faidherbe's tenure was followed by a much quieter period, similar in some ways to the first half of the nineteenth century. The excesses of the Second Empire, the defeat by the Prussian army in 1870, and epidemics in West Africa made it difficult for the government to invest in its colony. In 1871 the School of Hostages was closed (for two decades). Recruitment for the Tirailleurs slowed. But the mid-century plan and some of the structure for establishing French control remained in place. Most importantly, Faidherbe's modus operandi remained the standard for future administrators: hierarchical control, limited and carefully selected advisers, and a willingness to manipulate information to obtain desired goals.

One new institution did emerge during this period: the Direction of the Interior. It had jurisdiction primarily over areas that were "French" territory: the communes themselves, military and commercial posts, rights of way, and areas that had been annexed to the colony, as distinguished from the protectorates and independent zones, where the Direction of Political Affairs held sway. The director of the interior was designated to serve as interim governor, a measure of the importance attached to the position.[20]

Brière de l'Isle took over the reins of administration in 1876, ushering in the period with which I am concerned in this book. Regarding himself as Faidherbe's successor, he received considerable support from Paris. His main direction of expansion was to the east, where he helped establish the Commandement Supérieur of the Soudan, initially under the aegis of the governor of Senegal. This command, based in Medine and then Kayes in the upper valley, eventually extended the flag to the Niger River.[21] But Brière was also the first governor who had to deal with the criticism and potential opposition of the electoral institutions created by the Third Republic (see chapter 5).[22]

Brière's successors completed the conquest of Senegal and the northern bank of the river.[23] In 1885–86 the French opened the rail line that linked Saint-Louis to Dakar and eliminated the last quasi-independent rulers of Cayor. They established their control of much of Salum in 1887. In 1890–91 they eliminated some of the last pockets of independence in Jolof and Futa Toro. They established telegraph lines along the coast and up the river and presided over the inauguration of steamboat service from Bordeaux to Dakar. The new technology made it possible for Paris to monitor the initiatives of its administration in Senegal more closely, but also facilitated contacts among other parties as well—a fact not always to the liking of the imperial chain of command.

In 1895 the French reorganized their West African holdings into four colonies (Senegal, Soudan, Guinea, and Côte d'Ivoire) and put them under a governor-general. This official retained the title of governor of Senegal and for several years continued to reside in Saint-Louis. He had expanded jurisdiction, but few additional staff or resources to deal with the affairs of the other territories. In 1902 the two positions were separated and the government-general moved to Gorée, and then to its permanent location in Dakar. Roume, the first governor-general under the new dispensation (1902–8), obtained significant new investments and took over the biggest source of local income: customs revenues.[24] These changes sped the decline of Saint-Louis. The DSL, the railroad from Dakar to Saint-Louis, was already a recognition of the more favorable port facilities of the emerging capital.[25]

But Saint-Louis was the staging area for the new frontier of conquest to the north. Coppolani, the "Algerian expert" on Islam who became the delegate and then commissioner of Mauritania, established his headquarters on the spit of land by the sea, opposite the island that housed the government of Senegal. Coppolani was able to establish a measure of French control of southern Mauritania before his assassination in 1905. Gouraud conquered central Mauritania in 1909. With the death of the leading resistance figure in 1910, the French became the dominant power in the region.[26] Although Dakar became the federal capital, Saint-Louis had the unusual distinction of being the capital of two colonial territories for more than fifty years.

Only the judicial system enjoyed some autonomy from the governor.[27] Paris created a judiciary based on French law and applicable to the communes and French citizens in other areas. A *tribunal de première instance* heard civil and criminal cases involving small claims. A *chef de service judicaire* presided over an appeals court, which also had original jurisdiction over larger claims. He was appointed by the ministry and did not fall directly under the authority of the governor.[28] The head judge dealt with two vexed issues of particular concern here: the application of metropolitan legislation on slaves and slavery, in areas that were "French soil,"[29] and the rights of African citizens of the communes, called *originaires*, when they operated in the interior. A number of judges showed considerable independence from the wishes of the governor—particularly West Indian appointees in rulings on the issue of slavery. In 1903 the appeals court was transferred to Dakar as part of the government-general's effort to centralize the system and control legal contestation.[30]

During World War I the beleagured French government intensified its demands on its subjects: France needed military recruits and increased food production. This had the effect of consolidating the control that the administration had been exercising for several decades. After the war the regime had more confidence in its knowledge and domination of all the territories, including Mauritania. It established bureaucratic routines and gained substantial control over some of the electoral institutions of the communes.[31]

INTENSIFICATION OF COLONIAL RULE: THE CONFLICTS

In the 1880s, after the departure of Brière, the strong governor cast in the mold of Faidherbe, the French were not able to sustain an expansive policy. The colonial administration in Saint-Louis had a succession of short-term and ineffective governors. Part of the problem was disease, in particular an epidemic of yellow fever. Another part of the problem came from inadequate metropolitan resources and indecision about the course of action to follow. A final cause came from the electoral institutions based in Saint-Louis. The mayor, his city council, and the General Council gave close scrutiny to administrative initiatives.[32]

The most troubling case for the administration in the 1880s was a sequence of events culminating in the revocation of Governor Genouille in 1888. Genouille made several controversial decisions that his opponents exposed in Saint-Louis and France. The first occurred in 1886, when the governor dispatched military units against the last two damels of Cayor. Lat Dior and Samba

Laobe were both killed in October 1886, evoking considerable protest in Saint-Louis and comment in the metropolitan press. The second event occurred the following year, when the governor and his director of political affairs confiscated and sold cattle herds of a French ally, the emir of Trarza. The emir was interfering, in the administration's view, in affairs south of the river. The final event occurred in 1888 after Genouille posted a small contingent of soldiers on a barren island off the coast at Conakry, with a limited supply of food and drink. The governor forgot about the deployment, whereupon the men died of thirst and starvation.[33]

The event that led to the arrival of a metropolitan inspector and the recall of Genouille was the confiscation of cattle, rather than the discovery of the bodies of the abandoned men. The lesson that administrators learned from Genouille's experience was to be more careful and consistent, without abandoning the intensification of French rule. Paris appointed Léon Clément-Thomas as governor in 1888, with a mission to expand and consolidate French colonial rule in Senegal. Clément-Thomas, his successor Henri de Lamothe, and the Direction of Political Affairs followed this mission over the next seven years, until the formation of the government-general in 1895. They were not always careful, but they did receive consistent metropolitan support.

The biggest challenge for Genouille's successors, and the one that propeled the process of centralization more than any other, was the Jeandet Affair. The precipitating events, an assassination and three executions, occurred in September 1890; the judicial inquiries—local and metropolitan—lasted another year.[34] Abel Jeandet had arrived in Senegal in 1887 with a background in the French prefectural service. His intelligence, loyalty, and ability to make quick decisions made a favorable impression on the administration. He joined the Direction of Political Affairs as a troubleshooter on critical issues. In 1890 Clément-Thomas sent Jeandet to the Podor area as the French mobilized their resources against the central part of Futa Toro—the last "pocket of resistance" in what was about to become colonial Senegal.[35] In the midst of this rapid mobilization, a disgruntled soldier, just demoted to the status of porter, gunned down Jeandet in his tent.

Clément-Thomas and his political director, Louis Tautain, ordered a rapid inquiry, established a plot, and then decapitated the assassin and two "accomplices" in the public square in Podor—French territory.[36] Their bodies were thrown into the river. One of the three men was the former chief of the protectorate of Toro, Lam Toro Sidikh, whom Jeandet had removed from office three years before.

At this juncture, a coalition of Saint-Louis interests, led by the métis family and firm of Gaspard Devès, intervened. The Devès had close links with traders and chiefs in the river valley, and especially in the Podor area. Appalled at the summary justice and execution on French territory, anxious about their constituency in the interior, and eager to gain advantage against the administration, the Devès mobilized a protest. They worked with the director of the interior, who served as interim governor in the days between the departure of Clément-Thomas and the arrival of de Lamothe. They notified the chef de service judiciaire, an *antillais* named Ursleur, who quickly saw the implications of the affair and launched an inquiry into the actions of Director Tautain, the commander of the Podor post, and one other official. The Devès also alerted Alexandre Isaac, the humanitarian activist and senator from Guadeloupe, and Admiral Aristide Vallon, the deputy whom they had put forward in the 1889 elections. Vallon's support was essential to counter the efforts of the Ministry of the Navy to dismiss the inquiry.[37]

The ministry, certain Bordelese interests, and Governor de Lamothe moved with equal urgency. Ursleur was recalled; his successor, another *antillais* named Henri Larrouy, and two other members of the judiciary were transferred before the end of the year. The administration decapitated the judiciary as surely as they had the alleged plotters. The inquiry was dismissed in Senegal. De Lamothe revoked the city council of Saint-Louis, which was under the leadership of a Devès ally, and put in its place a commission under the French lawyer Jules Couchard. Deputy Vallon was persuaded to drop the affair.[38]

Empire triumphed over commune and citizen, but the opposition pushed the French hierarchy to the limit. Alert individuals, autonomous institutions, and clear distinctions between judicial procedures in "French" and "imperial" territory made this challenge possible. The administration had to take extraordinary steps to cancel a procedure that could have led to intense embarrassment, the possible imprisonment of Director Tautain, and censure of two governors. The effect could well have been to delay the enterprise of conquest in West Africa.

De Lamothe remained in the governorship for four years (1891–95), well above the average tenure for the nineteenth century. He used his position and strong metropolitan support to consolidate the conquest, establish new procedures for colonial rule, and move against the opposition that had caused such discomfiture to the administration. He continued to interfere in the electoral process and the affairs of the Saint-Louis city council. He had other members of the judiciary and the interior reposted to other colonies. He took every opportunity to diminish the power of the Devès clan.[39]

De Lamothe's replacement was Jean-Baptiste Chaudié, the first person to serve as governor-general and to combine that post with the governorship of Senegal. He came from a position of inspector in the Ministry of Colonies, a background similar to Roume's and designed to reinforce metropolitan control of the emerging federation. But he brought few additional resources to his much larger task.[40]

Chaudié continued the campaign against the Saint-Louis "opposition." He launched an inquiry into the Banque du Sénégal, a venerable Saint-Louis institution that served the métis community and had just made huge loans to the Devès. Behind the authority of a metropolitan inspector, the administration put the bank into receivership, confiscated its records, and incorporated the surviving interests into the Banque de l'Afrique Occidentale, with strong metropolitan control.[41] In the communes, Chaudié maintained the interventionist posture of his predecessors, backing particular candidates and coalitions. He sought to intervene in the civil war that enveloped Trarza and Brakna during this period. In his search for mediators and solutions, he established direct contact with Sidiyya Baba and persuaded him to visit Saint-Louis for the first time. In this respect he laid the groundwork for Coppolani's campaign.[42]

The conquest of Mauritania was the next major battleground within the administration and the francophone community. The opposition here went far beyond the Devès party and the métis community, including a broad array of Saint-Louis interests and some officials in the Ministries of Colonies and Foreign Affairs.[43] Governor-general Roume, from the beginning of his tenure in 1902, gave critical support to the campaign of "pacification."[44] Through alliance with Saad Buh and Sidiyya Baba, Coppolani hoped to avoid significant combat and instead establish a series of protectorates and posts by processes of negotiation, threat, and rapid deployment of small military units. He was largely successful in the southwest, corresponding to the exhausted areas of Trarza and Brakna, where his allies were most influential. When he moved further east, into the Tagant, he faced a wider array of forces who were much less influenced by the Saint-Louis networks. It was there that he was assassinated in 1905 by a small group hostile to French domination of a Muslim land.[45]

The "pacification" plan challenged a modus operandi that the merchants had been using for some time. As Bakre Waly (see chapter 6) explained to Coppolani in 1904, the traders would exchange munitions and other manufactured goods from Saint-Louis, as well as grain and slaves from a variety of sources, for gum, animals, and other products.[46] The slaves, along with those the *bidan* acquired directly by raiding, provided labor of all kinds: farming in the cultivable zones, gum collection, porterage, and domestic chores. The whole system, including advances made to Moorish traders, was enforced by the emirs and other chiefs of the Trarza and Brakna. French conquest would undermine the system by ending the sale of slaves and munitions and weakening the authority of the enforcers. Coppolani played on the French commitment to antislavery in his mobilization campaigns.[47]

Coppolani's death produced intense discussion in the meeting of the General Council of 27 May 1905. Some members hoped that the French might even abandon the conquest of Mauritania. Theodore Carpot, brother of the Deputy François Carpot, presided; Camille Guy, the lieutenant governor, represented the administration. Georges Crespin expressed reservations about the Coppolani policy and his fear that the event would be used as a pretext for a more massive campaign of conquest. Hyacinthe Devès went further:

> A death such as this one is the fruit of a ruinous policy. We are not here to express condolences but to assure that the acts of the administration do not compromise the vital interests of the colony. When the death of an important functionary is the result of a policy which has made the economy of Saint-Louis stagnant, closed shops in Guet N'Dar [a special fief of the Devès and the *bidan*], and taken away the employment of a number of people, one should ask if it is not appropriate for the General Council to express a strong opinion to the decision makers of the colony.
>
> We must recognize that we have very little say in the combinations and conceptions which are supposed to create our happiness but in fact consummate our ruin. But, as they say, the situation is not a loss for everyone. The Mauritanian enterprise will produce ribbons, promotions and other advancement. . . . Mr. Coppolani was not one of ours, he did not even belong to the government-general. He belongs to the group which sent him, to Waldeck-Rousseau [president of the Republic], Delcassé [minister of foreign affairs] and others.

Devès proposed that the council recommend that Trarza and Brakna be reattached to Senegal, restoring the traditional Senegalo-Mauritanian zone, and that troops and police be withdrawn. His motion was not passed, but he expressed the sentiments of many Saint-Louisians.[48]

The government-general and the Paris ministries went forward with the conquest of Mauritania, but with some delay and with considerable attention to circumventing the opposition in commercial and administrative circles in

Saint-Louis.[49] They moved relentlessly against the most conspicuous members of the local opposition, the Devès. The métis and African communities had a strong sense of impending decline and marginalization, and they were determined to use whatever resources were available to make their protest heard. I take up these issues again in chapters 4, 5, and 6.

INTENSIFICATION OF COLONIAL RULE: INSTITUTIONAL INNOVATIONS

Governors Clément-Thomas and de Lamothe took important steps to intensify French power. First, they "disannexed" areas that were parts of the Colony of Senegal, where French law applied. Included in this measure was most of Walo and some of Cayor. The areas were reconstituted as protectorates, insulating the government from challenges such as those mounted in the Jeandet Affair. It also allowed the administration to circumvent legislation favoring emancipation; in short, to support the slave-holding elites, their labor force, and patronage.[50] The protectorate became the favored form of control in the whole Senegalo-Mauritanian zone.

Another problem was solved in 1892 when de Lamothe managed to wrest budgetary authority for the protectorates away from the General Council.[51] This change diminished significantly the financial resources and scope of the council's authority, the necessity for governors to consult, and the flow of information into potentially hostile hands.

With this accomplished, the governor and his director of political affairs, Martial Merlin, put in place their plan for the creation of a new corps of chiefs to fill the lower levels of the administrative hierarchy.[52] They reconstituted Faidherbe's School of Hostages as the Ecole des Fils de Chefs et Interprètes (EFCI), with sections for chiefs and interpreters.[53] Over the next two decades, the school would train most of the colonial chieftaincy. By 1895 the administration was already turning down, for lack of space, candidates recommended by some of its closest allies.

In 1893 the most promising students and future chiefs were sent to a Franco-Arabic secondary school in Tunis. The governor expressed his hopes for this project in terms that recall the innovations of Faidherbe at mid century: "It is to be hoped that these young men will come back to us with the conviction, based on their experience in Tunis, that there is no incompatibility between their beliefs and European science, and that they can become precious auxiliaries of . . . a Muslim civilization which expresses itself in French."[54] The nine persons sent to Tunis ranged in age from thirteen to seventeen years.[55] Merlin escorted them, kept in close touch with the school staff, and brought them back to Senegal in 1895. Four of the nine were conspicuously successful as colonial chiefs and brokers.[56]

The Senegalese who came to the Saint-Louis school in this period had good credentials in the ruling classes of Wolof, Serer, Futanke, and Mandinka societies.[57] They were young, usually unmarried, subject to the constraints of their families at home and the administration in Saint-Louis. They quickly found hosts and sponsors in town; some married local women and established residence there. When they started their appointments in the interior, they used these contacts and their overall experience in the colonial capital to keep informed about the administration. They were often a match for their administrative superiors, despite relatively low levels of French education. They became important mediators and disseminators of knowledge about Senegalese society. While they worked within the framework of the colonial hierarchy, most of them retained some autonomy and sensitivity to the interests of their constituents. In short, they accumulated considerable social capital to go along with their aristocratic credentials and administrative salaries.

The next major watershed in the intensification of French colonial rule came in 1902, when Ernest Roume took charge of Senegal's custom revenues and forced the territory to rely on a more systematic collection of the head tax to finance its activities.[58] Specialized services for education and native affairs were established. In accordance with Republican *laïcisation,* most of the Senegalese schools still under church control were taken over by the government. In many ways this was a culmination of the secular orientation to education that Faidherbe had started in the mid nineteenth century.

Two of Roume's innovations bear directly on the issues in this volume. First, the creation of a Muslim Affairs Bureau to collect, channel, and disseminate information about Muslim societies and their marabouts. Islamicists with experience in French North Africa gave the colonial regime, for the first time, the capacity to survey the Muslim communities, differentiate among them, and establish coordinated practices of control.[59] I mentioned this in chapter 2 and expand on it in chapter 4.

Even more important was the government ban on war, raiding, and the importation of firearms. This prohibition was implemented more consistently than the ban on slave trade and slavery because it directly affected the new colonial order and the security of French forces. It weakened the power of the old aristocracies in the Senegalo-Mauritanian zone since it threatened the acquisition of booty and the patronage networks. It cut down on slave raiding and trading and diminished the practice of slavery.[60] Perhaps most of all, the ban created opportunities for marabouts, who in theory and by profession did not carry weapons or engage in raiding. They could transform slaves into followers and disciples and accumulate even larger amounts of economic, social, and symbolic capital in the colonial era.

William Ponty replaced Roume in 1908. Ponty has a more liberal and paternalistic image in the historiography, but he essentially continued and elaborated on the policies of his predecessor.[61] He brought Paul Marty in to head the Muslim Affairs Bureau in 1912. He continued the support of the conquest of Mauritania and worked out the arrangements that brought Amadu Bamba to Diourbel. By the time of his death in 1915, France was plunged into World War I and forced to depend, in ever more intensive ways, upon its West African colonies. The Muslim orders, now allies of the colonial regime, did not hesitate to affirm the French cause, condemn the Ottoman position, and supply disciples and followers for the battlefields of Europe. This support, together with the needs of the colonial authorities and their growing confidence in their knowledge and control, ushered in a new, calmer collaboration, just as the generation of the founders of the orders was passing away.

All of these processes—centralization, rationalization, secularization, diminishing the role of the military, budgetary constraints, and specialized services in the cultural and social spheres—intensified the practice of colonial rule.

MEDIATORS, DISSEMINATORS, AND ACTORS IN THE PRACTICE OF COLONIAL RULE

Chapter 2 has indicated how closely the French related knowledge and power. It did not ultimately matter how accurate the knowledge was or how it was obtained, as long as it had some correlation to realities within the Senegalo-Mauritanian zone. The mediators and disseminators of that knowledge—African and European, black, métis, and white—were recognized, appreciated by some and contested by others. Many of these mediators were also significant actors in the creation of colonial rule.

One can identify "teams" who played critical roles: one around Faidherbe in the mid nineteenth century; a group of *soudanais* around the Commandant Supérieur; and the associates of Coppolani in the conquest of Mauritania.[62] Here I wish to emphasize French officials who spent considerable time in the

Senegalo-Mauritanian zone, had an impact on events, and shaped the frameworks of colonial practice. Because of their competence, loyalty, and ability to interpret facts in a certain way, they received key appointments during the period of conquest and establishment of colonial rule.[63]

The oldest and most "local" of the four men was Victor Allys (born in 1849, retired from administrative service in 1907). He served in central Futa in the late 1880s, when that zone was not yet under French control. He supervised the suppression of the movement of a Muslim reformer in 1890, participated in the drive against Albury Ndiaye in Jolof and the Jeandet events later that year, and helped shape the column that completed the conquest of Futa in 1891.[64] He served in boundary negotiations with the British on Gambia, became interim director of political affairs in 1894, and was back in Futa in 1895 to deal with "Mahdist" agitation and the return of the Umarians from Karta.

Allys became administrator in Kaolack as the French were extending their control in eastern Salum at the turn of the century. When a small group of Muslims revolted and burned the village of the official Senegalese resident, he ordered an investigation, conducted summary trials, and decreed draconian punishments: the execution of several offenders, forced labor for a much larger group, and severe fines for villages that had ostensibly failed to inform the authorities of the threat. When his decisions became known, he was transferred without censure to another post.[65]

The new assignment was even more critical: administrator in Tivaouane, the central post in the heart of the old peanut basin. There Allys played a key role in several important cases. He made decisions on the succession of Demba War Sall, who served as the president of the Confederation of Cayor from 1886 until his death in 1902. Allys, who spoke Wolof fluently and was a close confidante of the chief, helped decide to break up the confederation into smaller units. More important were his actions in monitoring the return of Amadu Bamba from Gabon and carrying out the second arrest and deportation of the Murid leader in 1903.[66]

Robert Arnaud (born in 1873, retired in 1934, died 1950) was a member of the Coppolani team from the beginning.[67] Son of a government translator, Arnaud grew up in Algeria, bonded with Coppolani, learned Arabic, and mastered the rudiments of Islamic law, theology, and history. He accompanied his friend to the Soudan in 1898 on a mission to survey the northwestern frontiers of the territory and the nomadic populations thereof—specifically the Moors and Tuaregs. It was there that Coppolani conceived of the project for the western portion of the Sahara and gave it the name Mauritania.

Arnaud joined his colleague in the "pacification" of southern Mauritania. He was present in Tijigja at the time of the assassination and wrote his version of events in his biography of Coppolani.[68] Roume then incorporated him into the service of the government-general as the Muslim Affairs officer. In this capacity, he traveled on a secret mission to Morocco to explore the influence of Ma El Ainin, interviewed a brother of Amadu Bamba, and wrote the first statement of Muslim policy for French West Africa—a precursor to the works of Marty a decade later.[69]

Jean-Baptiste Théveniaut (1870–1956) had a wide range of experience. After serving as a military officer in Madagascar and Soudan, Théveniaut participated in the efforts to demarcate the frontiers among French possessions in the Sahara—Algeria, Soudan, and Mauritania, an enterprise fraught with potential for intra-French conflict.[70] In 1905 he resigned his commission and became a civilian administrator, with responsibility for eastern Trarza. He had his headquarters at Boutilimit, the residence of Sidiyya Baba. He organized the first "camelry" units. He collected documents of historical interest from Saad Buh, which were translated, published, and became part of the French framework for understanding Mauritania.[71] Théveniaut undoubtedly became acquainted with Amadu Bamba, who was spending his second period of exile (1903–7) in the sphere of Baba.

In 1908 the administrator was assigned to Diourbel, the post closest to the Murid heartlands. Amadu Bamba was now in his third exile (1907–12), in a remote area of Jolof; the preparation for his return to Diourbel, his final residence, was well under way. Théveniaut helped complete the process of "domestication" of Bamba. He was relieved of his post in 1913 because he sought to intervene too sharply in the growing relations of accommodation between the administration and the Murids (see chapter 11).[72]

The final figure I will mention was even more closely linked to the fortunes of Amadu Bamba. Martial Merlin (1860–1935) moved further up the administrative ladder than any of the others. Beginning in the Political Affairs Bureau, he designed the system of chieftaincy described above and was promoted to director by Governor de Lamothe. It was as director that he wrote the reports that called for the deportation of Bamba to Gabon.[73] Merlin remained at Political Affairs and played a large role in the reorganization of Baol, which was rapidly becoming a Murid fiefdom.[74] After service in Congo and Guadeloupe, he returned to Senegal to the position of secretary-general to Roume.[75] In that capacity he made the critical decisions to arrest and exile Bamba to the Sidiyya enclave in Mauritania in 1903. Merlin made other important contributions to the tenure of Roume; he filled in as interim governor-general on several occasions. He then served as governor-general of Afrique Equatoriale Française and Madagascar. Just after World War I, Merlin returned to Dakar as governor-general of the federation. His chief antagonist in the effort to centralize authority in French West Africa was Blaise Diagne, the deputy and inheritor of the remnant of the Republican tradition.[76]

— —

THE STANDARD INTERPRETATIONS OF the history of Senegal in the first two decades of the twentieth century feature a nationalist or protonationalist sequence: the mobilization of African voters in the four communes, culminating in the 1914 election of Blaise Diagne as Senegal's first black deputy.[77] This is certainly an important story, and the beginning in one sense of the move toward independence. But it too often has concealed the sequence of continual contestation, growing administrative control, and a steady erosion of the autonomy of local civil society.

As a defining moment of this period one should juxtapose, alongside the election of Blaise Diagne, the replacement in 1921 of the General Council by the Colonial Council. The new council contained appointed as well as elected members. Among those appointed were chiefs such as Buna Ndiaye and Abdussalam Kane. Its architect and spokesman was none other than Martial Merlin, now the governor-general. The new council would never challenge the administration in the manner of its predecessor.

The intensification and centralization of French colonial authority occurred over several decades and against considerable opposition. The process was ultimately successful, forcing chiefs, marabouts, and their followers to deal with non-Muslim rule. At the same time, the French accommodated themselves to the reality of subjects who were overwhelmingly Muslim. The practice of "Muslim Affairs" played a large role in shaping the "paths of accommodation" that they and their subjects took. That is the preoccupation of the next chapter.

—4—

France as a "Muslim Power"

AT CERTAIN TIMES IN ITS HISTORY, one might think of France as a Christian power.[1] At no time would one think of it as an Islamic power. But by the early twentieth century, French authorities were actively discussing and evaluating their policies as a *puissance musulmane*, by which they meant an imperial power with Muslim subjects. They controlled the Maghreb, through the colony of Algeria, the protectorate of Tunisia, and an emerging sphere of influence in Morocco. In West Africa they were taking over many Muslim societies. They had established interests and clients in the declining Ottoman Empire. They published the *Revue du Monde Musulman* to deal with questions of knowledge and power. The French compared themselves to Great Britain, the Netherlands, Germany, Italy, and Spain—other countries with "Islamic" dominions or interests.[2]

The point of origin of the concept of "Muslim power" is Napoleon's invasion of Egypt in 1798. He controlled a significant portion of the country for about two years. He took a range of scholars with him, presented himself as a friend and respecter of the Islamic faith, and gave a stimulus not only to Egyptology but also the study of Islam in France.[3] But it was only after the invasion of Algiers in 1830 that the French had Muslim subjects and developed institutions for governing them. Algeria became the litmus test of France as a Muslim power.[4] Algerian precedents were invoked in the Senegalo-Mauritanian zone, and never more frequently than in two periods: during the "creation" of Senegal by Governor Faidherbe in the 1850s and at the time of "pacification" of Mauritania in the early 1900s.[5]

By the Anglo-French Agreement of 1890, France fell heir to northwestern Africa—the area that became the French North and West Africa. This required an effort to become an "Islamic power," since the overwhelming majority of the inhabitants were Muslim, or fast becoming Muslim. The French feared Islam, recalling its long history of opposition to Christendom as well as its "incursions" into southwestern and southeastern Europe.[6] But they had no illusions about rolling back the Muslim identity of most of their subjects.[7] They would have to establish institutions of control. If they were successful in institution building, and in establishing a certain hegemony as a "Muslim power," they might reduce investment in the apparatus of repression.

In the 1890s the French expanded their African empire and capacity as a "Muslim power." Much of the initiative came from Jules Cambon, the activist governor-general of Algeria, who embarked on the conquest and consolidation of the Sahara and the establishment of links and boundaries with the colony of the Soudan. He sent a number of Algerians to serve as interpreters and guides in the emerging French domains in West and equatorial Africa.[8] It was on Cambon's watch that Xavier Coppolani and Octave Depont wrote the large study of Muslim brotherhoods and recommended close relationships between colonial government and Sufi leaders. Cambon supported Coppolani's request for assignment to survey the nomadic societies of the Soudan, a project that gave birth to the campaigns of "pacification" of Mauritania.[9] One of the governor-general's most significant achievements, for France as a Muslim power, was to secure decrees *(fatwa)* from the leading authorities of Mecca saying that submission to European rule was acceptable for Muslims.[10] The Muslim tradition of fatwa could now be used as an instrument of legitimation for French rule.

Morocco presented the strongest ideological challenge for France in North and West Africa. Unlike Algeria and Tunisia, it had never been a province of the Ottoman Empire. There could be no rationale of "liberation" from foreign rule, for Morocco was a rival of Istanbul in stature and independence within the Islamic world.[11] In the eighth and ninth centuries, it had a Muslim state with strong claims to descent from the Prophet; this "Sharifian" principle was sustained by most of the subsequent dynasties—including the Alawites, who have controlled the country since the seventeenth century.

Morocco was the base of the reform-minded Almoravids and Almohads, both of whom resisted the Christian reconquest in Spain. In more recent times, its dynasties fought the coastal incursions of the Portuguese and Spanish, who dressed themselves in Crusader clothing. The court laid claim to hegemony in the south, as far as the Senegal and Niger Rivers. While these claims did not evoke much local response, they could be important in a time of crisis. When the French were conquering West Africa, local Muslims did call upon the Moroccan sultan for assistance.[12] In all these ways the Sharifian kingdom upped the ante for any would-be "infidel" force. It is not surprising that, for reasons of prestige as well as location, Morocco was the last piece of the northwest African puzzle to fall to the French, nor that the challenge that it presented would have a significant impact on Islamic practice in West Africa.

The emergence of France as a Muslim power in the Senegalo-Mauritanian zone occurred in the late nineteenth century, thanks in part to influence from the North African experience. The emergence was critical to the "paths of accommodation."[13] Amid all the puffery and pretention, this conscious effort to control Islamic societies, select Muslim leaders and allies, and put a secular and tolerant face on imperialism was essential to whatever success colonial rule enjoyed. When the anciens régimes fell, the French could point to their acceptance of the institutions of Muslim civil society, particularly Islamic law and Sufi orders. To put it in Gramscian terms, the French sought to create an hegemony to parallel their domination.

In this chapter, I look at the ethnography that the French used in the nineteenth century, the growth of an established practice of relating to Muslim societies, and some of the individuals and families upon whom the French relied. I then turn to the early twentieth century, when that practice was elaborated into a full-blown policy, when France became fully a "Muslim power" in the Senegalo-Mauritanian zone.

FRENCH ETHNOGRAPHY IN THE NINETEENTH CENTURY

After the French resumed their commercial activities in West Africa, they developed close relations with the Moorish, Fulbe, Futanke, and Wolof peoples of the Senegalo-Mauritanian zone. On the basis of their experience, and the formulations of local mediators and disseminators of knowledge, they assumed that all four groups, in varying ways and degrees, were Muslim.[14] They extended that assumption to other groups who lived to the east, as they expanded over the course of the nineteenth century. Saint-Louis was not unlike the rest of the zone. It had significant Muslim communities but not a very strong Islamic identity in the earlier parts of the century. Over time it became more Muslim, both in the sense of numbers and with respect to the depth of learning and practice. The French also extended their dominion into the wetter, forest zones of the south. There they concluded, not inaccurately, that the inhabitants were practitioners of "ethnically based" religions—which they labeled paganism, fetishism, or animism.

The colonial government, a very modest operation based in Saint-Louis, worked with versions of this ethnography throughout the nineteenth century. It became the basis for deciding where Roman Catholic missionaries would work and what areas they should avoid. By and large, the missionaries shared the same conceptual framework, even when they protested what they often called the "pro-Islamic" practices of the government. They concentrated their efforts on the Serer and Diola in the central and southern parts of Senegal, and the profile of the Catholic community in Senegal today reflects that deployment.[15]

With few exceptions, the French made no effort to contest the Muslim identity accorded to ethnic groups; nor did they oppose the process of islamization in which they were engaged. Rather, they sought to channel the process, classify Muslims into "tolerant" and "fanatical" groups, and limit the influence of the latter.[16] As they expanded their knowledge, they became more confident in their ability to establish their authority. Over the course of the late nineteenth century, they realized the limitations of that knowledge, the need to improve their ways of collecting and interpreting data, and the imperative of finding their own "path of accommodation" for ruling over Muslim subjects.

For the French, the Moors were camel-and-cattle nomads who lived in siba, or dissidence, in the desert. They were "natural" Muslims. They were Arabic-speaking, and some of them claimed descent from the Prophet or the Quraysh. They called themselves *bidan,* "white," and considered themselves superior to the *sudan,* the "blacks." The French tended to accept these constructions of religious and racial identity and superiority.[17] It was the conquest of these "natural" Muslims in the early twentieth century that pushed the French to develop their capacity as a "Muslim power"—as I will show later in the chapter.

The Fulbe posed a special problem: they often claimed to be "white" or "red" and had more Caucasian features than the *sudan,* yet they spoke a language and practiced a culture that were obviously indigenous to the region. The French speculated on the possibilities of external origin as a way of attributing superior intelligence and physical appearance to them. The Fulbe raised cattle and followed paths of transhumance, like the Moors, and they were not attached to particular states. They were Muslim, but not particularly devout and certainly not fanatic. In general, they seemed opposed to reform movements.[18]

The Futanke, labeled Tokolor by the French and Wolof, were a different matter altogether. They spoke the same language as the Fulbe, but they were "fanatic" Muslims attached to the jihad and Islamic state. This stereotype grew from the experience of dealing with the sedentary farmers of Futa Toro and their leaders—Almamy Abdul Kader and Al-Hajj Umar. Umar came to personify fanaticism and the equation between Futa, Tokolor, the Tijaniyya order, and militant Islam. The French maintained this stereotype well into the twentieth century, and in some ways it survives to this day.[19]

The Wolof image was more nuanced. There was obviously an Islamic presence at the main courts, in the form of qadis, teachers, and other advisors, but they shared center stage with the ceddo, the crown slaves who consumed alcohol, pillaged the peasantry, and in other ways resisted the discipline that Islam was reputed to impose. Indeed, in many ways they behaved like the warrior *bidan*—raiders, highway robbers, outlaws—except that they were obviously "black." Ceddo and court often fought against the Muslim villages and minirepublics in their midst.[20]

These images were remarkably resilient over the course of the nineteenth century. The French usually found ways to attach resistance to the Futanke and Tijaniyya "branches" of Islam, until they encountered the threat of Ma El Ainin, the Qadiriyya and *zwaya* leader of Mauritania in the early twentieth century. The basic racial categories, "white" and "black," persist to this day.

Muslim Institutions and Officials in Saint-Louis

Over the course of the nineteenth century, the process of islamization was most marked among the Wolof. That process paralleled what occurred in Saint-Louis, the Wolof-speaking town at the edge of the old kingdoms of Walo and Cayor. By the time of Faidherbe's appointment in 1854, the Muslims of Saint-Louis had formulated a rudimentary plan for their community. They wanted a mosque, and had actually constructed one in the northern part of the island with the acquiescence of the colonial government.[21] This disturbed the Catholic priests and some parishioners, but the government's attitude was consistent with the religious ethnography, the traditions of toleration from the Enlightenment, and the secular orientation of French regimes since the time of Napoleon.

The Muslims also sought a court where Islamic law could be practiced on questions of family and property. The request was fulfilled when Faidherbe issued a decree for the establishment of a Muslim Tribunal in 1857.[22] This official sanction for the practice of Islamic law occasioned, as one might expect, a protest from the Roman Catholic community, but again it was entirely consistent with

French traditions and a recognition of the Muslim identity of the town and region. It would be hard to overestimate the importance of the tribunal for the image of Saint-Louis as a Muslim center—and the image of French toleration.

Faidherbe took other important initiatives in the educational and military arenas, as I indicated briefly in the preceding chapter. He took over the Ecole des Otages, the School for Hostages, where a lay Christian society provided rudimentary French education to sons of the aristocracy, and made it into a more secular institution for training chiefs and interpreters.[23] He refashioned local military recruitment by creating the Tirailleurs Sénégalais, under French officers. By changing the dress to more "Algerian" and "Ottoman" styles, allowing families to accompany the soldiers in some situations, and providing significant rewards for loyal service, the governor created a valuable instrument for conquest at much less expense than metropolitan units. Faidherbe also inaugurated the practice of the "sponsored" pilgrimage to Mecca for selected friends of the colonial regime—a way of demonstrating the consideration for the Islamic faith. He made sure that these achievements, and the exploratory missions that he commissioned, were widely publicized.[24]

Faidherbe put these institutions under the Direction of Political Affairs, the service next to his office and under his close control.[25] This agency was also the location of another innovation: a translation service for Arabic correspondence. In time, this service became a diplomatic operation and reception center for chiefs and marabouts in the Senegalo-Mauritanian zone. In great part this was because of the local Muslim notables that Faidherbe enlisted for this work—persons who had clear credentials of piety, learning, and prestige in the faith. The leaders of the translation service and the Muslim Tribunal burnished the Islamic image of Saint-Louis. They gave substance to the French claim of tolerance. They were able to work for the government without compromising their Islamic practice or their standing among most Muslims in the Senegalo-Mauritanian zone.

In effect it was two men and their descendants who served in this capacity for most of the late nineteenth century. The older one was prominent in Saint-Louis affairs for almost forty years. Hamat Ndiaye Anne (1813–1879) came from Futa Toro. His mother belonged to the family of Ndiak Moktar Bâ, a commercial and political broker in Podor. His father, Ndiaye Anne, hailed from a prestigious clerical lineage and settled in Saint-Louis in the early 1800s. He acquired a position of moral leadership over the Muslim community and functioned as a scribe for the administration in its dealings with chiefs and clerics in the interior. In time, the moral leadership was institutionalized in the title of *tamsir,* which in Saint-Louis translated into "head of the Muslim religion."[26]

Ndiaye and his son were the first to sign the 1843 petition calling for the creation of a Muslim judicial authority (the future Muslim Tribunal), and they may well have drafted it.

It was at about this time that Hamat took over the functions of his father in relation to the Muslim community and the French administration. When the Political Affairs office was created in 1845 to handle relations with the interior elites, he became its principal interpreter, accompanied expeditions into the river valley, and handled correspondence and treaty formulation. In 1857 Faidherbe made Hamat judge, or qadi, of the Muslim Tribunal, as well as third deputy mayor of the town. The Catholics struck out at Faidherbe and the tamsir; they called the governor a "marabout"; he was, they said, "trying to attract the good opinion of the Tamsir for whom he has a particular predilection. He proposed to create in Saint-Louis the famous Muslim Tribunal to the tune of 3000 francs for his dear Hamat and 2000 for his agents."[27] There was also division in the Muslim community: Muslims attracted to the preaching of Al-Hajj Umar criticized Hamat for his close association with the administration and they forced him to explain his actions in discussions at the main mosque.[28] Hamat's successful defense lent legitimacy to the idea of an Islamic practice compatible with French rule.

Over the 1860s and 1870s, Hamat continued to function as translator at the Direction of Political Affairs, interpreter for expeditions, and mediator in disputes in the interior.[29] He was engaged in correspondence with chiefs and clerics in other parts of the Senegalo-Mauritanian zone.[30] During the famine of 1865–66 and the cholera epidemic of 1868–69, he rendered great service to the administration by public appeals for calm. A grateful administration sent him on the pilgrimage, made him a knight and officer of the Legion of Honor, and provided prestigious gifts. His funeral in 1879 was almost a state occasion.

The Seck family played an even more critical role in supporting the French as a "Muslim power." Dudu Seck (1826–1880), better known as Ibnu-l-moqdad or Bu El Mogdad (see plate 2, made at the time Bu El Mogdad was making the pilgrimage and receiving decorations for his service to the French), took over the main responsibilities in Arabic correspondence when Tamsir Hamat became head of the tribunal.[31] His father Abdullay came from the Dagana area, on the western edge of Futa. He settled in Saint-Louis early in the century as a trader and cleric. In keeping with his Mauritanian connections, he sent his son to study in a Trarza school.[32]

Bu El Mogdad signed the 1843 petition, alongside Ndiaye and Hamat Anne. He began to serve the administration in the early 1850s. After 1857 he

helped train the corps of interpreters at the Ecole des Otages. He handled the
correspondence, treaties, and most of the diplomatic missions to the interior,
while the tamsir stayed in the capital. Given his education in southern Mauritania and fluency in Hassaniyya Arabic, he maintained close connections with
the *bidan*, offering his home to visiting marabouts, such as the Sidiyya of
Boutilimit.[33] He had an especially close relationship with Lat Dior for twenty
years. He also traveled to Futa Toro, Salum, and wherever the French had need
of his services. He journeyed to Mecca twice at administration expense, was
decorated as knight and officer of the Legion of Honor, and received a highly
publicized award from the Ottoman government.[34] When Hamat died, Bu El
Mogdad became qadi and tamsir until his own death the following year.

Bu El Mogdad had a larger and more aggressive view of his role than Tamsir Hamat. He accomplished a great deal for the extension of French hegemony
in almost three decades of service. He assisted Faidherbe with the development
of propaganda against "militant Islam" and Al-Hajj Umar, in particular. He and
Faidherbe developed the strategy for his pilgrimage in 1860–61 and portrayed
it as an effort to counter Umarian prestige.[35] In making the case to the director
of political affairs, Bu El Mogdad said:

> I think it would be most advantageous that some of the marabouts who are
> loyal to the French should achieve supremacy over those who still retain the
> old prejudices. As you know, the strongest marabouts are already those who
> serve French interests; but they would enjoy more influence still if they were
> not merely enabled to visit Paris and Algiers, but allowed to make the pil-
> grimage to Mecca, like Al-Hajj [Umar]. Such a pilgrimage might have very
> important results, because it would be known in the country that it was made
> under French patronage and that this patronage was as valuable as the best-
> established reputation as a good Muslim.[36]

In 1878 Bu El Mogdad took two of his sons, Abdullay and Dudu, to the Exposition Universelle in Marseille; he then performed the pilgrimage a second
time.[37]

At Bu El Mogdad's funeral in 1880, Governor Brière recognized his invaluable service in support of the French as a Muslim power:

> The qadi and tamsir can undoubtedly be replaced in the two functions he ex-
> ercised by two black clerics. But what cannot be replaced is the influential Al-
> Hajj, the devoted and eminently intelligent servant who was of such powerful

assistance in our relations with the Moors, the damel of Cayor, the sultan of Segu. This death occurring at the moment of inaugurating free trade on the river, and as we begin large undertakings on the Niger, can only be considered a calamity for the administration of the colony.[38]

Brière was right. The vacuum caused by the death of Hamat and Bu El Mogdad in successive years created problems of stability and credibility in the 1880s.

The administration sought to replace their services in a variety of ways. Ndiaye Sarr, a merchant based in Podor with a strong background in the Islamic sciences, became qadi at the tribunal.[39] Mambaye Fara Biram Lô and Abdullay Mar Diop filled in at the Interior and Political Affairs bureaus, and merchants like Pèdre Alassane Mbengue were pressed into service for particular tasks of negotiation (see chapter 6).[40] For the key position of translator and ambassador at the Direction of Political Affairs, the French went back to the Seck family and selected Abdullay, the oldest son. He took over assignments similar to those of his father until he was killed on a mission in Baol in 1887.[41] Within a month the French called on the next son, Dudu (1867–1943), or Bu El Mogdad II, to perform similar missions and translations. Dudu soon became a specialist in Mauritanian affairs and fulfilled the same role in French expansion in the Senegalo-Mauritanian zone that his father had performed so well and for so long.[42]

Dudu accompanied all of the key missions into the turbulent areas of southern and central Mauritania in the late nineteenth and early twentieth centuries. In 1893 he made the pilgrimage to Mecca, with stops in France, in the company of Ibra Almamy Wane, a chief of Futa. In the eyes of French officials, the pilgrim credential was more important for Dudu than for Ibra, and they made substantial use of it in the decades to come.[43] His most significant achievement, in terms of its impact on French policy and practice as a "Muslim power," was probably bringing Sidiyya Baba to Saint-Louis for the first time in 1898.[44] Dudu accompanied Coppolani on all of his campaigns between 1902 and 1905. He was present at the death of the Frenchman; family tradition says that, out of respect for the prestige of the Seck family, neither Dudu nor his mount was attacked by the assassins.[45]

The Anne and Seck households lived near the main mosque in the north. They developed close ties. Hamat's sister Kumba married Bu El Mogdad and gave birth to Dudu and Ainina; Hamat's granddaughter Indu married Dudu. Several of the ruling lineages from the interior sought the hands of women in the two families. A marriage tie to these established figures was a guarantee of access to the administration (see fig. 4.1).[46]

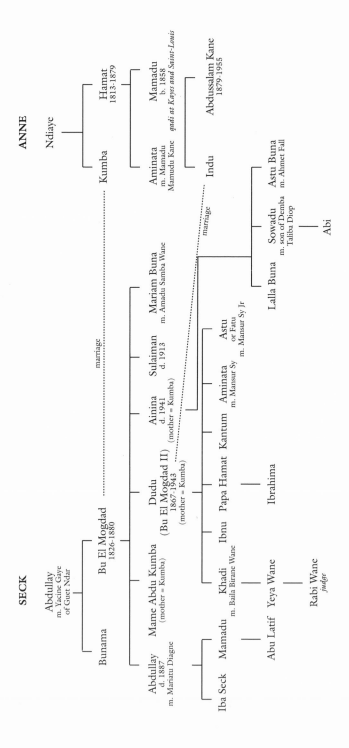

Fig. 4.1. The Anne and Seck Families

For the administration, the value of these Muslim leaders was incalculable. The Anne had their origins in the Futanke tradition, linked to the Almamate, while the Seck were formed among the *bidan* teachers of Trarza. Between them they represented the two most prestigious traditions of Islamic practice in the wider region. Their familiarity with Arabic, Islamic jurisprudence, and theology was unquestioned and helped to protect them from the potentially negative associations of cooperation with the French. As well as being actors on the Senegalo-Mauritanian stage, they were mediators and disseminators of knowledge par excellence. Their symbolic and social capital was durable and convertible, for themselves and the French regime.

The Anne and Seck were committed to the French presence and expansion, in whatever form.[47] The commitment and prestige were transmitted far and wide and carried over to the administration that they represented.[48] Hamat, Bu El Mogdad, and the latter's son Dudu were the precursors of the collaborative roles that Sidiyya Baba played at the beginning of the twentieth century and Seydu Nuru Tal a generation later.

FRANCE'S EMERGENCE AS A MUSLIM POWER: THE LATE NINETEENTH CENTURY

As the French expanded militarily in the 1880s, they made more attempts to understand Muslim societies, secure allies, and isolate enemies. They began to think in terms of a West African empire and to draw upon their North African precedents for dealing with Islamic communities. In time this exploration would become a full-scale "Islamic policy," yielding the Muslim Affairs Service launched by Roume and Ponty.

The geographical expansion that produced the Federation of French West Africa followed three directions: north, south, and east. The northern extension— Mauritania—came only in the early twentieth century. The southern extension was designed to consolidate control in the peanut basin.[49] The focus was the construction of the rail line from Saint-Louis to Dakar, completed in 1885. The French continued to use their basic ethnography of the Wolof—seen as a collection of Muslim and not-so-Muslim peoples. They did not anticipate the growing numbers of Muslims among the royals, crown soldiers, and peasants, something that became evident in their conflicts with Amadu Bamba and the Murids.

The eastern extension was led by the Commandant Supérieur, resulted in the establishment of the colony of Soudan, and produced the officers who often went by the name of *soudanais*. While the command became increasingly independent of Saint-Louis, it depended initially on the Direction of Political Affairs for its knowledge of custom, history, and religious affiliation. The most fundamental assumption of the bureau was the hostility of the Tijaniyya order to the French presence. The equation, Tokolor = Tijaniyya = fanatic, remained alive and well in the 1880s. Umar had evoked it in the Senegal River valley in the 1850s, and Ma Ba and the Madiyanke had strengthened it in the 1860s and 1870s.[50] The Tijaniyya was sometimes associated with the massacre of the second Flatters Mission in the Algerian Sahara in 1881, and even with the rise of the Mahdi in 1885 in the Sudan.[51]

The soudanais kept this image of hostility very much alive during the 1880s, as they used the Umarian dominions — or what remained of them — as the enemy against whom they were bound to struggle.[52] Amadu Sheku, from his capitals of Segu and then Nioro, could do little to stem the advance, but he was a convenient foil for ambitious officers in search of resources and promotion. It was this stereotype that largely motivated a rather curious episode in the mid 1880s.

A certain Abdel Kader, a Qadiriyya Muslim who claimed to be from the ruling circles of Timbuktu, behind the Umarian domain, arrived at the headquarters of the Commandant Supérieur. He assured the soudanais that one of Amadu's main lieutenants was on the verge of revolt, while the Grand Council of Timbuktu was prepared to grant exclusive commercial rights to the French. By the end of 1884, Abdel Kader was swept off to France and received by the Ministries of Colonies and Foreign Affairs. The next year he was sent back to Senegal, where he had to wait for two years for a mission to take him back to Timbuktu.[53] Abdel Kader was not heard from again, but the whole episode showed that the French, without much good information, or ability to check their informants, were thinking about rule over a large portion of West Africa and searching for allies for that purpose.[54]

The sense of a larger domain and the need for "Islamic" expertise led to the mission of Alfred Le Châtelier in 1887–88. Le Châtelier (1855–1929) was a well-educated military officer and Islamicist with considerable Algerian experience. He liked the challenges of crossing cultural and religious frontiers. He joined the first Flatters expedition into the Sahara, went up to the frontier of Mahdist control in the Nile Sudan, and spent time in Cairo collecting information on brotherhoods in the Hejaz.[55] Bored by garrison duty in France, he persuaded the Ministries of War, Foreign Affairs, and the Colonies to allow him to study Muslim orders in West Africa.

Le Châtelier's study confirmed some French predilections and contradicted others.[56] He came away convinced of the hostility of the Tijaniyya to the French presence. He confirmed the "fanatic" equation in the religious ethnography. He noted that Saint-Louis had become an important Muslim center and thought that most of its inhabitants were Tijani.[57] This finding was in some conflict with his other main observation: a rejection of the position of the "Algerian school" of Islamicists that Sufi brotherhoods were well organized in hierarchies and posed dangers for European control. Le Châtelier found the Sufis to be diverse and autonomous and he argued for policies of modernization and French education to bring them under colonial rule. In the absence of other studies of West African Islamic practice, Le Châtelier's work became the authority until Robert Arnaud and Paul Marty published their work in the early twentieth century.[58]

The stereotype of Tijaniyya fanaticism began to fade in the 1890s, after the conquest of the last Umarian bastions and consolidation of French control in the Soudan. Thousands of Futanke emigrants were forced out, back to their original homelands in the middle valley. The return journey was perilous and showed that the mailed fist was never far from the velvet glove of French imperialism.[59] While the "Umarians" disputed title to land and village leadership with those who had stayed behind, they posed no significant problem for the colonial chiefs and French administrators in Futa. Their main impact was to speed the transition of most Futanke to Tijaniyya affiliation.[60] At the beginning of the twentieth century, Amadu Moktar Sakho, member of a prestigious and learned Umarian family, became a colonial judge in Boghé, an important town in western Futa. For the Futanke, he was a role model of submission; for the colonial authorities he provided reassurance about the loyalty of the Tijaniyya (see chapter 7).[61]

At the end of the nineteenth century, the French administration in the Senegalo-Mauritanian zone had a well-established practice, if not always clear policy, toward Muslim societies. The core principles were straightforward. The French opposed Islamic states and reform movements, especially when the leadership was Tijaniyya and Tokolor and key interests were involved, such as the river valley and peanut basin. They sought out, in contrast, people like Abdel Kader of Timbuktu, Muslim leaders who rejected jihad and state building. These Muslims were often Mauritanian and members of the Qadiriyya Sufi order, and this was consistent with the French belief in the superiority of *bidan* to blacks. Finally, the French maintained the Muslim institutions of Saint-Louis, institutions that encouraged Muslims to accept the compatibility of foreign rule and Islamic culture.[62]

This practice was contained and transmitted through the Direction of Political Affairs, its oral traditions and archives, and its African translators and diplomats—most especially Dudu Seck. The direction and its African employees played host to visiting dignitaries, marabouts as well as chiefs. They could make much of the growing reputation of Saint-Louis as a center of Muslim learning and worship, and of the compatibility of Islamic piety and French rule. They also made use of "Islamic" resources from the Maghreb. One was a French translation of a compendium on the Maliki law dominant in North and West Africa. The *Mukhtasar* of Khalil ibn Ishaq was widely used by scholars in the Senegalo-Mauritanian zone. Colonial officials could now employ the French version for their own edification and relations with Muslim societies.[63] The other resource was the vast catalog of Sufi orders published by Octave Depont and Xavier Coppolani in 1897.[64]

The French had two important marabout allies in the interior in the late nineteenth century. Both were Qadiriyya and Moor. One was Saad Buh, who settled in Trarza in the 1870s, developed a following in Saint-Louis, and started his pattern of visits to the peanut basin and river valley (see chapter 8). During the last two decades of the century, he gave invaluable service to the administration—service that Dudu Seck, as a functionary, could hardly perform. Saad Buh received French missions, gave them his best advice, and sometimes helped them escape destruction. He made diplomatic missions for the French in Senegal—trying, for example, to persuade Lat Dior to accept the rail line or the successors of Ma Ba to submit to French rule. In return, the French allowed him to travel freely in areas under their control, nurture his clientele, and tap into the revenues of the peanut farmers of Senegal.[65]

A less-known but equally important ally was Bu Kunta, from a *bidan* family that had settled in Cayor. He helped Faidherbe in his campaigns in 1860. He assisted again in the final conquest of Cayor in 1886. In the words of Paul Marty, and despite his "maraboutic vocation," Bu Kunta "marched with several columns, took part in several engagements, and used all of his influence to restore calm among the natives who had revolted. When calm was restored, he gathered a great number of the former crown slaves and placed them in villages where they could live in peace and get accustomed to the new regime."[66] The people, villages, and fields belonged to Bu Kunta himself: he accumulated a massive fortune and pioneered the marabout-disciple pattern of peanut farming in Cayor—the essential structure for the colonial political economy.

FRANCE'S EMERGENCE AS A MUSLIM POWER:
THE EARLY MAURITANIAN CAMPAIGNS

After the turn of the century, well-established practice became full-blown policy. The causes were multiple. The competition among Western European nations for control of African space intensified. French officials felt an increasing urgency about occupying northwestern Africa, since Spanish, German, and British agents were active in Morocco and down the coast. The Saharan trade was changing dramatically, and many merchants, transporters, and security forces were moving south, toward the river and into Saint-Louis, disturbing the remnants of order in the French commercial sphere.

The western portion of the Sahara, the area that became Mauritania, was a land dominated by siba, "dissidence" or controlled chaos. Despite the absence of any central Islamic government, the ruling classes had no doubt about their Arab or Islamic identity. They were clearly part of the Dar al-Islam, and many claimed genealogies stretching back to the Hejaz. The French, to organize the occupation of this area, predictably searched their Maghribi experience. What better place to look than to Xavier Coppolani, the brilliant young Islamicist who had just completed a study of Sufi brotherhoods and a tour of the nomadic societies of the Soudan?

Coppolani was more than willing to distinguish himself in a new theater of operation. He was an advocate for the Algerian emphasis on networks of brotherhoods and the importance of controlling them. In the words of his close associate Arnaud, in the journal that they created together, the leaders of the Sufi orders

> should become agents of the state, entrusted in certain circumstances to distribute assistance to the poor, manage schools, and administer the areas around their *zawiya* [lodges]. With official titles and subsidies . . . with frequent visits and aid in the reconstruction of mosques and saints tombs . . . with confidence reestablished between the directors of Islam and the European regents, one could begin, with great delicacy, the work of improving Islam and moving it in the direction of our civilization.[67]

Coppolani formulated the concept of Mauritania and its frontiers and then proposed French occupation, not as conquest but "pacification." He built his strategy around the traditional vocational division in *bidan* society between the political and military leaders *(hassan)* and the religious and commercial entrepreneurs *(zwaya)*. He would ally with the second group, the "pacifists" responsible for trade and arbitration on the basis of their knowledge of Islamic law and Sufi stature.[68] The plan was a hard sell for metropolitan and local officials wary of the difficulties of establishing control of any part of the Sahara. It was a measure of Coppolani's ability to argue his case, as well as his obvious knowledge of Islam, Arabic, and the desert, that enabled him to win approval from the Ministries of Colonies and Foreign Affairs and the governor-general, Roume.[69]

On the ground in 1902, Coppolani set quickly to work. The "pacification" would have to occur from the southwest or Trarza. This meant that the campaign would necessarily challenge Morocco and its claims to control the Sahara, and that the conquest of Mauritania would be prelude to the conquest of Morocco itself. "Pacification" was built around the maraboutic allies of the Saint-Louis administration—Saad Buh and Sidiyya Baba. Before his assassination in 1905, Coppolani, with a relatively small deployment of French and African troops—including those of the "pacificist" marabouts—came close to achieving his plan in the southern tier of Mauritania.

When Coppolani called on the services of France's old ally Saad Buh, he found a reluctant collaborator (chapter 8). When he called on the new friend, Sidiyya Baba, he found the co-architect of "pacification" (chapter 9). One of Baba's most important initiatives, early in 1903, was to issue a fatwa in favor of colonial rule. Drawing on the jurist Khalil ibn Ishaq, and noting that the French controlled much of the Maghreb already, the marabout stated unequivocally that the obligation to wage jihad disappeared when Muslims were weak, had no treasury, and possessed inferior weapons. He claimed that the French had been supportive of Islam by their attitudes and actions.[70] The French could not have asked for a more timely and explicit endorsement—one from inside the Dar al-Islam and in the words of the prestigious West African marabout.

The key legacy of the Coppolani campaigns was the creation of enduring alliances with Muslim leaders in the interior.[71] Until the end of the nineteenth century, colonial authorities relied mainly on their Muslim functionaries in Saint-Louis and on the system of chieftaincy described in chapter 3. These chiefs, despite their ability to sustain some symbolic and social capital, exploited, bribed, and coerced their subjects.[72] On the other hand, the marabouts were becoming key allies. In Mauritania they were instrumental in the conquest. In Senegal they were already helping to solve significant problems of agricultural production, labor supply, and social control in the peanut basin. They could transform slaves and former slaves, who supplied so much of the agricultural labor, into followers. As disciples or clients of the marabouts, the former slaves would be contained within a sociopolitical structure and were less likely to attract the attention of antislavery activists.[73]

The French did not formalize this emerging alliance in any system of "official clergy" as they did in Algeria.[74] They allowed the relationships with Malik Sy and the Murids to develop over time. They saw the wisdom of not trying to include the marabouts in the colonial hierarchy, just as the latter sought to retain their autonomy in relation to the regime. After the "centralizing" Roume and the "pacifying" Coppolani moved into place in 1902, the French consolidated a policy of accommodation coupled with surveillance, a policy that would characterize the Senegalo-Mauritanian zone throughout the colonial era.[75]

France's Emergence as a Muslim Power: The Later Mauritanian Campaigns

When the French resumed the conquest of Mauritania in 1908–9, they concentrated on the Adrar, the commercial hub of the far western Sahara. The Adrar was a region of much more tangible Moroccan influence, and its occupation by an "infidel" power was bound to implicate the Sharifian kingdom. Morocco represented a great challenge. It was *makhzen*, "government," compared with a variety of forms of siba in the Atlas mountains and Mauritania. Its sultans were saintly as well as powerful—descendants of the Prophet, with their own place of pilgrimage in Mulay Idriss.[76] They could not be trumped by Ottoman forces nor the infidels of the West. If the French were contemplating conquest, they would have to use fictions and formulas of indirect rule to "protect" Morocco's prestige. If they could conquer the "Sharifian kingdom" and legitimate their action, they would enhance their status as a Muslim power.[77]

The prestige of Morocco did not prevent it from falling victim to European influence.[78] The army suffered defeats at the hands of the French and Spanish in the northeast, lost territory, and agreed to reparations. The court, in an effort to modernize its army, communications, and economy, sought European advisers. It borrowed money and used customs revenues to pay the debt. Mulay Hassan I (1873–94), remembered as the last "great" sultan of precolonial times, sought to modernize without losing control. He also made some effort to revive Moroccan claims to hegemony in the Sahara.[79]

Hassan's efforts at best slowed the pace of European encroachment. His vizir, Ba Ahmed, succeeded him as the de facto ruler. Ba Ahmed himself died in 1900, whereupon two of Hassan's sons sought unsuccessfully to maintain the country's prestige and independence. They were young and inexperienced. Moroccan and European advisors pulled them in many directions, and the inhabitants of the country were alarmed by a declining economy and the increasing presence of European agents. The French penetrated progressively into the country, finally declaring a protectorate in 1912. The delay in establishing the protectorate was more the result of European competition than of the strength of Moroccan government.[80]

Despite its weakness, Morocco loomed large in the minds of Frenchmen eager to enlarge and consolidate their holdings in West Africa. They brandished the Moroccan menace, to make the metropole provide the resources necessary to conquer Mauritania. At the same time, they were haunted by the "fear of Islam," by the possibility that someone would marshal modern firearms, the traditional hostility to a European presence, and the still substantial prestige of the Moroccan court to produce a massive jihad in the dangerous unknown of the Sahara desert. After the death of Coppolani, that apprehension was personified in Ma El Ainin, an older brother of Saad Buh.[81]

Ma El Ainin (1838–1910) left his native Hodh in the 1850s to make his way to Morocco and on to the pilgrimage. His learning, miracle working, and wise counsel impressed many, including members of the Moroccan court, where the cleric enjoyed direct access for the rest of his life. For them, Ma El Ainin was not only a way of asserting Moroccan influence in the Sahara, but also a spiritual and social resource in the turbulent times of the late nineteenth century. By 1870 Ma El Ainin had established his headquarters in Smara, in the Saqiyat al-Hamra—an area that would become part of the Spanish Sahara. Gifts from the Moroccan court and his own followers enabled him to establish an elaborate zawiya, or lodge, for what some were calling a new branch of the Qadiriyya Sufi order, the Aininiyya. Over the decades his influence grew, as well as his determination to resist European encroachment.

At the turn of the century the French knew of Ma El Ainin's reputation for learning and sanctity, but did not anticipate his opposition to European imperialism.[82] It was the assassination of Coppolani, the arrival of a Moroccan envoy in the Adrar in 1906, and the ensuing turbulence that turned the French definitively against Ma El Ainin. They then demonized him as the incarnation of resistance and fanaticism that threatened the French mission in northwestern Africa.[83] To a significant degree, Ma El Ainin conformed to this image. He became increasingly committed to the jihad of resistance, and he distinguished the threat of the French from the activities of the other European powers in northwestern Africa.[84] He criticized the sultans for their compromises with the European powers and may even have considered becoming sultan himself.

In the pause between Coppolani's death and the Adrar campaign, French officials linked the conquests of Mauritania and Morocco as never before. They made Ma El Ainin into the enemy of both. Their answer to the propaganda of Ma El Ainin and the link with Morocco was twofold. The first and irreplaceable response was force, in the form of the Henri Gouraud's conquest of the Adrar. A column went up through Trarza, and was joined by a supporting unit marching up from the Soudan. They made short work of the fragmented resistance in early 1909.

The second and equally important response was the mobilization of French prestige as a Muslim power. This campaign echoed the rhetoric of Bu El Mogdad's pilgrimage of 1860, over against the threat posed by Al-Hajj Umar. But this time the stakes were much higher. The strategy took the form of promoting Sidiyya Baba. If the Moroccan sultan could receive Ma El Ainin in his palace in Marrakech, the government-general could host the learned, eloquent, and charismatic leader of the Sidiyya coalition in its "palaces" in Saint-Louis and Dakar. Commissaire Montané-Capdebosc put the case very effectively in a 1907 letter to Roume, the governor-general.

> At his request I authorized Shaikh Sidiyya to come see me in Saint-Louis. In giving this authorization to the most venerated religious leader of Islam in French West Africa, whose influence and prestige, which has been put entirely in our cause, has counteracted effectively the efforts of opponents of our Mauritanian penetration, I was working for two political purposes. First, to annihilate as much as possible the influence of Shaikh Ma El Ainin in Mauritania in giving him a serious rival across all of the country of the Moors. Second, to accredit Shaikh Sidiyya to the Moorish groups as the principal religious leader on whom we have based our policy in Mauritania. If the sultan of Morocco received Shaikh Ma El Ainin with great esteem and gifts before all of his subjects . . . we cannot, without making a grave mistake, fail to take advantage of the opportunity to oppose the influence of Shaikh Sidiyya to that of the favorite of the sultan.[85]

Baba did not hesitate at the comparison. In fact, Gouraud and Baba jointly made the case for the campaign to the minister of colonies, Milliès-Lacroix, at a meeting in Dakar in 1908. Baba argued persuasively, on the basis of his own intelligence networks, that the people of the region were disillusioned with Ma

El Ainin and the Moroccan court. With a forceful policy and proper direction, they would support the new regime of colonial Mauritania.[86] Gouraud took the key towns of the Adrar, whereupon Baba traveled to the region to give his seal of approval and receive expressions of submission.

THE RESULTS: ISLAM NOIR AND ISLAM MAURE

The close relationship between Baba and French authorities was unusual and enduring. It started after the first visit to Saint-Louis, became intimate during the years of Coppolani, and lasted through the next generation of Sidiyya. The relations with Saad Buh, Malik Sy, and Amadu Bamba were marked by greater reserve, on both sides of the equation. But the policy of simultaneous accommodation and surveillance applied to all four relationships. The policy became full-blown under the impetus of the conquest of Mauritania and Morocco. France could now portray itself, in internal relations with subjects and external relations with European rivals, as a Muslim power in West Africa. Its North African experts could provide guidance to the administration of the federation.

In 1905–6, Governor-general Roume gave institutional shape to the policy by selecting Robert Arnaud as his Islamic specialist within the Political Affairs Bureau and commissioning his *Précis de la politique musulmane,* a kind of handbook for the administrator of "Muslim" West Africa.[87] Governor-general Ponty brought in Paul Marty from Tunisia in 1912 and issued the decree creating a separate Service of Muslim Affairs.[88] The service had a vast repository of files and the above-mentioned *fiches* going back to the Direction of Political Affairs, as well as continuing information coming in from the field.[89]

Most of the elements of surveillance were already in place: the intelligence reports, the forms on the various marabouts, the checks on the Muslim courts, and the monitoring of the various kinds of school systems.[90] To this apparatus was added, especially during the tense conditions of World War I, control of the pilgrimage by sea and monitoring subscriptions to Arabic newspapers. The war was also the occasion to elicit a series of declarations from the "main marabouts" of French West Africa. These were published in the *Revue du Monde Musulman,* the journal founded and edited by Le Châtelier, to demonstrate loyalty to France, over against the menace of Pan-Islamism and the Ottoman Empire.[91]

The evidence of accommodation—encouragements given to the marabouts and their constituencies, the correspondence, and personal contacts—is spread through the archival record, the oral tradition, and the spaces between the lines of both. It was expressed in the exchanges of visits, the French presence at important celebrations, and in a new confidence—expressed by marabouts and officials alike—about a working relationship that left considerable autonomy to each side.

It was Marty, the North African in the tradition of Le Châtelier, Coppolani, and Arnaud, who analyzed the vast information inherited from the Direction of Political Affairs and the *fiches de renseignement.*[92] He was strongly influenced by Sidiyya Baba in his approach to the subject. With the data, the tradition, and the influence, he then formulated the histories and constituencies of the Fadiliyya and Saad Buh, the Sidiyya and Baba, the Tijaniyya of Umar and Malik Sy, and the Murids of Bamba. His influence at the time, as the assistant of Governor-general Ponty and his successors, was substantial. His impact on subsequent generations of administrative practitioners and Africanist scholars is incalculable.

Marty codified what was fast becoming operative practice in colonial circles. It responded to the old religious ethnography of the nineteenth century, but was now placed in tighter compartments.[93] The main section, *Islam noir,* was epitomized by the Murid innovations in Muslim practice, but could be applied to the Futanke and other ethnic groups. It was operative in the *sudan* ("black") societies of West Africa. At its "worst," or in its least "Muslim" variants, it faded into the "paganism" of societies to the south.[94] The minor variant was *Islam maure,* as framed by Baba, Saad Buh, and the other Saharan interpreters, and it was operative among the *bidan.*[95] It corresponded more or less to Islamic orthodoxy, in the official mind.

This compartmentalization reflected contemporary French racial thinking. It provided a convenient set of stereotypes for the actions of colonial administrators. It enabled the West African federation to take its place, alongside the versions of indirect rule established in Tunisia and Morocco, as one of the "success" stories of French imperialism. European administrators of other nationalities would know that France was a Muslim power in West Africa with a coherent Islamic policy based on carefully collected facts, systematic analysis, and solid publication.

It is ironic that a practice and policy, constructed with considerable arrogance and under the direct control of an authoritarian administration, would yield enduring relations of collaboration without compromising either side in any significant way. The might of the administration, and its increasing ability to control the flow of arms and slow the pace of raiding, certainly opened the way to the new pattern. But alongside force emerged a sensitivity to the need to accommodate to Muslim societies and their institutions of civil society—especially

Islamic law and Sufi orders. This made it possible for distinguished local functionaries to adjudicate, translate, and conduct missions for more than sixty years
and for Saint-Louis to develop a strong Muslim identity. The challenge of conquering Mauritania then forced the development of an intense collaboration
with the *zwaya* class of *bidan* society, and this in turn transformed an established
practice into a full-blown policy. Over the late nineteenth and early twentieth
centuries, the French developed their own "path of accommodation" and their
symbolic capital as an "Islamic power."

It is not surprising that the French would look to North African precedents
and experts in the elaboration of this policy. Coppolani, Arnaud, and Marty
played key roles in that elaboration, under a much stronger and more hierarchical
administration.[96] At the same time, local interests ensured that the new policy
was not a copy of a Maghribi model but responded, in some measure, to West
African traditions. This partial approximation to local realities was the key to its
endurance.

Alongside the challenge to govern Muslim societies, the administration
faced the task of interpreting and defending its imperial expansion to several
French audiences. The most difficult audience consisted of the inhabitants of
the four *communes de pleine exercice* of Senegal, and especially those of Saint-
Louis. These people were not subjects but citizens, whatever their color. They
were very aware of their rights, expressed through institutions created by the
Third Republic, and had their own ideas about how imperialism should be
practiced. They formed a civil society capable of challenging the administration and opening up additional space for accommodation. That is the story of
the next chapter.

—5—

Civil Society

Saint-Louis in the French Imperial Sphere

IMPERIALISM AND COLONIAL RULE were processes of domination, not participation. While democratic institutions and universal suffrage might advance on the home front, the nations of Western Europe did not entertain the idea of extending the rights of citizenship to their colonies. Colonies consisted of subjects, not citizens.[1] Consequently the concept of civil society, that is institutions that function within nation-states and have substantial autonomy from the government, has not often been evoked for the empires created in the nineteenth century.[2]

It was nonetheless true that in most colonies some subjects were more empowered than others. Chiefs who had real local constituencies had some influence on the colonial regime, as did Western-educated Africans who knew the language and the system. Such Africans organized delegations, circulated petitions, and conducted campaigns in a variety of ways. Colonial authorities were obliged to seek African allies and auxiliaries to assist in administration, reduce costs, and extend the reach and legitimacy of the regime. The British colonies typically had "Legcos," legislative councils. Some of their members were African, and some were elected—by a very restricted electorate.[3]

The four communes of Senegal had much more than this in the late nineteenth century. They benefitted from the Republican ideology of universal male rights, first articulated in the French Revolution of 1789 and then again in 1848, and extended to a few island or urban communities in the empire. These rights inspired African, métis, and French inhabitants of the communes throughout the nineteenth century, but they were not seriously practiced until the

Third Republic created electoral institutions—city councils, mayors, a deputy to the French Assembly, and a General Council—in the 1870s. These institutions started in the oldest settlements—Saint-Louis and Gorée—and then in Rufisque and Dakar. They were never extended to other towns, much less the countryside.[4] In the four communes, however, this expression of citizenship produced feverish participation, heated competition, and headaches for the authoritarian administration of the governor and governor-general, as seen in chapter 3.

Saint-Louis, the location of the governor and his administration, produced the biggest headaches. It had the largest population, the best French schools, the headquarters of the General Council, and the most seats on that body. With the emergence of the telegraph and regular steamship service, the citizens of Saint-Louis had the means to provide alternative sources of information to their interlocutors in France and, on occasion, to challenge the interpretations and actions of the colonial administration.

In this chapter, I divide what is usually called civil society into two.[5] The "public sphere" refers to the electoral institutions created and maintained by the Third Republic in the four communes. The "private sphere" refers to the social, educational, and religious organizations and institutions. The private sphere was where the political coalitions mobilized their networks of support. Both spheres could oppose the third element in the West African equation: the administration and the military.

Here I wish to demonstrate the importance of the public and private spheres for the paths of accommodation. I am not suggesting that the citizens of Saint-Louis or the other communes were opposed to French colonial rule and its extension in West Africa. Most of them supported that expansion, most of the time, under most conditions. But some of them had a great deal to say about how, where, and when that extension occurred, and they did have some ability to force changes. This is why the administrators of Senegal and the federation, beginning with Léon Clément-Thomas in 1888, worked so assiduously to reduce the powers of the electoral institutions.

Nor am I suggesting that the African Muslim citizens—called *originaires* in the debates of the early twentieth century—were the most active participants in the Republican institutions. Through most of the nineteenth century, the local French and, especially, the métis populations dominated the electoral institutions. They had the educational equipment and the metropolitan connections for the task. They were children of the Enlightenment and the French Revolution, and not beholden to Islamic law and culture. But by the early twentieth century, Western-educated Muslims had completed their apprenticeship and learned to organize themselves in Republican terms. They then came to dominate the electoral institutions.

Finally, I am not suggesting that the leading figures of civil society were particularly linked to marabouts and Muslims in the interior. Indeed, many of the prominent members of Saint-Louis' métis population were conservative Roman Catholics who protested against the "Muslim institutions" and "pro-Islamic" policy of the administration. Others, of a secular cast, opposed established religious institutions of any kind. But the practice of electoral politics, the conflicts of coalitions in the communes, and the search for networks of support in the interior created the opportunity for diverse interpretations of what French intentions were. The institutions of civil society created space for accommodation to colonial rule.

THE INSTITUTIONS OF THE PUBLIC SPHERE

The Third Republic of France (1871–1940) followed two conflicting practices in its West African holdings. On the one hand, it resumed the process of imperial expansion; on the other, it reinforced the electoral institutions of the Senegalese communes. These institutions consisted of the mayor and city councils, chosen in each of the four communes, one deputy to the French National Assembly, chosen by voters in all of the communes, and the General Council, a quasi-legislative body with representatives from all the communes. All three were based on metropolitan models and male suffrage.[6]

Candidates had to be able to read and write French, but the vote was available to all males who had lived in the communes for five years.[7] Typically, the voting turnout was light (30 to 40 percent). The governor (later, the governor-general) had supervisory authority over the conduct of elections; from time to time, they intervened, delayed the vote, or found a way to suspend an elected official, but they were never able to stop the process.[8] Political clans and candidates made great promises and distributed money to gain the vote. The large and well-organized Bordeaux firms were at a particular advantage by virtue of their resources.[9] But political corruption was no more rampant in Senegal than in most parts of Europe and North America at the time. The electorate was interested, the competition serious, and the stakes significant.

Mayors had functioned at Saint-Louis and Gorée for some time.[10] They were ostensibly appointed by the governor and had authority over police, health, and other issues affecting the well-being of their citizens. Members of the older and wealthier métis families typically dominated these positions. The mayor of Saint-Louis was a particularly influential politician in the first half of the nineteenth century. Jean-Jacques Alin (served from 1829–47), for example, wielded more influence than the governor with the leading participants in the gum trade and the court in Cayor, which was the main source of grain for the town.[11] At mid century, Faidherbe and Second Empire officials were able to limit the influence of the mayors, transfer diplomatic duties to the Direction of Political Affairs, and to secure more tractable officeholders.

In 1872, the Third Republic decreed that the male inhabitants of Saint-Louis and Gorée had the right to elect councils just as did towns in France.[12] In 1882 they added the right to the direct election of mayors and assistant mayors.[13] Saint-Louis selected a council of fifteen, and members served for six years. The métis population dominated the council in Saint-Louis, and several of the town's most influential businessmen and functionaries created political machines to mobilize the voters and dispense patronage.[14] They did not hesitate to express their disagreements with the governor and his administration.

The most visible of the Republican institutions was the deputyship. In 1848, Durand Valantin, a prominent métis figure, became the first deputy, serving until the Second Empire abolished the position in 1852. The Third Republic reestablished the office in 1871. Saint-Louis, by virtue of its population and political activism, dominated the vote until the end of the century. French commercial firms played a considerable role in the choice of candidates and outcome of elections by their money and mobilization of employees, and they sometimes "parachuted" in individuals with rather tangential relations to Senegalese interests.[15] But over time the knowledge and ability to represent local interests became important, and the electorate became more discriminating. French and métis candidates competed actively for the prestige and patronage of the position, and for the African vote, until Blaise Diagne became the first African (that is, black) deputy in 1914.

The deputy was the main point of interaction between Senegalese and French politics. He spent a considerable part of the year in Paris at the Chamber of Deputies, with access to his fellow legislators and to the press. The wise official also spent time in Bordeaux to consult with the firms involved in West Africa; indeed, the Bordeaux houses and chamber of commerce were themselves active on the Paris scene, and they sought to make the deputyship their pawn and plum.[16] At the same time, the representative was subject to pressures from a variety of other sources, such as the Ligue des Droits de l'Homme, a humanitarian lobby that emphasized antislavery, liberty, and equality.[17]

If the deputyship was the most visible electoral institution, the General Council had the greatest local influence. Modeled on the departmental councils in France, it advised the governor, debated local questions such as taxes and customs, legislated on public works and other matters, and had substantial sway over the budget. The governor controlled mandatory costs, which included all operating expenses of his staff and public services, but the council passed on optional expenses, which meant most construction projects, scholarships for study in France, and a variety of other outlays, and it had the right to debate and approve the whole budget.[18]

In 1879, the Third Republic approved a General Council consisting of ten members from Saint-Louis and six from Gorée and Rufisque.[19] The same métis clans that dominated the city council of Saint-Louis competed for control of the General Council; they came to think of it as their fiefdom and means of checking the power of the administration.[20] To give substance to their vision, they established a permanent commission that met throughout the year in a handsome, new headquarters built to symbolize its role.[21] The rear of the building faced the river, the main artery of commerce, while the front looked toward the residence and offices of the governor.[22]

The métis spent most of the year in Saint-Louis and hence knew the local political scene more fully than the French businessmen or the administrators. They became masters of political mobilization, the manipulation of information, and the use of the French legal and judicial system. They resolutely defended their identity as French citizens. Some questioned anything that threatened to disrupt order and commerce, and this made them suspicious of expansion in the Soudan, consolidation in Senegal, and the conquest of Mauritania. The General Council was their most effective political instrument. Its transformation into the Colonial Council in 1921 symbolized the eclipse of the métis and the ebbing power of Saint-Louis in relation to Dakar.[23]

THE INSTITUTIONS OF THE PRIVATE SPHERE

The electoral process energized the private sphere. One of the key institutions was the Roman Catholic Church, a small but cohesive community in the capital. It fell under the leadership of a missionary order, the Congregation of the Holy Ghost and the Sacred Heart of Mary, and the Ploermel Brothers, a lay order based in Brittany.[24] In agreement with the administration, the priests, sisters, and brothers conducted little or no proselytization, at least not in heavily

Muslim areas.[25] Instead they constituted a community of worship around the church in the center of the island, a medical clinic, and several schools. They depended on government subsidies for the clinic and schools. The church did not exercise much direct influence on the administration, but through its most prominent parishioners, principally métis, had a significant impact on public life and politics. The church took a conservative approach on most questions and generally considered the administration too "friendly" toward Islam. These attitudes were reinforced when the Third Republic ordered the *laïcisation* of education and medical work in 1903.[26]

The Muslim community of Saint-Louis was much larger and less closely integrated. It, too, had a corporate identity, a leadership structure, and an architectural symbol. Since early in the nineteenth century, the government recognized the tamsir,[27] the "head of the Muslim religion," and sometimes gave him official status as an assistant to the mayor.[28] The Muslim leaders were concentrated in the Nord, or northern section of the island, in contrast to the Sud, sometimes called the *kretian,* or "Christian" quarter. In the Nord, they succeeded in constructing a mosque, over the protests of some Catholics. Under the tenure of Faidherbe they established another goal: a tribunal that applied Islamic law to disputes about family and property. The tamsir continued to preside, at least in a ceremonial sense, over the Muslim community of Saint-Louis.

The Muslims in Saint-Louis maintained a distinct cultural identity. Few of them could read or write French. Most of their signatures on petitions are in Arabic, a result of their education at the Quranic schools of the town. More advanced Islamic study was available in Saint-Louis, and students also had the option of going to schools in the interior. The Seck family sent their sons to *zwaya* schools run by the Awlad Daiman group, while some one hundred Saint-Louisians were studying in the school established by Saad Buh in the 1880s. Both were in Trarza, a region with a reputation for excellent Islamic education.[29] By the turn of the century, some of the more prominent Muslims were donating land and monies to build mosques, schools, and Sufi lodges in the city.[30]

Some inhabitants of Saint-Louis identified with neither the Catholic nor the Muslim persuasion. These "secularists" included French civilian and military personnel who expressed the Republican tradition of hostility toward the established church, and a small but significant number of métis. The Devès family, who are virtually absent from the Catholic registers of marriage of the nineteenth century, often espoused views that were critical of the church and its parishioners.

It is tempting to speculate on the links between some of these "secularists" and the Masonic orders. A lodge, the Union Sénégalaise, was established in Saint-Louis in 1873, dissolved by Governor François-Xavier Valière in 1876, and reestablished in 1881 with the encouragement of the city council.[31] Another lodge, the Etoile Occidentale, was set up in Dakar in 1893. The membership in both groups was small, but possibly quite signficant. Governor-general William Ponty was a member, as was the administrator Victor Allys. Some members of the Devès coalition belonged, and at some point Africans became members as well.[32] Additional research may eventually reveal that a number of other strategically placed individuals were Masons, but the significance of membership will remain difficult to assess.

Masonic interests were linked, in the minds of the Roman Catholic community, with the opposition press. Until the 1880s, the only newspaper published in Senegal was the *Moniteur du Sénégal et Dépendances,* launched by Faidherbe to disseminate official information and news of the colony.[33] Some French and métis began to publish *Le Réveil du Sénégal* in 1885 and *Le Petit Sénégalais* in 1886, both under the editorship of a French journalist, Auguste Foret. When the papers made insinuations about members of the Catholic community, some conservative métis parishioners brought libel charges, got the editor and manager fined, and embarrassed the financial backers. Both papers folded almost immediately.[34] But independent newspapers surfaced again in 1895 as Paris moved to reorganize its West African dominions in the government-general, and they soon became a permanent feature of the local landscape.[35]

The newspapers took a strongly assimilationist line. They were hostile to institutions that supported the autonomy of the non-French community, such as the Muslim Tribunal. They argued for a more complete system of education in the colony, and specifically the establishment of a *lycée* to complete the second (pre-baccalaureate) cycle of schooling. Local French education at the time consisted of several primary schools and one secondary school run by the Ploermel Brothers, but nothing that led to the baccalaureat, the principal degree and gateway to many careers.[36]

In proposing the lycée, the *Réveil* was critical of the system of awarding scholarships to boys and girls from the communes to pursue their secondary studies in France. The General Council made these awards amid intense competition that emphasized the family's record of service rather than the child's qualifications.[37] The scholarships permitted some of the métis to get a solid education and find alternatives to the old commercial tracks that had been the norm in their families. A few of them opened law or medical practices in the

communes, tested the political waters, and became critics of government practices.[38] The métis lawyers and their French counterparts played a critical role in
energizing civil society and, at some critical junctures, challenging the state.

One institution that enjoyed widespread support in Saint-Louis, among
métis and African communities, was the Banque du Sénégal.[39] Founded in 1855,
over some opposition from Faidherbe and the administration, it became a source
of savings and credit for a significant number of men and women in the town.
The director and his staff were influential members of the métis community. In
1895, the new government-general reacted to some large loans to the Devès interests, brought in an inspector, and put the bank under very tight control for the
next few years. In 1901 they dissolved it and transferred the remaining assets to
the Banque d'Afrique Occidentale. The administration used the inspection to
centralize control and to attack the autonomy of Saint-Louis. The campaign
probably did more to bring the métis community together than any other set of
events of the late nineteenth century.[40]

These institutions of civil society, based primarily in Saint-Louis until the
twentieth century, corresponded to no particular political or social orientation.
The electoral process had its share of corruption. The institutions defended
their own interests and were certainly not "pro-Muslim" at any time. The administration, in many ways, was a better "friend" of the faith, as I have suggested in chapter 4. But the networks of civil society did provide opportunity
for Africans, métis, and French to mobilize resources and pursue collective
goals, often with surprising effect.

Muslim Africans were at a disadvantage in terms of direct access to the
electoral, legal, and cultural systems, but their relatively low profile in the archival record before 1914 should not be confused with passivity. They developed and maintained their corporate identity and educational system. They
achieved a major goal: strengthening the Islamic culture of the town. By 1900,
Saint-Louis was an important center of Islamic education for students from all
over the Senegalo-Mauritanian zone.[41]

Over the forty years encompassed by this study, the Muslims took advantage of their knowledge and relations of confidence with chiefs and clerics in
the interior to bring pressure to bear upon the administration and the patrons
of trade. In Saint-Louis, they purchased land and buildings that they rented out
to the government and French firms. They forged coalitions with the métis
clans and the administration as the situation required. They learned to engage local lawyers and metropolitan groups such as the Ligue des Droits de
l'Homme to argue their cause. The number of Western-educated Muslims grew

dramatically, and it was they who created the conditions for Blaise Diagne's election in 1914.

THE PRACTICE OF POLITICS IN REPUBLICAN SAINT-LOUIS

Scholars have portrayed the political history of Senegalese communes before the election of Blaise Diagne as a struggle between the Descemet and Devès clans.[42] This competition is certainly a good beginning for the story, and it resonates for the 1880s and 1890s. It does not capture, however, the rapidly changing alliances, the intrusion of the administration, and the interventions of Bordelese interests. In what follows I sketch this broader picture, emphasizing the conflicts in the capital and the opportunities that they created for the processes of accommodation.

The Descemet clan enjoyed close relationships with the Catholic Church and the colonial administration. Its acknowledged leader was Louis Jacques Descemet (1839–1921), the grandson of a man who settled in Senegal after the Napoleonic period. The Descemet family did well in the gum trade, accumulated considerable wealth, and married into other prestigious métis families: the d'Erneville, Foy, Valantin, and Guillabert, in particular. In the late nineteenth century, several Descemet men, like their allies in other families, went into the professions, military service, or administration. Louis began a military career and then became Faidherbe's personal secretary. For reasons of health, he quit administration in the 1860s and devoted himself to his economic interests. He served as a member of the city council of Saint-Louis from 1872 to 1879, president of the General Council from 1879 to 1890, president of the chamber of commerce from 1881 to 1891, and mayor of Saint-Louis from 1895 to 1909. His political activity spans virtually the whole period under study. The colonial administration recognized his service by making him a knight of the Legion of Honor.[43]

Louis Descemet and his allies broke with the administration on rare occasion. The best-known instance was in 1881, when they successfully pushed for the removal of Governor Brière de l'Isle and demonstrated the power that the métis and Saint-Louis could wield.[44] Brière (1876–81) was the first expansionist governor since Faidherbe. Accustomed to military command, he was ill-prepared for the assertive communes with their deputy, mayors, city councils, and General Council. In the process, the governor created united opposition among constituencies that had conflicting interests: the large Bordeaux firms, the smaller métis firms and families in Saint-Louis, the local judiciary, and metropolitan humanitarian interests. It was no mean achievement.[45]

Three key issues were involved. The first was the legitimacy of the mayor and city council of Saint-Louis. Under pressure from the Bordeaux houses, who wanted to control local politics, Brière fired the mayor and assistant mayor and ordered new elections in 1878–79. He was not able to eliminate the city council nor subsume it under the General Council, where at the time he had more control.[46] On this issue, Brière succeeded in alienating a good portion of the métis community.

The governor was strongly committed to expansion to the east, the dream that Faidherbe had nourished.[47] In 1880 Brière used new metropolitan resources and local customs revenues to launch an offensive under an ambitious young officer, Gustave Bognis-Desbordes, as Commandant Supérieur.[48] The Bordelese and métis merchants were lukewarm about military campaigns at best. Their attitude turned to opposition when the governor confiscated their boats to ferry troops up-river, interfering with the trading season of 1880–81.

The third issue was the question of slavery and the slave trade. French governments made a variety of pronouncements against these practices during the nineteenth century. In 1848, they called for the abolition of slavery in French territory and enunciated the principle of *sol libérateur,* the "liberation" accorded to human beings on French soil. Administrators in Senegal struggled with the effective application of the principle,[49] but they could ill afford to ignore accusations of slavery and slave trade in the face of metropolitan opinion. Early in his tenure, Brière had to deal with charges of continuing slavery in Gorée, Rufisque, Saint-Louis, and along the Senegal River. Inhabitants of those areas, some of them merchants themselves, were accustomed to acquiring and using labor of all kinds, and they knew how to get new workers from the interior networks.[50]

But the head of the judicial service, the *antillais* Darrigrand, took the emancipation decrees seriously, raising questions about the willingness of the administration to carry out its mandate. The Ministry of the Navy succeeded in having Darrigrand transferred to Guadeloupe, but by then the metropolitan press had picked up the issue. Senator Victor Schoelcher, the most prominent French abolitionist, brought the evidence to the attention of the parliament. In this case the Bordeaux firms used the persistence of slavery to embarrass Brière and push for his recall.[51]

The events surrounding Brière's departure in April 1881 indicate how thoroughly the governor angered the electoral constituencies.[52] The General

Council met in early April to prepare the annual budget. It presented this to the *conseil d'administration,* a body that the governor ordinarily controlled, for approval. At that meeting two persons who belonged to both councils withdrew because of the governor's insulting language. One of their replacements was not qualified, and this threatened the approval process. Three days later, when Brière left by boat for France, all of the electoral bodies assembled, as was the custom, at the governor's office. An unrepentant Brière then began to hurl gross insults in every direction, especially at the General Council. Two of the council members and the whole city council of Saint-Louis walked out. Descemet, as head of the General Council, concluded his account of the events as follows:

> The population in its entirety . . . is indignant about such conduct. We cannot believe that the government of the Republic will tolerate from one of its functionaries such absence of respect for the elected bodies and such neglect of basic human dignity. In the name of the outraged General Council, in the name of an indignant population, I ask you for justice and hope that you will make it quick and severe.[53]

Brière did not suffer any permanent damage to his career, but his recall shows the chasm between military and civilian styles of government, the capacity for mobilization of the electoral constituencies, and their close ties with the metropole.[54]

After 1881 the General Council and the métis community rarely expressed the same unity. For the next decade, the leadership was divided between the Descemet and Devès coalitions. The Descemet group generally supported administration initiatives, while their opponents tended to be more critical. They took opposite positions on the Jeandet sequence described in chapter 3. African leaders in the interior maintained contacts with both groups; they sifted the information they received on government intentions and asked their contacts to intervene with the governor when needed.

In the 1890s, the Saint-Louis elite became more aware of the weaknesses in its position. They observed the efforts of the administration to centralize control, intervene in elections, weaken the General Council's authority, and take over the Banque du Sénégal. They were among the first to know of French intentions to shift power to Dakar, with its superior port facilities and strategic location near the peanut basin. Dakar and Rufisque had larger numbers of French inhabitants, who could be mobilized to counter the influence of the métis of the old capital. The métis became more conscious of the racial and cultural distinctions that separated them from the powerful French minority and

the emerging African majorities in the communes. In the light of this awareness, they began to mobilize more effectively as a group. The result was the
election of François Carpot as deputy in 1902, with the support of most of the
Saint-Louis elite, including the African leaders.[55]

But the unity was short-lived. The Carpot and Devès clans soon divided the
métis again, and both sides sought out French and African allies. Meanwhile the
center of gravity of French operations shifted to Dakar, while Governor-general
Roume found means to take an increasing number of resources out of Saint-
Louis. During all of this time, Western-educated Africans were mobilizing politically. With the election of Diagne as deputy in 1914, and his reelection in 1919
with control of the General Council and most of the city councils, the political
initiative passed out of the hands of the métis. They became advisers and supporters of African politicians.[56]

WORKING THE SYSTEM: THE DEVÈS CLAN

The name of Devès recurs constantly in the treatment of the institutions of civil
society in the late nineteenth century. Gaspard Devès and his sons built a network of trade and consultation throughout the Senegalo-Mauritanian zone and
translated it into effective action in the arena of Saint-Louis. They established
shifting coalitions of French, métis and African supporters. They used civil society to sustain what I call an ancien régime: a mosaic of political, economic, and
religious leaders who were bound in a common social structure, a recognition of
French overrule, and a commerce built on local products and European imports.
The Devès often failed in the short term, and they ultimately failed to stem the
intensification of French power that culminated in the government-general and
direct control of the Senegalo-Mauritanian zone. But over several decades, they
mobilized impressive human and financial resources. They made the electoral institutions function in ways that the Third Republic never intended. In the process, they earned the implacable hostility of the colonial administration.[57]

Bruno (1797–1868) and Justin Devès came to Senegal shortly after the
Napoleonic period.[58] They started a business that took on a number of different partners and titles.[59] The two brothers returned to Bordeaux, raised most of
their families there, and entrusted management to family or associates. But
Bruno also started a second family in Senegal. His Fulbe mistress, from the Dagana area, gave birth to Gaspard (1826–1901), the founder of the métis branch
of the family and the "Devès network."[60]

After studies in France, Gaspard returned to Senegal and went into trade. By the 1850s he had established his own company, obtained contracts to supply the administration with grain, and developed an extensive set of contacts along the river and in the peanut basin. He capped this with marriage to Catherine Foy, daughter of a rich métis merchant. She gave birth to a baby girl and died shortly thereafter.[61] The daughter, Elisabeth, was consigned to a mental asylum at about age twenty, and the responsibility for managing and investing her inheritance passed to Gaspard. Foy property was the basis for much of the wealth of the Devès in the late nineteenth century.[62]

A few years later, Gaspard married Madeleine Tambe Diop, a woman from the Dagana area.[63] She gave birth to his three sons, Justin, Hyacinthe, and François.[64] Gaspard collaborated with the "white" branch of the family and visited Bordeaux frequently, but he consciously made Saint-Louis his base of operations. In the 1850s, Gaspard forged a coalition of Senegalese and Bordelese interests opposed to the expansion of Faidherbe.[65] He maintained this stance toward the campaigns promoted by Brière, Coppolani, and others in the late nineteenth century. At the same time, Devès kept his government provisioning contracts, which enabled him to profit from the French presence and military expeditions. In the early 1860s, Governor Jean Jauréguiberry gave an interesting portrait of Gaspard, consistent with his actions in the late nineteenth century as well as French stereotypes about Fulbe ethnicity:

> He (Gaspard) is the most skillful merchant, the most flexible, the most clever that Saint-Louis has perhaps ever seen. Very broad minded, he knows how to turn to his advantage every bad thing that befalls him. The blacks say that he is clever and wicked like a Peul [Fulbe]. He is the son of a white man and a Peule woman and so necessarily had that personality.[66]

In the 1870s, Gaspard began to translate his wealth into social and symbolic capital on the Republican stage. He served as mayor, councilman, and member of the General Council on different occasions. His ally and frequent spokesman was Jean-Jacques Crespin, a popular politician who also served as mayor. Together they led the Devès clan, in opposition to the Descemet coalition and the governors, who sought every occasion to discredit them.[67] After the challenge that the Devès marshaled in the Jeandet Affair, the hostility of the administration bordered on paranoïa.

By the 1880s, Justin and Hyacinthe had completed their studies in France and returned to the family business. François joined them in the 1890s, whereupon the three sons progressively took over activities from Gaspard. Hyacinthe often specialized in networks in Cayor and Baol, while François made Trarza his particular concern. All three sons served on the General Council and city council in Saint-Louis at different times, and all were active in the campaigns for the deputyship.

Justin, the oldest, was successor to Gaspard as political leader and strategist. His French law degree was instrumental to the social and symbolic capital of the family, and of incalcluable utility in the contestations of the early colonial period.[68] Justin battled Descemet and then François Carpot and finally succeeded in becoming mayor of Saint-Louis and president of the General Council. While he sensed the decline of Saint-Louis and the dangers of a centralizing administration, Justin, like his father and brothers, was too committed to his own role to create an effective métis and African bloc. He died in 1917.

What were the Devès interests? The gum trade was their mainstay throughout the period and made for close ties with producers and protectors in the Trarza and Brakna areas and in the upper river. For some time they were able to sustain important commitments in the peanut zone, despite the presence of better-financed French firms. They were active on the frontiers of the French presence: the Southern Rivers, the Umarian state in the east, and the southern Mauritanian belt. They conducted a thriving business in guns and ammunition, supplied grain and meat to the administration and military, and ran boats to transport passengers and goods along the river.

The commercial activities presupposed close ties with African leaders in the Senegalo-Mauritanian zone, both independent rulers and those under French protectorates. For most of these, the Devès firm was a major creditor. Lat Dior relied heavily on Devès advice and intercession in Cayor. Albury Ndiaye and Abdul Bokar Kane often wrote to Gaspard. The chiefs of Toro consulted the family frequently, and it was because of that relationship that the Devès intervened so quickly in the Jeandet Affair. The contacts with *hassan* interests in Trarza and Brakna were strong.

The Devès firm was a resource and creditor to African traders over the whole Senegalo-Mauritanian zone and the Southern Rivers. In 1883, one of these traders, Abdullay Dièye, died in Bakel. Within a few days, Gaspard and Justin wrote to the commandant in Bakel to state that Dièye owed them 350,000 francs, and his son Madièye Ely owed another 150,000. To make sure that their claims were given priority, they dispatched an agent to meet with the local conciliation commission. The record suggests that when the commission completed its inventory, the Devès acquired most if not all of the estate.[69] The

Bakel case typifies the relations and influence that this métis firm exercised in much of the Senegalo-Mauritanian zone. The Devès indeed were the largest investors in the ancien régime of local autonomy and French overrule, a system that was gradually coming to an end.

The family wielded considerable influence in the councils of power in the communes. They had a strong base in Gorée as well as Saint-Louis.[70] They could marshal support in Guet N'Dar, the fishing quarter on the ocean spit, and in Gandiole, a set of villages south of town.[71] They had ties with the director of the interior, who handled administration in the nearby annexed areas, and with the customs service. They were a major debtor to the Banque du Sénégal and a principal cause of its downfall.[72] All of these relations, together with their constituencies in the interior, gave the Devès the knowledge, experience, and confidence to defend their kind of regime in the Senegalo-Mauritanian zone.

Their strength and resourcefulness lent drama to the confrontations with the administration. During the Jeandet sequence of 1890–91, the Devès hired André Chadelle, a French lawyer based in Saint-Louis, and contacted Alexandre Isaac, a senator from Guadeloupe and cofounder of the Ligue des Droits de l'Homme. In 1894 they hired Isaac to defend François against charges of customs fraud. Before the lawyer left, the Devès gave him a tour of the region and a fat file on the modus operandi of the administration.[73] In 1902, Governorgeneral Roume and the ministry considered charging the Devès for their machinations in Trarza. They quickly decided that they would not be able to make an indictment stick under the penal code.[74]

In 1910, the administration made a bold strike against the clan. Lieutenant Governor Peuvergne claimed that Justin called himself the "king of Saint-Louis," bought votes on a regular basis, and took money for brokerage services from clients in Tivaouane, Gandiole, and elsewhere. He had boasted that in exchange for 1,500 francs he would tell the governor-general to liberate Amadu Bamba from house arrest. He promised the return of slavery. By closing a secondary school in Saint-Louis, he forced white girls to go to class with blacks.[75] Peuvergne brought in a metropolitan inspector to seek indictments against the mayor and persuaded Paris to remove him from office.[76] There was undoubtedly some substance to the charges, but most of them were not crimes, nor even reprehensible, and all were motivated by the bitter hostility that the administration had harbored for decades.

Justin, in typical Devès fashion, recovered from the suspension and won reelection in 1911. Two years later he became president of the General Council. But the influence of the family was waning. The administration secured a final victory: after Justin's death in 1917, the lieutenant governor vetoed the quest of his supporters to raise a monument in his honor.[77]

CASE STUDIES OF DEVÈS INFLUENCE

1. Cayor. Serious peanut production had begun in Cayor in the mid nineteenth century and, by the 1880s, the value of peanut exports far exceeded that of gum.[78] Métis and African merchants failed to preserve the ancien régime of trade across the frontiers of colony and independent kingdom and to safeguard the commercial and political importance of Saint-Louis, which was threatened by a rail link to the more accessible port of Dakar. In 1885, the French opened the line, which helped shift the center of production to the south and consolidate the hold of the Bordeaux firms, with their branches in Rufisque and Dakar. In 1886, they eliminated the last gasp of resistance, killed Damels Samba Laobe and Lat Dior, and reorganized the region.

The administration and firms exercised considerable control in Cayor. They received good information from a variety of informants about what was going on, and had powerful allies inside a very divided society. Demba War Sall had a large following, wielded considerable influence, and knew that his future lay in incorporation into colonial Senegal. His chief ally and spokesman was Ibra Fatim Sar, an official from Ndiambur, the northern region of large Muslim villages. Deputy Albert Gasconi was a strong advocate, and there was no metropolitan opposition to colonial control.[79]

Arrayed against these forces were many of the métis and African merchants of Saint-Louis under Gaspard Devès. In an 1883 letter, the governor acknowledged the web of relations that the métis entrepreneur had established:

> Around this person [Gaspard] are grouped all the African traitants who monopolize the trade with Cayor, Jolof, Futa, and the upper river, and who understand entirely how the railway, in putting the European producer in direct contact with the indigenous producers, is eliminating the intermediaries, [and] will inevitably end the effective monopoly that they have exercised up until now.[80]

The Devès were not able to carry the General Council on this issue: Descemet and the majority supported the administration.[81] Their allies and debtors in Cayor, especially Lat Dior, were far too weak and exposed to counter the combined onslaught of the administration, the French firms, and their Cayorian allies.

The Devès did, however, make life difficult for the governor. French and Saint-Louis newspapers criticized the expeditions of October 1886 that resulted in the deaths of the two kings. The *Réveil du Sénégal* reprinted an article that first appeared in a Bordeaux newspaper and added a commentary of its own. According to the journal, the government had prepared traps to capture and kill the two Cayorian leaders. The protests threatened Governor Genouille, who received extrordinary powers from the ministry to shut down the paper before the end of 1886.[82]

2. Fulbe Emigration. The ability of the Devès network to use the complex realities of the Senegalo-Mauritanian zone was revealed in many situations, but no where more clearly than in the large-scale Fulbe migration out of Walo and western Futa in the 1880s. The basic cause was the old issue of sol libérateur: those slaves who could get to Saint-Louis or other parts of the colony could claim their liberty. Slaveowners migrated to the east, outside of the French sphere, as a means of saving their human property. They took their cattle with them, and this threatened the supply of meat to the colony. It was only in the early 1890s that the administration finally "solved" the problem, as described in chapter 3, by putting the territories in "protectorate" status, where French law did not apply.

Beginning in 1885, the emigration became more intense. Al-Hajj Umar's son Amadu had moved from Segu to Nioro, not far from the trading posts of the Senegal River. From there he sought to enlist new followers in the traditional Umarian recruiting grounds of the river valley. His invitation to a holy act, migration away from a "polluted" area to join an Islamic cause in the east, now reinforced the grievance against emancipation. The result was the movement of at least seven thousand people between 1885 and 1888.[83]

According to the French officers in Podor and Dagana, Gaspard and his sons profited from this migration in several ways.[84] They expressed sympathy for the slaveowners' plight, encouraged migration, and gave the impression that the administration also favored it. They bought cattle and sheep from the emigrating Fulbe, for the butchery that they owned in Saint-Louis, in exchange for *guinées*, cloth that could be used as currency in the east. They then sold tickets for passage on Devès's boats to the Upper Senegal. In short, they profited from the dilemmas of both the Fulbe masters and the administration, an administration that was caught between its instincts for order and its public commitment to end slavery and the slave trade.

3. Trarza. The Devès family ran an alternative system of production, trade, cash flows, and information in the Senegalo-Mauritanian zone. For this reason they became increasingly anathema to an administration bent on intensifying its control. The Jeandet challenge of 1890–91 sharpened the administration's resolve, and the attack on the bank deepened the determination of the Devès to resist. By the start of the twentieth century, the family interests had been reined in considerably; they were now concentrated in the remaining "frontier" zone, southwestern Mauritania.

For some time, the family had cultivated the reigning family of Trarza. The endorsements of the emirs, despite the infighting and turbulence, were important for Devès operations in gum, salt, cloth, slaves, and other products. Gaspard succeeded in 1880 in actually purchasing from the emir the island of Arguin, in an area rich in fish and salt.[85] The validity of the treaty was confirmed by several independent legal authorities, and on that basis the family sought compensation as the French began to occupy the western portion of the Sahara. The administration never acknowledged Devès ownership, but it had to resort to a host of legal obfuscations in the process.

Justin and his brothers consistently opposed the "pacification" of Coppolani (as shown in chapter 3) and the much-less-disguised conquest of Gouraud. In the pause between the two campaigns, the Devès marshaled their resources against the conquest of the Adrar, which they feared would further diminish their trading networks and freedom of movement. Lieutenant Colonel Montané-Capdebosc, who served as head of Mauritanian operations between the Coppolani and Gouraud, wrote an extensive report in 1907 on these opponents of French control.[86]

In his report, Montané-Capdebosc accused the clan, known in Trarza as the "people of Gaspard," of encouraging anarchy in southwestern Mauritania by providing information on government plans, encouraging raids and migrations, and posing as powerful members of the ruling classes of Saint-Louis. The colonel noted that they used the post of Ndiago, the terminal point for most transsaharan caravans heading into Saint-Louis, as a place to collect their own customs payments, and operated in a host of other small posts across southern Trarza.[87] They sold slaves, often taken from the Upper Senegal and Niger regions, to *bidan* purchasers by avoiding the French riverine posts. They counseled some *bidan* groups to move to the south side of the river, to protect their herds and people from raiding, and collected payments from them in lieu of taxes, as though they were part of the administration.[88]

This was the most galling dimension to the colonial regime: the Devès encouraged the *bidan* to believe that the General Council was the government. They used the expression for council, or assembly, *jama'a,* or *djemaa,* in local parlance, for the institution that the métis community had dominated for several decades, and associated it with the jama῾a that was the supreme authority in Trarza and the other emirates.[89] The Devès, their agents, and other merchant families of Saint-Louis moved with relative ease in Mauritania, and with much more frequency than any representatives of the colonial regime. They thus had great latitude to interpret the intentions and commitment of the French — at least until the campaigns of Coppolani and Gouraud.

The immediate occasion for the colonel's alarm in 1907 was the effort by the Devès to dissuade Sidiyya Baba from supporting the Adrar campaign. As chapter 4 reveals, Baba saw the campaign as critical to Sidiyya survival; he was the co-architect with Gouraud, just as he had been with Coppolani. When he visited Saint-Louis at the end of March 1907, an agent sent by Hyacinthe Devès sought to persuade him to change his position. Baba immediately informed Montané-Capdebosc and described his reply:

> I responded that I was a simple man who did not get involved in politics. I
> said that the agreement between those who make decisions in the country
> and me was complete, and that I could not benefit from my property, in
> Trarza as well as Adrar, until peace reigned, and that such peace could only
> be provided by the French government.

Baba concluded his letter by telling Montané-Capdebosc he would keep him informed of any other efforts to obstruct the plans of the administration.[90]

The Devès realized that the conquest of the Adrar, and by implication the rest of what would become French Mauritania, would severely damage their operations and eliminate any chance of compensation for Arguin. Their ability to maneuver, negotiate, and represent was increasingly constrained. Justin had some final victories, as mayor of Saint-Louis and president of the General Council, but his death in 1917 symbolized the end of the "Devès era" in Senegalo-Mauritanian politics.

WHAT DOES THE PRACTICE of civil society in Saint-Louis have to do with islamization and the paths of accommodation? It slowed and altered conquest and colonial rule in several important ways. It forced the administration to defend its actions in many settings and to find ways to circumvent the authority of the General Council. It suggested to chiefs, marabouts, and the common people in the interior that the French spoke with many voices and that their actions might be modified. It said that Eurafricans and Africans might obtain status in Saint-Louis and have some impact on those actions.

The most important contribution was in creating space in which African Muslim residents could live, work, and develop in Saint-Louis and then circulate in the interior. It was fine for the French to have Dudu Seck or Ndiaye Sarr on the administrative payroll, to write letters in Arabic, and appear at ceremonies to demonstrate French prestige as a Muslim power. But it was even more important that the African men of Saint-Louis could mobilize around candidates who best met their needs—needs as they defined them. With Western education, these residents could run for office. The record at the turn of the century shows that the candidates for the various positions in the Republican institutions took African interests with increasing seriousness.

But perhaps even more significant was the sense that residents obtained of a polity full of conflict and debate. They could turn to the mayor and council, the General Council, the governor, the director of political affairs, or their own resources in order to build a mosque, establish a school, maintain a court, or celebrate Muslim holidays—in short, to defend their own interests. The next chapter will show that these Saint-Louis Muslims communicated the same sense of possibility to the inhabitants of the interior of the Senegalo-Mauritanian zone.

Specifically, what did the Devès network have to do with islamization and accommodation? The Devès were certainly not known for their piety or respect for any established religious practice; they were probably Freemasons. But by their posture, by their access to guns, cloth, and other manufactured items desired in the interior, by the loans that they could offer, and by their access to the colonial bureaucracy they could give reassurance to the traditional rulers and the emerging maraboutic elites about managing the transitions of the late nineteenth century—reassurance about the continuity of chieftaincy, tribute, slavery, and religious identity and about the compatibility of Islamic practice with French rule. Older and newer elites could see the ability of the Devès clan to use the structures of Republican civil society to challenge the structures of colonialism; they could thus have more confidence that the institutions of Muslim civil society would survive under the new regime.

Did the operation of these Republican institutions serve to extend the sway of the colonial regime in the Senegalo-Mauritanian zone? Certainly the administration did not intend to extend its domination or hegemony in such a way. Officials worked assiduously to limit the impact of the Saint-Louis elite and to narrow the chain of command. But these institutions and people operated for some time outside of their control and quite possibly with the benefit of making colonial rule appear more open, malleable, and plural than it ultimately became.

—6—

The Sons of Ndar

The Muslim Merchants of Saint-Louis

WHAT MADE THE POLITICAL AND CIVIL SOCIETY of Saint-Louis so complex and so unlike towns in Western Europe was its African Muslim majority. The town included not only Roman Catholics, not only secular products of the Enlightenment, but also people of another confession—a confession that Europeans disdained and feared. Its Wolof and Hassaniyya name, Ndar, implied that religious identity. The governors and mayors did not will the presence of Islam, much less control its growth. The Muslim presence in the town went back many centuries, but it was in the nineteenth century that Islam became the widely and fervently practiced faith of the free, the slave, and the former slave. The administration recognized the predominance of Islam and the process of islamization, as shown in chapter 4. So did the large commercial interests, whether Bordeaux firms or the Devès family. All of these decision makers knew that their key agents in the Senegalo-Mauritanian zone would be the "sons of Ndar."

Historians and social scientists have written at length on networks of long-distance trade, the traders that ran them, and the strategies of kinship, ethnicity, language, and religion used to increase solidarity and control precious products. In Muslim zones, they have often emphasized the scholarly or saintly credentials that reinforced the traders' effectiveness.[1] This analysis has not usually been applied to the African Muslim merchants who operated out of coastal ports. In the case of Saint-Louis, there are at least two reasons for this neglect. First, the merchants operated under the French umbrella, even in cases where they were independent entrepreneurs. They accepted the European overrule that characterized the Senegalo-Mauritanian zone from the time of Faidherbe and the colonial regime that followed it by the early twentieth century. Second, the Saint-Louis traders did not have any particular distinction within the Islamic arena. Some were of modest social origin and had only recently adopted the faith. Most were laymen and not clerics. It was only in the late nineteenth century, and under the influence of Muslims from the larger region, that they established their town as an important center of religious practice and learning.

Their role in spreading the message of the compatibility of Islam and European overrule was profound. They went out every year for months at a time. They worked from one market and settlement, where they developed networks to facilitate trade; frequently this included acquiring local wives and family. If the local language was not Wolof, they learned it. They became sources of knowledge about the French and possible intermediaries with them. For leaders in the interior, these members of the "private sphere" might be more trustworthy than functionaries such as Bu El Mogdad, and more comprehending than non-Muslims. It is the role of these Muslim traders and the ways in which they encouraged accommodation to the growing colonial presence that are the subjects of this chapter.

THE SONS OF NDAR

Like all of the inhabitants of the town, the Muslims were closely linked to commerce. Most of the men, whether as independent merchants, agents of the larger firms, interpreters, boat crews, or dock workers, were connected to the collection of exports, the dissemination of imports, and the purchase of foodstuffs for Saint-Louis. They spent much of the year out of town, in designated markets in the hinterland. They secured their stocks, renewed their contacts with local producers and authorities, and negotiated deals before returning to town.

The season of the *traite* varied according to the products, region, and particular conditions.[2] The river trade east of Podor, for example, occurred late in the calendar year when the rising water level permitted the boats to get upstream; the journey was long and arduous and the trader might be isolated from Saint-Louis for months at a time. The trading season in the peanut basin was shorter, around the harvest in the fall, and the displacement was less difficult — especially after the completion of the DSL railway in 1885.

After the harvests of gum and peanuts, the merchants, their agents, and crews returned to Saint-Louis. Boilât, a Senegalese priest writing in the 1850s about the convoy from the upper Senegal, described the boats laden down with goods, the passengers putting on their best outfits, and the blasts of cannon to announce the arrival. He stressed the continuous dancing and feasting "until they spend everything they have earned."[3] According to a Frenchman writing in 1871, the traders

> can be recognized by their luxurious dress, their assertive demeanor, their re-laxed stroll. . . . They came to rest from their arduous commercial campaign and let loose in a relentless burst of costly fantasies that astound their more sedentary co-citizens. Frivolous and vain, their greatest pleasure is to fill up their huts with furniture and gee-gaws bought at all the sales, and to dress up their concubines in flashy clothes and sparkling jewels.

He went on to note the less agreeable reality of the off-season:

> Much of their time is spent at court. Every year the reckoning of accounts between agent *[traitant]* and boss *[patron]* causes numerous disputes, and their resolution often ends in the ruin of the agent, who usually then emigrates to the Southern Rivers [Guinea coast, there to start again].[4]

The disputes were frequent. Most African traders were vulnerable to the fluctu-ations in price, the circumstances of production, and the conditions set down by the large French firms. But they knew how to hedge their bets and could often get a new start in a frontier zone like the Southern Rivers.

Commerce was conducted according to the hierarchy of functions and fees outlined in chapter 1. Gaspard Devès was an exception to the hierarchy: a *métis négociant*. Most of the African Muslims fell into the traitant and sous-traitant categories. They worked on the basis of credit advances from the large firms, advances that they were supposed to repay at the end of the trading season.[5] A careful reading of the archival record suggests that, despite the dominance of the French businesses and the volatility of trade, a number of African entrepre-neurs were able to establish a solid network of contacts in their areas, build their reputations and economic capital, and transmit their profession to the next generation. I call them merchants rather than traitants, the official cate-gory in which most of them fell, because of the multiple ways in which they used the system and crossed its boundaries. They might serve as agents for a Bordeaux house and work for themselves at the same time.[6] They invested in urban real estate, owned and rented out houses, warehouses, and boats, and established gardens outside of town to produce food.

In the late nineteenth century, these merchants constituted the class of notables of Saint-Louis, referring to themselves as the "good families" of the town. The genealogical depth of their lineages was often shallow, perhaps to conceal "modest" origins, but they replicated the general social stratification of the Senegalo-Mauritanian zone and contracted occasional marriages with the interior aristocracies. All of this was important for their role as mediators of knowledge and actors on the local stage. In contrast to the European merchants, administrators, and the métis, who lived in the southern half of the island, the notables settled principally in the northern section. They avoided the spit of land beside the ocean (the neighborhoods of Guet Ndar and Ndar Toute) and the mainland area to the east (the various sections of Sor). They developed a solid Muslim identity around three institutions: the main mosque in the Nord, the Tribunal Musulman, and their educational system.[7] In effect, the Muslim traders were part of a diaspora comparable to those that have dominated cross-cultural trade in many periods of world history.[8] They had a distinctive identity, dress, and manner. They were urban Muslims, the "sons of Ndar," wherever they served.

It was in this capacity that Al-Hajj Umar challenged them during the confrontations over trade goods in 1855. He addressed the merchants who worked the Upper Senegal in particular and Saint-Louis Muslims in general to explain his confiscation of "Christian" merchandise. He challenged them to keep their distance, as good Muslims, from the "tyrant" governor of Saint-Louis.

> From us to all the sons of Ndar. Greetings, good will, and honor [be with you]. We have not destroyed your hope in us but rather increased and strengthened it, because we have not taken what belonged to you, not one coin, and we never will. Instead, we have taken the possessions of the Christians. We have returned to the sons of Ndar everything that belonged to them. If you ask the reason for the seizure of the Christian property, it is because they have committed injustices against us many times. . . .
>
> Now we are victorious by the power of God. We will not quit until we receive a plea of peace and submission from your tyrant, for our Lord said: "Fight those who believe not in God nor in the Last Day, nor forbid that which God and His Messenger have forbidden nor follow the religion of truth, out of those who have been given the book, until they pay the *jizya* in acknowledgement of superiority, for they are in a state of subjection."[9] Sons of Ndar, God forbids you to be in relations of friendship with them.[10] He

made it clear that whomever becomes their friend becomes an infidel, and one of them, through His saying: "Take not the Jews and Christians for friends. They are friends of each other. And whomever amongst you takes them for friends he is indeed one of them." Greetings.[11]

The challenge was not easy to dismiss. As outlined in chapter 4, Hamat Ndiaye Anne had to defend publicly his association with the French at the Saint-Louis mosque, while Bu El Mogdad couched his pilgrimage in 1860 in terms of countering the propaganda of Umar.[12]

Fortified by these reassurances from the highly visible leaders of the Muslim community, the merchants rejected the Umarian stance. They operated within a system of European overrule, charting their own "path of accommodation." They recognized French authority, but they also knew its limitations and welcomed the mediating and diplomatic roles that they were called upon to play. They were not a unified or homogenous group, in the sense that Abner Cohen gives to the Hausa traders in colonial Ibadan, but they shared and projected a common culture for those living in the Senegalo-Mauritanian zone.[13]

Indeed, these entrepreneurs possessed considerable symbolic, economic, and social capital. They operated most effectively and profitably on the frontiers of the zone, in areas where the French firms were less dominant. Many achieved success in the gum trade along the river, where their experience, resourcefulness, and networks could compensate for small initial capital. Some accumulated considerable wealth in the Upper Senegal in the late nineteenth century, particularly through trade in gum, cattle, and slaves with the Umarian dominions.[14] Others operated in southern Mauritania, around the fringes of the peanut basin and in the Southern Rivers area.[15] Independent operators had a more difficult time in the heart of the peanut region. There the Bordeaux firms could supply large quantities of credit, move goods quickly, and keep the attention of the administration; they preferred to have their own agents.[16] But even these agents were part of the Saint-Louis network, establishing contacts that went well beyond their responsibilities as employees.

By 1888–89, when Alfred Le Châtelier conducted his tour of what was becoming French West Africa, Saint-Louis had acquired a distinctive Islamic culture and reputation.[17] The Islamic "expert" was impressed with the combination of sophistication about Western institutions, knowledge of Islam, and sense of cultural distance communicated by the local Muslim community. He saw this culture as the product of the previous fifty years, and noted that the Saint-Louisians followed the example of Bu El Mogdad:

[They] were not naturally disposed toward intellectual tasks or moral improvement. But it has become fashionable to follow the example of Bu El Mogdad, the qadi and the indigenous interpreters. Piety, the knowledge of Muslim law, the *hadith,* and the commentaries have, bit by bit, acquired an important place in the world of the Muslim traders, after their professional occupations, and the same concerns have spread among the larger populace.[18]

The traders were important forces for islamization and incorporation into the colonial framework at the turn of the century. I will return to these important themes later in the chapter. At this point I wish to suggest the outlines of the trading networks across a series of family biographies that demonstrate how these men, their wives, and descendants served as mediators of knowledge and actors on the Senegalo-Mauritanian stage.

MERCHANT FAMILIES

Constructing the biographies of selected French officials in chapter 3 was relatively easy, thanks in part to personnel files in the colonial and military archives. Sketching the profiles of the "official Muslims" of chapter 4 was not a great deal more difficult, given their prominence in diplomatic missions and the public life of Saint-Louis. The vignettes of the merchants who follow require more diligent research. What I have done below, for a few selected families, is to piece together brief citations in the archives and official publications such as the *Annuaire du Sénégal et Dépendances,* and brief recollections in oral history or memoir, to make a kind of collage. Most of the individuals and families developed their careers in the "river" network, extending from the Upper Senegal down to Rosso, at the edge of Walo, Trarza, and Futa. The reconstructions show patterns of remarkable continuity and development across the generations, a strong Saint-Louisian identity, close relations with the administration and the Saint-Louis elite, and the accumulation of several kinds of capital over time.[19]

The first family under consideration are the Gueye (see fig. 6.1), best known in contemporary Senegal as the maternal ancestors of Lamine Gueye. The founder was Waly Bandia, who set up his operations in Bakel in the upper Senegal. By the mid nineteenth century, he had a large store well located near the main square and principal Bordeaux houses. He was conducting a thriving business in gum, cloth, guns, millet, and other products with the *bidan* of the right bank. His

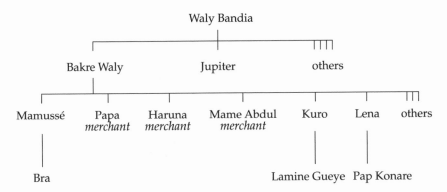

Fig. 6.1. The Gueye Family

name, written in clear Arabic, appears on an 1843 petition of Muslim inhabitants of Saint-Louis requesting the creation of a Muslim tribunal.[20]

By 1859 Waly had passed away and his son Bakre (1834–1904) had taken over. Bakre Waly worked initially as an agent for Rabaud & Company, but he also inherited his father's network. His name heads a letter of complaint to the governor in 1867 about conditions of trade.[21] He placed some of his goods in small factories between Matam and Bakel, under the care of his own agents, and he maintained close ties with chiefs in the region. He profited from the famine conditions that followed the massive emigration orchestrated by Umar in 1859: the Bakel record shows him receiving a woman pawned by one of the chiefs of the Upper Senegal.[22] He served on the conciliation council of the town and put one of his sons in the local French school.

In about 1868, Bakre shifted his activites to Podor, leaving his younger brother, Jupiter, in charge at Bakel.[23] He probably sought the year-round access to Saint-Louis that Podor offered. In association with Ndiaye Sarr, the future qadi of the Muslim Tribunal of Saint-Louis, he became an independent merchant. He soon created a similar network of relationships, joined the conciliation council by 1874, and eventually became the acknowledged dean of the Ndar community in Podor.[24] He continued to do some work at the post for the rest of his life.[25]

By 1880 Bakre Waly began spending most of his time in the colonial capital.[26] He became a member of the chamber of commerce, the municipal council of Saint-Louis, and the General Council of Senegal—the first African member of that body.[27] He commanded a part of the local militia that participated in military expeditions and local police work. In return for his services, the administration offered scholarships to permit his sons to study in France; he apparently decided not to accept the assistance for fear that education in France might produce cultural alienation.[28]

Bakre remained an ally of the administration in the 1880s and 1890s. He was on close terms with Abel Jeandet. He was active in the 1893 election of a French lawyer, Jules Couchard, to the position of deputy in the French National Assembly, at a time when the métis were badly divided.[29] When the Descemet and Devès clans finally joined forces to take the city council in 1896 and the General Council in 1897, in a kind of métis and African triumph over French commerce and the administration, Bakre was not part of the celebration. Indeed, during the 1897 visit of André Lebon, the minister of colonies, the local crowd singled him out for particular attention: "The demonstrations continued the next day, 9 November, on an even bigger scale. At 4:30 in the afternoon, the home of Bakre Waly, a native and former *conseiller général* . . . recently decorated by Mr. Lebon, was entirely sacked; doors and windows, everything was broken."[30] By this time, Bakre's oldest son Mamussé was taking an active role in the family business interests, in both Bakel and Podor.[31] His daughter married a wealthy merchant based in Medine and gave birth to Lamine Gueye.[32]

This skeletal outline, compiled from a wide variety of sources, begins to suggest the mediating functions of the family. Bakre Waly was wealthy and influential, sought out by post commandants, chiefs, and traders along the river and by political factions in Saint-Louis. He consistently served on the conciliation councils, which arbitrated commercial disputes and consisted of two titular and two substitute members in each post. His services to the administration were considerable, earning the offer of scholarships and his decoration during the visit of the minister. He did not have sufficient training in Arabic to handle treaty negotiations or correspondence. He studied French at one of the Saint-Louis schools and could function in meetings, but his competence in the language was limited. He sent his sons to local Muslim and French schools, but hesitated about sending them to a non-Muslim milieu such as France. The sons probably acquired a better education in Arabic and Islamic studies than he had obtained, and certainly in French. They stayed in the commercial sector, but the succeeding generation, in the unpropitious conditions of the early twentieth century, shifted into government service or the professions.[33]

An analagous pattern emerges from the Mbengue family (see fig. 6.2). A certain Alassane, ostensibly of noble extraction, left the Jolof area and settled in Saint-Louis in the early nineteenth century. His son, Pèdre Alassane (1821–1889), broke into the trade in Dagana in the 1860s and 1870s. Like Bakre Waly,

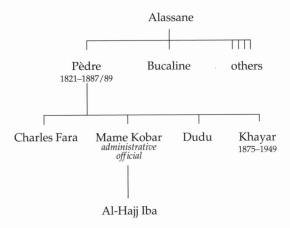

Fig. 6.2. The Mbengue Family

he served for years on the local conciliation council and enjoyed good rapport with traders, chiefs, and French officials. His prosperous gum business enabled him to open branches in the Southern Rivers, in Saint-Louis, along the lower river valley, and as far north as Mederdra in Trarza.[34]

Mbengue purchased oceangoing vessels that permitted him to trade directly with Marseille and Bordeaux. This in turn allowed him to become the "king of tea," the leading importer of what was consumed in increasing quantities in the region.[35] He ran a bakery and shop in Saint-Louis and had a large farm at Ross-Bethio, northeast of Saint-Louis. Pèdre had close ties with important chiefs who functioned under the French umbrella. Ibra Almamy Wane, the Futanke ally of the administration, and Amar Salum, the amir of Trarza, owed him considerable sums of money.[36] He transmitted a small fortune to his son Khayar, who maintained the family wealth and became influential in local politics in the twentieth century.[37] Of the merchants described in this chapter, Mbengue probably comes closest to the level of activity of Gaspard Devès.

Like Bakre Waly, Pèdre had close ties with the administration and the Direction of Political Affairs, and probably belonged to the same Descemet political "clan."[38] He had strong rapport with the Catholic community of Saint-Louis. In the mid 1880s, in the midst of the quarrels between anticlerical and "Catholic" interests, he made a public statement in support of the work that the priests, brothers, and sisters of the church had done in Saint-Louis throughout the nineteenth century. According to the parish journal, he said that "for more than sixty years the Christians have respected us, and much more than the Freemasons who do not even believe in God."[39] Mbengue was obviously not afraid to speak out, and his opinion carried weight.

Pèdre Alassane performed his most conspicuous service as a broker in the early 1880s. On three separate occasions he conducted prolonged negotiations with Abdul Bokar Kane, the prominent leader of central Futa Toro, over the plan to construct a telegraph line to the upper valley (see below).[40] Mbengue's ability to inspire Abdul's confidence, and to transmit the government's stipend, was instrumental in the achievement of the 1885 treaty that allowed the line to be completed. Abdul recognized Pèdre's labors by building a special river dock for him near Kaédi, which lies fully two hundred kilometers upriver from Dagana and Rosso—an indication of how far Mbengue ranged from his principal base.[41]

The careers of Pèdre's sons indicate the changing options of Saint-Louis Muslims. Mame Kobar became a government employee. Khayar Mbengue (1875–1949) also obtained a Western education, became active in the *originaires* and Jeunes Sénégalais movements that mobilized for Blaise Diagne, and combined support for the deputy with his own commercial activities into the interwar period. He took a more critical stance toward the administration than his father.[42]

The Lô family (see fig. 6.3) demonstrate an even closer tie to the administration in Saint-Louis. Fara Biram, who was probably of slave origin, became a trader in the early nineteenth century. He acquired considerable wealth, much of it in slaves, and his name appears on several petitions and delegations at mid century.[43] The names of his sons Mambaye (1820s–ca.1890) and Sidi first appear on the 1843 petition to create the Muslim court in Saint-Louis. Both sons went into the river trade, but neither had his own firm. Sidi worked primarily out of Bakel. He won the plaudits of the administration by participating in campaigns against the Umarian forces in 1857 and he became a member of the conciliation council in the 1860s.[44]

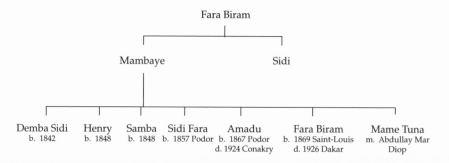

Fig. 6.3. The Lô Family

Mambaye was an extraordinary entrepreneur in Podor. The base was trade with *bidan* and Futanke customers. He supplied information about the politics of Brakna and Futa, interceded with the commandant of Podor and the governor on behalf of the chief of Toro province, and occasionally obtained a contract to supply a French military column.[45] He served as qadi of Podor in the early 1870s,[46] became a roving interpreter for the administration after 1875, and finally attached himself to the Interior Department in Saint-Louis in the middle of the 1880s. There he did some translation, received important visitors from the interior, and handled some administration for the immediate environs of Saint-Louis. The records of his conflict with the head of the Muslim Tribunal in 1885 reveal a self-assured notable, living on the island but with close ties to the ward chief and inhabitants of Guet Ndar.[47]

For his time and place, Mambaye was well educated in Arabic and the Islamic sciences, on the one hand, and in French, on the other. He moved further up the ladder of colonial administration than his African contemporaries because of his language skills and the confidence that he inspired in the government. Mambaye did not have the hesitation of Bakre Waly about the cultural alienation of his male children. He enrolled his sons in the French schools at Podor,[48] and they went on to the highest levels of Western education available at that time to Africans. They went further up the administrative ladder than he. Amadu (1867–1924), the older son, was born in Podor, studied in Saint-Louis and then at a lycée in Algiers, thanks to a scholarship from the General Council.[49] He did additional work in Paris and then became the first Senegalese accepted into the Outre-Mer administrative service. He worked in Côte d'Ivoire, French Congo, and Guinea, where he died in 1924.[50]

The younger son, Fara Biram (1869–1926), was born in Saint-Louis, did his secondary schooling in Saint-Louis, and became an interpreter in the province of Walo in the late 1880s. He was sufficiently fluent in Arabic to translate important letters from the *bidan*.[51] Because of his ability, connections, and loyalty, he was given some sensitive assignments in subsequent years. He served as official resident in Jolof after the expulsion of Albury Ndiaye in 1890 and played a major role in the arrest of Amadu Bamba in 1895. In 1903 he had the task of accompanying Bamba to Saint-Louis prior to his second exile. These assignments were undoubtedly made by his friend Martial Merlin, as director of political affairs and then general secretary to Governor-general Roume. Fara Biram continued to work with the administration and was appointed to the Colonial Council in 1921.[52]

The Diop family (fig. 6.4) started in a fashion similar to the Mbengue but

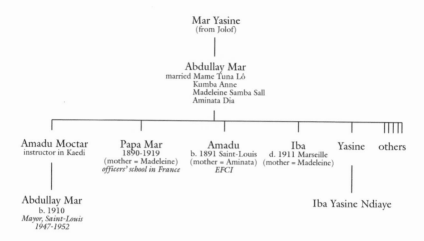

Fig. 6.4. The Diop Family

took on the pattern of the Lô. A certain Mar Yasine, of aristocratic Jolof origin, appears in the 1843 petition and several similar efforts at mid century.[53] His son Abdullay Mar (ca. 1834–1911) acquired a French as well as Islamic education. He began his career in Dagana as a teacher and trader, but soon abandoned the teaching to build up his business in the 1860s and 1870s. He was selected to join the conciliation council of the post. He operated independently and also as an agent of the powerful Bordeaux house of Maurel and Prom, along with Abdullay Seck, the son of Bu El Mogdad. It is likely that both of them played a role in persuading Malik Sy to come to Saint-Louis.[54]

After the mid 1870s, and much like Bakre Waly, Abdullay Mar spent most of the year in Saint-Louis. There he served as a city councilor, deputy mayor, and member of the chamber of commerce. He married the daughter of Mambaye Fara Biram; he also married two other Saint-Louis women of good standing, and took the hand of Kumba Anne after her husband, Bu El Mogdad, passed away.[55] His niece, Rokhaya Ndiaye, married Malik Sy and became the mother of his sons Amadu and Babacar. Abdullay accompanied Malik Sy on his pilgrimage in 1889 and may have helped finance the journey.[56] He sent his sons to the best schools Saint-Louis had to offer. Amadu Moctar became a teacher in Kaedi.[57] Papa Mar (1890–1919) joined forces with Lamine Gueye and other young Western-educated Saint-Louisians to push for the election of Blaise Diagne in 1914.[58]

From his base in Saint-Louis, Abdullay Mar moved progressively into work for the administration. He became an interpreter, with skills in Arabic as well as other languages, and was attached to the Political Affairs Bureau in Saint-Louis for several years. He performed a number of sensitive missions, especially for Governor Henri de Lamothe (1890–95). In his assignment as resident of Ndiambur, he supplied some of the information that led to the arrest of Amadu Bamba in 1895.[59] What is conspicuous in his case, as with the Lô, is the acquisition of French education and the move across the frontier between trade and administration. In both families, the men became functionaries fully a generation ahead of members of the Gueye family.

Mamadou Diouf has provided a case study of Hamat Gora Diop (1846–1910), an entrepreneur who emerged at a slightly later time than Abdullay Mar.[60] Hamat received a solid Muslim education, more than most traders, and started business under the umbrella of his father and the Devès family. Out of his store in Rosso, on the north bank of the river, he began to accumulate considerable wealth through trade in gum, millet, sugar, and other goods. He established ties with Saad Buh and Sidiyya Baba.

In 1882, Hamat shifted his headquarters to the eastern frontier at Medine, where he kept registers of his operations that profile his accumulation and strategy. He developed a network of sous-traitants along the upper Senegal, between the Bakel area and Bafoulabe, as the French were expanding toward the Middle Niger and creating their colony of Soudan. His agents ventured as far as the Umarian capital of Nioro and the Niger. He acquired some twenty barges and a number of canoes that were insured with Pellegrin, a métis firm of Saint-Louis; one large canoe provided free ferry service at Medine. He dealt in a variety of goods: gum, certainly, but also tobacco, which was prized by non-Tijaniyya Muslims, and munitions—at least until their interdiction in the 1890s.

By the turn of the century, Hamat had established his own import network and collaborated directly with Bordeaux firms. He used an accountant in Bordeaux and another in Saint-Louis to help with the books. He borrowed from some of the French firms, but as part of his overall strategy of investment and cash flow. When the agent of the influential Maurel and Prom firm sought to fix the price of gum in Medine in 1895, Hamat protested and maintained his own price in the face of administration pressure. He was a catalyst for petitions from the African trading community of Medine. In the absence of registers for other African merchants of the late nineteenth and early twentieth centuries, it is difficult to know how typical he was in his willingness to resist French pressure.

In Saint-Louis, Hamat acquired considerable rental property, most of it in the Sud. It was there that he built a mosque in which special provision was made for the poor. He also constructed mosques in Medine and Tivaouane and provided assistance to *bidan* friends during famine. He made the pilgrimage three times, visiting Jerusalem and Alexandria. He married well: one wife was a relative of Pèdre Alassane, another of Bakre Waly, and a third was from a noble family of the upper river region.

Hamat's headquarters in the Sud served as a meeting place for Saint-Louisians. In 1905, he hosted the discussions between the members of the Muslim community and the métis elite on the subject of the restoration of the Muslim Tribunal, and in 1913 his home was the venue for a meeting about the status of the originaires in the light of Mody Mbaye's arrest (see below).[61] His sons, raised and accustomed to life in Saint-Louis, went to work for the administration; it would have been very difficult to maintain a prosperous business in any area, "frontier" or other, after the first decade of the twentieth century.[62] But Hamat is an excellent example, for his generation, of the positive relationship between learning, piety, and entrepreneurial success.

THE COLLECTIVE ACTION OF THE SONS OF NDAR

1. The Telegraph Line. Where the documentation permits, it is possible to see the concerted action of the Muslim Saint-Louisians for specific goals. One instance involves the construction of the telegraph line across Futa Toro, a situation in which Muslims and métis collaborated effectively. With the establishment of the Commandement Supérieur of the Soudan, the French needed telegraphic communication between the upper river headquarters and the capital in Saint-Louis. They completed most of the construction in 1880. The missing portion lay between Salde, an important post of observation in central Futa Toro, and Bakel.

This was precisely the domain controlled by Abdul Bokar Kane, the masterful politician of Futa. He was an able military leader, effective administrator, and shrewd negotiator. He prided himself on the independence that he had demonstrated relative to the French, the Umarian movement, and all other comers in the river valley. In the 1880s, his symbolic and social capital were at their height. No telegraph line could be constructed or maintained without his support.[63]

Governor Brière and his successors tried the carrot and the stick. They conducted serious negotiations in 1880, 1881, and 1883. Brière went to Futa for the first negotiations; when he was kept waiting in the ceremonial capital of Futa for six days, he left in disgust. In 1881 and 1883 the administration mounted extensive military campaigns that caused significant destruction but yielded no political or diplomatic benefits.[64] Each time Abdul eluded their grasp and waited for the troops to withdraw from the harsh conditions of Futa. He repeated his demands: recognition of his dominion, a stipend to maintain the telegraph, customs duties, and decent wages for the Futanke workers on the line. Each time his patience paid dividends: he secured treaties that recognized his authority in return for the construction and maintenance of the telegraph. None of the agreements was implemented, however, and the telegraph poles stayed in bundles on the ground.

The conflict was finally resolved in 1885, when the French realized that they could not force their will on the Futanke leader. They were concerned about large-scale migration to the Umarian dominions by the Fulbe, who supplied a major portion of the cattle market of Saint-Louis, a situation discussed in chapter 5. Only Abdul had the capacity to stem the tide. In addition, the French had just suffered significant reverses at the hands of Samori in the Soudan. Consequently they negotiated an agreement that met Abdul Bokar's conditions in exchange for guarantees on the telegraph. This time the treaty was implemented: the line was built and maintained, the stipends paid, and customs duties collected.

Over five years, the administration strategy, if such it can be called, was formulated by a succession of governors and directors of political affairs. They were inclined toward force. The Hotchkiss machine gun used in the 1883 campaign showed the effects of European weapons, but yielded no ongoing control. The Commandant Supérieur of the Soudan, desperate for communications and a secure line of supply, pushed for the forceful solution. The Ministry of the Navy and Colonies provided the manpower and finances for the campaigns, but chafed at the failure to achieve the objective, especially in the wake of negative French opinion.[65]

It was the Saint-Louis commercial community that moved into the chasm between the administration and Abdul Bokar. Muslim and métis traders, concerned about the disruption of commerce in the middle and upper valley of the river, intervened on both sides over the entire period. In Saint-Louis, they used the General Council as well as private contacts with the governor and his political directors. They succeeded in canceling a proposal to construct a new post at Kaédi, on the north bank in the middle of Abdul's domain, realizing that the project would produce hostility and saddle the budget with heavy expenses.[66]

Out of Podor, Salde, and other markets along the river, the merchants kept in constant touch with the Futanke leader. They exercised influence over the commandant of Podor, who shared his instructions with them and a Saint-

Louis lawyer named Gillet. Some of that information was communicated to Abdul Bokar and enabled him to plan his strategy and minimize his losses.[67] Gaspard Devès was one of those who maintained contact; he even encouraged Abdul to threaten massive emigration to the east to dissuade the French from attempting the telegraph line.[68]

The key leaders in the negotiating drive over the whole period were a métis merchant named Raymond Martin, ally of Louis Descemet, and Pèdre Alassane Mbengue. Mbengue received a gold medal from the administration, as the head of the negotiating team, and the boat dock from Abdul Bokar.[69] In 1881, Pèdre, writing on behalf of the Saint-Louis community and after the recall of Brière, approached Abdul through common religious identity and shared commitment to peace and prosperity:

> We are coming to see you in Futa, for the purpose of avoiding the continuation of a war whose results would be disastrous for Futa and bad for our commerce. God has just sent us a new governor, a just man who seeks only the good of the country. Taking advantage of his open attitude, we have explained to him how you have always had good relations with the traitants and protected their boats and goods. He listened closely and, upon our request, consented to let us come to make you understand that it's impossible for you to continue the war against the French and in your interest, as well as that of the traitants, to make it end. We hope that, since the governor—who can ravage Futa and the whole country—has accepted our offer of mediation, we will find with you, our brother in religion, a warm welcome and that a most durable peace will result from our discussions.[70]

The sons of Ndar combined recognition of Abdul's authority with the ability to influence a clumsy administration. When news of the agreement reached Paris in September 1885, Deputy Albert Gasconi drove the essential point home with the Colonial Department: that the governor and director of political affairs would never have been able to reach a treaty by themselves; indeed, the governor's arrival for the signing of the treaty almost destroyed the careful preparations. Martin and Mbengue had conducted difficult negotiations with aplomb, assisted by two other merchants from Saint-Louis.[71]

2. The Bakel Siege. The very next year, the newly constructed portion of the telegraph line was cut by the forces of Mamadu Lamine Drame, a Soninke pilgrim of Tijaniyya affiliation. Mamadu Lamine was intent upon waging jihad against the dominant classes of the Upper Senegal.[72] These classes were mainly Fulbe and Futanke—the Sy dynasty of Bundu and the Umarians who dominated the other side of the river. Mamadu Lamine soon put the French forces of Bakel in his sights and laid siege to the fort and town in early April 1886. The captain of the fort mobilized a handful of French soldiers and the local militia, which included the able-bodied Muslim merchants, and finally put the jihadists to rout with the help of cannon and superior small-arms fire. Over the next eighteen months, the forces of the Commandant Supérieur and governor of Senegal tracked, cornered, and decapitated the *mujahid*. They used a combination of French troops, *Tirailleurs Sénégalais,* and "auxiliary" units supplied by their traditional allies.

This was the last major struggle in Senegal between a "jihadic" army and the French forces. For Muslims in the interior it demonstrated the weakness of the Islamic banner of resistance and the hopelessness of war against European-led armies and weapons. For the French and the sons of Ndar, the meaning was a common fight against "Tijaniyya fanaticism" and for the compatibility of French overrule and Islamic practice. The French would put Mamadu Lamine's campaign down in the mantra of militancy that included Umar, Ma Ba, and the Madiyanke, and that could be used as needed for new threats.[73]

The Saint-Louis Muslims had a searing memory of loss in the siege. At least sixty-four people in the town were killed during those four days, and ninety-seven wounded. Among the five merchants who died were Jupiter Waly Gueye, the younger brother of Bakre, and John Legros, the father of Galandou Diouf. The Saint-Louisians also witnessed the execution by firing squad of Alpha Sega, the lead interpreter of the post and a "loyal" ally of the administration for many years.[74] They came away from the encounter with a stronger sense of Saint-Louis identity, dependency on the French, and commitment to colonial rule. For them the siege was another experience of militant Islam, comparable to the threat contained in Umar's letter of 1855.

3. The Muslim Tribunal. The sons of Ndar also organized effectively to defend their hometown interests. Over the nineteenth century, they had campaigned for the Muslim Tribunal and used it as a place to adjudicate family and property matters on the basis of Islamic law. For them the recognition of their corporate religious identity was as important as their status as citizens, and they saw no reason why the two should not be compatible. The Catholic community remained hostile to the maintenance of an autonomous Muslim system, as part of their opposition to any official recognition of the rival faith, but they did not

have significant impact on administrative decisions.[75] The more radical and secular métis and French were sometimes opposed as well, because they favored a
more intensive policy of assimilation.[76]

The most serious threat to the community's status came when Ernest Roume
began to centralize services in Dakar. He suspended the Muslim Tribunal and
transferred its functions to another court, the *tribunal de première instance.* Persons
wishing to depose a case for adjudication according to Islamic law would have
to hire a lawyer competent in that area, something well beyond the means of
most inhabitants.[77] The Muslims of Saint-Louis mobilized in force, signed petitions, and convened their elected representatives to take up the case with the
governor-general and the ministry.[78]

In April 1905, 150 Saint-Louis Muslims, many of them now property owners in the Sud (the southern half) of the island, assembled at a building owned
by Hamat Gora Diop. With them were the leading métis members of the General
Council: Théodore Carpot, the president, Louis Descemet, the mayor, Louis
Guillabert, future president of the Colonial Council, Georges Crespin, son of the
old Devès ally, and Hyacinthe Devès. The members of the council supported the
protest.[79] Deputy François Carpot, Théodore's brother, intervened as well. In
May, the government-general issued a decree restoring the Muslim court in
Saint-Louis, as well as in Dakar, Kayes, and Rufisque.[80]

What is unusual about this case is not the willingness of the Saint-Louis
Muslims to organize for their own communal ends, but their alliance with the
métis leaders, many of them active members of the local Roman Catholic parish. The two groups, of such different cultural backgrounds, felt a common
threat in the intensification of power around the government-general in Dakar.

4. The Rights of Originaires. The sense of Saint-Louis identity and the evocation
of republican citizenship grew rapidly in the early twentieth century. Some
Muslim citizens began seeking alternative careers to the trading profession by
the late nineteenth century. This usually meant obtaining a French education
and learning the intracies of the colonial administration. In the process, these
individuals sharpened their consciousness as citizens as well as Muslims. They
learned to organize through the public and private spheres and to bring effective pressure to bear upon the colonial authorities. It was these developments
that culminated in the election of Blaise Diagne in 1914.

The Mody Mbaye sequence is a good illustration of the process. Mody was
born in Saint-Louis in 1871 and received the *brevet élémentaire* in 1893.[81] He
then worked in two capacities over the next decade in Baol, where most of his

family lived: as a schoolteacher and a secretary to some of the superior chiefs appointed by the French during this period. After 1902 he lost his access to positions within the administration, ostensibly because of embezzlement. But he was also a critical observer of the practice of the administration and its chiefs, and knew how to embarrass the colonial authorities.

At this point, Mbaye established his base in Tivaouane, the rail station and center of peanut cultivation in southern Cayor. He became a public letter writer who specialized in intervening with the administration for clients in the interior who were not literate in French and had little experience with the bureaucracy. He remained an advocate of French rule and modernization. He helped in 1904 in the capture of those involved in the death of a junior-level administrator in Thies.[82] He was critical of the conduct of chiefs appointed in the peanut basin and of administrators who ruled arbitarily.[83] Mbaye traveled widely across western Senegal, working closely with François Carpot, the métis deputy and lawyer, who was based in Saint-Louis, and Galandou Diouf, merchant and member of the General Council from Rufisque.

In 1913, Mbaye became a test case for republican citizenship. The rights of originaires, those born in the communes, had become a hot topic in the years just before World War I. The administration sought to limit those rights and the number of residents of the communes who could qualify for French citizenship. They were never able to overcome the practice of many decades, in which those who were born in or had lived in the communes for five years qualified for the vote. In 1913, Mbaye wrote an article in the liberal journal *Le Petit Sénégalais,* criticizing the authoritarian practice of Administrator Paul Brocard of Kaolack in relation to one of his clients. When Mbaye traveled to Kaolack, Brocard put him in prison on the basis of the *indigénat* code, the command system that prevailed everywhere outside of the communes. Mbaye wasted no time in contacting his allies and getting to Governor-general Ponty, and he was freed the next day. He then brought charges against the administrator and alerted the Ligue des Droits de l'Homme, which forced the Ministry of Colonies to look into the affair.[84]

Mbaye's case illustrates not only anxiety about rights but also the growing confidence of the African inhabitants of the communes in their ability to challenge the administration on its own terms. In these cases it was especially important to gain the support of the deputy to the French National Assembly, who could galvanize the metropolitan interests who monitored the rights of citizens, wherever they might live. For François Carpot and Blaise Diagne, the protection of the rights of originaires was a critical issue, and one that affected their identity as well. Under Diagne's tenure, legislation was passed that affirmed the citizenship of those born in the communes.[85]

PATTERNS ACROSS SPACE AND TIME

The families and events described here reveal a number of important patterns. The merchants were closely tied to the administration and the French commercial houses, even when they protested against specific practices. They were associated with the more conservative elements of métis society, symbolized by the Descemet clan and the Bordeaux firms, but also had ties to the Devès. In a word, they hedged their bets and managed their debts from a variety of sources. Their sense of an urban republican identity increased over time. By the end of the century, the sons of Ndar were ready to ally with the métis or use French procedures to defend their interests. Some were prepared to sack the home of Bakre Waly for his overt alliance with the administration.[86]

Several of the merchants profiled here were born in the 1820s and reached their adult careers by the 1850s, before the age of thirty. This was true of Pèdre Alassane Mbengue and almost certainly of Sidi and Mambaye Fara Biram. Bakre Waly fell one decade later, and Abdullay Mar and Hamet Gora Diop about a decade later still. All of the families enjoyed wealth and prestige in the wake of Faidherbe's expansion and before the renewed conquests of the 1880s, and all were able to sustain their positions for some time despite the increasing intervention of the administration and French firms.

It was in the *escales*, and over considerable periods of time, that the merchants established their Muslim identity,[87] developed their clienteles, accumulated wealth, and "proved" their reliability to the administration. Their expertise was particular to a geographical sphere.[88] Two emerged in Dagana, two in Podor, others in Bakel and Medine. Rosso, the market used by Mbengue and Diop, was on the "frontier" of Trarza; like Dagana and Podor, it was accessible to Saint-Louis throughout the year. One key index to status was membership on the councils at the posts: the conciliation commission, which adjudicated property questions, and the consultative commission, which advised the commandant. All the merchants could expect to serve in the local militia.

In time, these entrepreneurs could transfer their economic, social, and cultural capital to another location. As they grew older, they were likely to make Saint-Louis their year-round residence, leaving the interior operations to younger members of the family. In this setting, they could more easily sustain contact with the mayor, city council, and members of the General Council, or run for office, as Bakre Waly did. The Nord remained the quarter of choice for elite Muslim families, but some—such as Hamat Gora Diop—acquired property in the Sud or outside of the island altogether. The wealthier merchants expanded their investment in land and buildings. Many of them burnished their credentials as Muslims. Abdullay Mar and Hamat Gora made the pilgrimage. Hamat Gora and others gave land for mosques, schools, and zawiyas. They were also interested in bringing prestigious marabouts to Saint-Louis to visit or live. Malik Sy, a well-educated and "unfanatical" Tijaniyya cleric, was the most conspicuous case.

The Muslim elite could arrange marriages appropriate to their station. The data for marriage strategies is very incomplete, but there are certainly indicators of patterns among the notables of the town. An interesting example comes from three interrelated families: the Gargny, Ndiaye, and Seck.[89] Makha Gargny, a prominent Saint-Louisian with some connections to the Catholic parish in the mid nineteenth century, had several very eligible daughters. One married into the Blondin family, a métis line closely tied to the church. Another daughter, Yaba, married Makonne Seck (d. 1895), an important trader in Podor and Salde and the third signatory in the 1881 letter to Abdul Bokar cited above. She gave birth to Dame Seck (1874–1925), who started out as a trader in Dagana, made the pilgrimage to Mecca, and became one of the most learned Muslim clerics of Saint-Louis. It was Al-Hajj Dame Seck who gave the plot for the zawiya of Malik Sy in Saint-Louis. Dame Seck was also on good terms with Amadu Bamba.[90]

Abdu Ndiaye was a successful trader in Bakel. Most of his children were female; they married extremely well. Magatte married Al-Hajj Dame Seck. Diaw married Mamussé, one of the sons of Bakre Waly Gueye. Marie Pierre married Abdussalam Kane, the chief of Kanel in eastern Futa from 1896–1955 and grandson of Hamat Ndiaye Anne. Mariama married Buna Albury Ndiaye, the powerful chief of Jolof from 1895–1935. Both Abdussalam and Buna were close associates of Martial Merlin and pillars of the Colonial Council.

While these merchants maintained relations with independent chiefs and might oppose specific plans for expansion, they adjusted to increasing French control of the Senegalo-Mauritanian zone. By the end of the century, they realized that the era of economic entrepreneurship, Islamic diplomacy, and frontiers of opportunity was coming to a close. They directed their sons toward Western education and careers in the administration, professions, or politics. Some moved to more promising locations for commerce, such as Tivaouane,

Rufisque, and Dakar, but they usually had to function as agents of European firms. A few could carve out careers as "letter writers" in the fashion of Mody Mbaye. While Islamic education was more important than ever, it could no longer yield the prestigious and challenging diplomatic experience enjoyed by the Anne and Seck.

All of the individuals and families offered invaluable services to both the colonial administration and the interior leaders in the late nineteenth century. The merchants, in their various implantations in the hinterland, participated in the local militias that might have to defend a post, courier, caravan, or fleet of boats.[91] They joined the local garrison as auxiliaries for military campaigns, and might pick up booty—slaves, cattle, grain—in the process. The 1886 attack on Bakel resonated through their ranks and drove home their dependence on the colonial regime.

The commercial operations of these Saint-Louisians brought in a variety of information about local and regional developments. Some merchants were close to the commanders and other official personnel in the post. They communicated to their networks in Ndar, especially when they moved back to the capital for the off-season. They served as couriers for letters in every direction. They helped sort out the estates of their deceased colleagues, and this gave reassurance that wealth accumulated would be passed along.

The informational services were invaluable to the chiefs and clerics of the interior as well. In the case of the telegraph line, the flow of useful information was primarily in the direction of Abdul Bokar, not the governor. Traders sufficiently literate in Arabic might actually write letters for these leaders. Some became the confidants of particular chiefs.[92] In many cases, the traders, often debtors themselves, made loans to the leaders, and they provided a precious supply of arms and ammunition.

For several decades in the late nineteenth century, the merchants used their capital to provide reassurance about patterns of revenue and patronage to ruling classes anxious about the labor supply. The traders communicated that concern to the administration, and they were accomplices in the slave trade, which continued to supply workers to the wealthy and powerful into the early twentieth century.[93] The chiefs were also worried about their position under colonial rule, involving patronage and clientship, rights of taxation, and customs collection. Again the sons of Ndar had a calming influence. They could point to the administration's preference for a protectorate rather than annexation and to the ability of protectorate chiefs to continue to exploit their subjects. Ultimately, the Saint-Louisians gave reassurance by the values that they shared with the leaders of the interior: the practice of Islam, a hierarchical social structure that emphasized tribute and labor service, and a wide-ranging commerce in many goods. Their contribution to the extension of French hegemony was invaluable.

In the early twentieth century, some of the urban Muslims shifted their alignment. Thanks to more extensive French education, a greater consciousness of citizenship, and a decline in their economic capital, they became more critical of the colonial authorities and the appointed chiefs and more aware of the marginalization of Saint-Louis. Acting in concert with the métis, the press, or other parts of the private sphere, they could use their still considerable social and symbolic capital to embarrass the administration, achieve limited objectives, and organize for the election of Blaise Diagne. But they were not in a position to challenge the intensification of power of the administration. The only groups capable of negotiating with the colonial authorities on equal terms were the emerging Muslim authorities—the subject to which I now turn.

PART 3

Patterns of Accommodation

—7—
The Obstacles to Accommodation for the Umarians

BY THE LATE NINETEENTH CENTURY, all of the reformers and the Islamic states had disappeared, with one exception. The exception was the Umarian enterprise, which was still alive in the minds of the Tal family and thousands of disciples well after the destruction of its garrison capitals. But the inheritors faced a daunting task of adjustment as the Europeans took over the Dar al-Islam of West Africa and established their rule over Muslim societies.[1]

Shaikh Umar had grown up amid the memories of an Islamic state in Futa Toro, well before the French became the "masters of the land." He forged his community through the pilgrimage, the return journey, and teaching in Futa Jalon. All of these events transpired by the mid nineteenth century, before the tenure of Governor Faidherbe.[2] In contrast, the founders of the "paths of accommodation" lived two generations later. Born at mid century, they grew up amid the turmoil of the anciens régimes and the growing strength of the French in the late nineteenth century.

The Umarian community, once forged, had embarked on an all-consuming campaign to destroy the outstanding examples of "paganism" in the Dar al-Islam: the small Mandinka state of Tamba and the larger and more powerful Bamana ones of Karta and Segu. While the Umarians recruited heavily all along the Senegal River valley, the focus of their efforts was to the east, in what became French Soudan. After their initial victories, they settled into garrison towns as a ruling aristocracy, fueled by new recruits and supplies of munitions from the west. Their position, as a minority within an often hostile majority,

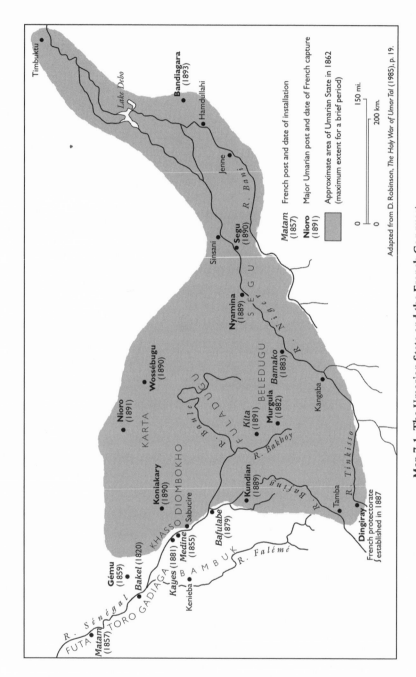

Map 7.1. The Umarian State and the French Conquest

Timbuktu

Bandiagara
(1893)

Hamdullahi

Lake Debo

Jenne

R. Bani

Segu (1890)

Sinsani

S E G U

Nyamina
(1889)

BELEDUGU

Bamako
(1883)

Murgula
(1882)

Kita
(1891)

Kangaba

R. Niger

Wossébugu
(1890)

KARTA

Nioro
(1891)

F U L A D U G U

R. Bakhoy

Koniakary
(1890)

DIOMBOKHO

Sabucire

KHASSO

Kundian
(1889)

R. Bafing

R. Tinkisso

Tamba

Dingiray

French protectorate
established in 1887

Gému
(1859)

Bakel (1820)

Kayes (1881)

Medine
(1855)

Bafulabe
(1879)

Kenieba

B A M B U K

R. Falémé

R. Sénégal

FUTA

Matam
(1857)

TORO GADIAGA

Matam French post and date of installation
(1857)

Nioro Major Umarian post and date of French capture
(1891)

Approximate area of Umarian State in 1862
(maximum extent for a brief period)

0   150 mi.

0   200 km.

Adapted from D. Robinson, *The Holy War of Umar Tal* (1985), p. 19.

forced them to rely heavily on their ideology of religious and ethnic superiority—at least until the conquests of the Commandants Supérieurs reduced them to submission or flight.

By contrast, none of the marabouts and constituencies treated in the coming chapters embarked upon, or even seriously considered, careers of jihad, state building, or hijra. They observed the annihilation of the Madiyanke in 1875 and the disintegration of the inheritors of the Ma Ba tradition. They were not attracted to the Umarian enterprise. Even Malik Sy, the marabout of Tijaniyya affiliation, framed his Umarian relationship around distant links: a memory from childhood about a maternal uncle.[3]

The Umarians had also staked out an interpretation of the Tijaniyya that was hard to sustain amid the great transformations of the early colonial era. Following the main teaching of the founder, Ahmad al-Tijani, they construed the order as a special Sufi revelation, directly from the Prophet. The revelation was exclusive and final; a Muslim could "convert" to the Tijaniyya, but could not then join a different affiliation, nor combine more than one. Within West Africa, they believed that Umar was the appointed representative. Other knowledgeable Muslims, including the founders of the paths of accommodation, accepted multiple affiliation, the spiritual equality of the Sufi orders, and a variety of legitimate ways to access the Tijaniyya.[4]

Another problem came from the great fragmentation of the Umarian community. Shaikh Umar had not been able to devote energy to the institutionalization of Islam in the conquered lands or to training his sons and disciples in the arts of rule. The Masina debacle wiped out much of the leadership and propelled Amadu Sheku into responsibilities for which he was not prepared. For almost thirty years he held some of the Umarian dominions together, but at great cost in enmity among the Tal and the principal *talibés,* or disciples. For many West African Muslims his reign was an example of *fitna,* "civil war." After his departure for the east in 1893, the fragmentation grew dramatically, across space, generation, and ideological persuasion.

The final problem for Umarian accommodation came from the positions that Umar wrote and preached in the 1850s in relation to the French; these became standard fare in the decades to follow. Umar warned against *muwalat,* "close association" with Christians. He had recruited on the basis of hijra, or "emigration" from a land "polluted" by non-Muslim authorities. Indeed, he had called for the restoration of the customary tributary relationship of non-Muslims to Muslim authorities.

His son was loyal to these traditions.[5] In 1893, as the archenemy Archinard

approached Bandiagara, the last bastion of Umarian control in the Middle
Niger, Amadu wrote a desperate plea to Mulay Hassan I in Morocco:

> And now, O lieutenant of God on earth, successor to the Prophet for his
> people, descendant of the chief of the Prophets, make haste, make haste! Your
> friends have been abandoned, your country is ruined and your subjects are dis-
> persed. Death, captivity, and pillage, that is the end which awaits them. The
> enemy has destroyed mosques, burned Qurans, thrown our scientific books
> into the desert, and has transformed our places of prayer into churches—the
> church bell has replaced the muezzin. He has kidnapped the daughters of the
> shaikh and forced his sons into his service. The children of Muslims have been
> divided among the chiefs of the army that has taken the whole country.[6]

A few days later, Amadu himself, with perhaps a thousand followers, embarked
on the hijra from the "pollution" created by the French colony of Soudan. He
died in 1897 near Sokoto, the capital of the still independent Muslim regime
close to the original home of his mother.[7] His actions strengthened the tradition of Umarian opposition and distance from European rule.

By the end of the century, the Umarians had lost much of their luster and
leadership, even for Tijaniyya initiates. They were dispersed and torn by rival-
ries. In the eyes of some, they were discredited. Most of the Tal men neglected
the scholarly career and specialized in politics—a politics that ended emphatically with the French conquest.[8] Their discomfiture and disarray allowed other
Tijaniyya leaders to come to the fore—foremost among them, Malik Sy.

The Tal had to make radical adjustments to cope with the new realities of
colonial rule in their three principal areas of occupation. The Dingiray area of
Guinea was the birthplace of the holy war and the site of the early Umarian
community. The Middle Niger, now the heart of French Soudan, was the theater of most of the combat and the fragile Islamic state that the French dubbed
the Tokolor Empire.[9] Senegal was Umar's place of origin, the source of most of
his soldier disciples, and the area with the most favorable view of the jihad and
state. And yet it is the area where Tal and Umarians were least conspicuous during the early colonial period.[10]

A PROBLEMATIC HERITAGE

Intellectual and spiritual leader, destroyer of "paganism," resistance hero. These
three expressions summarize the positive achievements of Al-Hajj Umar, as
outlined in chapter 1. The negative ones were no less apparent to Muslims in

the late ninetenth century: the attack upon another Muslim state and the great destruction wrought in Masina; the failure to develop institutions of integration in Karta and Segu; and fitna, the "civil war" among the sons.

Fitna was the biggest problem for Muslims in the Senegalo-Mauritanian zone. They knew that Amadu Sheku attempted to preside over the Umarian dominions from Segu for about thirty years. He never had any control over Masina, his cousin Tijani, or the garrison capital of Bandiagara. He exercised some influence over Dingiray, the main center from the days of the early jihad, but this disappeared in the 1880s. He placed a great deal more emphasis on maintaining his authority in Karta and the fort of Nioro, which lay along the route of recruitment and supply from Senegal. But controlling Karta was not an easy task. The indigenous inhabitants were in frequent revolt. The younger brothers who had been appointed to positions of power often disobeyed his commands. On two occasions, from 1869 to 1873 and again in 1885, Amadu marched on Nioro and fought against them. In the first instance, he arrested Habib and Mokhtar, Umar's sons by the daughter of Muhammad Bello,[11] and took them back to a Segu prison, where they died some years later. In the second instance he laid siege to the fort and brought another brother, Muntaga, to the point of destruction.[12] Like his father in the campaign against Masina, Amadu had his justifications, but they did not take away the sting of fitna. Indeed, the two conflicts in Nioro did more than anything else to diminish the Umarian leadership of the Tijaniyya; informants are still reluctant to talk about the situation.[13]

The French conquest dealt a further blow to Umarian prestige, both moral and political. Louis Archinard defeated the Umarian garrisons of Segu, Nioro, and Bandiagara in rapid succession (1890–93). The colonial Soudan was carved out of the old "Tokolor Empire." The conquest of Segu, which was the symbol of Umarian and Tijaniyya distinction, was a bitter blow for Muslims of many persuasions.[14] Archinard captured it without losing one soldier. He transported the Umarian library, some jewelry, and memorabilia to Paris, enrolled one of Amadu's sons in military school in France, and distributed women and children to African allies.[15]

Amadu recouped some prestige at the end through resistance and hijra. But even the Umarians who moved out of Bandiagara in 1893 were divided and ambivalent about their course of action. By a reconstruction of the available sources, one can see at least two major periods of hesitation: a first one around Aribinda, shortly after their departure, and a second before moving into Hausaland in 1897, just before Amadu's death. A substantial number of the migrants returned to Bandiagara in 1894–95 and made their accommodation to the colonial regime.[16] Bassiru, Amadu's brother, and Madani, his son, stayed in Hausaland and made their peace with British colonial rule. Alfa Hashimi, Amadu's cousin, went on to the Holy Lands. His fortunes are discussed below.

The fragmentation of authority started in the 1850s with the preoccupation with the prosecution of the jihad. At that time, Umar appointed some *muqaddam*, the "authorized representatives" of the Tijaniyya order, as well as some emirs to rule over specific administrative entities. He entrusted overall responsibility for the territory, command structure, and the Tijaniyya to the young and inexperienced Amadu. The unity that Dingiray had imposed on the Tal family and the Umarians at the very beginning of the jihad dissipated. Umar had wives, concubines, slaves, and children across the Upper and Middle Niger regions. When he died, these women and their families organized their lives and ambitions as best they could. All of this made for the fragmentation of what the French called the Tijaniyya Omaria in the early twentieth century—a situation in which they took a measure of satisfaction.[17]

Umar did not reveal clearly his intentions relative to the Tijaniyya. He may have appointed as many as ten muqaddam while he was alive: Amadu; his slightly younger brother Makki, who died in Masina; Agibu; Seydu Anne from the Sokoto region; and others.[18] Amadu then named muqaddam at several different times over his career and played an active role in the dissemination of the Tijaniyya. He played this role at annual ceremonies in Segu and encouraged his brothers and other Umarians to come for the occasion.[19] In 1892–93, Amadu made a point of naming muqaddam from Bandiagara, as he considered his options and decided to make the hijra. He appointed his brother Murtada in person and dispatched a disciple with a license of authorization to his son Muntaga Amadu.[20]

After Amadu departed on the hijra, authority within the Umarian Tijaniyya became even more diffuse. None of those appointed by Amadu moved into the Senegalo-Mauritanian zone. In Bandiagara, Agibu seems to have been the most prominent official for some time, and he passed the mantle on to his sons.[21] After World War I, Seydu Nuru Tal gradually assumed leadership in the family, along with the authority to appoint other muqaddam.

It is difficult to discern any Umarian pattern of marriage. Umar's first wives came from Bornu and Hausaland. Some were of noble, even illustrious birth, while others were slaves given to honor his distinction. These women became the mothers of the principal contenders for his succession: Amadu, Makki, Habib, Mukhtar, and Agibu.[22] During the 1850s they resided in Dingiray. Umar seems to have taken his later wives primarily from the families of chiefs, whether allies or enemies, perhaps as a way of seating his authority more firmly in the conquered territories. Umar's sons continued this practice, and consequently the grandchildren or third generation of Tal had widely diverging experiences. If the Agibian tradition is to be believed, Umar encouraged his sons to avoid marrying Futanke women: they were supposedly greedy and treacherous, with agendas of their own.[23]

The Umarian women were kept in seclusion and isolation. They supported themselves by spinning, weaving, dyeing, and other productive activities. Many had their own attendants. In the case of Segu, they numbered in the hundreds; some never had sexual relations with Amadu and were probably kept to be given to other Tal, disciples or allies of the moment.[24] If they rebelled against the discipline of the harem, they could be brutally beaten. But they were certainly not passive. In Dingiray and other centers, they plotted the fortunes of their offspring.[25] In the 1860s, Segu became the principal location of wives and children, while smaller groups of women and children lived in the palaces of Nioro, Bandiagara, and the other capitals. Agibu collected a large number of Umarian survivors in Bandiagara in the 1890s.

The French conquest accentuated the leadership vacuum. The Umarians looked first to the sons of the founder of the movement for leadership. Most of them had passed away; many died in the traumas of Masina in 1863–64, others at the hands of Amadu in the conflicts for control of Nioro. In addition to Amadu, Bassiru and Mubassiru departed on the journey to the east. This left only three sons, by my count, in the areas that had now fallen under French control: Agibu, who accepted French appointment as "king of Masina"; Murtada, who was closely watched by the government at Nioro; and the erratic Naziru, who enlisted with the French military.[26] These sons, and even more the grandsons of the founders, were heterogenous in every respect: age, language, Islamic culture, and orientation toward the colonial authorities.

At the next level, the sons of Umar's older brothers—Eliman Gede, Alfa Amadu, and Cerno Bokar—the situation was similar. Eliman Gede's descendants were mainly confined to Dingiray, the original Umarian center in colonial Guinea, and had little impact beyond the local scene. Alfa Amadu exercised some influence at Dingiray, Nioro, and Bandiagara in the 1850s and 1860s. His oldest son Tijani reigned at Bandiagara until his death in 1887. Tijani seems to have kept many Tal there, safe from the designs of his cousin and rival in Segu.[27] His younger son Alfa Hashimi departed on the hijra in 1893. Cerno Bokar also had some impact in Nioro and Bandiagara at mid century. Most of his descendants probably lived in Bandiagara. His son Seydu Habi reigned over the fiefdom briefly after the death of Tijani, while Salif counseled Amadu and

Madani in Segu, came to Bandiagara in Amadu's entourage, and joined the march to the east.[28]

In addition, most of the experienced talibés had disappeared.[29] Many died in the battles around Nioro at the beginning of 1891, others made the trek to the east, while still others went underground. There was little reason for them, whose skills were primarily those of waging war or adjudicating disputes according to Islamic law, to expect any particular consideration from the new French regime.

The French supervised the surviving foyers of Umarians very closely. They had manufactured the myth of the Tokolor Empire and exaggerated the hostility of the Umarians.[30] Even in the 1890s, they found it useful, on occasion, to trot out the old "fanatic" equation. This was especially true in the Soudan, where the French saw the Umarians as exploitative settlers. They sent thousands of them back to Futa Toro and watched the others very closely, often under conditions approximating house arrest.

The Options of Hashimi and Agibu

Two of the Tal framed the extreme options for the inheritors of the Umarian enterprise. Alfa Hashimi, the nephew, represented the option of "resistance"—in its form of hijra away from European control. Agibu, the son, represented the choice of collaboration, as a colonial chief within the new order of French West Africa (see plate 3). In the early colonial period, no Umarian was able to mobilize a significant constituency around a "path of accommodation."

Alfa Hashimi (ca. 1866–ca. 1939), the younger brother of Tijani, became the most celebrated Umarian leader at the turn of the century. He made the hijra, lived in the arena of the Sokoto caliphate until the British conquest, and then continued on to the Sudan. In 1904–5 he crossed the Red Sea and settled in Medina for most of the rest of his life. He lived, it was said, in the old hostel established by Askiya Muhammad of Songhay for West African travelers. It was there that he received the pilgrims of the early twentieth century who came overland or by the French steamships working out of West African ports. It was from there that he completed or circulated the account of the Amadu's hijra and came to the attention of French and British authorities.[31]

Alfa Hashimi emerged as a leading actor in Hausaland, after Amadu's death and as a counselor to Bassiru in the years immediately prior to the British conquest (1898-1903).[32] He survived the battle of Burmi, where the British killed Caliph Attahiru of Sokoto, who was engaged in a hijra of his own. In the company of Fulbe, Hausa, and members of the ruling classes of northern Nigeria, he moved east to the Nile over the next year, and then to Medina. His reputation seems to have grown quickly from this time on. He traveled to Yemen and through much of the Anglo-Egyptian Sudan. He wrote treatises, including his account of the hijra and texts emphasizing the special role of the Fulbe within the Islamic world.[33] He became a leading muqaddam of the Tijaniyya in northeastern Africa, particularly for the West African Muslims who had migrated to the east.[34] His reputation extended back to Nigeria.[35]

It was this growing reputation that troubled the colonial authorities in the years leading up to World War I. Hashimi's hostel became a gathering point for West African pilgrims. In 1909, the French authorized the pilgrimage of Sulaiman and Ainina Seck, brothers of Dudu and teachers at the government Medersa, and asked them to examine Hashimi's operations in Medine.[36] The Seck produced no evidence of propaganda hostile to French rule, but the administration's concern was not put to rest until 1919. At that time, the French and British learned that Hashimi had supported their position in favor of the Arab revolt against the declining Ottoman regime.[37]

Hashimi's prominence for the Umarian and Fulbe communities should not surprise. He had performed the hijra away from infidel control on two conspicuous occasions: from the French in 1893, and from the British as they moved into Hausaland in 1903.[38] He made the ultimate emigration in those troubled times of aggressive imperialism by going to the one region that was not falling under European control, transforming his hijra into the most sacred obligation, the *hajj*. He was scholar, author, and counselor to Umarian and Nigerian elites. He was a Tijaniyya muqaddam and leader of the West African affiliates in northeastern Africa and Arabia. For Muslims in the new French federation, and especially the Futanke, he had fulfilled all of the obligations of Islam and the Umarian tradition.

It would be hard to imagine a greater contrast to Hashimi than the "king of Masina." Agibu (ca. 1843–1907) was probably the ninth son of Umar; his mother was the prestigious Mariatu from Bornu.[39] In the 1860s, he lived in Segu on good terms with his older brother. When these relations deteriorated in the 1870s, Amadu appointed him governor of Dingiray, but kept his wife and part of his entourage as a guarantee of loyalty.[40] By the end of 1878, Agibu had established himself in the original Umarian capital.

Over the next decade, Agibu sought to cope with the rapidly changing realities of the Upper Niger region. His policies and practices make sense from two perspectives: trying to rule over Dingiray and the domains of the old state of Tamba, and trying to carve out a situation for himself as a talented son of the most prestigious Tijaniyya and jihad leader of his day.[41] It was the pressure from Samori that precipitated his alliance with the French. In 1887, Agibu agreed to a protectorate, and in 1891 to a French garrison. When he obtained custody of many of the women captured in the Segu campaign, including his wife Assa Kulibali, he began to harbor hope of serving as successor to Amadu. In 1892, he entrusted Dingiray to his son Alfa Makki and traveled to Kayes to meet Commandant Supérieur Archinard, never to return. In 1893, Archinard installed him on the "throne" of Bandiagara as Fama, or king of Masina, while Amadu, Alfa Hashimi, and other Umarians fled to the east.[42]

Agibu probably expected to rule in a manner similar to the virtually autonomous practice of Dingiray: small-scale raids and military actions, taxation, confiscation when necessary, and considerable deference. He had been able to live with the protectorate arrangement after 1887. But the military garrison and civilian administrator of Bandiagara cramped his style. The French were not about to entrust major responsibility to an African ally in a frontier region near Timbuktu, the Sahara, and a host of uncharted areas. Agibu soon realized that the French would not provide significant resources or permit much latitude in his responsibilities. It mattered little whether he was "king of Masina" with a large jurisdiction (1893–1902) or a simple chief of Bandiagara (1902 until his death in 1907).

Agibu was not very popular; indeed, he needed the protection of his patrons. He did not have much support in the local Umarian community, most of whom had lived in Bandiagara from a much earlier time or who had strong attachments to Amadu Sheku. For the first two years, he very much wanted French support against the emigrants, who might return from the east at any time. Agibu ultimately did integrate several hundred returnees into the life of Bandiagara. He presided over a very divided Futanke community, which in turn had very complex relations with the Fulbe, Dogon, and other groups, who had long inhabited the area and were marked, in quite different ways, by the Masina-Futanke struggles.

By the time of his appointment in 1893, Agibu had developed the rationale for his actions that he and his descendants have used ever since. According to his grandson, he had even worked out an understanding with Amadu after the fall of Segu. On the basis of this arrangement, Agibu composed his differences with the French in order to rescue forty-five young Umarians from their grasp. He then wrote to his older brother to indicate that he had done everything requested and would provide protection for Amadu should he decide to stay in Bandiagara.[43]

Agibu articulated this rationale in his traditional speech to the chiefs and other notables of Bandiagara in 1895 after the ʿId al-Kabir: "The French killed the Futanke they found in Segu, and they cut the throats of all those they found at Nioro. They did not do that at Bandiagara; on the contrary, they welcomed those who submitted, even those who left Amadu [and came back from the hijra]. This is because I asked them, and I intercede for you every day."[44] To this, the fama often added the most important justification: how he had saved from slavery or death the women and children captured by Archinard in Segu in 1890.[45] Many of them came to Bandiagara, accepted the protection that he offered, and tempered their judgments about his collaboration.

Many Umarians were publicly critical of Agibu. They considered him a traitor to his father, older brother, and the Umarian cause. Where Umar had waged the jihad of resistance to European rule, where Amadu had resisted through jihad and hijra, Agibu now ruled the last capital with heavy dependence on the French. He made no effort to hide that dependency: he sent his sons to French schools, openly wore his Legion of Honor medals, and enjoyed presiding over 14 July celebrations. He transferred his family and entourage from Dingiray. He established his sons as successors over the Futanke community of Bandiagara. He was greedy, cruel, capricious, and plaintive.[46] Most of the French officials who served in Bandiagara agreed with these judgments.[47]

Some of the same Umarians were more kind in their private communications. In my interviews with descendants of Umar, I found a consensus that Agibu played a key role in taking care of the family at a very critical juncture.[48] Bandiagara became, and in some respects has remained, the most visible Umarian center in francophone West Africa. Many people took refuge there. For Aissata, the wife of Salif Bokar, and her young son, the future Cerno Bokar, Bandiagara was a place where one could obtain a proper Islamic education, practice the Tijaniyya rituals, and celebrate the Umarian heritage.[49] Agibu helped to preserve that heritage; he presided over the place where Umar had died or disappeared (Degembere) and over the objects that Umar had bequeathed to his successors.[50] He exercised the greatest single influence over the formulation of traditions about Umar and Amadu.[51] He had known Eugène Mage, Paul Soleillet, and Louis Archinard, the three main European interpreters of the Umarian movement. In sum, he was the only surviving son who had lived through the critical watersheds and could relate them to his Futanke and French interlocutors.

OTHER FOYERS OF THE SOUDAN AND GUINÉE

While Hashimi and Agibu framed the limiting options for Tal and talibés in the early colonial period, and Bandiagara became the foyer most closely identified with the cause, most of the Umarians lived elsewhere, scattered through Soudan, Guinée, and Sénégal. A surprising number lived in the old garrison cities of the "Empire," where they constituted a small but visible minority. Leadership often fell to a Tal, usually a descendant of Umar. Some of the more prestigious and experienced disciples, such as the Cam of Bandiagara, Segu, and Dingiray, established their own autonomous networks of support.[52]

Segu had been the main Umarian capital and remained a key center. It was part of a larger Bamana culture and much closer than Bandiagara to the emerging center of colonial Soudan. The community had no obvious leadership there after the French conquest until Muntaga (born ca. 1873), the son of Amadu, was allowed to return in 1905. Muntaga Amadu, as he was called, became a very prominent leader in Segu and Soudan during the early colonial period.[53]

With Archinard's approach in 1890, Muntaga fled, but he did not follow his older brother Madani to Nioro, nor was he at Bandiagara at the beginning of Amadu's hijra. Instead, he joined the forces of Samori and stayed with the Mandinka leader until they were captured by the French in 1898.[54] The French recognized Muntaga's potential influence by keeping him under surveillance for several years in Timbuktu. When he returned to Segu, it was thanks to the intervention of two prominent Umarian women who had influence in colonial circles. One was his mother, Binta Kulibali, who was captured and handed over as booty to the interpreter Hamady Kumba Sy after the fall of Segu. The other was his sister, Jeynaba Umu, who had been given to Mademba Sy, colonial functionary and chief.[55]

Muntaga's influence in Segu grew steadily over the next decades and by the interwar period he was probably the single most widely respected member of the family. This was especially remarkable because he had very little literacy in Arabic.[56] His impact can be explained in several ways. Muntaga had continued resistance against European encroachment by joining the campaigns of Samori, in stark contrast to Agibu. He was the oldest son of Amadu in the region.[57] He had been designated muqaddam, with the power to appoint other muqaddam, and was living in Segu, the main capital of the old Islamic state. Above all, his prestige stemmed from his political acumen. Muntaga allied with the descendants of Seydu Jeliya Ture, Amadu's principal counselor, and thus replicated the relationship of chief and counselor that had existed before. He enjoyed a close relationship with his brother-in-law Mademba Sy, the redoubt-able "fama of Sansanding," who exerted enormous influence over the Middle Niger until his death in 1918. Muntaga's daughter Madina married Mademba's son, Lieutenant Abdul Kader Mademba.[58]

Tijaniyya and Umarians looked to Muntaga for leadership in the early years of colonial rule. When his uncle Murtada died in Nioro in 1922, Muntaga played the decisive role in the choice of a new muqaddam. According to a French report, Muntaga consulted with his older brother Madani in Nigeria and then agreed to the appointment of Shaikh Hamallah, the popular choice in Nioro. Shaikh Ha-mallah became the leader of a branch of the Tijaniyya called *onze grains* and chief rival to Umarian leadership of the order in French West Africa.[59]

Another critical foyer was Nioro. Symbol of the first great victories against the Bamana, the struggle between Amadu and his brothers in 1869–73 and 1885, it was forever marked as an Umarian center. Nioro and the surrounding area had received a very large influx of Senegambians between 1855 and 1890. These settlers went further in the direction of creating Islamic institutions and mechanisms of control of the indigenous populations than any other Umarian center.[60] Thousands remained after the forced repatriations engineered by Archi-nard in 1891 and 1893, but in a situation of internal division and difficult rela-tions with their former subjects. The French, as in the case of Segu, left the Nioro community without visible leadership until the early 1900s.

The approved candidate, properly chastened, was Murtada Tal, one of the oldest surviving sons of Umar. Almost as old as Agibu, Murtada had spent many of his earlier years in Nioro. Amadu appointed him governor of a province of Karta and sent him on a recruitment mission in Senegambia in the late 1880s.[61] Amadu then named him muqaddam in 1893, just before leaving Bandiagara for his hijra.[62]

Murtada endured a period of exile and close surveillance—in his case in Bandiagara and Jenne—for more than ten years. In 1906, he was allowed to settle near Nioro. There he allied with the influential Kaba Diakité family and other Umarian disciples. In concert with them, he supported the deportation of Shaikh Sidi Muhammad Lakhdar, practitioner of the onze grains, predecessor and patron of Shaikh Hamallah, and marabout of the sons of Ndar who had settled in Nioro. Sidi Muhammad was exiled to Saint-Louis and Trarza for two years before returning to die in Nioro.[63]

Murtada married three women of important Futanke and Fulbe families near Nioro. He raised cattle and engaged in trade. He was popular in Karta and Senegal. He enjoyed the favor of his French patrons, making the pilgrimage by sea in 1910–11 with their approval and probably with their financial support. He participated actively in the French effort to recruit soldiers during World War I.

The other obvious foyer in the wider region was Dingiray. The town and surrounding area were heavily colonized by talibés from Futa Toro and Futa Jalon and by Umar's wives and family; it has a "Tokolor" character in the archival accounts of the twentieth century. Alfa Makki, son of Agibu, reigned as a *chef de province* until 1899, when the complaints of subjects persuaded the French to send him to Bandiagara. At the same time, the colonial authorities moved Dingiray from the jurisdiction of the Soudan to that of Guinée and attached it to Futa Jalon. The effect of all these actions was to reduce the visibility of the Tal, enhance the leadership of some of the talibés, and accentuate the isolation of the Umarian heritage.[64]

No other towns in Soudan or Guinea had such visible symbols of the heritage as Bandiagara, Segu, Nioro, and Dingiray. Kayes and then Bamako were the capitals of colonial Soudan, and had never served as Umarian centers. Konyakary, a few miles from Kayes, had been an important garrison, but the prominent leaders there were talibés, such as Alfa Ibrahima Wane. Disciples and Tal alike accommodated to the pace and tone of activities in these colonial centers.

THE SENEGALESE SPHERE

It is significant that no single member of the Tal family became prominent during the early colonial period in the Senegalo-Mauritanian zone. One of Umar's daughters settled in the Podor area of Futa, another in Kaolack, another in Diourbel. His son Naziru worked out of a village in Gambia. His grandson Seydu Nuru was studying and working for Amadu Moktar Sakho, the qadi of Boghé, and married Khadijatu, daughter of Malik Sy. He divided his time between Tivaouane, Saint-Louis, and Boghé on the north bank of the river in Futa. Neither he nor any other descendant had any significant influence at the time.[65]

The reasons for this invisibility are not difficult to find. In the late nineteenth century, the Umarian Tijaniyya had relatively few partisans in Senegal. As long as the garrisons held out, and recruiters could evoke the jihad and the Islamic state, Senegalese responded to the call and left for the east.[66] Once the French eliminated the last vestiges of the state and established their colony of Soudan, enlistment in the cause had no purpose. The Umarian mission was attached above all to an independent state.

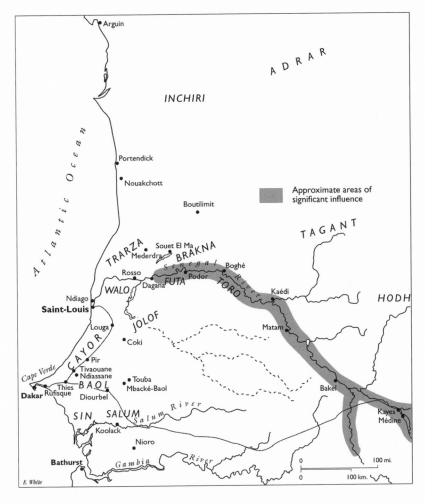

Map 7.2. The Umarians and the Senegalo-Mauritanian Zone, ca. 1880–1920

It was inevitable that Futa Toro, the birthplace of Umar and the crucible of recruitment for the jihad and hijra, would become a vital foyer of Umarian tradition. But that transition did not come until the end of the century. Before the French conquest, the Tijaniyya order had a very limited presence in Futa Toro and was attached primarily to the Fadiliyya tradition propagated by Saad Buh (see chapter 8).[67] The decisive factor in seating the Umarian Tijaniyya in Futa Toro was the return of the migrants, specifically the *fergankobe* or *muhajirun* whom Archinard expelled from Karta in 1891 and 1893. Some of these disciples had been born in Futa, some in the Nioro region. Most enjoyed considerable prestige for responding to the Umarian call to jihad and hijra. At the same time, their experience with Archinard's power and the forcible eviction from Karta prepared them to accept submission to the new political authorities.[68]

The numbers of returnees from the east was considerable. Some 7,500 made their way back in 1891, and a roughly comparable number returned in 1893.[69] Many were able to get access to family and lineage lands, but others became embroiled in disputes. Some occupied lands on the north bank in the conditions of relative security that followed the French conquest. What stands out in the return and reinsertion is the prestige factor, absence of members of the Tal family, and overwhelming predominance of disciples originating from western Futa Toro-Umar's original home.

The leading Umarian families in colonial Futa were talibés: the Cam, Sakho, and Ture of Toro, the Ba of Hore-Fonde, the Wane of Kanel, and a few others. They had been prominent in the east, were related by marriage to the Tal, and were usually received as heroes in the middle valley.[70] The "*talib*-ization" of the Umarian movement, the transfer of leadership from Tal to talibés or disciples, went furthest in the confines of Futa Toro.

One of these talibés established an important foyer for rehabilitating Umarians and easing accommodation to the new colonial regime. Amadu Mukhtar Sakho (1860s–1934) came from a lineage of scholars and teachers of eastern Toro. Lamine Sakho taught Umar and married his sister. Several members of the lineage, including Amadu's father, died fighting in the jihad. Amadu Mukhtar himself was born in Segu, came to Futa for some of his studies, and then completed his training in Trarza.[71] When he returned to Futa at the turn of the century, he had a firm foundation in Islamic law and a network of contacts from Saint-Louis to the Upper Senegal. He combined commerce and teaching for several years. In 1905 he was appointed as qadi of the new *tribunal noir* by Coppolani.[72]

Sakho established a zawiya and school around his home and court in Boghé, on the north bank of the river. It was there that many returnees came to study and take counsel. It was there that Umar's grandson, Seydu Nuru, did his apprenticeship in the early twentieth century, as a kind of secretary, librarian, and teacher under the patronage of the qadi. Amadu Mukhtar continued to travel, maintain his network of contacts, and develop a particularly close relationship with Malik Sy. It would be hard to overestimate the key role played by Sakho for the first generation of Umarians under colonial rule.

Amadu Mukhtar's rationale for his initiative was very similar to that of Agibu: to save the tradition from destruction and spread the faith under new conditions. According to family accounts, he expressed this rationale when he was finally able to make the pilgrimage in 1929 and encounter Alfa Hashimi, whom he had known in childhood days in Segu. When they met, Hashimi asked him if he were a French qadi. Sakho denied the accusation, indicating that he facilitated contact between subject and regime and made the situation of subject easier.[73]

Amadu Mukhtar also played an important role as a mediator of knowledge, particularly about the Umarian heritage. He developed a bond with Henri Gaden (1867–1939), a member of the "Gouraud" team and subsequently lieutenant governor of Mauritania.[74] Gaden spoke Pular and became deeply interested in the historical and cultural traditions of Futa. Sakho gave him two copies of the long poem of a talibé, Mamadu Aliyu Tyam, about the jihad; Seydu Nuru Tal supplied another. In 1935, Gaden published this work, in Pular transcription, French translation and commentary, as *La Vie d'El Hadj Omar: Qaçida en Poular*.[75] The *Qacida*, more than any other single work, helped established the jihadic and resistance credentials of Umar. By this time the French and what we could call an emerging Umarian establishment could agree on the greatness of the pilgrim, warrior, teacher, and Sufi leader. The symbolic capital associated with jihad could now be translated into accommodation.

— —

THE UMARIAN MOVEMENT WAS IN substantial disarray during the early colonial period. In part this was because of the intense French rhetoric about the "Tokolor Empire" and the close surveillance of their former enemies. In part it stemmed from the predation, dissension, and loss of vision of the Umarians themselves, and the bitterness and resistance that they generated among the peoples of colonial Soudan. The Umarians knew no single leader and no single course of action to follow in new and troubled times. In effect, there was no Umarian Tijaniyya at the turn of the century, only competing clusters of Tal and talibés who nurtured their memories and made their separate terms with the new colonial order. There was no path of accommodation.

Several forces ultimately enabled the Umarians to find a significant place within the colonial order after 1920. One element came from the French authorities, who declared the existence of the Umarian Tijaniyya,[76] paid homage to its precolonial resistance to European conquest, and elevated its leaders into the colonial Islamic establishment. The critical internal initiative came from Amadu Mokhtar Sakho and Malik Sy, who offered a rationale to submit and participate in the colonial enterprise. The transition was completed under the leadership of their apprentice, Seydu Nuru Tal. After World War I and from his base in the federal capital of Dakar, he began to address the needs of the family, establish effective linkages among the different foyers, and fashion a tradition. By this time, a perceived threat was bringing colonial authorities and Umarians even more closely together. Shaikh Hamallah and his followers were preaching a different interpretation of the Tijaniyya in Nioro, in the old heartlands of the "Tokolor Empire." Soon the colonial authorities and the new Umarian establishment found themselves collaborating against a common enemy.[77]

—8—

Saad Buh and the Fadiliyya Way

In the early twentieth century, the French portrayed their old ally, Saad Buh (see plate 4), in unflattering terms.[1] He was fat; twelve men were required to lift him off his camel. At one point he could no longer enter the Saint-Louis train cars to make his annual tour through the peanut basin. He was materialistic, constantly begging for more support or more freedom to coax contributions from gullible followers in the peanut basin. He performed miracles that impressed his "black" constituency in Senegal but not the "whites" of Mauritania, who understood what Islamic faith and learning were really about.[2]

The French were not completely off the mark. Saad Buh was obese, accustomed to administration support of all kinds, and increasingly dependent on a constituency in the peanut basin. He lost some of his luster when his older brother Ma El Ainin began to organize resistance against the French conquest of Mauritania in the early 1900s. He had been surpassed, in utility to the colonial cause, by his Trarza rival, Sidiyya Baba. He had strong reservations about the French conquest of Mauritania and he expressed those reservations quite openly.

But the French officials were not fair to their long relationship with the man, his network, and the whole Fadiliyya tradition out of which it came. Saad Buh established ties with the administration in Saint-Louis soon after moving into the southwestern part of the Sahara in the late 1860s, when he was less than twenty years old. He became the dominant figure in a configuration of teachers, schools, and lodges that stretched across the Sahel and Sahara in the late nineteenth century. Time after time, the French called on his mediating

services and the prestige that he enjoyed across frontiers of language, social status, and even religious identity. Each time Saad Buh did his best, and on several
occasions, such as the 1900 Blanchet mission, he averted disaster.[3] For these
reasons he has appeared frequently in the previous chapters.

It is therefore appropriate to begin the description of the successful "paths
of accomodation" with a network that was quintessentially adapted to the anciens régimes of the late nineteenth century. Saad Buh, his family, and disciples
functioned brilliantly in the Senegalo-Mauritanian setting, as long as the
French dealt in treaties and protectorates and tapped the gum, peanuts, and
other products of the region. The failures of the aristocracies and the Islamic
states made his pragmatic approach to Islamic practice attractive. Even as the
administration stamped out the last bastions of autonomy in Senegal, chiefs
such as Lat Dior, Albury Ndiaye, and Abdul Bokar Kane were willing to listen
to Saad Buh's interpretations of French purposes.[4] The Fadiliyya leader had
substantial social capital, reflected in part by his demonstrated ability to navigate the colonial bureaucracy.

When the French sought to intensify their power and extend it north of
the river among the *bidan,* with their strong sense of Arab and Islamic identity,
Saad Buh warned them of hostile reactions. He found it more difficult to employ his stature and skills. For some, he became the *marabout chrétien* in contrast
to Ma El Ainin. But he adjusted to the new reality, preserved substantial autonomy, and continued to render important services to the colonial regime.[5]

ORIGINS

Saad Buh always said that his only shaikh was his father.[6] He knew him for
only eighteen or nineteen years, but came to appreciate his piety, learning, and
charismatic power. Muhammad Fadil had grown up at the end of the eighteenth century in the Hodh, a collection of rocky plateaux at the edge of the
desert in what is today eastern Mauritania. Challenged by the revival of the
Kunta family network, led by Sidi al-Mukhtar, he established a rival branch of
the Qadiriyya that emphasized his Sharifian descent, knowledge of the law,
and ability to provide initiation into several Sufi orders.

The Fadiliyya were probably of Berber origin, but in keeping with the aspirations of many West African clerics, they developed an Arabic lineage that
took them through the Idrissids of Morocco to the Prophet's family.[7] It is not
clear how and when this genealogical manipulation developed, but it was a

common occurrence among Saharan and Sahelian Muslims of the day.[8] The Fadiliyya version was apparently widely accepted in the nineteenth century. Muhammad also established his reputation on his knowledge of *fiqh,* Islamic law or "external" knowledge. He built this base by studying with a number of members of his family, who were well-known teachers,[9] but he seems to have quickly become his own master. Knowledge of the law enabled him to arbitrate disputes and defend himself against clerics who were critical of "esoteric" knowledge, or Sufism, the third strand of his symbolic capital.[10]

Muhammad obtained his Qadiriyya initiation from his father. It is not clear, in the present state of research, when he received initiation into other Sufi orders, but the practice of multiple affiliation was already established in his family. He claimed initiation to the Tijaniyya and authorization to initiate, in turn, based on his father's visit to Fez and direct contact with Ahmad al-Tijani. He used this authorization as the basis for his interpretation of the Tijaniyya as a nonexclusive order compatible with multiple Sufi allegiance.[11] He developed a practice of *dhikr,* rituals for loud and public recitation that attracted popular attention as well as the criticism of more sedate and traditional Muslim leaders.[12] All of this became the practice of his son Saad Buh.

Muhammad impressed his contemporaries not just with his knowledge of things external and internal but with his capacity for working miracles, which showed his connection to sources of spiritual power. For his followers, the "miracle" power stemmed from the credentials of genealogy, learning, and Sufi affiliation, and in turn reinforced them all. His hagiographers contend that a great saint of the region predicted a brilliant future for the young Muhammad Fadil, that he led prayer at the age of seven, and that he saved the town of Walata from a divine curse. He was undoubtedly a man of great spiritual presence. In the words of Saad Buh, written several decades after his father's death,

> [Muhammad Fadil] was filled with humility and ignored all spirit of ven-
> geance. Constantly submissive to God's will, he took the harassments of his
> enemies as divine signs to be accepted. He was uniquely occupied with the
> contemplation of the divine, absorbed by meditation on the works of God as
> manifestations of His attributes. He really believed the verse: "It is God who
> has created you, you and what you are," and "They would not have done it
> had God not wished it."[13]

Shaikh Umar sought his support during the difficult campaign against Segu and may have received some aid through one of Muhammad's sons—but the traditional Qadiriyya and Fadiliyya hostility toward jihad and violence quickly reasserted itself.[14] By the time of his death in 1869, Muhammad Fadil was well known in Morocco, the Sahara, and much of western Sudan. His reputation created access for his sons and grandsons into many African societies in the late nineteenth century.

Saad Buh followed the paternal model quite closely. He was the thirtieth of forty-eight sons, born probably in 1850–51 when his father was sixty to seventy years old.[15] He spent his first fifteen years in close proximity to Muhammad Fadil in the Hodh. He quickly learned the Quran and assisted his father in the maintenance of the network. His hagiographers portray a precocious student, miracle worker, and favorite son.[16] At the age of about sixteen he had sufficient confidence in his credentials, and presumably the blessing of his father, to leave the Hodh, which was in turmoil and increasingly marginal to economic enterprise. Some of the older sons had already left for other regions.[17] Saad Buh went to the west, to the region of Trarza and Inchiri, near the Atlantic Ocean.

INSTALLATION IN SOUTHWESTERN MAURITANIA

For Saad Buh's settlement in the "west," we have two bodies of information. The first consists of material from the French and Shaikh Musa Kamara, the Futanke cleric who became a disciple of the Fadiliyya marabout in the 1880s. They indicate that Saad Buh wrote to the Saint-Louis Muslim community in 1867, stressing his Sharifian identity and spiritual powers.[18] He soon developed a pattern of annual visits to Ndar. It was there, in about 1872, that his followers, after singing the Fadiliyya chants with great gusto in the late hours, were arrested by the governor for disturbing the peace. Saad Buh performed one of his first "miracles" the following day, in persuading the administrator to let them go.[19] In the same period, he met the young and ambitious cleric Shaikh Mamadu Mamudu, who claimed descent from Abdul Kader Kane, the first Almamy of Futa Toro. Saad Buh introduced his pupil to French officials and the leading Muslim families of the town—especially the Anne and the Seck.[20] It was during these visits that Saad Buh established a residence in Ziré in the Maringouin area just north of the colonial capital. He married there, among the people called the "black" Ntaba, and used it as a base for his developing network.[21]

The other body of material comes from Arabic sources generated principally by the Fadiliyya themselves. They portray a precocious marabout trying to establish himself in Trarza, a region well known for its masters of Islamic law and theology.[22] Saad Buh came at a difficult time. Muhammad Lhabib had exercised substantial control as Emir up until his death in 1860. His son Sidi enjoyed considerable popularity, but he had a number of rivals and was assassinated in 1871, shortly after Saad Buh's arrival.[23]

Emir Sidi Muhammad consulted with the local Islamic establishment about the wisdom of permitting the young cleric to settle in their area. Accounts generated by the Fadiliyya picture a debate in which Saad Buh was questioned about his knowledge and practice of Islam amid rumors of sorcery. One source suggests that an older brother, jealous of the talents of his sibling, encouraged the opposition in hopes of finding proof of heresy.[24] The emir eventually granted permission for Saad Buh to stay, but by this time the cleric had apparently decided to move to the Inchiri region to the north.

In the present state of knowledge, it is difficult to determine exactly what happened and why. It is evident that Saad Buh aroused the hostility of the local Islamic scholars. He was, after all, a newcomer. But the hostility also focused on the Fadiliyya Sufi orientation that he represented and that ran contrary to the strict fiqh tradition of the establishment.[25] Saad Buh probably chose not to settle in the immediate area of Trarza because of this opposition and the threat of political instability. What is clear is that he used his new base at Touizikht in Inchiri, and his earlier installation near Saint-Louis, to crisscross the Trarza zone.[26] Over the period of the 1870s and 1880s, he established a growing network of disciples and alliances across the western side of what would become Mauritania, from the Senegal River in the south to Adrar in the north. Saint-Louis masons built his house in Touizikht, and one hundred or so pupils from Saint-Louis were studying there in the early 1880s.[27]

It is from this period that we get a first-hand impression of Saad Buh—an impression that confirms some of the internal hagiography and some of the later images of the French. In 1880, Paul Soleillet, an intrepid French explorer, sought to reach Timbuktu via the Adrar. This took him across Trarza to the Inchiri, where his host was Saad Buh. The marabout established a bond with the young Frenchman, of comparable age, and tried to dissuade him from going to the Adrar. Soleillet persisted. He had all of his possessions pillaged by a local band and had to be rescued by Saad Buh. The rescue became part of the discourse that Saad Buh rehearsed with the French to remind them of his value.

Soleillet, as quoted by Paul Gaffarel, left some valuable images of his host:

> [Saad Buh] had organized a sort of convent of disciples, young students who were completely devoted to him. Extraordinary powers were attributed to

him. It was said that he could read the most secret thoughts in one's eyes. He could see while sleeping everything that was happening on the land, and he was not limited by the laws of physics, for he walked on water. Saad Buh declared in his first meeting with Soleillet that "he had read attentively his eyes and found nothing but good in him, and that he would be treated with the same respect of members of his own family." A close bond developed between the two. Soleillet exposed his views about economic development, and the marabout associated himself with them, but counseled him to wait for several months, because the route was not secure.[28]

THE FADILIYYA NETWORK IN THE SENEGALO-MAURITANIAN ZONE

We know something of the shape of the network of disciples and relations established by Saad Buh in the 1870s and 1880s. We know that his camps became gathering points for his brothers and nephews, as they sought to establish themselves outside of the Hodh. He encouraged marriages between his sons and daughters and their Fadiliyya cousins, thereby strengthening the network. He established representatives in regions where he had an important following. Through all these men and women, the cleric managed networks of information across the Senegalo-Mauritanian zone, to the point that it is appropriate to equate his relations with the Fadiliyya as a whole.[29] For several decades, and despite very different orientations toward the European presence, Saad Buh maintained close relations with his elder brother Ma El Ainin, who moved between the Adrar and the coast in what would become the Spanish Sahara. Saad Buh gave two of his daughters to Ma El Ainin's sons, and at a slightly later time two of his sons married daughters of the older brother.[30] The marabout developed ties with the emiral families of Adrar and Trarza, ties that would make him invaluable to French initiatives in the region.[31] In the 1880s, he established his principal camp in the heart of western Trarza, at Nimjat.[32]

Relations with the older clerical establishment, those who opposed his original installation, are much less clear. Presumably these clerics maintained a certain distance against the unorthodox newcomer. Saad Buh developed a rivalry with another relative newcomer, the Ahl Shaikh Sidiyya. Sidiyya al-Kabir had established a very important network of mediation and commerce out of Boutilimit in the mid nineteenth century.[33] His grandson Baba began to build on the system in the 1880s (chapter 9). Sidiyya Baba was younger than Saad Buh, by more than ten years, but he inherited the Kunta mantle of his grand-

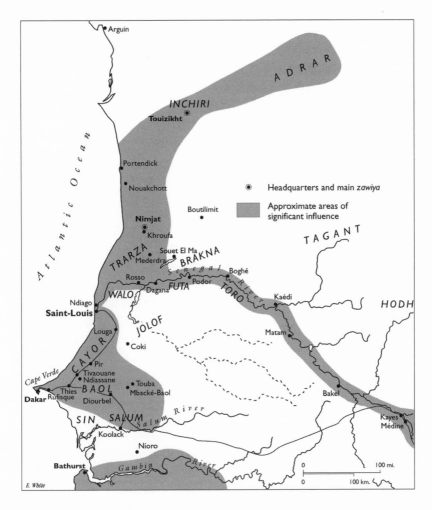

**Map 8.1. Saad Buh, the Fadiliyya Network, and the
Senegalo-Mauritanian Zone, ca. 1880–1920**

father, and thereby a certain "antipathy" to the Fadiliyya. When Saad Buh extended his influence among the *sudan,* it was often at the expense of the Kunta and Sidiyya—and vice versa.[34]

But the greatest friction with the Sidiyya stemmed from Saad Buh's close relations with the Awlad Bu Sba', a group of warriors and merchants from southern Morocco who had descended into the Adrar, Trarza, and Saint-Louis in the late nineteenth century. They operated across the traditional distinctions of the *hassan* and *zwaya;* they traded, protected their caravans, conducted raids, and fought pitched battles. They became an indispensable support for Saad

Buh and, a few decades later, the Coppolani mission.[35] Across the shifting alliances of the western Sahara, they maintained one consistent enemy: the Kunta and their allies in Trarza, the Ahl Shaikh Sidiyya. From his base in Touizikht, Saad Buh developed a good relationship with the Awlad Bu Sba‘. He wrote a treatise that supported their claim to Sharifian origins, an important legitimation as they moved into new regions.[36]

The Fadiliyya leader developed a considerable following of *sudan* from a wide swath of Senegambia and the Upper Niger.[37] He recruited especially from the river region, from Saint-Louis to Bundu. In Saint-Louis, he had many disciples in Ndar Toute, the quarter that was linked most directly to Trarza to the north, and good relations with the Islamic establishment that revolved around the Seck family. From Bundu he attracted a talented student who went on to a career as the leading counselor to Samori.[38] In the middle valley of the Senegal, Saad Buh became the most popular teacher and Sufi shaikh in the late nineteenth century, at least until the return of the Umarian *muhajirun* in the 1890s. In addition to Shaikh Mamadu Mamudu,[39] Saad Buh was revered by the Wane of Mbumba, Shaikh Musa Kamara, and Hamidu Kane, who became the French-appointed qadi of Matam.[40] He used the Fadiliyya practice of multiple affiliation to provide Tijaniyya instruction and initiation to some of his Futanke disciples. This incurred the hostility of the Umarians, who promoted the exclusivist interpretation.[41]

Affiliation to Saad Buh could foster the acquisition of positions within the emerging colonial order. Two vignettes set at the very end of the nineteenth century illustrate this. Both concern Muslims from Futa Toro. In the first case, Abdul Aziz Ly, member of a prestigious torobbe family of Diaba in the central region, was studying with Modi Mamadu Alimu, a teacher from Futa Jalon who had settled in Boki Diave in the eastern region. Modi Mamadu was a Tijani, but he had ties with Saad Buh. It was from his circle that Ly heard of the Fadililyya cleric. He then went to Saint-Louis, spent two months with his new shaikh, and became a muqaddam. Abdul Aziz soon became the imam of the Friday mosque in Kayes and an assessor in the colonial court.[42] An even more striking instance comes from the prestigious Ba family of Hore-Fonde. Shaikh Amadu, son of one of Umar's prize recruits, Bokar Sammolde, returned from the east after Archinard's conquests. Despite his Umarian credentials, he quickly made contact with Saad Buh, studied with him in Saint-Louis, and wrote poetry in praise of his new shaikh. Amadu Ba then became the colonial qadi at Kaedi.[43] Ba and Ly were probably both Tijanis, or principally Tijanis, but accepted their affiliation through the Fadiliyya. Saad Buh's ability to create enduring relations with these prestigious torobbe families speaks volumes for his symbolic capital and runs counter to the derogatory images put forward by the French in the early twentieth century.

Saad Buh also offered counsel to princes and kings, who were usually not free to study in his camps but who eagerly received him when he made his annual visits through Senegal. Abdul Bokar Kane sought him out in the troubled 1880s.[44] Albury Ndiaye of Jolof became a client during the same period, as did Lat Dior of Cayor. Saad Buh developed similar ties in Baol and Salum.[45] The cleric offered these political figures religious counsel and Sufi affiliation. He also provided reliable information about the French, and on occasion intervened between them and a client. These were no small assets in a time of heightened violence and considerable uncertainty.

The shape of the political economy of Saad Buh's network is instructive. Saad Buh's family and following took control of a number of wells and water holes; they raised herds of camels, cattle, and other animals to provide transport, meat, and milk.[46] They did not possess the productive land and assets that would characterize the Tijaniyya of Tivaouane, the Muridiyya, or the Sidiyya; they traded the blue *guinées* obtained in Saint-Louis for dates and animals in the Adrar; they controlled some oases with their palm groves and grain. But for most of their needs in grain and currency, and all manufactured imports, the Fadiliyya depended on the south. They received some gifts from the administration, for services rendered, but they relied principally upon contributions from disciples, transmitted through Saad Buh's representatives and the collection tours, organized with increasingly frequency through the peanut basin. Saad Buh's interventions with Albury Ndiaye, Lat Dior, and the chiefs of Baol and Salum were closely related to the collection tours and the extension of his symbolic capital in the new center of gravity in Senegal. His network was a dramatic illustration of "Mauritania descending": the increasing dessication of the desert and the Sahel, and the increasing pressure of their inhabitants upon the south.[47]

RELATIONS WITH THE FRENCH: THE LATE NINETEENTH CENTURY

The documentation on Saad Buh's relations with the French is far more abundant than information on the development of his network across the Senegalo-Mauritanian zone. It is sufficient, at this juncture, for sketching the ties between the man and his network, on the one hand, and French authorities and civil society, on the other — ties that lasted almost fifty years.[48]

In a 1985 interview with sons of two important disciples of the cleric, I obtained the following account of Saad Buh's visits to Saint-Louis and his relations with the administration:

> When Saad Buh or his sons came to Saint-Louis, they contacted the military man who headed the Bureau of Muslim Affairs of Mauritania. . . . This officer spoke Arabic and was trained in North Africa. He served as the intermediary with the governor, who listened to the grievances about villages, water holes, wells, roads, malnutrition, dispensaries, and so on. Often military trucks would carry sacks of rice, millet, sugar, and tea [to Saad Buh's camps in Mauritania].[49]

The informants were remembering the situation in the early twentieth century, when the French established a military administration for Mauritania, under the governor-general, with its base in Ndar Toute; they added the motor vehicles of a still later era. The Mauritanian administration typically included officers trained in the Maghrib and fluent in Arabic; they were affiliated with the Muslim Affairs Bureau based at the government-general.[50] The topics to be covered focused on provisions for the entourage and dependents of Saad Buh.[51]

The informants also give insight into the earlier period, before the French conquest of Mauritania. Visits then were annual, and the subjects to be discussed were part of a regular agenda. The interlocutor was the governor of Senegal, who handled protectorate and "foreign" affairs beyond the borders of the colony. Saad Buh performed critical services for the administration and mediated effectively for the needs of his followers. He translated his symbolic capital into social capital, in particular the skill of navigating the colonial bureaucracy.

My informants then went on to the increasingly vital dimension of the relationship: the authorization to receive gifts and alms in Senegal: "The collection tours in Senegal were necessary to provision poor Mauritania. The marabout fed a large number of people. [He and his entourage] would go to counsel and pray with the disciples [in Senegal], and in return would ask them to give to the poor."[52] The trips of the Fadiliyya into rural Senegal began in the 1880s. They typically occurred after the harvest, when Wolof, Serer, and other peasants were "flush" with the proceeds of their peanut crop.

By the 1880s, Saad Buh's relationship to Saint-Louis and Senegal and the links with his growing community in Trarza and Inchiri were fully established. The visits to the colonial capital were frequent, and the flow of Senegalese students to the camps in the north had been routinized. He went into debt to the merchants of Ndar in order to purchase needed supplies and undoubtedly had contacts with the institutions of political and civil society.

The ties were not ones of dependence but of interdependence: Saad Buh performed invaluable services for the administration. As the leader of a far-flung Islamic network, irreplaceable in his combination of genealogical, juris-prudential, and Sufi capital, the Fadiliyya cleric was a spectacular resource. For these reasons, the administration asked for his help wherever they were having difficulty establishing their control. This meant trying to calm the population of Cayor about the construction of the railway in 1881, provide information about Baol in 1884, and decipher the relations among the successors to Ma Ba in 1887. In later years, he and other Fadiliyya worked the newer and further frontiers of expansion.[53] In recognition of this contribution, the administration made gifts to him every year.[54]

In the 1890s, Saad Buh performed his most important services in Maurita-nia. His ability to mediate was certainly equal to his competence in Senegal, and the situations were more challenging. Earlier the Fadiliyya leader had saved the life and property of Soleillet. In 1891, he protected Lieutenant Léon Fabert, who was on a mission to explore the Adrar. The officer spent some time with Saad Buh in Touizikht, while the cleric corresponded with Emir Si Ah-med, waiting for the situation in the Adrar to clarify. Fabert was never able to make the journey, but he did lay the basis for a treaty the following year.[55] Of his host, the lieutenant was generous in praise: "I found our host to be not only well disposed but of remarkable insight, lofty thinking, and a loyalty [to our cause] that won me over." Dudu Seck, interpreter for the trip, emphasized the effectiveness of Saad Buh's relations among the *bidan*.[56]

In 1900, in extremely tense conditions, the governor and ministry gave Saad Buh a more daunting assignment: to protect the scientific mission sent to Adrar under the leadership of Paul Blanchet. Several powerful groups were competing for control of the Adrar. The Idawaish were pressing up from the southeast, the Awlad Bu Sba' had come in from the northwest, while the Kunta were trying to maintain their preeminence. The Moroccan court was expressing a much stronger interest and threatening to declare jihad. Ma El Ainin was the spokesman for this position, and his relationship with his younger brother was showing signs of strain.[57] The court and its counselor could point to the grow-ing interventions of European powers in an area that, despite its history of vi-olent conflict, was obviously a part of the Dar al-Islam. The Spanish were increasingly active on the northwest coast, the French were expanding their ac-tivities in the southwest, and the Germans were providing arms to all comers.

At this point, and just after a preparatory mission by Dudu Seck, the emir died and a succession struggle ensued.[58]

In precisely these perilous circumstances, an exploratory mission left Saint-Louis in March 1900. Blanchet, head of the group, was to study geography; his team included a geologist, several other Europeans, the ever-present Dudu Seck, and a contingent of soldiers from the Tirailleurs Sénégalais.[59] Their focus was the salt deposits of the coastal region and the Adrar. Saad Buh met the group in Trarza, accompanied them to the staging area of Touizikht, provided one of his sons as a guide and protector, and counseled them on the delicate situation. The mission journeyed to Atar, the main town of the Adrar, where they were attacked by the more radical members of the new emir's entourage. Some of the black soldiers panicked, killed eight *bidan,* including six *zwaya,* and fled back to Saad Buh, who gave them an escort to Saint-Louis. All the rest of the party were taken prisoner, Dudu having been injured.

At the urgent request of the governor-general, Saad Buh journeyed to Adrar at the height of the hot season, dissuaded the *bidan* from killing the remaining hostages or sending them to the sultan of Morocco, and paid a ransom—for which he was later reimbursed by the administration.[60] The mission members were freed after seventy-eight harrowing days of captivity. At one point the Europeans were buried up to their necks in the sand and forced to endure the dust and reverberations of the *fantasia*—horses riding by at full gallop.[61]

The Adrar intervention represented a turning point for Saad Buh vis-à-vis his *bidan* constituency. To save the lives of the members of the mission he had to put all of his considerable capital on the line. No longer able to rely on his letters, sons, and nephews, he had to intervene directly. For some he became the marabout chrétien.[62] This change was part of an overall pattern: as the French steadily expanded their control through the area of the Fadiliyya network, they forced Saad Buh into increasingly compromising situations.[63] For the most part, the area of Senegal was under effective control by 1891, and the references to Saad Buh in the archives accordingly become less frequent. North of the river he remained prominent through the first decade of the twentieth century, but he increasingly ceded center stage to Sidiyya Baba, the principal collaborator for the conquest of Mauritania.

Indeed, Saad Buh registered strong reservations to Coppolani in 1902 about the wisdom of a campaign to establish non-Muslim control over the *bidan,* an action that would threaten his symbolic and social capital. According to a trusted disciple, he expressed himself in the following way:

For twenty years I have put myself between you and the Muslims, forbidding the latter to cause you harm. I saved your compatriot Soleillet from the Awlad Delim, who almost killed him. I prevented Amar Salum [emir of Trarza] from killing your compatriot Fabert. I freed your fellow citizen and nobleman Blanchet and his companions from the people of Adrar, who were planning to kill them or send them to the sultan of Morocco. I did all of this in order that you have no reason to conquer the land of the Muslims or to make war upon them. Believing that you do not commit unjust acts, I did not allow anyone else to commit injustices toward you.[64]

Saad Buh failed to persuade his old allies and resigned himself to coping with the new situation.[65]

RELATIONS WITH THE FRENCH: THE LATER YEARS

The last fifteen years of Saad Buh's life, from the inception of the Coppolani mission of "pacification" until the cleric's death in 1917, constitute a different phase. The balance in the relationship with the French shifted from interdependence to dependence. The collection tours became occasions of contestation, between a military commander of Mauritania who favored them, on the one hand, and a governor of Senegal who opposed the extraction of resources from the peanut farmers, on the other. The decision was often made by the governor-general, usually in favor of the Mauritanian position.

The most revealing material about the collection tours comes from the archives of 1905-7.[66] In early 1905, shortly after the harvest, Saad Buh and an entourage of about fifty people, some of them armed,[67] circulated through western Senegal along the DSL railway. They used the train to visit Gandiole, Louga, Tivaouane, and Thiès, then traveled through Jolof and Walo on their way back to Saint-Louis. They collected well over 100,000 francs and gifts in camels, horses, and cattle. Saad Buh spent much of the money in Saint-Louis to buy new goods for his family and satisfy his creditors. The collection occurred after a difficult year in peanuts and millet and provoked protestations from administrators in Cayor and Baol and from the governor of Senegal. When challenged, Saad Buh cited the authorization of Coppolani, but he cut short his tour and returned to his campsite in Mauritania.[68]

The government-general arbitrated an agreement among the competing

sections of the administration for 1906. Saad Buh would be permitted to circulate, but with no more than ten people, without arms, and only after register-
ing with the appropriate authority in each *cercle*. Colonel Montané-Capdebosc,
Coppolani's successor in Mauritania, strongly supported the authorization to
tour, noting that most of the proceeds went into the coffers of the merchants of
Ndar, who had provided credit to the marabout over the years. Saad Buh was
able to circulate in 1906, beginning in April, a date later than usual. In March
1907, he asked to tour again at about the same time that Sidiyya Baba was being received in "royal" fashion in the colonial capital. The administration questioned Saad Buh's utility and loyalty at this moment, in the midst of Ma El
Ainin's initiatives in Mauritania, and apparently did not allow him to circulate
that year.[69] Later in the same year, however, the governor-general was quick to
reject the rumors of disloyalty and to reaffirm both the pattern of services and
the delicate negotiations in which he was engaged in the Adrar with members
of Ma El Ainin's entourage.[70]

There is no indication of subsequent interruption in the annual tours. Saad
Buh's role in the north was still critical to French fortunes, and the journeys
remained part of the landscape of colonial Senegal. The French now monitored
the annual event rather closely. In 1913, they compiled a list of contributors
and contributions, totaling 63,350 francs for the year.[71] They noted the increasing participation of sons, daughters, and nephews. The difference was in
the perspective of the administration. In the late nineteenth century, the trips
had served the purposes of the colonial authorities, to calm the troubled waters
of the frontier and show the compatibility of Islamic identity and French rule;
now they were to be tolerated because they nurtured dependent constituencies
in Mauritania, but they were "undignified" and the marabout was "grasping."[72]

North of the river, Sidiyya Baba became the architect for the conquest. He
even developed a group of warriors among the Awlad Abyayri, who played a
critical role as auxiliaries to Coppolani and Gouraud. As for Saad Buh, he remained more consistent to the Fadiliyya and *zwaya* tradition that rejected arms
and war; in the words of his disciples, he limited himself to the "power of the
rosary."[73] He supplied provisions for the missions and the administrators and he
gave his still considerable moral stature to encouraging submission to the French.
He also made a significant contribution to French knowledge of the *bidan* by
providing documents to Administrator Théveniaut in about 1907. The manu-
scripts and French translations were published in 1911 as *Chroniques de la Mauritanie sénégalaise: Nacer Eddine.*[74]

Saad Buh had one critical and unique role to play: to reaffirm the traditional Fadiliyya position against jihad to his older brother. Holy war had been tried and had repeatedly failed in Senegal and was not actively entertained in the most learned circles. In the early twentieth century, however, the idea was very much alive in *bidan* country, under the pressures of French, Spanish, and German outsiders. Ma El Ainin was becoming an increasingly visible and popular figure in the Sahara and Morocco, overshadowing the role of his siblings and challenging the image of mediation and tolerance of the Fadiliyya. In these circumstances, Saad Buh wrote an extensive *nasiha*, a letter of "counsel" to his older brother.

The "counsel" apparently never reached its destination. But it did received wide circulation, across the Senegalo-Mauritanian zone and into Morocco, by an arrangement between author and colonial regime. Saad Buh insisted that he wrote the document in 1906, when sons of Ma El Ainin and a representative of the Moroccan court arrived in Adrar; the governor had insisted on printing the letter before sending it to its addressee, and this accounted for the delay.[75] In 1909, Governor-general Ponty printed one thousand copies, published the French translation in the *Bulletin du Comité de l'Afrique Française*, and circulated original and translation in West Africa and Morocco. In 1910, Malik Sy cited the document from the pulpit of Tivaouane; other Muslim leaders undoubtedly did the same.[76]

The letter is testimony to the erudition of Saad Buh. He demonstrated his knowledge of the history of the Prophet, the early caliphs, and Spain—both Muslim and Christian. He reviewed the recent history of the Sahel and the Sahara, including criticism of the effort of Shaikh Umar to impose Islam by force on non-Muslims and the struggles among his sons. He developed the traditional *zwaya* critique of the *hassan* political leaders and their use of indiscrimate force to oppress their subjects.

Drawing on the tradition of his father, Saad Buh developed a strong argument against jihad. The Muslim *umma* was not unified and had no widely recognized imam to legitimate holy war. Jihad always led to exploitation and civil strife, which fell upon "just" and "unjust" alike, upon women, children, and the weak. It was often invoked for violence and expropriation of Muslims rather than for attacks against the French, who consistently defeated the proponents of holy war. It should never be waged when the Muslims were not in a position of force. The French were much stronger not only in weapons but also in general wealth. Moreover, they had treated Muslims and Muslim institutions with respect, for they believed in freedom of religious expression. If Ma El Ainin could persuade his entourage to cease the resistance, Saad Buh could guarantee that they would be well treated by the "Christians."

There is little evidence that the "counsel" had any impact on the resisters who had organized around Ma El Ainin. But it certainly helped restore Saad Buh's favor with the French, and it became the model for other statements of loyalty produced by other leaders in the paths of accommodation. While one cannot measure its precise influence on practicing Muslims in French West Africa, it is reasonable to expect that it had significant impact on believers searching for a rationale to submit and get on with their lives.

Saad Buh continued to work closely with the colonial administrations of Senegal and Mauritania until his death in 1917. His oldest son, Sidi Buya, became his successor, but he was not able to maintain the limited unity of the Fadiliyya network of his father.[77] Nimjat continued to serve as a gathering point for the faithful from all parts of the Senegalo-Mauritanian zone, but the Fadiliyya dispersed into the towns and villages of the French West African Federation. Many of them maintained considerable prestige, and continued to make tours and collect contributions, but they did not have the cohesion of the Muslim orders that I consider in the coming chapters.

— —

THE FRENCH IMAGES THAT BEGAN this chapter are a distortion of Saad Buh's relations with the colonial authorities. They are a product of the early twentieth century, when the Fadiliyya leader was less important to their strategies and eclipsed by the younger, more engaging, Sidiyya Baba. But even in his declining years, Saad Buh was an important symbol and advocate of accommodation with the French, and he remained effective even when some were applying to him the label of marabout chrétien. It would be difficult to overestimate his importance in preparing the way for colonial rule. He exceeded in influence and range the precious Muslim allies of the administration in Ndar. The Anne and Seck families wrote and translated letters, counseled compliance, and undertook diplomatic missions. But they were paid functionaries of the regime, and regarded as such by many of their interlocutors. Saad Buh used his quite distinct legitimacy and vast capital to encourage Lat Dior to accept the railway, to urge patience on leaders of anciens régimes confronted with the advance of colonial rule, and to portray Soleillet, Fabert, and Blanchet as simple explorers in quest of information.

At the same time, Saad Buh preceded by several decades the other Muslim architects of accommodation. His rival Baba did not enter the colonial center until 1898, and he did not begin effective collaboration until the installation of

Coppolani in 1902. Malik Sy spent many years in Saint-Louis in the late nineteenth century, but he had no relationship with the regime and provided no support for its activities. It was only after his move to Tivaouane in 1902, and not fully until 1910, that he became a leader in the practice of accommodation. As for the Murids, Amadu Bamba did not begin publicly to endorse obedience to the new authorities until 1910, near the end of his third exile in Jolof.

What were, then, the accomplishments of Saad Buh and the Fadiliyya network in terms of "paths of accommodation"? First, he set the pattern whereby prestigious marabouts from the interior stayed in Saint-Louis. He set the stage for Malik Sy and Sidiyya Baba, and all of them contributed immeasurably to the reputation of the town. Second, he intensified the Islamic identity of many Muslims in the Senegalo-Mauritanian zone. By providing access to various Qadiriyya and Tijaniyya litanies, he made the Islamic faith more public and vital in people's lives. By advocating multiple Sufi affiliations, he offered a wider range of choices in Islamic practice—choices that had special value in a time of dramatic change. By his Sharifian ancestry he encouraged others to make connections with the founders of Islam, in genealogical and intellectual terms. Third, Saad Buh assisted in the spread of the faith in less-islamized zones, such as the peanut basin and Salum and the areas of the Upper Senegal and Niger. The Fadiliyya constantly crossed frontiers of religion, ethnicity, class, and regime.

Finally, he gave a strong rationale, in terms of Islamic history and his own considerable symbolic capital, for accommodation with the colonial authorities. It was not only necessary to submit to superior force, it was also acceptable and recommended. The new order would produce more justice, peace, prosperity, and faithful practice than the turbulent times that were ending. It is significant that Malik Sy and Amadu Bamba issued their first written exhortations to accommodation in 1910, just after the dissemination of the "counsel," and that they followed the same arguments as the first great accommodator.

Plate 1. Ernest Roume, governor-general of French West Africa, 1902–8.
Bodleian Library, Oxford.

Plate 2. Bu El Mogdad I (also called Dudu Seck; 1826–1880).
From *Tour du Monde*, 1861.

Plate 3. Agibu Tal (ca. 1843–1907) in Bandiagara, ca. 1905, with one of his children. From the Photo Library of IFAN in Dakar, Senegal.

Plate 4. Saad Buh
(ca. 1850–1917) receiv-
ing disciples, with period
furniture and rug,
ca. 1900. From CRDS,
Saint Louis, Senegal.

Plate 5. Sidiyya Baba (1862–1924) traveling by camel with his entourage, 1903.
Institut de France, Fonds A. Terrier, no. 5942, Doctor F. l'Herminier,
August–September 1903.

Plate 6. Malik Sy (ca. 1855–1922), photographed in Tivaouane, ca. 1912.
From Paul Marty, *Etudes sur l'Islam au Sénégal* (2 vols., Paris, 1917),
vol. 1, facing p. 176.

Plate 7. Amadu Bamba (ca. 1853–1927), photographed in Diourbel, 1913. From Paul Marty, *Etudes sur l'Islam au Sénégal* (2 vols., Paris, 1917), vol. 1, facing p. 222.

—9—

Sidiyya Baba

Co-architect of Colonial Mauritania

IN JANUARY 1903, SIDIYYA BABA (see plate 5) composed and circulated the fatwa cited in chapter 4.[1] Drawing on the jurist Khalil ibn Ishaq and other sources with impeccable credentials, and noting that the Muslims of the eastern Maghrib were already living under French rule, Baba declared that the military jihad would only bring exhaustion to Muslim societies. It was especially to be rejected when Muslims were in a situation of weakness:

> It is evident that the obligation [to wage] holy war disappears in the face of the inability to accomplish it. . . . The inability of this land [of Muslims] to fight against the force of the Christians is obvious. Any sane man who hears and sees is aware of the absence of unity among Muslims, the absence of a public treasury necessary for any action, and the inferiority of their weapons in comparison to those of the Christians.[2] . . . [There is also no obligation] to emigrate, en masse or in part, from the territory conquered by the "infidel", because of poverty as well as the absence of destinations where the necessary security and resources exist.[3]

Baba did not stop there. He noted that the French had demonstrated that they would not interfere with the practice of the faith; indeed, that they would give positive support to the institutions of worship, education, and law. Their rule promised an end to the conditions of anarchy *(fitna)* that had plagued the societies of northwest Africa, and the beginning of conditions of peace and stability that would enable Islam to consolidate its position:

It must be said, in addition, that the conduct of the Christians . . . [is what is required by Islam]. They not only do not oppose the exercise of religion, they also provide positive support in the construction of mosques, appointment of qadis, and provision of a good organizational structure.[4]

An organizational structure, indeed, in which Islam and islamization would thrive. In other words, the French were a good "Muslim power."[5]

The French could not have asked for a more explicit endorsement from inside the Dar al-Islam. At precisely the moment when they expanded into the area that lay between their colony of Senegal and Morocco, they could count on the support of the young, vigorous, and brilliant head of a network of interests that stretched across the Senegalo-Mauritanian zone. Sidiyya Baba, Sufi leader and accomplished jurist, joined forces with Xavier Coppolani, "Algerian" Islamicist and author of *Confréries religieuses musulmanes*, to design the conquest of Mauritania.[6] Baba appeared in a public ceremony in Saint-Louis with Coppolani in November 1902, traveled with him along the river and in Trarza, and then issued the fatwa at the beginning of January.[7] Baba and Coppolani worked in harmony as the architects of the "pacification," which relied on the *zwaya* rather than the warrior classes, until Coppolani's assassination in May 1905. Baba then established an equally effective collaboration with the man who completed the conquest of southern and central Mauritania, Henri Gouraud.[8] For all these reasons, he has been prominent in the earlier part of this work, especially chapter 4.

THE SIDIYYA NETWORK

Baba's statement and support were all the more impressive because of their provenance: a well-established scholarly and Sufi lineage of southern Mauritania with a history—at least in the traditions of the French colonial authorities—of distance from the European presence. Sidiyya al-Kabir (ca. 1780–1868), Baba's grandfather, had brought a small group of obscure clerics, merchants, and herders, the Awlad Abyayri, into great prominence in the Senegalo-Mauritanian zone. The Abyayri were classed as *zwaya*, but they claimed descent from Barkanni, the *hassan* founder of the Brakna confederation of southwestern Mauritania.[9]

Sidiyya al-Kabir studied with Sidi al-Mukhtar al-Kunti and his son Sidi Muhammad in the Azawad, north of Timbuktu. With these illustrious credentials, he returned to the southern Mauritanian zone in the 1820s. There he constructed a network of trade, production, legal consultation, diplomacy, and Sufi leadership along the lines of the Kunta model.[10] The shaikh participated in the commerce of gum, salt, animals, and slaves. He acquired interests in lands, wells, and oases in southern and central Mauritania.[11] He resolved disputes, arranged marriages, and gave a wide variety of counsel, all with the goal of establishing greater peace and prosperity in the Saharan and Sahelian areas. He extended that counsel to the emirs of Trarza, Brakna, and the other kaleidoscopic confederations of southern Mauritania—including the provision of sanctuary to opposition candidates for the emirship. Finally, he helped to spread allegiance to the Qadiriyya order, the dominant Sufi affiliation of the Sahara and Western Sudan. Initially, he emphasized the Kunta version of his mentors; over time he put his own stamp on the Qadiriyya. Like Muhammad Fadil, he developed a multifaceted and eminently transferable capital.

Sidiyya al-Kabir established his main base at Boutilimit, an area of pasturage some two hundred miles north of the Senegal River. Boutilimit was in eastern Trarza, and it was well positioned to encourage influence across a broad swath of nomadic societies in southern and central Mauritania.[12] Sidiyya achieved his visibility and a bit of notoriety with the French by his intervention in the struggle for the emirship of the Brakna confederation at mid century. In 1856, he helped organize a coalition in opposition to the candidate of Saint-Louis. Governor Faidherbe duly noted his mobilization skills in accounts to Paris and articles in the *Moniteur*.[13] From these reports it was but a short step to the classification of Sidiyya al-Kabir as a "resistance" foe for the French—and a "resistance" hero for many Mauritanians in the twentieth century.[14]

In fact, Sidiyya al-Kabir had different priorities. The French in the mid nineteenth century were but one contender, albeit a strong one, for commercial and political preeminence along the Senegal River. The major preoccupation for the emerging Sidiyya network was the maintenance of influence and wealth in the Senegalo-Mauritanian zone. The influence extended all along the Senegal River, into Saint-Louis, and as far south as the Gambia and Futa Jalon. The archives and oral tradition give glimpses of the operation of this influence. One disciple, Cerno Falil Talla, opposed the jihad of Al-Hajj Umar in Futa Toro in 1858–59 and apparently paid for it with his life.[15] Another, Cerno Brahim Kane, preached hijra with some anti-French overtones and attracted followers to his community of Maqama, a "sanctuary" on the north bank of the Senegal, in the 1860s. Abdul Bokar Kane eventually led a coalition of forces that defeated and killed the cleric in 1869, thereby ending the threat posed to the Islamic regime of Futa.[16]

Sidiyya al-Kabir also had important disciples among the chiefly lineages of the region.[17] One of the most prominent was Bokar Sada Sy, the almamy of Bundu for most of the late nineteenth century and a consistent ally of the French. Bokar maintained close ties with Shaikh Sidiyya and called upon the French to facilitate the travel of Sidiyya's envoys. In 1865, he made the following request to the local French commander at Bakel:

> The bearer of this letter is Fode Salum, a disciple of Shaikh Sidiyya, my marabout for all time. [Sidiyya is] unlike the other marabouts who declare war on everyone. I am requesting that you give him [Fode Salum] transport [along the river] to Podor, in order that he return to Shaikh Sidiyya [in Boutilimit]. He is carrying my gifts [to Shaikh Sidiyya].[18]

Bokar Sada's letter and continuing relations with Boutilimit suggest that the French and Sidiyya cooperated selectively and effectively in their overlapping spheres of influence in the mid nineteenth century.[19]

Sidiyya al-Kabir was not without his opponents within the *zwaya* constituencies of southern Mauritania. Indeed, he and the Awlad Abyayri were upstarts in the eyes of the clerics of the Tashumsha fractions who had dominated scholarship, adjudication, and diplomacy in Trarza since the Sharr Bubba conflicts of the late seventeenth century.[20] The Tashumsha maintained a strong position at the emiral court, among Muslims of Saint-Louis, and through much of the Senegalo-Mauritanian zone. Some of them gradually accepted the distinction and influence of Sidiyya al-Kabir and by the late nineteenth century were linked to Boutilimit through marriage and collaborative networks.[21]

THE DESPERATION OF THE SIDIYYA IN THE LATE NINETEENTH CENTURY

Sidiyya al-Kabir died in 1868 and was succeeded by his son, a noted poet.[22] A cholera epidemic swept the poet away in 1869, leaving Baba to be raised by other members of the family and by a Kunta shaikh.[23] The family kept a low profile for the next two decades.[24] In the late 1880s, Baba began to change that profile. He was a brilliant student of the Islamic sciences and Sufism; he soon projected a career on a broad canvas similar to that of his grandfather, and like him he assumed the name Shaikh Sidiyya.[25] He probably launched his diplomatic career in 1886, when he gave sanctuary to the two sons of the recently assassinated Trarza emir, Mohammed Fal.[26]

Baba faced a much more precarious situation than his grandfather had

faced: the increasing violence and disruption of *bidan* society. To the east, in
Tagant, Sidiyya influence was threatened by Bakar wuld Su‘aid Ahmad, the
head of the Idawaish coalition. Bakar maintained an active network of war,
production, trade, and protection extending from the Senegal River into the
Adrar.[27] He took a clear stand of opposition to the "pacification" of Mauritania
by the French, a policy that eliminated the "customs" payment that he had long
received for transporting and protecting gum caravans along the Senegal
River.[28]

In Brakna Sidiyya, hegemony was contested by the Ijaydba, a *zwaya* group
that had long-standing claims on key resources in the region, including wells,
pasture, and fields ranging from the river to the desert, and opposed the Sidiyya
claims to religious and legal supremacy in southern Mauritania. The Ijaydba
tended to ally with factions of the emiral houses of Brakna and with Futanke
groups that were opposed to Sidiyya interests.[29]

The broader context was the transsaharan trade, which was changing rapidly. Warriors, herders, and traders pressed increasingly into the southern
zones, closer to the river, sources of grain and gum, and to the French trading
sphere headquartered in Saint-Louis. The Abyayri and their Sidiyya leadership
encountered increasing competition for resources at the end of the nineteenth
century. In this connection, the worst enemy of the Sidiyya were the Awlad Bu
Sba‘, a group with origins in southern Morocco and what was becoming the
Spanish Sahara. By the end of the century, they had moved with force into the
Adrar and all of the coastal region down to Saint-Louis.[30] They laid claims to
zwaya Sharifian status; they ran caravans but also provided their own protection; they acquired modern weapons from Spanish, German, and French
sources. Like the Awlad Abyayri, they ignored the traditional boundaries of
bidan society, between "warrior" and "marabout," and engaged on all fronts.
They had absorbed a particular hostility to the Kunta network, which was very
important to trade and production in the Adrar and Tagant, and they classed
the Sidiyya as part of the Kunta system. By the position they acquired in Saint-
Louis and across a wide range of central and southern Mauritania, they became
indispensable to the French designs of conquest.[31]

Sidiyya Baba was also preoccupied with the situation in the reigning house
of the Trarza. The emiral confederation of southwestern Mauritania played a
large role in control of river traffic, farming in the lower river valley, the supply
of gum, and access to central and eastern zones of Mauritania. The royal family
was related by marriage to the ruling house of Walo; they continued to maintain claims to tribute and lands in the lower valley despite the "renunciation"

clauses in the treaty signed with Governor Faidherbe.[32] They had similar interests in Jolof and Cayor and were monitored closely by the French during the process of construction of the railroad from Dakar to Saint-Louis.[33]

Emir Muhammad Lhabib, remembered as the great foe of Faidherbe,[34] dominated the Trarza confederation until his assassination in 1861.[35] Thereafter, his descendants engaged in a bitter struggle for the succession. Sidiyya Baba and other *zwaya* provided sanctuary and mediation, but they were not able to unify the family around any one figure. Lhabib's son Sidi, who organized the "examination" of Shaikh Sa`d Buh in the late 1860s, maintained a semblance of unity until his assassination in 1871.[36] A decade of struggle followed until another son, Amar Salum, emerged in the 1880s as a candidate capable of bringing peace to the disrupted region.[37] But a grandson of Lhabib, Ahmed Salum, assassinated Amar and became the leading contender in the 1890s. During most of the 1880s and 1890s, Baba supported another candidate, one to whom he had given sanctuary some years before. When Ahmed Salum married the sister of Ahmeddu, the emir of the Brakna confederation, Baba feared that he would be overwhelmed by a vast coalition uniting all of his enemies: the Awlad Bu Sba`, the Ijaydba, and fractions of the two emiral houses where he had the least support.

It was this threat and strife, expressed as fitna, which Baba had in mind when he wrote the fatwa at the beginning of 1903. By the late nineteenth century, he was prepared to explore radical new options for the stabilization of southern Mauritania. Indeed, it would not be an exaggeration to say that he was desperate to save the Sidiyya heritage. The Ijaydba, allied with the Brakna emiral fraction of the Awlad al-Sayyid, almost captured him in 1896. Baba considered migration with his entire camp to the left bank of the river, in search of security.[38] In this context, the French, concerned about the stability of their trading interests in the Trarza and Brakna zones, intervened in 1897–98. They helped establish some order in the emiral houses and in the distribution of wells contested by the Ijaydba and Sidiyya. In the process, Sidiyya Baba came to Ndar for the first time, in 1898, in the company of the distinguished colonial functionary, Dudu Seck.[39] This marked the beginning of a long and consistent cooperation with the French authorities.

Seck, in his memoir written a decade later, has left some precious images of the visit to the colonial capital. Baba was given an excellent reception by the administration and its allies in the town. He was impressed with the freedom of religious practice, the respect for Islam, and the support of Islamic institutions — themes that he stressed in the fatwa of 1903. Governor-general Chaudié organized a tour by horse-drawn carriage, with Dudu as his guide. Afterwards Baba said that "If my father [*sic*; grandfather] Shaikh Sidiyya al-Kabir had known the French and seen what I witnessed today with my own eyes, he certainly would not have given his benediction and prayers to the Moors in their quarrels with Faidherbe." The visit certainly prepared the way for active collaboration at the time of Coppolani. It was an important breakthrough in the maraboutic or *zwaya* classes of *bidan* society, which were traditionally more hostile to Europeans than the political elite. Baba also expressed his racial attitudes: in confiding to Dudu his respect for the Islamic civilizations of North Africa, he emphasized his disdain for the little "black kinglets" in the south that had never known civilization.[40]

In 1900, Baba played a minor role in the liberation of the Blanchet mission in the Adrar. The following year he was again on the defensive. The Abyayri, Awlad Daiman, and Idawali, all *zwaya* groups in the *bidan* classification, had to take refuge from the Awlad Bu Sba ͨ.[41] In the same year, Xavier Coppolani, the Algerian Islamicist fresh from a tour of the Hodh and Timbuktu regions, came to Saint-Louis to sketch out a model of "pacification" of a new territory, to be called Mauritania and to be constructed with the "pacifists" of *bidan* society. In Sidiyya Baba he found an immediate ally.

Sidiyya Baba and the Creation of Colonial Mauritania

As outlined in the preceding chapter, Saad Buh had serious hesitations about the "pacification" campaign. His sphere of operations and relations did not require such extreme measures. He feared a massive countermobilization of the *bidan* of this Dar al-Islam and a loss of symbolic and social capital. When he realized that his view would not prevail, he adjusted and became a loyal soldier in the conquest.[42]

Sidiyya Baba did not hesitate. He supported the Coppolani *pacification*, the Gouraud *conquête*, and the consolidation of colonial Mauritania. Indeed, as the fatwa suggests and the narrative of Gouraud's campaign reveals, Baba pushed openly, consistently, and intensively for French control. His situation at the outset of the French campaigns was so desperate, and the forces arrayed against him so multiple, that it was fully a decade before he could be secure about his investments and relations — in other words, the diverse forms of his and his family's economic capital. More than any of the other grands marabouts in this book, Baba was closely attached to a particular colonial configuration and to continuing support from authorities in Saint-Louis and Dakar.

Beginning in 1902, Baba was very active along the river and in Saint-Louis.[43] He came to Dagana in April to discuss the situation in Trarza, especially regarding the emiral family. At Coppolani's request, he joined Saad Buh in Saint-Louis in November for a highly publicized meeting at the governor's office to announce the campaign of "pacification." Immediately after the meeting, the two clerics accompanied Coppolani by boat to Dagana and then traveled through Trarza. Along the way they explained the new plan and pressed members of the emiral family into signing treaties of protection with the French.

Baba then became the key human resource for subsequent campaigns: in Brakna in 1903–4, Tagant in 1904–5, and the Adrar in 1908–9.[44] Boutilimit became the most important staging area for the campaigns. For some time it was the most advanced telegraph post connected to Saint-Louis. Under Administrator Jean-Baptiste Théveniaut, it became the training point for the *meharistes,* or camelry.[45] Baba made his own camels available for the effort along with mounted troops from the Awlad Abyayri. He provided constant and invaluable information to the French effort from his own networks. Indeed, Baba actively strategized with most of the French officers who organized the conquest and establishment of colonial Mauritania. In addition to Coppolani, Gouraud, and Théveniaut, their number included Montané-Capdebosc, Louis Frèrejean, Henri Gaden, and many others who passed through Boutilimit and depended upon its logistical services.[46]

Over the course of the first decade of the twentieth century, Baba made a very positive impression on most of his European interlocutors: curious, open, modern, sophisticated, nonmaterialistic. The images recorded by Commandant Frèrejean in late 1904, just before the Tagant campaign, are a typical example:

> He is a completely different type of human being than the marabouts that I
> have seen up until now. He is strikingly different from the fat materialistic
> man who is Shaikh Saad Buh. I had my proof right away. He launched into a
> scientific conversation with *Capitaine du génie* Gérard, who gave him some in-
> struction in astronomy and physics. . . . He shows that he understands. . . .
> Even in Europe, he would appear sophisticated, well-spoken, cool, and calm.
> He is a schoolmaster, a moral authority, an Arab scholar of the olden days, a
> "marabout for the Whites."[47]

In almost every respect, the French drew a contrast between Baba and Saad Buh.

Baba invested heavily in the Coppolani venture. He committed his resources to the Tagant campaign: one thousand camels, Abyayri units, and envoys to his

Kunta allies. He was deeply affected by Coppolani's assassination in 1905 — and by the freeze on operations for three years. He and the French Islamicist had come to rely on each other and believe in their ability to bring stability to *bidan* society through the role of the *zwaya*. Now the forces of resistance threatened to gain the upperhand.[48] Ma El Ainin now became more visible as the champion of jihad; he was received with pomp and circumstance in Marrakesh in 1906. At the same time, the sultan sent a relative, Mulay Idriss, into the Adrar to test the attitudes of *bidan* toward Moroccan and French interests. From this point on, the policy of "pacification" and reliance upon the *zwaya* was called into question. The French began to talk of *conquête* and to consider reaching out to the *hassan* classes.[49]

The uncertainty about the French ability to control their Mauritanian holdings, combined with the difficulty of holding the southern regions without possessing the Adrar, added to the insecurity of the Sidiyya. The Ijaydba pressure continued.[50] The conflicts with the Awlad Bu Sba[c] intensified in 1905; the French forced a truce, because they needed both sides in their effort to establish the new colony.[51] At the same time, Baba received letters from distinguished clerics in the Adrar urging him to break his alliance with the infidel and return to the "Muslim fold," or alternatively to leave the Dar al-Islam that was the country of the *bidan*.[52]

The pressure on Baba from these Muslim sources was intense. It was also recognition of his prestige among the *zwaya* of the Saharan region. In one letter, Hassana, a son of Ma El Ainin and director of his network in the Adrar, evoked the Moroccan hegemony in the south and challenged the Sidiyya leader's commitments very directly:

> The sultan [of Morocco] told the Christians that the country of the Moors belonged to him and that they must not try to take it. . . . [He] told them that the contested territory belonged to him since Ali Shandor [emir of Trarza] . . . and that he had a seal given him by the sultan. . . . These events motivated the sultan to send a mission headed by his cousin. . . . This mission will receive the submission of Muslims and provide arms and troups to those who desire it. Once submission has been made to the representative of the Sharifian court, it will serve as proof of the sultan's argument. If then the Christians leave the country, everything will return to normal. Otherwise it will be jihad. Those who defend the cause of religion will be supported and those who ally with the French will be considered enemies. I wanted to alert you in time and to ask your aid for the defense of religion.[53]

At this low point in the fortunes of his high-stakes wager, Baba did not hesitate. He went to Saint-Louis for several weeks in March 1907 to celebrate his five years of service to the colonial cause and mark the return of Montané-Capdebosc from France.[54] Baba welcomed the extension of the telegraph line and the appointment of a French doctor to Boutilimit. He sent one of his sons to accompany a scientific mission along the coast.[55] All of this was preparation for the big effort in 1908: to gain French commitment to the conquest of the Adrar.

During his stay in Ndar, Baba rebuffed the overtures made to him by the Devès, as outlined in chapter 5.[56] He was an active protagonist for the conquest of the Adrar. He could not afford to rely on the traditional commercial lobby and General Council of Saint-Louis. In order to save the fortunes of his family, he needed the French to assert themselves through the creation of colonial Mauritania. Nothing less would do.

Governor-general Roume, his general secretary, Martial Merlin, and his director of Muslim Affairs, Robert Arnaud, had already given considerable thought to the conquest of the Adrar and to Sidiyya Baba as a counter to Ma El Ainin. In June 1908, Baba traveled to Dakar, to the government-general, to meet Minister of Colonies Milliès-Lacroix. His role was not ceremonial. As indicated in chapter 4, he made the case, together with Gouraud, for the conquest of the Adrar.[57] Gouraud and Baba made a significant impact on the minister and began a long relationship that resembled that of the Sidiyya leader and Coppolani in many respects.[58] Preparations for the campaign began in the last half of 1908. Again the Sidiyya and Abyayri provided indispensable logistical support. Gaden, member of the Gouraud "team" and future lieutenant governor of Mauritania, was stationed at Boutilimit to ensure the maximum flow of information between the forward troops and Saint-Louis. Supply columns were organized from Saint-Louis and northwestern Soudan. In January 1909, Gouraud defeated the forces of resistance, built a post at Atar, and installed a member of the emiral family as the French representative.[59]

Baba mobilized his entire network on behalf of the campaign. He sent envoys on missions and supplied a steady stream of good information on tribes, their alliances, and intentions. He visited the Adrar twice in 1909; he received expressions of submission from warrior and clerical leaders almost as though he were the new ruler.[60] Gouraud used Baba's support for the French in his declaration of sovereignty in January,[61] and in his memoirs gave a fitting tribute to his ally after Baba arrived in early June: "In making this tiring and dangerous journey, the shaikh gave a stunning proof of his pro-French sentiments."[62]

With the conquest of the Adrar, Baba could consolidate Sidiyya holdings in the south. He maintained his flocks and transhumance zone. He strengthened his agricultural holdings in the river valley. He sent his sons and disciples on collection tours in the peanut basin, on the same basis as Saad Buh. And he received frequent cash gifts from the administration.[63]

THE SIDIYYA AS CUSTODIANS FOR AMADU BAMBA

Sidiyya Baba quickly became a strong ally and confidant of the colonial administration. He was ready to intervene on matters outside of his jurisdiction and to assist the French in difficult situations. The most striking example of this unusual level of cooperation concerned Amadu Bamba, the subject of chapter 11, in his second exile.[64] Bamba had returned to Senegal and his Baol homeland in 1902, thanks to the intervention of Baba, Deputy François Carpot, and other influential people. His presence proved disruptive to several chiefs who were seeking to consolidate their authority under the colonial system. Their complaints affected French thinking in 1903.[65] Martial Merlin, secretary-general of the government-general, organized the arrest and second exile of Bamba, this time to Trarza and the orbit of the Sidiyya. Baba's son-in-law Shaikhuna was present at the arrest and facilitated the transfer in May 1903 — indicating close consultation over the entire period of Bamba's stay in Senegal in 1902–3.

The period of Bamba's residence in Mauritania is not well documented. Bamba apparently moved around eastern Trarza, beginning with Souet-El-Ma, at the northeastern extremity of Lac Rkiz, where the French had a post. He probably followed the movement of the Abyayri tents for a time, but grew tired of the transhumance pattern and settled in one or two places.[66] Bamba spent considerable time in reflection and writing. He decided, in about 1905, to give the name Muridiyya to his approach to Islam, without rejecting the Qadiriyya influences that had shaped much of his search.[67] His disciples came in considerable numbers to visit him. The complex logistics of these displacements and surveillance persuaded the administration to transfer his residence a third time, in 1907, to an isolated village in Jolof.

The nature of the influence of the Sidiyya on Bamba is not clear. Baba himself was certainly preoccupied with survival and orchestration of the colonial campaigns for the conquest of Mauritania; the news of Coppolani's assassination arrived while Bamba was in Trarza. It is said that Baba discouraged Bamba from any further pursuit of Tijaniyya affiliation.[68] What is clear is that the four-year stay in Trarza sealed the bonds of friendship and respect between the two men and their respective entourages. Baba's sons often visited the Murids in Baol, provided instruction to Bamba's children, and received the traditional gifts due to saintly and learned persons. What is equally certain is that the stay convinced Bamba of the necessity, if not the virtue, of working within the colonial structures. By 1910, Bamba was willing to write exhortations to his followers to accept and take advantage of French rule, along the lines of Baba's own fatwa of 1903.[69] From Baba's perspective, Bamba's residence was at least as important: it gave the Sidiyya unparalleled access to the expanding Muridiyya networks in the Senegalese peanut basin.

What is most striking about this Bamba episode is the enormous confidence that the French authorities placed in Sidiyya Baba. Only five years after his first visit to Saint-Louis, only a year after the beginning of active cooperation in Mauritania, at the very beginning of "pacification," the French were willing to entrust their ally with the custody of the marabout who posed the most serious problems for control of a vital part of the colonial economy — the newer peanut basin developing in eastern Cayor and Baol.[70] The colonial authorities were satisfied with the result and they continued to seek Baba's advice about Muslim communities in Senegal.[71]

THE SIDIYYA HOUSE AND THE FRENCH IN BABA'S LATER YEARS

By World War I, the Sidiyya had restored their position in Trarza and established considerable influence in other regions. They enjoyed prestige and support as winners in the struggle for the creation of colonial Mauritania. Baba could claim credit to a hegemony equal to that of his grandfather, and one obtained in very different conditions. He consolidated the Sidiyya position among the Abyayri and other groups through carefully designed marriage strategies. Like his grandfather and father, he encouraged alliances within the Awlad Abyayri group, increased its size through descendants and assimilation, and made the Ahl Shaikh Sidiyya the dominant fraction. Most of his daughters married prominent members of Abyayri fractions. Mahjuba married Shaikhuna wuld Dadda, a close counselor who made frequent visits to the Murids, Bu Kunta, and Malik Sy; it was Shaikhuna who escorted Bamba from the peanut basin to Trarza in 1903. Bettul, also called Fatima, married into the prominent Tashumsha tribe, the Awlad Daiman. Her husband, Bu Mediana, was another important agent for Sidiyya interests.[72]

The Sidiyya accumulated considerable wealth in animals, fields, and oases

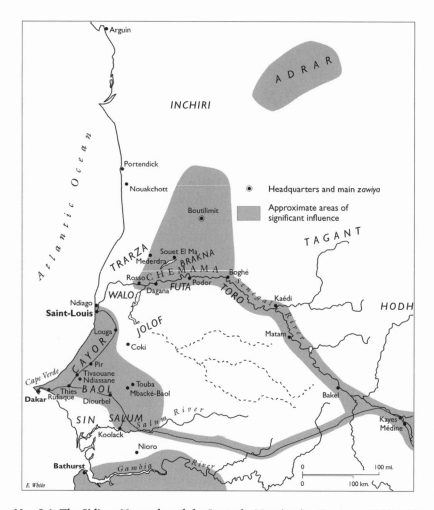

Map 9.1. The Sidiyya Network and the Senegalo-Mauritanian Zone, ca. 1880–1920

and a large following of disciples, subjects, and servants.[73] This wealth extended from grain farms on the north bank of the river valley, known as the Chemama, to date palms and oases in the Adrar. It included property taken at the expense of the Ijaydba and other groups who had opposed the Sidiyya at the turn of the century. Baba sent his sons, sons-in-law, and disciples on regular collection tours among the Muridiyya and in other areas where his family exercised influence.[74]

The Sidiyya enjoyed unquestioning support from the administration. In part this was evident in the "political" gifts and the authorizations for collection tours in Senegal. It was also expressed in the presumption of support that the Sidiyya made, and that their potential opponents made, in cases of conflict—such as the fields of the north bank of Futa Toro or the wells that the Abyayri secured at the expense of the Ijaydba.[75] Boutilimit, with its administrative center, military garrison, and French doctor, was a visible sign of the alliance. The French Orientalist, Louis Massignon, cataloged the vast library established by Sidiyya al-Kabir.[76]

Baba was a "modernizer" and admired the efforts that Muhammad Ali had made in Egypt in the early nineteenth century.[77] He was a pioneer in Western education. In 1912 he encouraged the establishment of a *medersa*, or "franco-arabe" school in Boutilimit, and a few years later welcomed a school for girls.[78] The medersa was one of the few colonial Muslim schools that was maintained in French West Africa, and over the decades it produced a significant portion of the intellectual and political leadership of Mauritania—many of them from the Ahl Shaikh Sidiyya themselves. After World War II, it was elevated to the status of Institut Supérieur d'Etudes Islamiques, a kind of modernized "Al-Azhar" for West Africa.[79]

Baba gave unquestioning support to the French World War I effort. He was among the first to condemn the Ottoman links to the Axis forces and to decouple Ottoman actions from Islamic obligations. He wrote and circulated a special prayer for the troops in 1914 and supported the recruitment that the French conducted among the "black" populations of Mauritania and Senegal. The colonial authorities nominated him for the Comité consultatif des Affaires Musulmanes, a body designed to demonstrate France's distinction as a "Muslim power." In 1916, as the French and British wrestled with the issues of reauthorizing the pilgrimage and encouraging Arab nationalism against the Ottoman Empire, they sought prominent Muslim allies across their imperial possessions. When the French constituted a commission of prominent Muslims to handle the movement and stays of pilgrims in the Holy Lands, they considered Baba to be one of only two marabouts in West Africa who fulfilled the necessary conditions. But they esteemed that "Sidia's absence [would be] . . . too damaging to the maintenance of order in Mauritania where his personal intervention [might be] necessary at any moment."[80]

The Sidiyya leader continued to travel to Saint-Louis and Dakar on special occasions, despite declining health. He went to Dakar in 1916 to see Governor-general Clozel and his assistant Maurice Delafosse.[81] At about the same time, his son Abdallah was in Diourbel visiting Amadu Bamba. Baba was back in Dakar at least one more time, in 1919, when the well-known son of Ma El Ainin, Taleb Khiar, made his submission to the French. Through his sons and agents, and his own correspondence, he remained influential in French policy and practice in the Senegalo-Mauritanian region until his death in 1924.[82]

The very positive impression that Sidiyya Baba made on Coppolani and Gouraud carried over to Paul Marty.[83] Marty exercised enormous influence over Islamic policy, the images of the marabouts and brotherhoods, and the interpretation of twentieth-century history in French West Africa. He carried the praise of Baba to new heights:

> By his clearly francophile attitude, Shaikh Sidiyya rendered, as much to our authority as to the faithful of his Way and by extension to all Moors, a great service. We owe to him the possibility in Mauritania, from the beginning, of collaboration between Christian and Muslim, between the French chief and the director of a Muslim order. In responding enthusiastically and loyally to the political genius that was Coppolani, he permitted two peoples, two civilisations, and two religions to know and respect each other. He took a giant and positive step for the evolution of our relations with the inhabitants of the Sahara.[84]

The affection and esteem did not always carry over to the next generation, but the sense of obligation certainly did. The Sidiyya were a colonial investment. Mauritania was inconceivable without them. Mohamed, Ahmed, Abdallah, and the other sons became regular visitors to colonial offices in Saint-Louis and Dakar.

Baba made some effort to organize his holdings and distribute labor among members of his family. He turned administrative tasks over to his brother al-Mukhtar in 1911, but took them back in 1916 after some complaints.[85] In his last years, he began to distinguish between the political, administrative, intellectual, judicial, and mystical dimensions of the Sidiyya heritage and to make different allocations to his sons. Mohamed took over the overall leadership at Baba's death in 1924.[86] When he in turn died in 1927, Ahmed withdrew into contemplation and the management of his flocks, so that overall religious and administrative leadership passed on to the third son, Abdallah.[87] Sulaiman shared in the administrative work, while Ya'qub carried much of the *baraka* and organized many of the collection tours to Senegal and beyond. Isma'il and Harun became the scholars of the family, and it is thanks to Harun's indefatigable work, not finished at his death in 1977, that we owe much of our knowledge of the Sidiyya enterprise.[88]

— —

Throughout his life, Sidiyya Baba effectively and consistently pursued a strategy of consolidation of his family's position. For his last twenty-five years, he pursued that strategy in open cooperation with the colonial authorities. He ensured the prominence—indeed the preeminence—of his family among the Mauritanian elite during the colonial period.[89] He saved the symbolic capital of the Sidiyya, translating it into varied forms of economic and social capital, including access to the colonial administration. He shaped French attitudes and the historiography of Mauritania. More than his contemporaries and his rival Saad Buh, he foresaw the end of the anciens régimes of the Senegalo-Mauritanian zone, including the one managed by his grandfather. More than any other grand marabout described in this volume, he comes close to being an "organic intellectual" of colonial rule.

Baba was not able to translate effectively the multifaceted capital of the Sidiyya beyond the colonial setting. Preoccupied for many years with simple survival, he was not able to devote sufficient energy to the preparation of his children. The colonial setting, in the form of French sovereignty, presented a difficult problem for the citizens of the Dar al-Islam. Some of the most articulate Muslims saw Baba as "official clergy," in the sense intended by Coppolani and Arnaud, and as one who refused to "defend the cause of religion." The limits of Sidiyya cohesion appeared shortly after his death. His zawiya disappeared. His sons and daughters began to go their separate ways, with their tents, followers, and flocks.

While Sidiyya influence remained considerable in the early years of independence,[90] thanks in part to their relatively high level of Islamic and Western education and considerable experience in administration, it could not easily withstand the ideological commitments of subsequent decades. An Islamic Republic of Mauritania, based in Nouakchott, committed to arabization and attachment to the Mediterranean "heartlands" of the faith, could not easily accept the importance of a colonial Mauritania, created from the south, administered from Saint-Louis, and dominated by a maraboutic family from Trarza. The Sidiyya have experienced a dramatic decline in influence in recent decades.

~IO~

Malik Sy

Teacher in the New Colonial Order

OF THE FOUR PATHS TO ACCOMMODATION sketched in this book, Malik Sy's (see plate 6) was the least visible and the most steady.[1] The cooperation, when it finally developed, was extremely useful for the colonial authorities—and recognized by them as such. But the grand marabout of Tivaouane was never an instrument of the administration, and he worked consistently for his own purposes and those of his constituency.[2] Malik Sy is also the hardest of the four leaders to "historicize." He scarcely appears in the French archival record before the last decade of his life. His own works consist of poetry and treatises on law, theology, and pedagogy; they rarely mention dates or events, and nothing that would position him relative to the sequences of colonial rule. The knowledge of most of his life comes from internal traditions in the Sy family and among disciples, traditions recorded at different periods over the twentieth century. Two of the major compilations were done by Paul Marty, just before World War I, and by Ravane Mbaye in a doctoral thesis defended in 1993.[3]

Malik had a difficult path to trace. He belonged to the order founded by Ahmad al-Tijani, who made controversial claims to revelation and authority that aroused considerable polemics among Muslim scholars. He grew up at a time when the Tijaniyya order of West Africa was closely associated with the jihad of the sword and the careers of Umar, Ma Ba, the Madiyanke, and Mamadu Lamine. As indicated in chapters 4 and 7, the French retained the association of Tokolor, Tijani, and "fanatic" Muslim for most of the nineteenth century, even when the evidence contradicted the stereotype, and even when

194

they collaborated intimately with Tijaniyya zawiyas in Algeria.[4] It is a measure of Malik Sy's achievement that, by the early twentieth century, he convinced Marty and the French to distinguish between his constituency, the Tijaniyya *ouolofs*, and the still suspect Tijaniyya *toucouleurs* derived from Al-Hajj Umar.[5]

The Early Years

The sources for Malik Sy's biography are scarce compared with those for Saad Buh, Sidiyya Baba, and Amadu Bamba. His origins are obscure. The prodigies often associated with the childhood of a great religious leader are virtually absent. This suggests that he came from a family with little distinction in wealth or learning, and it is consistent with the slow but impressive development of his career.[6]

Malik was born about 1854 in the village of Gaé, near Dagana in Dimar, the westernmost province of Futa Toro. Dimar was the theater of heavy propaganda and recruitment for Umar's holy war in the 1850s. It had a large, agricultural Wolof population as well as significant pastoral Fulbe. Malik's family was sedentary and Wolof. They established links to the Umarian cause, but primarily at the level of Sufi affiliation rather than through participation in the jihad.[7] As suggested in chapter 7, Malik sought to keep a respectful and respectable distance from the Umarian cause, break the Tijaniyya-jihad connection, and establish a Tijaniyya constituency in a Wolof milieu.

Dimar was the first setting of his early years. He spent most of the time in Gaé, where his mother Fatimata lived and took care of the pupils in a Quranic school. Her brother Mayoro Wele, who had received his Sufi initiations from Umar and the Idawali of Mauritania,[8] was a prominent influence upon Malik. The other setting was Jolof, the kingdom to the south that was home to his father, Usman Sy. Usman had studied in Gaé, married Fatimata, and died not long after the birth of their son.[9] His brother and other members of the family helped raise and educate Malik in Jolof.

The situation was extremely turbulent in both areas. In the mid 1850s, the French waged a war with the emir of Trarza for control of Walo; they then competed with Umar for domination in Futa Toro. In the 1860s, Ma Ba Diakhu attracted a large following in Rip and Salum.[10] By 1865, he had swept into Jolof and sent missionaries and refugees into the whole Senegal River region. In 1867–68, a cholera epidemic struck the whole Senegalo-Mauritanian region; it provided the crisis that enabled the Madiyanke, the reformers who preached about the end of times, to establish their supremacy throughout western Futa, Walo, Jolof, and Cayor. It was only in 1875 that the coalition of French, Cayorian, and Jolof forces defeated them and "restored" the traditional order and dynasties.[11]

Malik Sy's connection to these events is much less obvious than that of Amadu Bamba. In his writings at the turn of the century, Malik does not reflect directly on these troubled times, but they undoubtedly played a significant role in his development. My observation emerges from his negative judgments about the anciens régimes and the unfavorable comparisons that he made between them and the colonial order.

In the 1870s, Malik traveled widely to study law, theology, and Sufism with a variety of teachers. These years marked the beginning of his search for a Sufi master and framework, a search that he conducted largely within the Tijaniyya options available in the Senegalo-Mauritanian region. He placed great emphasis on strengthening his connections with the Hafiziyya Tijaniyya tradition of Mauritania. Through them he established relations with Fez, site of the tomb of the founder and the leading zawiya of the order. In the process he became a muqaddam of the Tijaniyya, authorized to initiate and to license muqaddam of his own.[12] It was during this period, and probably while he was teaching near Dagana, that he attracted the attention of the Muslim merchants from Saint-Louis.[13] By the latter part of the decade, he had established a residence in Ndar, created close relations with several leading Muslim teachers, and married into one of its prominent families.

THE EMERGENCE OF MALIK SY

It is difficult, in relation to later oral and written traditions, to pinpoint any event sequence or moment when Malik Sy became prominent among his Muslim contemporaries or the colonial authorities. Like many clerics, he passed gradually from being a student to being a teacher, from being an initiate of a Sufi order to being an initiator. Unlike some of his contemporaries, he did not participate in jihad, express any significant political ambition, develop close relations with traditional courts, or establish a reputation for performing miracles.[14] He was more scholar and teacher than saint; to put it another way, his saintliness emerged from prolonged contact and exposure to his wisdom. But one can say that by 1880 Malik had established a reputation as a learned scholar who traveled and studied through the Senegalo-Mauritanian zone, encouraged the spread of Islam, and enhanced the religious reputation of Saint-Louis.

We know this through the oral traditions of Saint-Louis in particular. He created a pied-à-terre in Saint-Louis thanks to several sponsors in the Muslim community.[15] One was his teacher, perhaps the most famous in Saint-Louis at the time, Amadu Ndiaye Mabeye. Another was Mor Massamba Diery Dieng, a merchant of Cayorian origin who had amassed wealth and a reputation for piety; a decade later Malik would take Dieng's daughter Yasine as his third wife. The most illustrious sponsor was Abdullay Seck, oldest son of Bu El Mogdad. Abdullay completed his Islamic studies in a Trarza *zwaya* school and then began trading in the Dagana area.[16] It was there undoubtedly that he made Malik's acquaintance. Abdullay was also being groomed to replace his father as an interpreter and translator for the colonial administration.[17] Malik had periods of residence with the Seck and Amadu Ndiaye Mabeye before establishing his own place in Saint-Louis.

With this support, it is not surprising that Malik was able to marry well in Saint-Louis society. In about 1879, he took as his first wife Rokhaya Ndiaye, member of a prestigious local family and niece of the merchant discussed in chapter 6, Abdullay Mar. Malik had four children by her. The oldest son, Amadu, was born in 1883; his second son, Babacar, came along in 1885.[18] By the late 1880s, Malik had acquired a considerable reputation for piety and learning, opened a Tijani zawiya, and obtained some property on the island.

What, therefore, is one to make of traditions of opposition to his presence in the colonial capital? One strand emphasizes his Tijani affiliation as the cause. This is credible in terms of administration attitudes, especially in the wake of the Madiyanke episodes, but it makes little sense in relation to his local sponsors.[19] Indeed, Abdullay Seck came from the most prestigious Muslim and Qadiriyya family on the island; presumably he and other notables stressed Malik's learning and piety more than his Sufi affiliation. The more believable strand is a class difference: that Malik felt unsophisticated in the presence of the Saint-Louis community. He came from a relatively poor, rural background and was accustomed to the disruption and wars of the interior. He certainly did not have the urban polish of the local notables, not at the beginning. But in time he acquired the bearing, carriage, and property that characterized the Ndar elite.[20]

During this period, from the late 1870s to the late 1880s, Malik Sy did not stay in Saint-Louis for extended periods of time. He traveled frequently through the Senegalo-Mauritanian region, continuing his search for Tijani masters, especially among the Idawali and other *zwaya* of southern Mauritania.[21] He spent some time in Jolof, apparently at the request of Albury Ndiaye, the king and former protégé of Ma Ba, to help with the islamization of the unruly ceddo (crown slaves) of his court. It was perhaps partly in return for his services that, in 1887, Malik contracted another important marriage, with Safiatu Niang. She was cousin to both Malik and Albury.[22] His Jolof journey aroused concern among administrators preoccupied with Mamadu Lamine and a series of supposed "Tijaniyya enemies."[23]

Malik spent part of each growing season in Gandiole, a cluster of villages and farms just south of Saint-Louis close to the mouth of the river. In fact, it would not be inappropriate to call this the "Gandiole" period, because of the emphasis that he placed on farming and the values of work and self-sufficiency. His followers cultivated his fields. According to Mbaye it was two good successive harvests that enabled Malik to undertake the pilgrimage in 1888–89.[24]

The pilgrimage set Malik apart from most of his contemporaries and the other marabouts featured in this book. It gave him the same distinction, unusual for the time, as Umar Tal, Hamat Ndiaye Anne, and several members of the Seck family. He became "Hajj Malik" from this event forward, and commemorated his journey in a poem.[25] In the traditions collected by Mbaye, Malik traveled by ship with Abdullay Mar Diop and one other man from Saint-Louis. They sailed from Dakar to Marseille, Alexandria, and Jedda, and returned by way of Marseille and Casablanca.[26]

What is most striking is the scarcity of detail about this signal event.[27] I have not found any contemporary archival record of the pilgrimage. This suggests that the French did not sponsor the trip nor consider it particularly noteworthy at the time. But the configuration of the voyage, by boat from Dakar, with stops in Marseille, indicate that they approved the journey and may have used the escales to influence the young scholar. There is no record of a trip to Fez to visit the tomb of Ahmad al-Tijani. It is not likely that a French ship would have stayed for a long time in the port of Casablanca, nor that French authorities would have looked kindly on a journey to the main Moroccan zawiya at this time.[28]

So how should one understand this event? Certainly as part of the development of Saint-Louis as an Islamic center. Certainly as part of the development of the administration as a "Muslim power" that provided the infrastructure for accomplishing a fundamental religious obligation. And surely as testimony to the respect and prestige of Malik Sy in Saint-Louis at this relatively early date. According to the traditions collected by Mbaye, some of the leading Muslims of the town helped to finance his journey.[29]

The pilgrimage also inaugurated the period of his most sustained residence in Saint-Louis, from 1890 to 1895. "Hajj" Malik had considerable symbolic capital, and this in turn enhanced the reputation of the town as an Islamic center. It was during this time that he married his third wife, Yasine, the daughter of Mor Massamba Dieng.[30] He acquired new patrons and new property. A well-known Muslim notable, Al Hajj Dame Seck (see chapter 6), built him a house, while two prominent and pious *saint-louisiennes,* Sokhna Anta Ndiaye Gueye and Marietu Sikithior, provided land for the construction of his mosque and zawiya. Both were in the northern, predominantly Muslim quarter of the island. Thanks to his learning, piety, and support, Malik watched his following grow considerably during this period.[31]

THE TIME OF CONSOLIDATION

The internal sources for Malik Sy single out a period of about five years (ca. 1895-1900) as key to the consolidation of the network of disciples. They call this the "period of Ndiarndé," after the name of a village in the interior of Cayor. Mbaye, in his extensive collection of materials, lists the "ninety-nine disciples" of Malik in conjunction with this period of teaching and training. He is undoubtedly right in portraying this as a time of testing—there were periods of food shortage, for example—and as a critical juncture, both for the career of the marabout and the emergence of the "Wolof Tijaniyya" that has been typically associated with Tivaouane.[32] Whether it constitutes a kind of hijra from engagement with the colonial administration and commerce in Saint-Louis, or even a kind of extended retreat, or *khalwa*, in the Tijaniyya tradition, is open to question.[33]

The last years of the nineteenth century represented a period of dramatic change for Muslims in the region. The railway between Dakar and Saint-Louis led to an "intensification of power" in the peanut basin, increased exports of peanuts, and closer communications between the new and old capitals. It speeded up the process of transferring the administrative center to Dakar, with its superior port facilities and proximity to the developing peanut zones. The authorities, under a governor-general from 1895, were more interventionist, more determined to reduce the influence of the electoral institutions dominated by métis interests, and more paranoid about the influence of potentially "fanatic" Muslims.[34] It was in August and September 1895 that Amadu Bamba was arrested, summarily tried in Ndar, and exiled to Gabon.

The internal traditions make no specific link with these developments, but it is possible that the atmosphere of intensification and suspicion affected Malik Sy's decision.[35] He took his entire family to Ndiarndé, by stages, and brought in his key disciples. He invested heavily in teaching and training his following, and in agricultural labor, as he had done in earlier years in Gandiole. He had fields at Diaksaw and Fass, and his followers grew millet for their own consumption as well as peanuts for exportation. The work ethic was always prominent in his teaching. While it is impossible to date the poetry and treatises of Malik, much less the stages of composition of particular works, it is likely that the basic pedagogy, reflected in the *Kifaya al-Raghibin*, the *Ifham al-Munkir al-Jani*, the *Diwan*, and the *Nasiha*, was established during this period.[36]

But this place and period were not as isolated as the internal traditions suggest. Ndiarndé was only twenty kilometers from the rail depot of Kelle and in the middle of the flourishing peanut basin. Malik was undoubtedly aware of the nearby community of Bu Kunta, which was deeply involved in the cultivation of millet and peanuts by the 1880s. Bu Kunta, member of the prestigious Kunta lineage but with little learning, was also engaged in commerce across the whole Senegalo-Mauritanian zone and made large-scale purchases of rural and urban property in the Niayes, Saint-Louis, Dakar, and Rufisque. He was a model, in other words, for maraboutic enterprise in the emerging colonial economy.[37]

During the Ndiarndé years, Malik continued to travel through western Senegal. He was the marabout of the traitants, the African Muslim merchants described in chapter 6. While the Tijaniyya order was still not free of the stereotype of "fanaticism," administrators were beginning to realize that no single Sufi order had a monopoly on militancy or cooperation.[38]

It is interesting to note the groups identifiable among the "ninety-nine disciples" of the master.[39] They include a number of people originally from Saint-Louis, Gandiole, western Futa, Walo, and Jolof; that is, disciples across the area of Malik's movement during his years of learning and teaching—with the exception of Trarza. The Jolof contingent included a number of brothers and relatives from his father's side. Descendants of participants in the Ma Ba Diakhu struggles and inhabitants of the Cape Verde peninsula, especially Lebu and Layennes, are significant. The most important feature of the group, however, is not their origin but their deployment, principally in the villages and towns of Cayor, Baol, and western Senegal, and particularly along the railway line. His disciples would hold positions as teachers, imams, or judges in Rufisque, Dakar, Kaolack, and other towns connected closely to the colonial structures. Malik Sy further cemented this system by the marriages arranged for his daughters and sons.[40]

THE EARLY YEARS AT TIVAOUANE

By 1902, "Hajj" Malik was ready to move even closer to the heart of the colonial infrastructure. He chose Tivaouane, which was located on the rail line, in

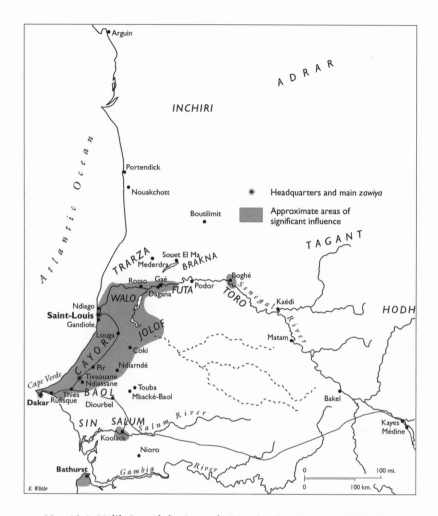

Map 10.1. Malik Sy and the Senegalo-Mauritanian Zone, ca. 1880–1920

what could be called the older peanut basin. It was in the old Muslim area of Saniokhor in southern Cayor.[41] It served as headquarters for the colonial administrator of the Cayor region, who worked through a number of French subordinates and Senegalese *chefs de canton* over a large zone.

It was a conspicuous moment for such a move. It was the time when the machinery of the French West African Federation moved to Dakar, leaving Saint-Louis under a lieutenant governor.[42] The economic center of gravity had already shifted from the river valley to the peanut basin. The commercial community of Saint-Louis had anticipated the change for some time. The year 1902 also marked the return of Amadu Bamba from his first exile in Gabon. He spent the last months of the year and the first months of 1903 in Baol and southern Cayor. Victor Allys, the administrator in Tivaouane, was assigned to supervise his activities.[43] The year was significant for yet another reason: it marked the death of Demba War Sall, the head of the crown ceddo of Cayor, who, by casting his lot with the French, had become the president of the Confederation of Cayor. Demba War had dominated Cayor, with a salary superior to the head French administrator, for sixteen years. The French did not put anyone in his place, signaling a more direct administration of the area. They now limited Senegalese to positions as chefs de canton.[44]

Alongside the heavy reliance on chiefs chosen from the traditional aristocratic lineages, the colonial authorities now considered enduring relations with maraboutic communities linked to the peanut basin. Saad Buh and Sidiyya Baba were the precursors to this new pattern of alliance. Malik Sy and Amadu Bamba would now develop the pattern in the peanut basin itself. The administrative leadership for this arrangement came from Governor-general Ernest Roume (1902–8), Xavier Coppolani, and Robert Arnaud. The events that drove the new pattern were the "pacification" and conquest of Mauritania, described in chapter 4.

Malik's choice to settle in Tivaouane, to move to the heart of the colonial administration and economy, was quite deliberate.[45] He knew the area well. Ndiarndé was not far away. He traveled frequently through the region, often using the railroad. His disciples cultivated fields in central Cayor that the marabout had obtained over the years. Now they also cultivated around Tivaouane, where Malik, his brothers, sons, and disciples practiced the pedagogy designed at Ndiarndé.

At this juncture, "Hajj" Malik made some critical choices about the deployment of his family. His first and third wives, both from Saint-Louis, went to the old colonial capital and raised their families there. Babacar, the oldest surviving son of Rokhaya and Malik's successor in 1922, lived most of the time in Saint-Louis. He had casual but cordial relations with the administration, who saw him as the likely successor to leadership.[46] It was the third wife, Safiatu, the Jolof aristocrat, who made her home in Tivaouane with her sons Mansur, Abdulaziz, and Habib. Over the years, she became a very dominant influence in the life of the order, even while Babacar was serving as khalifa (1922–57).[47]

Malik continued to travel from his Tivaouane base, particularly along the rail line. He visited Dakar and established a strong presence there through his lead disciple, Abdullay Ndur. He established a zawiya in Ndur's home, and eventually married his widow.[48] He had an important community in Rufisque and often purchased books from a Moroccan bookseller there. In Kaolack he exercised his influence through Abdu Kane, whose daughter Astu had married Babacar.[49] He visited Gambia and Sierra Leone and had disciples there.[50] He was frequently in Saint-Louis, for religious, medical, and administrative reasons.[51] As outlined in chapter 7, he had close ties with Amadu Moktar Sakho, the French-appointed qadi of Boghé. Through him, Malik Sy established a connection to the Umarian heritage, especially for the thousands of persons who returned from the Soudan in the 1890s.[52] These early years can be dated from 1902 to about 1910, but the record is extremely sparse about "events."

"Hajj" Malik expanded his symbolic and social capital. He instituted the Gamu, to celebrate the birthday of the Prophet, as a regular event. It was an occasion for his disciples from all over the region to pay tribute to his influence, visit fellow Tijanis, and make contributions to the order. Malik had certainly established his reputation as a master teacher with a pedagogy that could function within the colonial order. This reputation attracted Muslims from a wide zone, and considerable energy was deployed in sustaining these Muslims in the towns and villages where they taught and worked.

As for the order's relations to the French, there are almost no records— which is in sharp contrast to the quantities of data on the Murids. This indicates that Malik Sy, while under some observation from the administrative offices on one side of Tivaouane, and presumably from the rail and road agents where he passed, posed no problems for the authorities. By the same token, he was not called upon by them for any particular service.

THE LATER YEARS AT TIVAOUANE: MORE ACTIVE COOPERATION

It is really in the second decade of the twentieth century that the period of active cooperation began. The closer ties began effectively in 1910, when, at the Friday prayer, Malik built a sermon around the "counsel" that Saad Buh wrote to Ma El Ainin and that the French distributed widely to Muslims in West Africa (see chapter 8). The document bristled with reasons why the jihad of the sword was not an appropriate response to European conquest.[53] Malik Sy's reading of the letter and commentary on its contents suggested to the colonial authorities how valuable an ally he might be, and this impression was only reinforced in the crises that were soon to come, especially during World War I. It was also at this time that he persuaded Abdullay Niasse, the Tijaniyya leader with growing influence in Salum, to settle in the town of Kaolack in the full view of the French administration.[54]

For the later years it is important to establish two trajectories. The internal "Malikiyya" path continued at a steady pace. The order itself was growing, around the wisdom and teaching of Malik Sy. It was undoubtedly the dominant Tijaniyya brotherhood in the Senegalo-Mauritanian zone, an umbrella under which disciples could comfortably and openly practice its special rituals.[55] Malik Sy was aging, and losing his eyesight progressively.[56] Increasingly his brothers, sons, and disciples began to handle the routine affairs of the order. Malik continued to exercise the principal authority over his network, apparently until the very end of his life.[57] He received distinguished Tijani visitors from Mauritania, Morocco, and Algeria, maintained epistolary and personal contact with friends in the administration, and traveled on a limited basis.

The second or "colonial" trajectory was not closely tied to the first. The French made a rather abrupt "discovery" of Malik Sy, his prominence in general Islamic pedagogy, and his "pacifist" form of Tijaniyya teaching and practice. This involved closer relations between administration and order, a kind of "exchange of services," and in turn closer surveillance of the man who was now a grand marabout.

The French needs were more sharply exposed as war became likely in the European and Mediterranean theaters. By 1912, Paris was concerned about reactions to their new protectorate over Morocco and to Pan-Islamic threats emanating from Istanbul. At this key juncture, "Hajj" Malik made a strong public exhortation to loyalty that emphasized the same points as the fatwa of Baba and the *nasiha* of Saad Buh. The administration circulated copies of his text widely, with claims that it was unsolicited. Malik Sy came quickly to the point:

> Support the French government totally. God has given special victory, grace, and favor to the French. He has chosen them to protect our persons and property. This is why it is necessary to live in perfect rapport with them. . . .
>
> Before they came here we were living in a situation of enslavement, murder, and pillage. Muslims were no better than infidels on that point. Had they not come we would still be in that state. . . .
>
> My brothers, do not let yourselves be seduced by the words of those who say: "Soon the day will come when French authority will collapse." Those are pernicious words. . . . Do not complain that you have to fulfill the requirements which they have established. . . .
>
> Have confidence in the French, as they have confidence in you. The compensation for good deeds, is it not other good deeds? Cling to divine

wisdom, your hearts will enjoy peace. The hour for him who knows that will be blessed. . . .

Know that the French have given great assistance to our religion and to our country. The intelligent will understand that.[58]

One could hardly imagine a warmer endorsement for France as a "Muslim power."[59]

During the war, Malik Sy made numerous declarations of loyalty. He exhorted his followers to enlist in the army. He lost his oldest son Amadu in the fighting at Salonica in 1916. He gave money to support medical care for the wounded. The colonial authorities consulted him about recruiting Muslims as soldiers and about declaring war against the Ottoman regime. As outlined in chapters 7 and 9, the French assisted the Arabs against Istanbul, constituted a Habus Commission for the Holy Lands, and sought representatives from the "Muslim" parts of the empire. They considered naming Malik Sy, but realized his failing health would not permit him to travel to North Africa. They appointed his disciple, Abdu Kane of Kaolack, instead.[60]

The principal return that Malik Sy received for these services was the freedom to continue the teaching and training of the dominant Senegalese Muslims of early colonial Senegal.[61] In the account given by Marty, which can be dated to the period at the beginning of World War I, Malik's relatives and disciples ensured the teaching of pupils whose numbers fluctuated between 80 and 250, depending on the agricultural and trading seasons. The teachers stressed the Quran, its exegesis, and Islamic law. Malik himself taught the upper levels, despite his failing eyesight. He and his fellow teachers drew from an impressive library, much of it obtained from Moroccan booksellers in Senegal or Mauritanian Tijaniyya scholars. Some works were the gifts of the governor-general, obtained from various parts of the Mediterranean Muslim world. Indeed, the administration arranged for the publication of twenty-six of Malik's own works in Tunis.[62]

The years that followed the war were not eventful for relations between Tivaouane and the colonial administration. The close relationship continued while Malik Sy's health declined. The French certainly watched closely over the succession on his death in 1922, but there is no evidence that they intervened. Babacar, the oldest surviving son who had spent most of his life in Saint-Louis, moved to Tivaouane and took over the reins of the order for the next thirty-five years. This produced some strains with Safiatu Niang and her sons, who had resided in Tivaouane since the beginning of the century.[63]

—·—

ACROSS HIS ENTIRE CAREER, Malik Sy stressed learning about Islam and the dissemination of Islamic knowledge and practice. He understood that the conditions in the old "order," which was a kind of "disorder," or siba, were not conducive to that learning and dissemination. Over time, through his contacts with Muslims in Saint-Louis, and through them with the administration, he came to appreciate the advantages that the emerging colonial order offered to his goals.

In this register of ideas, the "Saint-Louis" and "Gandiole" periods involved exploration. The "Ndiarndé" period was one of consolidation. The "Tivaouane" years were devoted to expansion and generalization. Only toward the end of the latter period did Malik Sy work closely with the administration, and that without sacrificing anything truly important to his objectives. There is no reason to doubt the sincerity of his declarations of support for the colonial regime.

From the Ndiarndé period, "Hajj" Malik secured his credentials, developed his pedagogy, and communicated it to the core of disciples who would play critical roles of islamization in Senegal. Through his writings and teaching, the marabout became an important mediator and disseminator of knowledge about Islamic practice within the emerging colonial order. He kept his distance from the colonial authorities until late in his life, intruded rarely into the record, and made no overt attempts, in ways comparable to Saad Buh or Sidiyya Baba, to shape the historical or ethnographic accounts. But this should not obscure the message that he communicated consistently to his disciples and those involved in the civil society of the towns: the compatibility of devotion, learning, and orthodoxy with submission to French rule.

Malik Sy retained much of the simplicity of his origins, while acquiring some of the sophistication of Saint-Louis. He consistently emphasized the importance of work, by which he particularly meant the growing of food crops and peanuts, and his followers were encouraged to labor in the steadily growing number of fields at his disposal. He did not, however, accumulate great wealth in his lifetime. His personal fortune, and that of his family, could not compare to that of the Murids.[64]

Not the least of Malik's achievements, and one that endeared him to the colonial authorities, was to transform the construction of the Tijaniyya in the Senegalo-Mauritanian zone. He defended the order and its founder, but without the polemical zeal of some of his contemporaries.[65] He decoupled the old equation *Tijaniyya = jihad of the sword,* the stereotype that was the tired but still powerful Umarian legacy. It was not difficult, at the turn of the century, to manage the decoupling with local Muslims, Futanke, and others, weary of military struggle. Among staunch Umarian families like the Sakho, or the descendants of Ma Ba Diakhu, he found a ready audience for understanding the Tijaniyya as primarily a teaching order.

It was more difficult to do the delinking with the French, who seemed to need a "devil" in dealing with Islam. In this case, it was the "devils" of Amadu Bamba, Ma El Ainin, and finally the Ottoman sultanate in its last crumbling stage, that opened the way for a new understanding of the West African Tijaniyya. When the authorities in Saint-Louis, Dakar, and Paris finally made the shift, they warmly embraced Tivaouane as an important support for the colonial economy and polity, and this paved the way for cooperation with Seydu Nuru Tal.

While the relationship between the French and Malik Sy became cordial after 1902 and close after 1910, I would not call the marabout an "organic intellectual" of the new colonial order, in the sense intended by Antonio Gramsci.[66] It is preferable to think of the Tivaouane leader and the colonial government operating along parallel trajectories. Each understood the other very well, respected the other's sphere, and cooperated in an overlapping arena. The authorities did not interfere in his mission to disseminate and ameliorate the practice of Islam; indeed, by the early 1900s they saw the advantage for themselves in that mission. Malik Sy, for his part, benefited from the conditions of stability that the colonial regime enforced. He knew that cooperation would always be accompanied by surveilliance. By living in Tivaouane for the last twenty years of his life, and making it the center of his order, he reduced that surveillance to a reflexive habit.

⟶II⟵

Amadu Bamba

A Complex Path to Accommodation

OF ALL OF THE "PATHS OF ACCOMMODATION" between Muslims societies and French colonial authorities, the one followed by Amadu Bamba Mbacke (see plate 7) and the Murids is ostensibly the longest, hardest, most complete, and most enduring.[1] For these reasons, the Murid movement has been more fully documented and studied, by Paul Marty of the colonial Muslim Affairs Bureau in the early twentieth century and by social scientists in recent decades.[2]

The Murid trajectory was not fundamentally different from its less dramatic predecessors. For this reason it needs to be considered in conjunction with the same broad developments in the Senegalo-Mauritanian zone where Muslim leaders acquired social and economic capital, in the form of constituencies, wealth, and insertion into the new colonial economy. Amadu Bamba and his followers witnessed the same processes: the decline of the anciens régimes, the growing turbulence and displacement of people, and the search for new structures in a new order. Bamba's movement deserves to be placed last in the sequence for several reasons: the Murids participated more actively in those processes, over a longer period of time; their accommodation was completed later, and it put the seal on a new pattern of relations between Muslims and colonial authorities.

The French made the process of accommodation with the Murids — or with Bamba, as opposed to his key relatives and disciples — longer and more complex. At a time when French control of the peanut basin was still fragile, Bamba developed a reputation as teacher, saint, and rallying point among a large number of displaced persons. That reputation included an attitude of opposition to the practices and agents of power, whether they were members of the anciens régimes, the rulers of "Islamic" states, or the emerging colonial order.

When the French developed their rationale for colonial rule of Senegal in the 1890s, they were still suspicious of Muslim leaders and of Islam itself.[3] Their first approach to the administration of territories was a modified system of chieftaincy (see chapter 3). For Bamba and his followers, the methods of rule employed by these chiefs were not significantly different from their precolonial predecessors, and they sought to keep social and geographical distance from the new centers of power.[4] This attitude, combined with French fear about controlling the critical peanut basin, go a long way to explaining the exile of Bamba in 1895.

In this chapter, I suggest that the path to accommodation was less long and more complex than the standard interpretations suggest. The conventional historiography focuses on the person of Bamba and makes the entire period of his exile (1895–1912), in three different locations, into a time of opposition, followed by a rather intensive collaboration (1912–27) from his return to Baol until his death.[5] I argue that understanding the pattern of accommodation between Murid and colonial authorities requires a different approach.

1. One must make a distinction between Bamba and his key associates. While Bamba was in exile, some of his brothers and disciples were developing relations of cooperation with the administration.
2. One must acknowledge the simultaneous combination of close surveillance by the French, constant communication between the two sides, and collaboration in the economic development of the peanut basin.

By the early twentieth century, both French and Murids were making the distinction and recognizing the coexistence of surveillance and cooperation. Bamba's return to Baol in 1912 marked not the beginning but the consolidation of this understanding.

BAMBA AND THE CRITIQUE OF THE EXERCISE OF POWER

To ground the Murid "path" to accommodation, one must go back to the formative years of the founder. The biography of Amadu Bamba, in its broad outlines, is relatively well known. Like Malik Sy, he was born at mid century, grew up amid the conditions of disruption, and developed a following, a pedagogy, and a place in the new colonial economy by the end of the nineteenth century.

But Bamba came from a well-established maraboutic family of eastern Baol. His great-grandfather Maharram founded the village of Mbacké-Baol, and it was there that Bamba was born in the early 1850s. His father, Momar Antasali, was a well-known teacher, and his mother, Diarra Busso, came from a prestigious clerical lineage. His father served from time to time as counselor and secretary to chiefs in Baol and Cayor. Because of this insertion, Bamba had a more intimate experience with the power brokers of central Senegal than did Malik Sy. He formed his views on the exercise of power in relation to the careers of Ma Ba Diakhu in Rip, the movement of the Madiyanke, and the aristocrat Lat Dior (sequences I explored briefly in chapter 1).

Martin Klein and Boubacar Barry have portrayed Ma Ba as providing the most fundamental critique and the most challenging Islamic resistance to the anciens régimes and the embryonic colonial order.[6] Certainly, the reformer attracted a large following and exerted great influence, over such ambitious aristocrats as Lat Dior of Cayor and Albury Ndiaye of Jolof. He developed a severe critique of the regimes based on ceddo power, and established his preeminence over the Wolof and Serer states in the 1860s.

But the movement had serious weaknesses. First, the haste. Ma Ba took little time to prepare his teaching or following, much less to formulate a program to replace the practices of those he was condemning.[7] Second, the coercion of participation. His invasions of the Wolof kingdoms resulted in the death of Bamba's grandfather and the forced deportation of Momar Antasali and his young son to the Rip. Third, Ma Ba's own strong political ambitions, even while he was delivering the traditional Muslim critique of power. These dimensions may help to explain the defeat at the battle of Somb in 1867, when Ma Ba was killed. They certainly go a long way to explaining the struggle among his successors, a struggle that has gone down as an example of fitna, internecine strife that weakens the fabric of Islam.[8]

After the death of Ma Ba, Lat Dior returned to Cayor. He became Damel with the support of the administration in Saint-Louis. During the 1870s, the king struggled with a variety of opposition to his power. The fundamental contradiction was between his agents of power at the court and his constituents in the countryside.[9] He persuaded Momar Antasali to join him as a counselor and judge in a regime where he would attempt to establish Islamic law.[10] It was in this environment that the young Bamba continued his studies with local specialists, most notably Ma Diakhate Kala, the qadi and secretary of the Damel.

The strongest opposition to Lat Dior came from the Madiyanke.[11] Amadu Madiyu and his brothers formulated a commentary on contemporary society, the exploitation of the royal courts, and the close relations of certain chiefs with the French administration in Saint-Louis. They pushed this critique further than Ma Ba and Umar Tal. In so doing they won a considerable following in northwestern Senegal. The pressure forced Lat Dior into closer ties with Saint-Louis, where he helped persuade Governor Valière to intervene with colonial troops in 1875.[12] The combined army routed the "Muslim" forces at Samba Sadio. The Madiyanke leaders and most of the followers were killed, whereupon the victors confiscated their possessions and enslaved the survivors, as was the custom. The confiscation provoked controversy among Muslim scholars in Cayor.

On one side of the debate was Ma Diakhate Kala, the well-known cleric, author, and qadi of Lat Dior. For him, the Madiyanke, by their "Messianic" claims, had forfeited their status as Muslims; their possessions and their persons were fair game.[13] On the other side was Amadu Bamba, who was coming into his own as a Muslim authority. While he had little patience with the grandiose claims, he did not feel that the Madiyanke had committed apostasy; the victors consequently had no right to the booty. According to one version,

> Ma Diakhate said to Bamba: "The one [Amadu Madiyu] defeated at Samba Sadio had proclaimed himself the Prophet. He waged war to give material realization to his prophetic pretensions. Consequently it was legitimate to spill his blood, confiscate his property, and enslave those taken prisoner." Bamba replied: "Who told you this, that he claimed to be a Prophet?" Ma Diakhate responded: "Why the people of Cayor." Bamba replied: "Those were his enemies, those waging war upon him. You, a judge, did not take into consideration that the accusations brought against him came from his enemies."[14]

The debate sharpened Bamba's criticism of the practice of power. He kept his distance from the Damel. When Lat Dior brought a gift of slaves to ask for his blessing for a male heir, Bamba refused the slaves but gave the invocation. The next year, a son, Mbakhane Diop, was born—the future colonial chief who had such a complicated relationship with the Murids.[15] Bamba reserved a harsh judgment for his father. He reputedly said: "If my father does not leave the king, I will leave him."[16] Under this pressure, Momar withdrew increasingly from his association with Lat Dior and lived in the village of Mbacke-Cayor, which he had founded a few years before.

The relationship between father and son remained close, however. Momar, just before he died in 1883, called in Amadu and entrusted to him the care of his younger sons:

> Continue to learn the Quran and the sacred texts, without forgetting grammar and jurisprudence. It is only in this way that you will be able truly to understand religion and serve God and His Prophet. The country at this moment is in a very confused state. The only way in which you can aid others and yourself is to flee from the things of this world. Watch over your brothers; I entrust them to you, because it is in you that I have the greatest confidence. Help them to acquire the qualities that you have already.[17]

Bamba took his father's message to heart. Not long after Momar's death he returned to eastern Baol with the Mbacké family, his father's disciples, and others who wished to flee the turbulence of Cayor in the 1880s.[18]

Murid sources and their Western interpreters have often portrayed an encounter between Bamba and Lat Dior, not long before the Damel's death in his last confrontation with the French in October 1886. According to this tradition, Lat Dior came to Bamba for advice. Bamba supplied the blessing, but gave no support for Lat Dior's cause.[19] The effect of these versions is to link Bamba to the tradition of Cayorian resistance, which is the strongest strand of Senegalese opposition to French rule. If such an encounter did happen, it occurred in eastern Baol, where the desperate king sought out the reluctant marabout.

Bamba attracted a number of the survivors from the courts of the anciens régimes to his base in eastern Baol. There he had the opportunity to develop his teaching and train his following for the next several years. His experience with the traditional courts, and with those who wished to reform those courts, had been discouraging. It is small wonder that this long-developing and deeply-lived attitude would carry over to the colonial regime and its minions.

AMADU BAMBA AND THE SEARCH FOR A NEW WAY

At the same time that he was dealing with the practitioners of power, Bamba was engaged in his own search for vocation and meaning. He followed the traditional peripatetic pattern of scholarship and Sufi affiliation. Gradually the student gave way to the teacher, but even in the early twentieth century Bamba was still learning, at the feet of those who had some dimension of understanding that he did not yet possess.[20]

The tremendous outpouring of Murid literature in the twentieth century makes it difficult to illuminate the pattern of Bamba's search across the last two decades of the nineteenth century. We hear that he affiliated to the Shadhili and Tijaniyya Sufi orders as well as the Qadiriyya. He traveled around western or Wolof Senegal, to Saint-Louis, and into the Trarza region of southwestern Mauritania, known as the most important center of scholarship in the larger zone. Bamba was certainly acquainted with the Bu El Mogdad family of Saint-Louis. He followed his father's precedent by spending time with the Sidiyya family of Trarza, which had not yet developed the close ties with colonial authorities discussed in chapter 9.[21] In each of these places he sought out the most enlightened teachers and Sufis of his day. Murid tradition suggests a certain dissatisfaction with these mentors.

Bamba developed his framework for a Muslim community in the 1880s, after his return to eastern Baol. He established the leadership core of the community. His foremost confidant was his half-brother Ibra Fati, about five years his junior. Shaikh Ibra Fall, a disciple from Cayor, appears in the traditional sources at this time as the symbol of submission as well as the apostle of hard work.[22] With these supporters, Bamba forged an economic and religious community. It included peasants, crown soldiers from Cayor, Baol and Jolof,[23] and slaves or former slaves who would transform their bondage into religious loyalty.[24] The economic dimensions of the community were undoubtedly influenced by the patterns of millet and peanut cultivation practiced by Bu Kunta.[25]

It was during this period, in the late 1880s and early 1890s, that Bamba wrote much of his poetry in praise of the Prophet, odes recited by disciples today. He wrote often about the *murid,* the "seeker after God," and that expression began to be used for the community. He began to cast himself as the *khadim Rasul Allah,* the "servant of the envoy of God." Bamba claimed a visitation from Gabriel when he turned forty, the age of the Prophet at the time of his initial revelations, and in commemoration he established the new village of Touba on the site.[26]

Bamba also developed a new Islamic pedagogy.[27] He retained the traditional practice of *ta'lim,* or learning, built around the Quran. He also proposed *tarbiyya,* an adult learning that was linked to action, work, and loyalty. Finally, he developed *tarqiyya,* a kind of apprenticeship of student to teacher, to prepare the next generation of leadership. Bamba put a premium on autonomous Muslim communities that would live, work, and reproduce themselves in conditions of stability, in contrast to the conditions of turbulence that he had experienced in Cayor. Perhaps the most important dimension of his pedagogy was the diversity of options. Bamba recognized the variety of backgrounds of his constituents, their different needs, and the importance of forming a new and durable social order.

The French were not well informed about these developments. They operated at a distance, in geographical and social terms, from the Murid milieu. They heard more about the external trappings, the Sufi affiliations, or about the former ceddo who had gravitated into his circle. The mediators of this "knowledge" were usually the interpreters and chiefs who felt threatened by the influence of the Murid movement. The French, when they arrested and exiled Bamba a few years later, apparently thought that they could disperse his community—or at least restrain its growth.

EARLY CONFLICTS BETWEEN COLONIAL AUTHORITIES AND BAMBA

At the end of the 1880s, the French government began effectively to "intensify its power" over the interior areas of Senegal and the local republican interests of Saint-Louis. The initiative for this effort came from Governors Clément-Thomas and de Lamothe (see chapter 3). With strong support from Paris,[28] the governors removed areas from the purview of the General Council and diminished that body's budgetary authority. They prepared the way for a more hierarchical and elaborate colonial regime, which in 1895 took the name of government-general and in 1902 moved to Dakar.

As the key to the administrative hierarchy of Senegal, the French put in place a more systematic version of an old policy: a set of chiefs who were strongly influenced by the colonial administration (chapter 3). Governor de Lamothe and Martial Merlin, director of political affairs, used the Ecole des Fils de Chefs et Interprètes to provide the key training.[29] By the mid 1890s, these young men were functioning in many Wolof and Futanke areas of Senegal. Replacing the old courts, they soon incurred similar criticisms about their exercise of power from their subjects—and from the Murids. The chiefs provided much of the push for the arrests and exiles of Bamba, with the help of their big defender, Merlin.

The administration gathered its first direct information about Bamba in 1889, on the eve of the conquest of Jolof. The Political Affairs Bureau expelled some Murids from Ndiambur, the heavily Muslim area between Jolof and Saint-Louis.[30] In 1891 the bureau apparently summoned Bamba to the capital. The best evidence suggests that the marabout sent an emissary in his place.[31] Saint-Louis did not become overly alarmed about Bamba at this time.

The developments that led to his arrest occurred in the early months of 1895, when the marabout moved his core following from Baol to Jolof and acquired significant influence over Samba Laobe Penda, the chief appointed by the administration in the wake of the exile of Albury Ndiaye. Jolof bordered on the peanut basin and was not yet under effective French control. It was in this context that Saint-Louis sent the column that arrested Bamba in August 1895.[32]

Bamba put up no resistance.[33] As far as we know, he did not speak up in his own defense in the procedure that the French organized in Saint-Louis. Merlin, director of political affairs, directed the performance.[34] He brought the case not before the General Council, where he would have been closely questioned, but to the *conseil privé*, which the administration dominated. He marshaled his case in terms of the "warrior" following of the marabout, the flow of arms into the peanut basin, and the high level of agitation that made the task of the colonial chiefs impossible. It was this level of "agitation" that motivated the administration and threatened the apparatus that they had set so carefully in place.[35]

In his brief to the interim governor and council, Merlin declared that since

Amadu Bamba, pupil of Shaikh Sidiyya, Moorish marabout of the Qadiriyya sect,[36] had professed in the last few years the Tijani doctrine which involves preaching holy war. Anyone with experience in the country and with the preachers of holy war will immediately understand that Amadu Bamba, without seeming to, was preparing very adroitly to act in the near future, almost surely during the next dry season.

Having applied the Tijani label to the founder of the Murid brotherhood, Merlin could then write that Amadu Bamba had followed the same pattern of action as the leaders of several important Muslim movements led by Tijani clerics,

such as Ma Ba, Amadu Sheku [of the Madiyanke], Mamadu Lamine, and Samba Diadana. One is struck by the similarity between the protestations of friendship which he made to us in 1889 and 1891 and those which Ma Ba made in 1864, Amadu Sheku before 1868, Mamadu Lamine at Goundiourou in 1885 and in Goye in 1886, just before preparing their campaigns in Rip and Salum, or Jolof, or finally in Bundou and Bakel.

Merlin invoked this history once again as he moved to his final argument for deportation:

Thus it is of utmost importance, Monsieur le gouverneur, in order to bring calm back to Ndiambur, Jolof, and Baol, and in order to avoid the reproach of "excessive tolerance" that Faidherbe used with reference to our attitude toward

Mamadu Lamine in 1886, to remove Amadu Bamba not just from the region
. . . but from Senegal itself and to intern him, for at least several years, in a distant land, such as Gabon, where his fanatic preaching will have no effect.[37]

Merlin showed that the standard religious ethnography, as well as the influence
of Faidherbe, were still alive in the repertory of stereotypes at the end of the
century.

Soon Bamba was en route by train to Dakar and then by ship to Gabon.
This first exile was a frightening trial.[38] The visions and revelations recorded
by Bamba confirm the efforts of the administration to undermine the mission
and confidence of this man whom they had translated into a threat. At some
point, Bamba gained access to books, pen, and paper. He corresponded with
members of his family. He received some visits. While he never expressed open
resistance to his treatment by the French, he apparently never gave them the
affirmation of colonial rule that they sought. On his return, he reportedly said:
"I have left behind in Congo the robe of misery which I was wearing. I will
never voluntarily put it back on, and if anyone tries to force me it will cost
him a great deal."[39]

The most lasting contribution of this seven-year exile was Bamba's writing
about the tribulations and how he survived them. This material in turn spawned
a hagiographic literature from his followers and a set of images that have inspired
Murids throughout the twentieth century: Bamba was Daniel in the lion's den;
Bamba prayed on the ocean to the amazement of the French authorities; Bamba
could never be reduced to a state of submission. It is obvious that some of this
reputation and "cultural" resistance was known in 1902, when Bamba was
greeted as a hero at the docks of Dakar.[40]

What tends to be forgotten in treatments of the exile is the survival and
growth of the community. Bamba's absence forced the growing community to
develop its own resources of leadership and fostered a division of labor—as
well as some tension—among his brothers and key disciples. Ibra Fati maintained correspondence with Bamba and gave spiritual and educational direction to the community.[41] Two other key Murids handled relations with the
"external" world, which meant the administration and the leading figures of
civil society. Bamba's half-brother Shaikh Anta developed his competence in
the economic and political fortunes of the order. He traveled widely, married
equally widely, and became the "minister of external affairs," to use the designation of Marty. The leading disciple, Ibra Fall, nurtured his own following, the
Baye Fall, and a network of contacts throughout the peanut basin and the

coastal cities. Shaikh Ibra developed ties with the Saint-Louis milieu and became the "minister of economic affairs."[42]

CHANGING RELATIONS WITH THE COLONIAL AUTHORITIES

The economic and social capital of the two "shaikhs" played an important role in Bamba's return from exile in 1902. They concentrated on the position of deputy, the office with the greatest influence in metropolitan and local circles. Their contributions helped elect the métis leader François Carpot, who in turn intervened with the authorities.[43] The administration, under the influence of this pressure, agreed to bring Bamba back. This is the standard explanation for the return from the first exile. It goes on to suggest that the second exile, beginning in 1903, demonstrates that French practice had not significantly changed.[44]

Without rejecting this interpretation of the return, I emphasize four other dimensions: the decade of experience of working with the Murid leadership; the emergence of a strong government-general under Ernest Roume; the decision to move ahead with a program of pacification of Mauritania under Coppolani's leadership; and the intervention of Sidiyya Baba.[45] Roume and Coppolani took up their positions in 1902. With a stronger administration, centered on Dakar, less opposition from the republican interests of Saint-Louis, and the model of relations from French North Africa, the administration saw the value in enduring links with marabouts in Senegal—without abandoning the colonial chiefs.[46]

One example of "maraboutic bond" was Malik Sy, who in 1902 settled in Tivaouane (see chapter 10). Another was Bamba. It is likely, in my judgment, that they brought the marabout back in 1902 to strengthen the existing bonds with the Murids and in the hope that Bamba would be able to join in that collaboration—albeit with close supervision. They were encouraged by their new ally, Sidiyya Baba, who interceded strongly for Bamba's return and vouched for his cooperation. Baba assigned his disciple and son-in-law Shaikhuna to remain with the marabout during most of his stay in Cayor and Baol in 1902–3.[47]

The apparatus of surveillance remained operative. It was, after all, part of North African and Senegalo-Mauritanian practice. Merlin, now secretary-general to Roume, retained the instinct for protecting his cohort of chiefs. One of his closest collaborators was Victor Allys, the old colonial hand with a penchant for difficult assignments, who was placed in Tivaouane with significant military resources.[48] The monitors were in place when Bamba returned to a tumultuous welcome in Dakar in November 1902. He spent about a month in Saint-Louis and then was allowed to travel in Cayor and Baol.

In June 1903, Bamba submitted to a new arrest and a second deportation—this time to nearby Trarza and the care of Sidiyya Baba. The cause of the second arrest and exile was similar to the first: the excitement of the former crown soldiers, slaves, and others in the peanut basin, the disruption of tax payments, and the general difficulty experienced by the new generation of colonial chiefs.[49] But the intention and solution were quite different, and the impact on Murid hagiography was much less substantial. Roume acknowledged that the 1903 measure was motivated by the "turbulence of fanatic disciples of the marabout rather than by his personal hostility."[50] In his second exile, Bamba would not be far away; indeed, he would be accessible to his followers. Baba could provide Bamba with an example of the kind of benefits of collaboration with French authorities.

But quite apart from the second exile and the patronage of Baba, it was clear that the Murids were already a necessary part of the infrastructure of central Senegal. They helped to solve significant problems of agricultural production, labor supply, and social control. They produced growing quantities of peanuts. The economic contribution was recognized in a 1904 report written by Allys, the man who had organized the arrest of Bamba the year before:

> At this moment they [the Murid farmers] concentrate only on their fields, which are immense and magnificent. These natives do not work the soil in the same way as other cultivators. For example, working by the light of the moon, they stay in their fields until eleven o'clock in the evening, then go to pray at the mosque, and only then eat their meals.[51]

The movement also solved a social problem in ways that the chiefs could not: it transformed the slaves and former slaves, who supplied so much of the agricultural labor of precolonial Senegal, into followers. As disciples, or clients of the marabouts, the former slaves would be "free" but contained within a structure; they were much less likely to attract the attention of humanitarians or antislavery interests.[52]

During Bamba's absence, the core leadership remained in place. The French authorities did not expect the community to collapse, nor did they anticipate a prolonged exile of the founder. Indeed, they hoped that he would return to the peanut basin, more aware than ever of the bonds of cooperation. Just before Bamba's departure for Trarza, they permitted him to write a letter to

Ibra Fati naming four "commissions" for his followers in his absence: to consult Ibra Fati if they wished to learn; to see Shaikh Anta if they wished to work without learning; to see Ibra Fati if they wished to do both; finally, to leave the community if they wished to do neither.[53]

CONSOLIDATING THE RELATIONSHIP OF ACCOMMODATION

By the early twentieth century, the structures for accommodation between colonial regime and Murids were in place — just as they were for the other movements discussed in this book. This is not to say that there were no turns in the

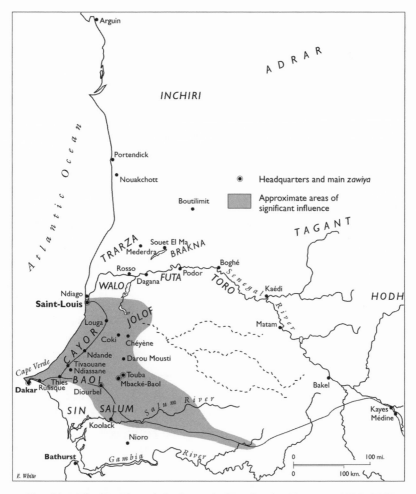

Map 11.1. The Murids and the Senegalo-Mauritanian Zone, ca. 1880-1920

path in subsequent years, nor that events, communications, and relations over the next twenty-five years were not highly significant in consolidating the tentative, exploratory bond established at the turn of the century. It is to this sequence of events in the developing relationship that I now turn.

Merlin, as the acting governor-general, dispatched Bamba to Trarza in the company of Shaikhuna, the son-in-law and representative of Sidiyya Baba. Shaikhuna had been with Bamba during most of the months in Senegal and was present for the critical conversations between marabout and administration in Saint-Louis. In the letter that Shaikhuna transmitted to Baba, Merlin explained that he had told Bamba the reason for the second arrest—the refusal to restrain his disciples and to come to Saint-Louis. The threat of permanent return to Gabon was still present, but since Bamba had not resisted arrest, he could be treated less harshly than in 1895. The administrator then continued with his requests to his friend:

> I thus decided that Amadu Bamba would be entrusted to you for placement in one of your zawiyas. In that way he can consecrate himself entirely to the service of God and spend his time in prayer. You will give him counsel drawing on your deep religious commitment and experience. You will prevent him from communicating with the people of Baol and Senegal who could trouble his time of reflection and inspire him with the same ideas that have led to his exile before. You will remind him that it is because of you especially that I have shown mercy and generosity toward him.[54]

Baba was preoccupied by the "pacification" of Mauritania and not able to carry through on all of Merlin's fronts.[55] The period of residence in Trarza (1903–7) nonetheless played a key role in the consolidation of the relationships between Bamba, Baba, and the administration. Members of the Sidiyya family and entourage interacted a great deal with their guest. Relations between Baba and Bamba and their respective cohorts remained cordial, and would endure long after Bamba's return to Baol. The Murids were already sending gifts to the Sidiyya, and this tradition continued through the twentieth century.

Bamba did remain in correspondence with his followers and received many of them in Trarza. Murid sources are careful to indicate that Bamba made a strong impression of learning and saintliness on his hosts; he was not the rapt pupil that the colonial authorities might have wished him to be.[56] But this should not obscure the "lessons" that were undoubtedly absorbed—including the French determination to control Mauritania, the last "frontier" of West Africa.

In 1907, Bamba communicated to Administrator Théveniaut his desire to return to Senegal.[57] He was allowed to move to Chéyène in Jolof, under the surveillance of two administrators: the French commandant at Louga and Buna Ndiaye, the most successful and loyal of Merlin's cohort of chiefs.[58] The stream of followers who visited the marabout at the new site persuaded the authorities, were persuasion still needed, of the multifaceted symbolic capital of their detainee. The pressure to bring Bamba back to Baol continued from many quarters. Shaikh Ibra Fall wrote a pleading letter to the lieutenant governor in Saint-Louis in early 1909:

> On this matter which I am submitting to you, I have already asked MM Descemet and Carpot to act on my behalf. I now beg you directly to liberate Shaikh Amadu Bamba, our guide in the spiritual life. It will be a gesture of mercy that will never disappear from our hearts. For fourteen years he has been in the hands of the French because of the false rumors circulated against him. It has never occurred to him to break the laws of the French.[59]

It was in late 1910, during this third exile, that Bamba wrote a long letter to his followers. The context was Ma El Ainin's struggle against the French in Mauritania and Morocco. It is likely that the administration suggested to Bamba that he make the declaration, and it may have been part of an arrangement for the eventual return to Baol. In any case, Bamba agreed for the first time to express public praise for the French and their attitude toward the practice of Islam.[60]

His letter picked up on the main themes already articulated in the declarations of his *zwaya* contemporaries, Sidiyya Baba and Saad Buh. He began:

> After realizing the situation of the French government and what it comports of justice, benevolence, and power . . . and convinced that no people, however powerful, can rival the French government or oppose it, unless they be blinded by their ignorance . . . [and unable] to distinguish between the smallest ant and the elephant, between night and day, I have decided to give . . . some advice to my Muslim brothers in order that they not be drawn into wars.

Bamba went on to say that, since Muslims were not in a position of strength and since no universally recognized Muslim leader existed to declare jihad, the believer should reject that course of action. Muhammad had lived in peace with Christians and other nonbelievers, made pacts with them, and exhorted his followers to have patience.

The Murid founder then moved to an even more positive affirmation of the colonial regime:

> The French government, thanks to God, has not opposed the profession of
> faith but on the contrary has been friendly toward Muslims and encouraged
> them to practice [their religion]. We have noted that in many of the lands of
> the blacks that, thanks to French occupation, the inhabitants who, far from
> being Muslim, were pillagers, living at the expense of travelers and the weak,
> have changed to become calm and peaceful and that now, among them, the
> sheep and the jackals march together.

Bamba mentioned the improved communications that had allowed Islam to spread. He declared, perhaps tongue-in-cheek, that throughout his ordeal of exile he could not complain of French conduct toward him: "The truth is that I am sincerely attached to the French and always satisfied to live in the place in their land which they will designate for me, knowing how happy are those that live with them and in peace." Bamba concluded with a special exhortation to his Saharan brothers to reject the violence that had characterized their land and submit to the French.[61] This strong statement certainly played a role in the return to Baol and the consolidation of a relationship of accommodation with the founder of the Murid order.

EXPANDING THE RELATIONSHIP OF ACCOMMODATION

The year 1912 marked the return of Bamba to his native Baol. In some respects the surveillance was even closer—confinement to his compound in Diourbel. The keeper was now Jean-Baptiste Théveniaut, who had worked with Baba and Saad Buh. Théveniaut completed his service at Boutilimit in 1907 and became the administrator in Diourbel in the following year, probably to assess the situation and prepare for Bamba's return.[62] This suggests that the French had anticipated the return of the Murid founder to the peanut basin and wanted to assure proper monitoring, by a trusted official, when that time came. Who better than a former military officer, member of the Coppolani team, and confidante of the zwaya marabouts?

But in the very same year, Théveniaut's authoritarian manner ran afoul of the accommodation that the French and Murids had been building for some time. The administrator wanted to put Shaikh Anta in prison and intensify the surveillance of Bamba, because both opposed the establishment of a government agricultural cooperative in Baol. Governor-general Ponty warned the lieutenant governor not to take any action that would create martyrs or jeopardize the long-established bond:

> As to the measures suggested by M. Théveniaut . . . they do not seem wise. They are perhaps energetic and certainly severe, but I have always thought that our policy toward the native Muslims should reflect more nuance and tact than severity, especially when it concerns our policy toward a Muslim group with numerous followers. We must not, above all, forget that Amadu Bamba is a pupil of Shaikh Sidiyya [Baba], the most revered of chiefs among the Moors. Shaikh Sidiyya was the prime mover of our action north of Senegal, the pivot of the policy of my predecessor and of myself in Mauritania. The Murid sect was launched in Senegal by Amadu Bamba, and Murid means the "disciple of the faith." This is to say that Amadu Bamba still submits to the great authority of Shaikh Sidiyya, the most devoted artisan of our influence beyond Senegal.[63]

Ponty's patronizing view of Murid Islam cannot conceal the concrete interests in the bond with community.[64] Théveniaut was soon relieved of his post.

The French were now prepared to acknowledge publicly the positive relations between movement and government, and between Bamba and the administrators. In 1913, the governor of Senegal wrote:

> Our relations with Amadu Bamba have entered a normal path, and the attitude of the Murids has in general been very proper. One can therefore hope that the chiefs of this powerful organism, who are already waiting for the division [of the estate] at the death of Bamba, will not attempt to stray from the economic path in which they certainly make their contribution to the development of the country.[65]

A "normal" path meant that the Murids paid their taxes on time and provided recruits for the colonial army. Mamadu Mustapha, the oldest son of Bamba, was hosted by the administration in Saint-Louis. These observations come from Paul Marty, the Islamic "expert" from North Africa in the tradition of Coppolani and Arnaud. He completed the draft of his report on the order in the same year, 1913.[66] His study of the leaders and followers gave the regime greater confidence about its position than ever before.[67]

World War I provided a unique opportunity for strengthening the relationship. The French needed all of the resources of the empire to survive the German offensive. They sought the support of Bamba to sustain their cause, and the Murid leader rose to the task. He continued his declarations of loyalty. Along with Shaikh Anta and Shaikh Ibra Fall, he encouraged Murids to enlist in the army and he was even awarded the cross of the Legion of Honor for his efforts.[68] The valor of the Murid soldiers, and the inspiration that they received from Bamba's poetry, were visible in the terrible fighting in the Dardanelles campaign of 1915:

> Several hundred Murids . . . assemble in the evening, pray or chant hymns to the accompaniment of the tam-tam, say their prayers, and explode in frenetic dances. Despite the insistence on the "fanaticism" and strange religious behavior, these activities did not worry the officers in charge of the black units preparing for the Dardanelles campaign because these *tirailleurs* had demonstrated "their discipline, intelligence, zeal, level-headedness, and resistance to fatigue.[69]

By this time, the administrators were attending Murid ceremonies and communicating with the leadership on a more frequent and open basis.[70]

Immediately after the war, the order and the administration had another striking opportunity to expand the collaboration. The railroad from Thiès to Bamako was completed and it opened up new areas for peanut cultivation to the east. Bamba, his family, and leading disciples encouraged Murids to spread in this direction. Many of the younger leaders took their followings, founded new villages, and increased peanut production. In the process they often evicted the pastoralists who had dominated the region heretofore.[71]

At the same time, the surveillance continued. Bamba's requests to settle in Touba were refused. Even his requests to build a mosque that would also serve as his own tomb were refused for several years. After he made a contribution of 500,000 francs to support the French government in 1925, permission was granted and disciples began to quarry the stone. Work was soon halted with the discovery of the diversion of funds, about 1 million francs, to a French administrator and some members of the Mbacke family.[72] By this time, Bamba's health was rapidly declining, and he died in 1927. Within a week, a Murid council chose his eldest son, Mamadu Mustafa, to be his *khalife*, or successor.[73]

The confinement of Bamba contrasted with the freedom of movement of Shaikh Anta, Shaikh Ibra Fall, Mamadu Mustapha, and the other core leadership. They accumulated great wealth and considerable followers and maintained their ties with elected officials and the administration. The two "shaikhs" were the most effective intermediaries, honing the skills that they had developed from the time of Bamba's first exile.

Shaikh Anta was the most active in political terms. He maintained ties with the administration, French-dominated commerce and the Senegalese deputies. He supported Blaise Diagne for a number of years and then shifted his support to Galandou Diouf. In the Murid "tradition" he provided significant contributions to the campaigns in exchange for intervention in favor of his interests and those of the Murids. The Diourbel administrator in 1926 described him in this way:

> Shaikh Anta Mbacke impresses by his imposing stature. Businessman, active
> intelligence, frequent visitor to the land registry, this noteworthy man is con-
> stantly looking for new deals and challenges. Advantageous locations and
> long-range possibilities, nothing frightens him. One can be sure, when with
> a nonchalant air he proposes something banal, that he has already envisioned
> profitable results. I confess that I have no confidence in him.[74]

It was Shaikh Anta, even more than Shaikh Ibra, who used his wealth, social capital, and prestige to manipulate the institutions of civil society. It was because of this entrepreneurship that in the 1910s and 1920s the French began to monitor Shaikh Anta as closely as Bamba. After the founder's death, the "businessman" continued to scheme against Mustapha and to support Galandou Diouf against the establishment figure that Blaise Diagne had become. He incurred the wrath of the administration, who deported him to Soudan from 1930 to 1934.[75]

The surveillance of the Murids was always more severe than the monitoring of the other movements described in this work. But eventually it also became a kind of reflex, the product of a very significant investment over the decades in the fortunes of the order—and those of the colonial economy itself.

——

THE FRENCH ADMINISTRATION HELPED to create an enduring and "productive" colonial order in the Senegalo-Mauritanian zone by learning to work with the Muslim authorities and their growing constituencies in the early twentieth century. The most important of these bonds with Muslim leaders was with the Murids, because of their cohesion and central location in the expanding peanut basin.

The example of less formal cooperation had been prepared with Bu Kunta and Saad Buh in the late nineteenth century. The example of formal cooperation was provided in the tight bond with Sidiyya Baba, who intervened not only for the continued "pacification" of Mauritania but to work out terms of accommodation with Bamba. With the return from Gabon and the nearby exiles to Trarza and Jolof, the administration intensified the practice that combined close surveillance of the founder and intensive collaboration with his brothers and disciples.

Bamba, like the other grands marabouts discussed in this work, bore no stigma for the excesses of the anciens régimes and had no official role in the new colonial order. He could justify cooperation in terms of the old order's violence, which affected Muslims as much as non-Muslims, and the weakness of Muslim societies relative to the new regime. He saw the opportunity for islamization provided by the new conditions of stability when the colonial authorities controlled the supply of firearms, clamped down on raiding, and reduced the resources on which indigenous chiefs and warriors had relied upon. He came to understand that the administration would not interfere with the practice of Islam; indeed, the colonial authorities might even encourage it, once they felt a stronger measure of control.

Bamba had a more difficult adaptation to this new reality than his contemporaries. This was partly because of his constituency. His crown soldiers, slaves, and former slaves required more adjustment and aroused more suspicion for the colonial authorities—in contrast, for example, to the urban and commercial Muslims who loomed so large in the entourage of Malik Sy. Bamba was also slower to realize the increased capacity of the emerging new regime and its deep investment in an apparatus of chiefs. The colonial authorities were gathering strength and were able to reach much further into the spaces where marabouts and their communities had found autonomy in the past. They were also gathering knowledge, much of it from unreliable and anxious sources, and this knowledge sometimes propelled them to take precipitous action.

But Bamba survived both the effort to break his spirit in Gabon and the severity of years of exile. He saw that his movement had survived in his absence. These realizations, along with the pedagogy that he developed and refined over the years, gave him a special symbolic capital, a kind of protection from accusations of collaboration. The protection carried over to his brothers, disciples, and followers.[76] It enabled them to accumulate social and economic capital with relative freedom, even as early as Bamba's first exile.

For the administration, the Murids offered a major solution to problems of social control. Former warriors could be demobilized; former slaves could be incorporated as followers and clients. The labor power of both groups could be turned to the growing of peanuts, millet, and other work. Bu Kunta had shown the way. Malik Sy had expanded on his example in the older peanut basin. Saad Buh and Sidiyya Baba knew how to tap into the agricultural revenues of Senegal. But it was Bamba and the Murids who completed the transformation of the old disintegrating regime into the new colonial order.

Conclusion

THIS BOOK INCLUDES BOTH THEMATIC and biographical chapters, and often they have run across the same period and space. There has necessarily been some repetition about events, institutions, and personalities. I hope that the work also has woven a convincing argument about the conditions of the emergence of a new generation of Muslim leaders and their constituencies, the difficulties of an administration bent on domination, and the patterns of accommodation that the various parties forged. The paths sketched here converge in significant ways. At the same time they have different textures, timing, and turning points.

BASES OF ACCOMMODATION

The sources available for this work are not passive documents waiting for collation and examination. They are the product of diverse interests across a range of time and contestation. Numerous agents, African and European, appear again and again. They were often in positions to translate their "knowledge" into a certain kind of "power," regardless of where they sat in colonial or indigenous hierarchies.

The materials are full of lacunae, distortions, stereotypes, telescoping, and rereading. But with careful contextualization and analysis, a study can yield rich description and solid interpretation. It is possible to identify regular informants, the hierarchies along which information flowed, the constellations of interest, the traditions transmitted through the Direction of Political Affairs, or the clichés and discourses designed for particular audiences. It is easier to do this for the abundant French archival record, and some of the early secondary sources written around this record, such as those of Paul Marty. But the analysis of oral tradition and Arabic documentation can yield similar insight. It is also critical to remember the "oral" and "aural" dimensions of the archival record—the observations and instructions that were not written but that often determined action.

The concept of repertory is useful in this analysis. In taking the example of Martial Merlin's brief to the governor and the *conseil privé* for the deportation of Amadu Bamba in 1895, one could say that the director of political affairs was wedded to stereotypes about the Tijaniyya, fanaticism, and danger to the fledgling colonial regime. But it is certainly more useful to see that Merlin was "working" his audience, both the one in Saint-Louis and another in Paris, by drawing from a repertory of images to achieve the desired effect: approving deportation with a minimum of debate and reassuring the fledgling apparatus of colonial rule.

The French administration, in its local and metropolitan manifestations, did not face an easy task in bringing the diverse constituencies of Senegal and Mauritania under its control. They faced opposition on several fronts—from the indigenous societies, the larger francophile community, and within their own ranks. Institutions like the judiciary interfered with the military command system. Officials in Paris imposed restrictions on cost and procedure. Astute governors and political directors learned how to avoid scrutiny, package information, advance incrementally, provoke the casus belli, and justify the fait accompli. But all of this required shrewd planning, and some administrators were not up to the task.

The societies that I include in the "Senegalo-Mauritanian zone" were all Muslim. They were in the process of becoming more fully and determinedly Muslim in the late nineteenth century, and were recognized as Muslim in the operative French ethnography. A few perspicacious administrators saw the need for France to develop a reputation as a "Muslim power" in order to dominate this space. France must be capable, and be seen to be capable, of controlling but also respecting the practice of a faith with a long history of opposition to Christianity and European domination. Beginning with distinctions between "good" and "bad" Muslims, governors and political affairs directors developed institutions and cultivated prestigious allies from their headquarters in Saint-Louis. They helped the town to become a center of Islamic learning and Sufi affiliation. They enlisted marabouts from the interior, such as Saad Buh of the prestigious Fadiliyya network, to soften the angles of expansion. In the process, these administrators helped themselves to a kind of social and symbolic capital as a "Muslim power."

The intensifying drive to occupy northwestern Africa — the desert labeled Mauritania and the august old kingdom of Morocco — pushed the French further down the road of Islamic practice. Mauritania had to be conquered from the south, from areas under French control, and to be incorporated into the French West African Federation. But it was also a stepping-stone to Morocco. It was an area of nomadic peoples who presented new problems for European control. The *bidan* regarded themselves as Arab and "natural Muslims," obviously superior to the *sudan* to the south. The French joined in that judgment and constructed Mauritania around *bidan* identity.

To provide leadership in the task, they brought in "Maghribi experts" in Islam, Arabic, and nomadic societies. The experts helped design enduring relationships with a new generation of Muslim scholars and Sufis, in contrast to the older ties with the political aristocracies. Two brilliant men, each in a sense desperate about his career, pushed this process further and faster than many might have wished. One was Coppolani, who imported himself from Algeria and France with his credentials as Islamicist and negotiator. The other was Sidiyya Baba, immediate friend, colleague, and co-architect in the "pacification" program. Baba was the equivalent of the "Bu El Mogdads" in an earlier era, but as a *bidan* cleric from a prestigious tradition he moved into a relationship of trust that was possible only for "Arabs" and "whites." The mutual admiration between Baba and Coppolani carried over to Gouraud and then Marty, who codified France's credentials as a Muslim power and consolidated the religious ethnography of *Islam maure* and *Islam noir*.

The administration had other problems, and opportunities, on its hands. Precisely at the time that the governors and the Ministry of the Navy and Colonies determined to dominate subjects in French West Africa, the Third Republic created institutions of citizenship in the four communes of Senegal. French, métis, and African inhabitants became avid practitioners of electoral campaigns, machine politics, budget negotiation, and public relations — including publicity in local and French newspapers. This was particularly true in Saint-Louis, the largest of the towns, the seat of the administration and the most politically sophisticated community.

Republican practices were hardly what a militarily minded administration wanted as it drove its legions into Senegal, Soudan, and Mauritania. The officials could not eliminate electoral institutions, but they could weaken them with selective interference. They set about this process with a certain vengeance, directed particularly against the hydra-headed Devès firm. By the end of the period, they had succeeded in eliminating or controlling every republican creation but one—the post of deputy.[1] The deputyship remained the one alternative appeal for Muslims in the Senegalo-Mauritanian zone, and the Murids learned to use it with a vengeance of their own. The Muslim citizens of Saint-Louis and the other communes were less knowledgeable and more reluctant to jump into the republican cauldron. But in time they became astute practitioners of electoral politics, at a time when the position of deputy was clearly the prize. They applauded the 1914 election of Blaise Diagne as the first African representative to the French National Assembly, and they dominated this part of the political arena from that time forward.

Well before this, they had learned how to exercise their influence as a Muslim community on the mayor, the city council, the General Council, and the administration, and to combine Muslim identity with French citizenship. As merchants they took this model of compatibility to the chiefs, marabouts, and inhabitants of the interior. In their various places of insertion, along the river, in the peanut basin, or at the edge of the Sahara, they developed enduring relationships and accumulated economic, social, and symbolic capital. As "sons of Ndar" they became informal ambassadors for French hegemony. It would be hard to overestimate their contribution to the seating of colonial rule.

COMPARATIVE BIOGRAPHIES

The documentation on marabouts and Muslim movements has usually taken a biographical form, and the sequences recounted in chapters 7 to 11 are no exception. The contemporary archival accounts, the Arabic documentation, and the oral tradition feature the exploits of famous men. The secondary literature follows in the same furrow. By careful collection, arrangement, and juxtaposition, one can see beyond biography and hagiography to the texture of constituencies, the conditions and causes of decisions, and the shape of the patterns of accommodation.

The marabout story is ultimately about the development of different forms of capital and their "interconvertibility" amid the dramatic changes of the late nineteenth and early twentieth century. The grands marabouts by definition succeeded across the whole range of forms. They spent their early years accumulating symbolic capital, often in the traditional ways of sitting at the feet of scholars and Sufi masters. Gradually they became practitioners of the arts of

arbitration, organization, teaching, composition, initiation, and other expectations of religious leaders. With the partial exception of Malik Sy, they benefited
from a significant inherited component, an anticipation that they would follow
in the tradition of the father, or lineage. These strands of symbolic capital created the foundations for a community.

At crucial junctures, the marabouts made decisions about how to translate
symbolic capital into economic and social forms. Social capital included strategic marriages, both inside and outside of the family, as well as the skills to work
with the emerging colonial order and deliver benefits to constituents. The marabouts learned how to shape the thinking of the French about local Muslim
societies and their relationship with the emerging colonial order. They were the
custodians of the institutions of Muslim civil society—institutions of learning
and Sufi orders—that survived the transition to European rule. Their prestige
grew at the expense of the old aristocracies, whose symbolic capital declined
with their failure to maintain conditions for the production and reproduction
of the social order. By the early twentieth century, the descendants of these
aristocracies, often now in the position of colonial chiefs, were seeking to reinforce themselves by marriage and other forms of alliance with the maraboutic
families.

By the twentieth century, the grands marabouts risked little of their symbolic capital in public statements of support for the French. The colonial regime
was a fact of life, and the marabouts benefited from the order that it imposed.
The authorities, for their part, recognized the immense value of fatwas and *nasi-
has* for their image as a "Muslim power," and gave them the broadest circulation
possible.[2] The content was essentially the same. Each statement emphasized the
anarchy and violence of the immediate past, including the risks posed for Muslims. The Muslim community was weak, relative to the Europeans, and no one
was in a position to mobilize the faithful for resistance. The French had shown
a benevolent neutrality to the faith. Indeed, they had provided support for worship, learning, and pilgrimage. The security of colonial rule provided conditions in which Islam could spread and Muslim societies could prosper. In my
judgment, such statements did not compromise the autonomy of the Muslim
communities, nor make the marabouts "organic intellectuals" of the colonial
regime—with the possible exception of Sidiyya Baba.

Saad Buh developed his ties with the French some two decades earlier
than the other grands marabouts. Not yet twenty years old, his symbolic capital
scarcely established, he made the bold move from the homestead in the Hodh
to the confines of southwestern Mauritania. In his new setting, he consolidated

his credentials in a kind of religious "transhumance," moving between his tents and disciples scattered across the Senegalo-Mauritanian zone. By using public recitation and multiple affiliation, by encouraging his kinsmen to study with him and marry into his family, he became the effective hub of the Fadiliyya network. He crossed the *bidan/sudan* divide better than any of the other grands marabouts, well before the crystallization into *Islam maure* and *Islam noir*.

Saad Buh integrated Saint-Louis into his travels early on. He opened the way for other clerics from the interior to sojourn or reside in the colonial capital. He gave his support to French exploration, diplomacy, and occupation of territory in the late nineteenth century. In exchange, he gained permission for annual collection tours and developed them into a fine art and source of sustenance for his home community. The tours went with increasing regularity into the peanut basin and integrated rail transport into their rhythm. Saad Buh also became a source of information and interpretation for the French, by his contact with governors, political affairs directors, explorers, and military men, by the materials that he supplied to Théveniaut, or again by the long document that he wrote in 1906 about the misfortunes of jihad and the benefits of cooperation. For indigenous Muslims, Saad Buh provided counsels of patience, intercession on specific needs, and the appeal of multiple and changing Sufi affiliations in a time of great turbulence. He developed a range of clients — and a flow of gifts — from the top to the bottom of the social ladder. He encouraged the spread of the Tijaniyya as well as the Qadiriyya, and this produced conflict with Umarians, who asserted exclusivity of affiliation and their own primacy.

As a *bidan* cleric, Saad Buh was prepared for the conquest of *sudan* Senegal, but he was very reluctant to see that impulse extended into his own territory, the "real" Dar al-Islam. He nonetheless adjusted to the French determination to create and conquer Mauritania. Already labeled the marabout chrétien after the Blanchet Mission of 1900, he struggled to maintain his symbolic capital in the face of two challenges — the frontal one of resistance formulated by his older brother Ma El Ainin, and the more subtle campaigns organized by his fellow "pacificist" Sidiyya Baba. Baba's insinuations, especially to the great codifier Marty, have distorted much of the record about the Fadiliyya leader.

The Sidiyya leader emerged later and more abruptly into the consciousness of the administration. He was forced out of the tradition of distance from European power by the dramatically altered circumstances of Trarza at the end of the century. Desperate to protect his constituency and property, desperate to survive, Baba probed the Saint-Louis milieu and then leapt into alliance with

Coppolani. Of all the grands marabouts, he took the boldest risk of symbolic capital.

Baba persevered across the assassination of his friend, sharp accusations of betraying Islam, and the more subtle manuverings of the Devès. He faced a stronger charge of collaboration with the "infidel" than Saad Buh. He worked with a succession of governors-general and commissioners to produce the conquest of the southern and central portions of Mauritania. At times, Baba seemed to be prodding the French to act. In the process, he pressed them to demonstrate their "Muslim power," and he presented himself, or let himself be presented, as the "most venerated religious leader of French West Africa."

Baba quickly acquired, from a grateful administration, a considerable economic capital through gifts, stipends, confiscations, collection tours, and support for his claims to land and palm groves. Boutilimit received a clinic, schools, and other investments. Sidiyya collection tours were rarely questioned in the ways that Saad Buh's were. Baba developed social capital in the form of unparalleled networks of access into the colonial apparatus. He evoked the strongest sense of collaboration in the colonial authorities, and the deepest sense of obligation to his successors. The openness of the alliance does not appear to have damaged his symbolic capital during his lifetime, but it did pose a problem for subsequent generations.

Of all the mediators and disseminators of knowledge mentioned in this volume, the Sidiyya leader had the greatest impact on the interpretation of Islam in the Sengalo-Mauritanian zone. His bond with the French began in a modest way with Dudu Seck during the first visit to Ndar. It blossomed with Coppolani: only months after their first meeting, Baba produced the fatwa that justified the "pacification." The relationship continued with soldiers and administrators such as Arnaud, Frèrejean, Théveniaut, Montané-Capdebosc, Gouraud, and Gaden, all persons of considerable influence in terms of documentation and power. The impact reached its culmination through Paul Marty, who quickly fell under the same spell of intellect, curiosity, and self-interest as his predecessors. Marty found how closely his views of Islam, civilization, and ethnicity corresponded to those of Baba, and he wrote them into the volumes produced out of the Muslim Affairs Bureau.

Malik Sy and his "path" emerged with the same slow pace as Saad Buh. He moved with almost imperceptible ease in and out of Saint-Louis, because his constituency came precisely from the mobile merchants who were also upwardly mobile Muslims. They brought him in, contributed to his zawiya, mosque, and pilgrimage, and basked in the glow of learning, tolerance, and wise counsel that

he offered them and their town. Saad Buh was the pioneer marabout who so-
journed annually in Saint-Louis, but it was Malik Sy who made Ndar into a permanent anchor of his community.

"Hajj" Malik, however, faced a significant problem of reconfiguring symbolic capital. It was not a case of reworking a dispersed network such as the
Fadiliyya, nor remaking a tradition of distance from European power expressed
in the figure of Sidiyya al-Kabir. In order to create stability for his constituents
in the emerging colonial order, Malik had to change a tradition of opposition
to European rule: the heritage that Umar had stamped upon the West African
Tijaniyya in the minds of many, African and French. The reconfiguring took
decades. He diversified his affiliations, Sufi and scholarly, along the Tijani path-
ways, and strengthened his ties with the "mother" zawiya of Fez. He married
into well-placed Saint-Louis and aristocratic families. He was the only grand
marabout to perform the pilgrimage, and this made a significant contribution
to his symbolic capital. He may have construed his "Ndiarndé" period as a hijra
from engagement, and a prelude to reengagement. He certainly used the time
in Ndiarndé to forge a pedagogy and develop a mission to people that he regarded as less islamized, such as the inhabitants of Dakar and the Cape Verde
peninsula. Over time, he put a new face on his version of the order.

The transformation of the Tijaniyya and the character of the Saint-Louis
constituency explain, to a significant degree, Malik's slow and surreptitious
route into the imagination of the administration. It is as though, one fine day
in 1910, the French awoke to the implications of the "treasure" in Tivaouane.
Malik Sy had carefully crafted his pedagogy and sphere of influence over the
years. By the time the French took notice, they could appreciate his symbolic
and social capital and their value for French control of Senegal.

By comparison with these paths, the Murid road seems bumpy and circui-
tous. Amadu Bamba started with a traditional Muslim hesitation about the exercise of power and deepened it into disdain. He fled the troubles of Cayor in
the 1880s, performing a geographical and internal hijra into the relative autonomy of eastern Baol. In the process, he took with him a diverse constituency of
believers and nonbelievers, of students, drinkers, warriors, and slaves, and began to fashion them into a a new kind of Muslim community. He seems to have
patterned his career around the life of the Prophet in ways that do not resonate
in the careers of the other marabouts. It was in these conditions that he consolidated a broad symbolic capital of genealogy, learning, quest, wisdom, composition, and personal courage.

More emphatically than the other movements, the Murid community was built around distance from the centers of power—any power. It thus ran afoul of an aggressive and anxious administration bent on controlling the entire peanut basin through a hierarchy of administrators and chiefs. This meant inevitable conflict and the perhaps inevitable deportation. At the same time, the deportation provided political cover for the administration to work out relations of accommodation with the brothers and disciples of the founder. On the Murid side, Ibra Fati, Shaikh Anta, and Shaikh Ibra could use the symbolic capital of their leader, now a martyr in far-away Gabon, to develop their own social and economic capital in Baol and Cayor, and even Saint-Louis, Rufisque, and Dakar.[3]

French action created a more "complex path of accommodation" (as is reflected in the title for chapter 11), but it also ensured a more durable "division of labor" of capital. Ibra Fati and Shaikh Anta might have their conflicts, but no one was in conflict with the founder. Bamba was free amid his confinement. He could pursue his prayer, poetry, pedagogy, and admonitions to a grateful and growing following. Unlike the other grands marabouts, this generous man did not need to develop the social capital of navigating the colonial bureaucracy. The lieutenants, with their own skills, mastered that agenda.

The Umarians represent an intriguing foil to the paths of accommodation. In their fragmented state they could not possibly reconfigure what was left of their symbolic capital, in the manner of Malik Sy. Most of the Tal were chiefs, not marabouts.[4] Their founder lived at almost the last possible moment when it was possible to wage jihad and carve out an Islamic state without a devastating confrontation with European forces. Umar chose the only workable formula for his enterprise: recruitment in the west, in the sphere of French influence, to wage war in the east, against the Bamana states. He took a critique of power that Sidiyya al-Kabir or Amadu Bamba might have formulated, attached it to "pagan" courts, and sought to destroy them by force. He was so successful, in the military and recruiting sense, that he left a set of Futanke and Fulbe communities scattered across French Soudan and Guinea.

But back in the Senegalo-Mauritanian zone, his example was impossible to imitate. The reformers who followed his model failed miserably, often against European-led armies able to marshal overwhelming force at a given place and time. The Umarian message of jihad and hijra resonated among many, but was applied by few. Alfa Hashimi was the "perfect" example, since he reached the holy and European-free city of Medina. Albury Ndiaye, tutored by Ma Ba early in his career and companion of Amadu Sheku in his latter days, was the best-known example in the Senegalo-Mauritanian zone. But the model offered little comfort for the vast majority, and no food for thought of the grands marabouts who had grown up in radically different conditions from Umar.

The inheritors of the Umarian mantle did not help matters with their internal struggles. But their legacy and community were not about to disappear in French West Africa. Once the militant and courageous achievements were recognized by friend and foe, African and European, once they were public in packages such as the *Qaçida* of Mohammadou Aliou Tyam, Umarians could find a way to public accommodation. During the early decades of colonial rule, they needed intermediaries and counselors such as Amadu Mokhtar Sakho at Boghé and "Hajj" Malik at Tivaouane. In the next generation they acquired a grand marabout of their own, a Tal of great stature, with a West African rather than Senegalo-Mauritanian field of operation. Seydu Nuru Tal was a "fitting" successor to Umar; he wore the prestige of jihad alongside the medals of the French empire, with equal pride.

OTHER FRAMEWORKS OF INTERPRETATION

In a recent article on the "Colonial Caliphate" of northern Nigeria,[5] Murray Last suggests that the Hausa-Fulani inheritors of the Sokoto regime quickly found a commonality of interest with their British overlords. Despite the abrupt and often bloody conquest and the massive hijra that Caliph Attahiru led in 1903, the two sets of elites worked out a compromise that kept the old apparatus of governance in place and allowed Europeans to impose their ideas of civilization.

One might be tempted to apply such a construction to the Senegalo-Mauritanian zone. Islamicists such as Coppolani and Arnaud advocated the creation of a kind of official Muslim clergy, and Sidiyya Baba might be taken as an example of this.[6] The Tijaniyya of Tivaouane and the Muridiyya certainly became fixtures in the landscape of the peanut basin, and they were widely consulted about a range of policies. But otherwise the analogy does not work. The marabouts and their disciples, with rare exceptions, were never part of the administrative hierarchy. With the partial exception of the Sidiyya, they maintained their autonomy, a certain social distance from the colonial regime.[7] Their orders were new, the product of agency and conditions of the late nineteenth century. The marabouts might have Qadiriyya or Tijaniyya antecedents, and significant genealogical credentials, but they represented no precolonial state, no Sokoto caliphate. The only thing remotely similar was the Umarian regime for a brief moment in the 1860s.[8] By the end of the century, it existed only in bits and pieces, and in memory. The French used it as a foil to justify conquest. They were not about to use its descendants in any capacity except as local leaders. At least not for a generation—not until Seydu Nuru Tal.

If the colonial caliphate analogy fails, the conception of the new orders as a form of civil society has more resonance.[9] The strong métis community had all but disappeared by 1920, and with it the strong General Council. The deputyship remained a pole of attraction for Senegalese seeking to affect the practice of the administration. But the orders were now more effective instruments, especially those of Touba and Tivaouane. They had significant numbers, recognized leadership, considerable wealth, and effective social networks. Normally they worked in conjunction with the colonial administration of Senegal and the independent regimes that succeeded it. But in recent decades, and particularly in the Murid case, they have exercised leverage, refused policies, and even supported opposition candidates.

The networks of Saad Buh and Sidiyya Baba have had more difficulty in functioning as "civil society" in Mauritania. Their relations with the colonial administration were too close, their dependence on permissions for collection tours too great, and their sphere of autonomy less clearly demarcated. The Islamic Republic of Mauritania has moved away from the southern, French and Trarza-centered identity of the colonial territory, and this shift has diminished the influence of these families.

The emergence of "brotherhoods" in the Senegalo-Mauritanian zone at the turn of the last century, sometimes called a "maraboutic industry," has too often been confused with the fortunes of Muslim societies in francophone West Africa as a whole.[10] This is a serious error. The other areas had no long experience with French merchants, administrators, and soldiers. They had no republican institutions or efforts to develop an Islamic practice or policy. The most that can be said about their parallels to the Senegalo-Mauritanian zone is that they were also subjected to *fiches de renseignement* and pilgrimage control, and they were also studied by Paul Marty and ushered into the category of *Islam noir*.

In summary, I conclude by asserting what I said at the beginning: northwestern Senegal and southwestern Mauritania constitute a meaningful zone, and 1880 to 1920 was a decisive period. From coastal and river bases, the French conquered Senegal; from the river valley and with Trarza allies they occupied Mauritania. That occupation forced the final development of Islamic practice in which the grands marabouts and their orders became allies of the colonial administrations of the two territories. Saint-Louis lost its West African preeminence

to Dakar, but it remained the headquarters for both territorial administrations.
The marabouts and their disciples continued to move across the whole zone to
provide counsel, collect gifts, and sustain their influence. With the death of the
founders between 1917 and 1927, the crystallization of the categories of *Islam
maure* and *Islam noir,* and the emergence of Seydu Nuru Tal as the grand marabout
for French West Africa, the accommodation was complete.

Notes

Introduction

1. Huntington, *The Clash of Civilizations and the Remaking of the World Order,* New York, 1996.

2. James Searing is critical of the way the precolonial literature abruptly stops with conquest, accentuating what was not such a sharp divide. "Accommodation and Resistance: Chiefs, Muslim Leaders, and Politicians in Colonial Senegal, 1890-1934," Ph.D. diss., Princeton University, 1985, 8 ff.

3. I have not dealt with Abdullay Niasse and the branch of the Tijaniyya that he formed out of Kaolack at the southern edge of the Senegalo-Mauritanian zone. Niasse did not become a significant factor with a considerable following until late in the period; it was his son Ibrahima who began to play a much broader role in the 1930s. See Christopher Gray, "The Rise of the Niassène Tijaniyya, 1875 to the Present," *ISASS* 2 (1988).

4. The deaths of the four founders constitute the end of a period in the history and historiography of the zone. Saad Buh died in 1917, Malik Sy in 1922, Sidiyya Baba in 1924, and Amadu Bamba in 1927. *Marabout*—derived from *murabit,* a Muslim spreading or defending Islam (cf. *Almoravid*)—has passed into general use in West and North Africa for a Muslim leader, often one with saintly credentials.

5. Chiefs, drawn mainly from the traditional aristocracies, were a vital part of the hierarchy, but they had interests of their own. The other element of the colonial picture consisted of the citizens of the communes, who were dominated by the political organizations of Blaise Diagne and his successors as deputies of Senegal to the French National Assembly.

6. For a short account of this, see Chris Harrison, *France and Islam in West Africa, 1860-1960* (Cambridge, U.K., 1988), pts. 2 and 3.

7. There are only two clear instances during my period of reformulating basic judgments about Muslim societies. The first came after the mobilization by Mamadu

Lamine Drame against the colonial authorities and their allies in 1886 in the Upper Senegal, a region that the French thought they knew and controlled. This lies outside of the Senegal-Mauritanian zone, but it reverberated through it because of the siege of Bakel in April of that year and the vast countermobilization made to eliminate Mamadu Lamine. See the treatment of this in chap. 6, and the judgment of "excessive tolerance" made by Faidherbe and recited by Merlin in 1895, in chap. 11 (n. 37). The second instance was the campaign of resistance mounted in Mauritania around the Qadiriyya leader Ma El Ainin, discussed particularly in chap. 4.

8. For a very useful interpretation of French actions and the knowledge upon which they were based, see Raymond Taylor, "Of Disciples and Sultans: Power, Authority, and Society in the Nineteenth-century Mauritanian Gebla," Ph.D. diss., University of Illinois, 1996, chaps. 5 and 6. For a similar situation of knowledge, power, manipulation, and "disinformation" in nineteenth-century North Africa, see Julia Clancy-Smith, *Rebel and Saint: Muslim Notables, Populist Protest, Colonial Encounters (Algeria and Tunisia, 1800–1914)* (Berkeley, Calif., 1994), 9–10 and passim.

9. For the increasing racism characteristic of French attitudes in the late nineteenth century, see William Cohen, *French Encounter with Africans* (Bloomington, Ind., 1980).

10. Here my definitions are close to those of Bourdieu. See Craig Calhoun, "Habitus, Field, and Capital: The Question of Historical Specificity," in Calhoun, ed., *Bourdieu: Critical Perspectives* (Chicago, 1993).

11. See, for example, the use of charisma in Donal Cruise O'Brien and Christian Coulon, eds., *Charisma and Brotherhood in African Islam* (Oxford, 1988).

12. See, for example, Christian Coulon, *Le Marabout et le Prince* (Paris, 1981); Jean Copans, *Les Marabouts de l'Arachide* (Paris, 1980); Donal Cruise O'Brien, *The Mourides of Senegal* (Oxford, 1971), and *Saints and Politicians* (Cambridge, U.K., 1975); and Cheikh Tidiane Sy, *La Confrérie sénégalaise des Mourides* (Paris, 1969).

13. I disagree with Ernest Gellner who, in *Conditions of Liberty: Civil Society and Its Rivals* (London, 1994), chap. 3, claims that Islam does not have "civil society."

14. See Walter Adamson, *Hegemony and Revolution: A Study of Antinio Gramsci's Political and Cultural Theory* (Berkeley, Calif., 1980), chap. 5.

15. I seek to avoid altogether the language of resistance and collaboration, which distorts the paths and the accommodation that Muslims—and the French—created in the late nineteenth and early twentieth centuries. For the sense in which the British and ruling classes of Hausaland forged a kind of "colonial caliphate" in which the sense of continuity with an Islam order could be maintained, see Murray Last, "The 'Colonial Caliphate' in Northern Nigeria," in David Robinson and Jean-Louis Triaud, eds., *Le Temps des Marabouts: Itinéraires et stratégies islamiques en Afrique occidentale française* (Paris, 1997).

16. Civil society and hegemony are rarely applied in colonial situations. The comment of Nicholas Dirks, in his reader *Colonialism and Culture* (Ann Arbor, Mich., 1992, 7), is typical of most of the thinking: "Hegemony is perhaps the wrong word to use for colonial power, since it implies not only consent but the political capacity to generate consent through the institutional spaces of civil society, notably absent in the colonial context." The republican institutions of the coastal communes present an opportunity to explore these concepts, which I do especially in chap. 5. The result is an obvious

modification of the distinction between domination and hegemony in Western Europe that Antonio Gramsci developed in his *Prison Notebooks.*

17. Bruce Berman and John Lonsdale, *Unhappy Valley: Conflict in Kenya and Africa,* book 1, *State and Class* (London, 1992), chaps. 4–7.

Chapter 1

1. Dakar was of course the capital of the French West African Federation. It became the capital of Senegal in 1960 just as it lost its jurisdiction over the other territories of the federation. In the 1950s, the outpost of Nouakchott was prepared to serve as the capital of an independent Mauritania. Nouakchott's location symbolized the very different orientation that the country has taken since independence. See Jean-Robert Pitte, *Nouakchott, capitale de la Mauritanie* (Paris, 1977).

2. The applicability of these corporate and economically embedded structures to other parts of francophone West Africa is extremely limited. This has often been forgotten by French administrators as well as recent scholars. See Jean-Louis Triaud, intro. to Robinson and Triaud, *Le Temps des Marabouts,* 22 ff.

3. Coppolani made contact with Black as well as Moorish leaders as he laid the plans for taking over Mauritania. Note his contacts, for example, with Amadu Moktar Sakho in Boghe and the significant infrastructure that the French placed in the Boghe area in the early years of the twentieth century. See Ibrahima Abou Sall, "Cerno Amadu Mukhtar Sakho, Qadi Supérieur de Boghe, 1905–1934," in Robinson and Triaud, *Le Temps des Marabouts.*

4. The most complete accounts deal with societies in Senegal. Abdoulaye Bara Diop (*La société wolof: Tradition et changement: Les systèmes d'inégalité et de domination,* Paris, 1981) gives a very useful analysis of Wolof society based on castes and orders. Paul Pelissier gives more of an overview in *Les paysans du Senegal: Les civilisations agraires du Cayor à la Casamance* (Saint-Yrieix, 1966), while Barry provides a synthesis in *La Sénégambie du XVe au XIXe siècle: Traite négrière, Islam, conquête coloniale* (Paris, 1988). Yaya Wane's *Les Toucouleur du Fouta Tooro, stratification sociale et structure familiale* (Dakar, 1969) is still the most complete look at the society of the middle valley, but an unpublished dissertation by Olivier Kyburz gives a fascinating picture of the way the social structures of Futa developed: "Les hierarchies sociales et leurs fondements idéologiques chez les *haalpulaar'en* (Sénégal)," thèse de docteur, de l'université de Paris 10, 1994. The best analysis of *bidan* society is Abdel Wedoud Ould Cheikh, "Nomadisme, Islam et pouvoir politique dans la société maure précoloniale (11–19 siècles)," thèse de doctorat d'état, Paris 5, 1985.

5. For useful descriptions of this code, see Taylor, "Of Disciples and Sultans," intro. and chap. 1, and Boubakar Ly, "L'honneur et les valeurs morales dans les sociétés oulof et toucouleur du Sénégal: Etude de sociologie," thèse de troisième cycle, the Sorbonne, 1966, 2 vols.

6. In fact, many of those taken into the Sahara were kept there, at oases and other strategic points, for agricultural, domestic, or other work.

7. Two recent statements on the slave trade take contrasting positions. James Searing,

West African Slavery and Atlantic Commerce: The Senegal River Valley, 1700–1860 (Cambridge, U.K., 1993) emphasizes the transforming effect of the Atlantic slave trade on Wolof political economies. He places a very useful emphasis on the provisioning trade, whereby slaves were producing for the slaves and crews engaged in the Atlantic slave trade. James Webb Jr., *Desert Frontier: Ecological and Economic Change along the Western Sahel, 1600–1850* (Madison, Wisc., 1994) stresses the impact of the Saharan and transsaharan trade. See E. Ann McDougall, "Research in Saharan History," *JAH* 39 (1998) for a review of Webb's book and the historical literature on Mauritania.

8. These "court clerics" ran the risk of being considered pawns of the ruling classes and ignoring the appropriate distance between scholar and sultan. This is a frequent theme in the Arabic scholarly literature. See, for example, the very conscious effort of Uthman dan Fodio and his contemporaries to portray his distance from the ruling circles, in M. Hiskett, *The Sword of Truth* (Oxford, 1973). This theme emerges very strongly in the career of Amadu Bamba (see chap. 11).

9. See Martin Klein, "Social and Economic Factors in the Muslim Revolution in Senegambia," *JAH* 13 (1972).

10. Tal Tamari, in *Les castes de l'Afrique occidentale: Artisans et musiciens endogames* (Nanterre, 1997) has built a strong case for Mande origins for blacksmiths, griots, and the whole caste system from the thirteenth or fourteenth century. The system and most of the particular castes spread to *bidan,* Fulbe, Tokolor, and Wolof society several centuries ago. Indeed, she suggests that the Wolof system is one of the most complete and may be almost as ancient as that of the Mande or Old Mali.

11. Tamari observes the infrequency of enslaving casted persons. *Les castes,* chap. 2, pt. 1, sec. a.

12. Searing (*West African Slavery,* chaps. 1 and 2) locates the development of autocratic regimes and slave armies, as opposed to more participatory, lineage-based societies, in the late seventeenth century and around the reign of Lat Sukabe Fall, who combined the thrones of Cayor and Baol.

13. The classic cases were those of the Bambara states of Segu and Karta established in the eighteenth century. See Robinson, *Holy War,* chaps. 5 and 7. The most relevant example in this work is Demba War Sall, head of the crown slaves of Cayor, who became the president of the Confederation of Cayor under French rule from 1886 until his death in 1902. His sons remained prominent within the ranks of colonial chiefs and in Senegalese society as a whole.

14. Lucie Colvin pointed this out in a useful article on Wolof societies, "Islam and the State of Kajoor: A Case of Successful Resistance to *Jihad,*" *JAH* 15 (1974): 587–606. It could also be applied to the Moors, the Fulbe, and the hal-pular.

15. The dhimmi image was the Islamic equivalent of the local metaphor that the Europeans were masters of the water but not the land. See n. 67 below, and Robinson, *Chiefs and Clerics,* 23–24.

16. See Louis Brenner, "Concepts of *Tariqa* in West Africa: The Case of the Qadiriyya," in Cruise O'Brien and Coulon, *Charisma.* For Kunta and Qadiriyya relations with the Islamic states created by Fulbe reform movements, see Robinson, *Holy War,* chap. 2.

17. The Tuareg were nomadic and largely Muslim societies of the central Saharan and Sahalian regions.

18. See Jean-Louis Triaud and David Robinson, eds., *La Tijaniyya: Une confrérie musalmane à la conquête de l'Afrique* (Paris, 2000).

19. See Colvin, "Islam and the State of Kajoor," and Robinson, *Holy War,* chap. 2. Ivor Wilks (in "The Dyula and the Southward Expansion of Islam"), in Nehemia Levtzion and Randall E. Pouwels, eds., *A History of Islam in Africa* (Athens, Ohio, 2000), develops the concept of the "Suwarian tradition" of Islamic practice in West Africa in which Muslims accepted the weakness of the faith relative to non-Muslim majorities or courts with very mixed constituencies.

20. Some of these reformers were incorporated into the dominant regime. This was the case for some autonomous villages and regions of Cayor from the time of Lat Sukabe: Coki, Louga, and Niomre in the north or Ndiambur, and Pir and the area of Saniokhor in the south. The Muslim village chiefs were responsible for the taxation, conscription, administration, and general loyalty of their subjects, in return for significant autonomy. Searing, *West African Slavery,* 25-26.

21. For West African instances, including Futa Toro, see my "*Jihads* in West Africa," in Levtzion and Pouwels, *History of Islam.*

22. Sharr Bubba, or Shurbubba, may mean "Babba's war," "Cry out assent!" or something else. I am drawing from the article of Abdel Wedoud Ould Cheikh, "Herders, Traders, and Clerics: The Impact of Trade, Religion, and Warfare on the Evolution of Moorish Society," in John Galaty and Pierre Bonte, eds., *Herders, Warriors, and Traders: Pastoralism in Africa* (Boulder, Colo., 1990), which in turn is drawn from Ould Cheikh's thesis, "Nomadisme." For a recent formulation, see his "La société Maure: Contribution à l'étude anthropologique et historique d'une identité culturelle ouest-saharienne." For a more standard interpretation, see Charles Stewart, "Political Authority and Social Stratification in Mauritania," in Ernest Gellner and Charles Micaud, eds., *Arabs and Berbers* (London, 1972). For the larger context of relations between Saharan Muslims, who typically understood themselves as "white," and Sahelian Muslims, who were identified as "black," see Brenner, "Qadiriyya"; Charles Stewart, "Southern Saharan Scholarship," *JAH* 19 (1976); and Webb, *Desert Frontier.*

23. This is the interpretation offered by Boubacar Barry in *Le Royaume du Waalo: Le Sénégal avant la conquête* (Paris, 1972), and by Carson Ritchie in "Deux textes sur le Sénégal (1673-77)," *BIFAN,* ser. B, 30 (1968). The French traders preferred to work with the warrior groups who were less likely to impose conditions on the commerce in gum. See the Ould Cheikh article cited in note 21. For a study of the importance of this to the later successful Islamic revolution in Futa Toro, see my "The Islamic Revolution of Futa Toro," *IJAHS* 8 (1975).

24. For discussions about the importance of the confederations or emirates, see Taylor, "Of Disciples and Sultans," chap. 5, and Abdel Wedoud Ould Cheikh, "Les fantômes de l'amir: Note sur la terminologie politique dans la société maure précoloniale," *Maghreb Review* 22 (1997).

25. See n. 19 above and Jean Boulègue, "La participation possible des centres de Pir et de Ndogal à la revolution islamique sénégambienne de 1673," in his *Contributions à l'histoire du Sénégal* (Paris, 1987), 119-25; Robinson, "Islamic Revolution."

26. See Timothy Cleaveland, "Islam and the Construction of Social Identity in the Nineteenth-century Sahara," *JAH* 39 (1998): 367 ff. Al-Yadali's views became widely

available in French with the publication of Ismaël Hamet, *Chroniques de la Mauritanie Sénégalaise* (Paris, 1911), on the basis of a copy of the manuscript supplied by Saad Buh. Sidiyya Baba refers to Sharr Bubba, al-Yadali, and the *hassan/zwaya* distinction often in the manuscript he prepared on the Idawaish; the manuscript was finished by his son shortly after his death. See Shaikh Sidiyya Baba, "A History of the Western Sanhaja," in H. T. Norris, *Saharan Myth and Saga* (Oxford, 1972), 160–217, esp. 205–11.

27. Before that they were Peul or Fulbe, like the other speakers of Pular who lived in the Senegalo-Mauritanian zone. Tokolor, the name that passed into common usage for the Futanke, comes originally from Takrur, the name that Arab geographers gave to a Muslim city and state of the eleventh century, probably in the middle valley. The nineteenth-century usage probably came from the Wolof term and was adopted by the French and inhabitants of Saint-Louis. Until the early 1800s, the almamy of Futa was often called the "roi des Poules." The people of Futa prefer to call themselves *hal pular*, "speakers of Pular." In *Encyclopedia of Islam*, 2nd ed. (1999), s.v., Robinson, "Tokolor," and Robinson, *Holy War*, 82, 143–44.

28. The most complete article on this subject is still my "Islamic Revolution." See also Oumar Kane, "Les unités territoriales du Futa Toro," *BIFAN*, ser. B, 35 (1973), and "Les Maures du Futa Toro au XVIIIe siècle," *CEA* (1975).

29. Most notably at Pir in southern Cayor or Saniokhor. Pir occupies an important place in the historiography of islamization in Senegal. See the Boulègue reference cited in n. 24. The reformers were also linked to the Muslim center of Coki in northern Cayor or Ndiambur. See Jean Boulègue, "La participation possible des centres de Pir et de Ndogal à la revolution islamique sénégambienne de 1673," in his *Contributions à l'histoire du Sénégal* (Paris, 1987), 119–25; Robinson, "Islamic Revolution."

30. Since the Denyanke rulers were also Fulbe, the torobbe accentuated the religious and moral failures of the regime, not their ethnic identity. For the best recent statement on the emergence of the different social classes and categories in Futa Toro, see Olivier Kyburz, "Les hierarchies sociales et leurs fondements idéologiques chez les *haalpulaar'en* (Sénégal)," doctorat de l'université de Paris 10, 1994.

31. Traditionally placed in 1776 but probably occurring a few years later. Almamy Abdul and his contemporaries did not leave a written record comparable to that of the other Fulbe-led Islamic movements. More Arabic documentation may come to light, however, with the publication of the French translation of the ethnohistory of Futa written by Shaikh Musa Kamara; see Jean Schmitz et al., trans. and eds., *Florilège au jardin de l'histoire des noirs: Zuhur al-Basatin*, 4 vols., with commentary (Paris; vol. 1 appeared in 1998).

32. The issue of land and rights on the north bank of the Senegal has become a heated debate in the last decade, fueled by the disputes and killings in Mauritania and Senegal. Most of the occupation of the north bank by hal-pular goes back to the early twentieth century, but there is also a an earlier history of habitation by them. Many of the lineages of the central region of Futa have had a fairly continuous occupation of the right bank. See Olivier Leservoisier, *La question foncière en Mauritanie* (Paris, 1994).

33. In the search for African resistance to the practice of enslavement and slave trade, historians have often seized upon this instance in the career of Almamy Abdul. The sovereign was not, however, expressing opposition to the slave trade and slavery

as institutions, but only to the victimization of Muslims in them. See, for example, Barry, *Sénégambie,* 156.

34. In particular, Ali Dundu Kane, the elector of Dabiya in Bossea, and Ali Sidi Bâ, the elector of Mbolo Ali Sidi, in Yirlabe. For an oral tradition of this encounter, see Moustapha Kane and David Robinson, *The Islamic Regime of Fuuta Tooro* (East Lansing, Mich., 1984), 53–63.

35. He used the Maliki formula, an invitation, usually in the form of a diplomatic mission, to "convert" and swear allegiance to the new Islamic regime of Futa Toro. This approach allowed his potential enemies to organize resistance. It is likely that the other reformers mentioned in this chapter, all of whom came from traditions of the Maliki school of law, followed the same practice. See Patricia Seed's demonstration of the impact of this Maliki practice on Spanish practice in the Iberian peninsula and the Americas in *Ceremonies of Possession in Europe's Conquest of the New World, 1492–1640* (Cambridge, U.K., 1995), chap. 3.

36. Abdul was captured at the battle of Bunguy in 1796–97. His fortunes in Cayor are a favorite subject of the oral traditions of Senegal; the perspective taken is typically that of the Damel. See Baron Roger, *Kélédor, histoire africaine* (Paris, 1829). For the conflict between the Muslims of Njambur and the Cayorian king, as well as the Futanke intervention, see Mamadou Diouf, *Le Kajoor au XIXe siècle* (Paris, 1990), 96ff.

37. Sire Abbas Soh, *Chroniques du Fouta sénégalais,* M. Delafosse and H. Gaden, trans. and eds. (Paris, 1913), 46.

38. For a Futanke perspective on this signal event, in which Almamy Abdul is portrayed as a martyr against the forces of reaction, see Kane and Robinson, *Islamic Regime,* 65–71. For a Bundu perspective, which regards Abdul's death as a liberation from foreign domination, see Michael Gomez, *Pragmatism in the Age of Jihad* (Cambridge, U.K., 1992), 81–85.

39. The Umarian phenomenon is treated later in this chapter. Futanke origin was virtually a prerequisite for "reform" identity in nineteenth-century Senegambia: Ma Ba Diakhu, Amadu Bamba, and Malik Sy all claimed Futanke origins. For other reform movements in Senegal, see Klein, "Social and Economic Factors"; Robinson, "An Emerging Pattern of Cooperation between Colonial Authorities and Muslim Societies in Senegal and Mauritania," in Robinson and Triaud, *Le Temps des Marabouts,* and Barry, *La Sénégambie.*

40. Karta had played the signal role in the death of Almamy Abdul. For studies of Umar, see Robinson, *Holy War,* and Madina Ly-Tall, *Un Islam militant en Afrique de l'Ouest au XIX siècle* (Paris, 1991).

41. See Robinson, *Holy War,* 93–98. In about 1845, Umar finished his long treatise in which he relates his pilgrimage, *Kitab Rimah Hizb al-Rahim ʿala Nuhur Hizb al-Rajim,* published in the margins of Ali Harazim, *Kitab Jawahir al-Maʿani wa Bulugh al-Amani* (Cairo, 1383AH/1963–64). For a somewhat less exclusivist interpretation of Umarian attitudes, see Dedoud ould Abdellah, "Le 'passage au sud': Muhammad al-Hafiz et son héritage," in Triaud and Robinson, *La Tijaniyya.* The main study of the Tijaniyya is Jamil Abun-Nasr, *The Tijaniyya: A Sufi Order in the Modern World* (Oxford, 1965).

42. He used the term *muwalat* to express association or friendship and called the

governor of Saint-Louis a tyrant *(taghi)*, a stock epithet for a Christian ruler who would not subordinate himself to Muslim authority. See Hanson and Robinson, *After the Jihad,* 106–11. I quote the letter at some length and deal with its implications for the Muslim merchants of Saint-Louis in chap. 6.

43. Umar's army lost half of its strength after his defeat in 1857, due primarily to desertion. To continue his enterprise, especially against the Bambara of Segu, he had to conduct massive recruitment in Senegal, especially in Futa Toro. During the recruitment campaign in 1858–59, he challenged his contemporaries, in the words of Mohammedou Aliou Tyam, to commit hijra, or *fergo,* "to leave the land of the European where life for Muslims would never be good." See Tyam, *La Vie d'El Hadj Omar: Qaçida en poular,* ed. and trans. Henri Gaden (Paris, 1935), 109 ff.; and Robinson, *Holy War,* 205–11, 219 ff. His message was embraced by tens of thousands of the faithful between the 1850s and 1890. For the use of the concept of hijra in eastern Algeria and Tunisia, see Clancy-Smith, *Rebel and Saint,* esp. chap. 5.

44. For Umar's justifications, see Sidi Mohamed Mahibou and Jean-Louis Triaud, *Voilà Ce Qui Est Arrivé: The Bayan Ma Waqa'a d'Al-Hajj Umar al-Futi* (Paris, 1984). For a summary of the conflict and its ramifications in the late nineteenth century, see Robinson, *Holy War.* chap. 8. The Marina conflict marked the height of conflict between Qadiriyya and Tijaniyya orders.

45. See John Hanson, "Generational Conflict in the Umarian Movement after the Jihad: Perspectives from the Futanke Grain Trade at Medine," *JAH* 31 (1990) and "Islam, Migration, and the Political Economy of Meaning: *Fergo Nioro* from the Senegal Valley, 1862–1890," *JAH* 35 (1994), and his book, *Migration, Jihad, and Muslim Authority in West Africa* (Bloomington, Ind., 1996).

46. Useful summaries of Ma Ba's career can be found in Tamsir Ousmane Bâ, "Essai historique sur le Rip," *BIFAN,* ser. B, 19 (1957); Martin Klein, *Islam and Imperialism in Senegal: Sine-Salum, 1847–1914* (Stanford, Calif., 1968), 63–93.

47. See Barry, *La Sénégambie,* 268–72, and chaps. 10 and 11 below. Ma Ba's son Saër Maty influenced another emerging figure, Abdullay Niasse. Brief summaries of Niasse can be found in Gray, "The Rise of the Niassène Tijaniyya," and Klein, *Sine-Salum,* 223–25. Lat Dior sought asylum with Ma Ba after Faidherbe's interventions in Cayor, following a pattern of temporary exile that had a long history in this region.

48. There still is no full-length work on this very interesting movement. See Robinson, *Chiefs and Clerics,* chaps. 4 and 5, and Eunice Charles, "Shaikh Amadou Bâ and Jihad in Jolof," African Historical Studies 8 (1975). Amadu Madiyu is often called Ahmadou Cheikhou in the sources. The movement that he and his brother Ibra led was resented and resisted by Amadu Sheku, the son of Umar, even though both families and movements claimed the Tijaniyya mantle. Amadu and Ibra's father, Hamme Bâ, was a scholar and Sufi who grew up near Podor in the early nineteenth century. He was a contemporary of Umar Tall. In the 1820s he formulated a critique of the Islamic regime of Futa Toro and took the name of Mahdi, the "rightly guided one" who comes at the end of time. He apparently carried through with the sacrifice of his son in imitation of the act that Ibrahim was willing to perform with Ishaq. He was then banished from Futa, lived in exile in western Senegal, and established close ties with the family of the Serigne Coki in Ndiambur. During the 1850s, Hamme opposed the Umarian emigration and

provided information to the French on Umar's movements — particularly during the momentous year 1858/59.

49. See Hanson and Robinson, *After the Jihad: The Reign of Ahmad al-Kabir in the Western Sudan* (East Lansing, Mich., 1991), docs. 13 A and B.

50. See the letter written in 1874 by Shaikh Muhammad Mahmud Kane from Saint-Louis to his relatives in the Umarian capital of Segu, ibid., doc. 13 C. Shaikh Muhammad, like many people from Futa Toro, was outraged by the assassination of many of the inhabitants of Pete in 1873. See Robinson, *Chiefs and Clerics,* 95–96.

51. Amadu Bamba judged his mentor Ma Diakhate harshly. See Amar Samb, *Essai sur la contribution du Sénégal à la litterature d'expression arabe* (Dakar, 1972), 429–30, and my chap. 11.

52. I have not included the movement organized by the Soninke cleric and pilgrim Mamadu Lamine Drame (except for a brief reference in chap. 6) because of its brevity (late 1884–87) and its concentration in the Upper Senegal valley. I have also not mentioned the dramatic but ephemeral movement of Diile Fatim Caam, a jeweler turned reformer who challenged the kingdom of Walo between 1827 and 1830, nor the challenges to the dominant classes of Futa Toro in the late 1820s from Hamme Bâ, the Mahdi and father of the Madiyanke discussed above. For a nationalist interpretation of these two movements, see Barry, *Senegambia,* 180–81, 230–34. For a treatment of Hamme Bâ, see Robinson, *Chiefs and Clerics,* 83–84. The French were not threatened by any significant Mahdist agitation, such as the British faced in northern Nigeria. See Lovejoy and Hogendorn, *Slow Death,* chap. 2.

53. This can be contrasted with the significant strength of Islamic reform and Mahdist movements in the area of the Sokoto caliphate at the turn of the century. See Paul Lovejoy and Jan Hogendorn, *Slow Death for Slavery* (Cambridge, U.K., 1993), chap. 2.

54. See Robinson, "The Islamic Revolution." For the critique that Cerno Brahim Kane made against the almamate, see my article "Historien et anthropologue sénégalais: Shaykh Musa Kamara," *CEA* 109 (1988). By contrast, the Sokoto caliphate still enjoyed considerable legitimacy in the late nineteenth century among the inhabitants of northern Nigeria in the twentieth century. See Remi Adeleye, *Power and Diplomacy in Northern Nigeria, 1804–1906* (London, 1971), and Paul Lovejoy and Jan Hogendorn, *Slow Death for Slavery.*

55. In some respects, hijra was the Muslim option that best translated the traditional obligation of honor of the royal lineages of the Senegalo-Mauritanian zone; the best example is Albury Ndiaye. In chap. 5, I explore briefly the large-scale migration of Fulbe owners of slaves and cattle from the lower Senegal valley. This was a case where Umarian recruitment coincided with grievances against the emancipation of slaves. For the massive emigration in northern Nigeria on the occasion of the British conquest in 1903, see R. A. Adeleye, "The Dilemma of the Wazir: The Place of the *Risalat al-Wazir ila Ahl al-ʿilm wa'l-Tadabbur* in the History of the Conquest of the Sokoto Caliphate," *Journal of the Historical Society of Nigeria* 4, no. 2 (1968).

56. Including the Idawali. See Dedoud, "Le passage au sud."

57. One of the proverbs of Futa captures this convergence very well: "The cleric gives birth to the chief, the chief gives birth to the pagan." Henri Gaden, *Proverbes et maximes Peuls et Toucouleurs* (Paris, 1931), 68.

58. For a good overview of the situation in the 1890s, from the perspective of the Direction of Political Affairs of the French administration, see ANS 9G 14, pièces 13 and 14, "rapport d'ensemble" dated 5 August 1895. The author was Martial Merlin, the director of political affairs and interim governor, who was about to order the arrest and deportation of Amadu Bamba.

59. Ali Shandora, his son Amar, and his grandson Ali Kowri (the one defeated by Almamy Abdul) exercised considerable authority across the entire eighteenth century.

60. See Paul Dubié, *La vie matérielle des Maures* (Dakar, 1953), 157–84; Paul Marty, chaps. 7 and 8 of *L'Emirat des Trarzas, RMM* 36 (1917–18): entire issue.

61. See Paul Marty, *Etudes sur l'Islam et les tribus Maures: Les Braknas* (Paris, 1921), 35–93; Raymond Taylor, "Warriors, Tributaries, Blood Money, and Political Transformation in Nineteenth-century Mauritania," *JAH* 36 (1995).

62. The one incident usually invoked took place in 1856, when Sidiyya al-Kabir convened an assembly of key Brakna *bidan* to forge a coalition. This is hardly a basis for a tradition of "resistance," but Sidiyya did keep his distance from the administration. The 1856 episode has been analyzed in some detail by A. Leriche in "Deux lettres du temps de la pacification (Mauritanie)," *BIFAN*, ser. B (1952). See chap. 9 for greater detail on the Sidiyya heritage. See also Taylor, "Of Disciples and Sultans," chaps. 4 and 5.

63. Robinson, *Chiefs and Clerics*, 43 ff.

64. The principal source here is Robinson, *Chiefs and Clerics*, passim.

65. Mbodj appears in a number of archival records beginning in the 1860s and extending until his death in 1914. For his short autobiography, see CAOM SEN 4 127 (11 November 1889, letter of Yamar Mbodj to Admiral Aristide Vallon, deputy of Senegal).

66. This compromise involved major French assistance with the defeat of the Madiyanke in 1875 and Lat Dior's surrender of the Walo chief, Sidia Diop, in the same year. Yves Saint-Martin, *Le Sénégal sous le Second Empire* (Paris, 1989), 575–76, 592–93.

67. See, for example, Vincent Monteil, *Esquisses sénégalaises* (Dakar, 1966). I discuss this in more detail in chaps. 2, 5, and 11. For the construction and impact of the Dakar–Saint-Louis rail line, see Paul Pheffer, "Railroads and Aspects of Social Change in Senegal, 1878–1933," Ph.D. diss., University of Pennsylvania, 1975). For the constant negotiations over the rail line between 1879 and 1886, see Guy Thilmans, "Lat Dior, Cheikh Saad Bou et le chemin de fer," *Saint-Louis-Lille-Liège*, no. 1 (1992), 1–36.

68. Albury joined forces with Abdul Bokar and then moved further east to link up with Amadu Sheku, Umar's son. See Robinson, *Chiefs and Clerics*, 153–58, and "The Umarian Emigration of the Late Nineteenth Century," *IJAHS* 20 (1987). Albury is a rival of Lat Dior as a Senegalese resistance hero and in some ways is a stronger candidate for the honor. See Barry's treatment in *Senegambia*, 234–42.

69. Searing, "Accommodation and Resistance," 75–79.

70. See, for example, Webb's treatment of the Idaw Al-Hajj or Darmankour in Walo and Cayor, *Desert Frontier*, 35–36.

71. The French had more abolitionist pressure applied to their West African holdings than did the British. It came from inside the administration in the form of the judiciary (see chap. 3) and from certain republican citizens in the four communes (see chap. 5). For the British "adjustment" in northern Nigeria, see Lovejoy and Hogendorn,

Slow Death. For general issues associated with the "end" of slavery, see Suzanne Miers and Richard Roberts, *The End of Slavery in Africa* (Madison, Wisc., 1988).

72. On gum, see Curtin, *Economic Change,* 215–18, 259–62, 338–39; Désiré-Vuillemin, "Essai sur la gommier et le commerce de la gomme dans les escales du Sénégal," thèse secondaire, Montpellier, 1961, passim; Robinson, *Chiefs and Clerics,* 29–30; Charles Stewart, *Islam and Social Order in Mauritania* (Oxford, 1973), 120ff. The French also made some experiments in agriculture, particularly around the area of Richard Toll. See Madina Ly-Tall and David Robinson, "The Western Sudan and the Coming of the French," in J. F. A. Ajayi and M. Crowder, *History of West Africa,* vol. 2 (new ed., London, 1987).

73. Some gum was also obtained in Bakel, Medine, and other parts of the upper river. See Hanson, "Futanke Grain Trade"; Robinson, *Chiefs and Clerics,* 109–10.

74. *Travels in the Interior of Africa,* French trans. (London, 1820), 137, quoted in Robinson, *Chiefs and Clerics,* 28.

75. Diouf, *Kajoor,* 119–20.

76. See George Brooks, "Peanuts and Colonialism: Consequences of the Commercialization of Peanuts in West Africa," *JAH* 16 (1975); Paul Pelissier, *Les paysans du Sénégal* (Paris, 1966), esp. chaps. 3 and 5.

77. See Marty, *Etudes . . . Sénégal,* 1:333–64.

78. See Geneviève Désiré-Vuillemin, ed., *Journal of Frèrejean, Mauritanie, 1903–1911: Mémoires de randonnées et de guerres au pays des Beidanes* (Paris, 1995), 105; A. Gruvel and R. Chaudeau, *A travers la Mauritanie Occidentale (de Saint-Louis à Port-Etienne),* 1, *Parties générale et économique* (Paris, 1909), 69; Pheffer, "Railroads and Aspects of Social Change," 165, 205–6. Pheffer mentions large groups of camels and donkeys from Mauritania and Gandiole, south of Saint-Louis, by 1881.

79. The most detailed exposition of railroad construction in Senegal is still Paul Pheffer, "Railroads and Aspects of Social Change."

80. For a general description of the layout of Saint-Louis, see Alain Sinou, *Comptoirs et villes coloniales au Senegal* (Paris, 1993), chap. 10.

81. Roger Pasquier, "Les traitants des comptoirs du Sénégal au milieu du XIXe siècle," in Catherine Coquery-Vidrovitch, ed., *Actes de Colloque 'Entreprises et Entrepreneurs en Afrique (XIXe et XXe siècles,'* 2 vols. (Paris, 1983).

82. For these trading operations, see Pasquier, "Traitants"; Robinson, *Chiefs and Clerics,* 28–31; and Taylor, "Of Disciples and Sultans," chap. 4.

83. Robinson, *Chiefs and Clerics,* 31. A case in point is offered in chap. 6 in the Lô family.

84. See Searing, *West African Slavery,* chap. 4.

CHAPTER 2

1. Charles Stewart deals with this theme in "Colonial Justice and the Spread of Islam in the Early Twentieth Century," in Robinson and Triaud, *Le Temps des Marabouts.*

2. In a sense they were frozen into the configurations *Islam maure* and *Islam noir* in the early twentieth century. See below. For these and other observations in this

work I have relied on Jean Schmitz's introduction to Schmitz et al., trans. and eds., *Florilège au jardin de l'histoire des noirs: Zuhur al-Basatin* (Paris, 1998), 1:32–51, and Emmanuelle Sibeud, "La naissance de l'ethnographie africaniste en France avant 1914," *CEA* (1994).

3. The *Revue* published virtually all of the volumes of Paul Marty. Le Châtelier made an important journey and study of Islam in West Africa before devoting himself to things Moroccan and a chair of "Muslim sociology" in Paris. See chap. 4.

4. The government-general was actually created in 1895 with four territories (Senegal, Soudan, Guinea [Conakry], and Côte d'Ivoire), but at that point the governor-general was based in Saint-Louis and also held the position of governor of Senegal. A 1902 decree created a separate lieutenant governor for Senegal, with headquarters in Saint-Louis. Roume worked out of Gorée for some of 1902–3, but by 1904 the government-general was located in Dakar.

5. Sydney Kanya-Forstner describes the process by which the Commandants Supérieurs of the Soudan wrested authority away from the governor over the decade of the 1880s. See his *The Conquest of the Western Sudan* (Cambridge, U.K., 1969), chaps. 4–6. From 1895 to 1902, the governor of Senegal was also the governor-general, but it was only with the appointment of Governor-general Roume in 1902 and the shift of the capital of the federation to Dakar that significant resources were invested in the federation.

6. As well as in the Southern Rivers region, which formed the coast of what became Guinea Conakry.

7. They included the main areas of classification that still dominate the francophone archival system today (discussed later in the chapter): general (political) affairs, military affairs, economic activities, slavery, labor, transport, health, etc. The original documents of the ancienne série, dealing with the period up to 1920, is still located at the Archives Nationales du Sénégal, as well as a considerable number of materials dealing with the period after 1920. For the history of the archives, which were taken under the custody of the Institut Français d'Afrique Noire (IFAN) in the 1940s, see Saliou Mbaye, *Guide des Archives de l'Afrique Occidentale Française* (Dakar, 1990), 11–15.

8. For Roume's critical roles, see Alice Conklin, *A Mission to Civilize: The Republican Idea of Empire in France and West Africa, 1895–1930* (Stanford, Calif., 1997), and Searing, "Accommodation and Resistance."

9. The principal works relevant for this study are *L'Islam en Mauritanie et au Sénégal*, published in RMM 31 (1915–16); *Etudes sur l'Islam maure: Cheikh Sidia, les Fadelia, les Ida ou Ali* (Paris, 1916); and *Etudes sur l'Islam au Sénégal*, 2 vols. (Paris, 1917).

10. After World War I, Hardy served under Resident-general Lyautey as the director of education in Morocco. See D. Rivet, *Lyautey et l'institution du protectorat français au Maroc, 1912–1925* (Paris, 1988), chap. 20.

11. In addition, a paternalistic and humanitarian journal, the *Revue Indigène*, was launched in 1906 under the direction of Paul Bourdarie.

12. Monod answered to the Ministry of Overseas France and not just to the governor-general. Beginning in 1943, central direction of research in the French African territories was accorded to ORSOM (later ORSTOM), the Office de la Recherche Scientifique d'Outre-Mer, part of the Ministry for Overseas France. Lord Hailey, *An African Survey Revised, 1956* (Oxford, 1957), 1604. Monod traveled constantly across

the federation and conducted regular research in the Sahara. His independence, curiosity, and breadth were manifested in the special interest that he took in two Muslim intellectuals who defied the established Islamic and colonial community. The first was Tierno Bokar Salif Tal, a member of the Umarian family in Bandiagara, Soudan, who sought out Shaikh Hamallah, the leader of a dissident branch of the Tijaniyya order in Nioro. Tierno Bokar "converted" to the Hamalliyya, which led to virtual quarantine by the colonial administration and other members of the family, and hastened his death in 1940. Monod became interested in Tierno Bokar through the second intellectual, Amadou Hampâté Bâ, a disciple of Tierno Bokar as well as a researcher at IFAN. While the Hamalliyya were still very suspect in the eyes of the colonial administration, Monod published two articles on the poetry and teachings of Cerno Bokar. He also gave considerable counsel and protection to Hampâté Bâ during the 1940s. See Louis Brenner, *West African Sufi: The Religious Heritage and Spiritual Search of Cerno Bokar Saalif Taal* (London, 1984), 8–9, and his article, "Amadou Hampâté Bâ, *Tijani francophone*," in Triaud and Robinson, *La Tijaniyya.*

13. One for the natural sciences (A) and one for the human sciences (B), titled *Bulletin de l'Institut Français d'Afrique Noire.*

14. Since independence, the vocation, energy, and resources of the institute, renamed the Institut Fondemental d'Afrique Noire, have steadily diminished.

15. See Jean Devisse, "La crise de 1968," a paper distributed in 1968; Mamadou Diouf, "Intellectuals and the State in Senegal: The Search for a Paradigm," in Diouf and Mahmood Mandani, eds., *Academic Freedom in Africa* (Dakar, 1994).

16. During the 1950s and 1960s, Lat Dior was the symbol of resistance par excellence. Subsequent research has revealed the very complex interactions of Lat Dior with the French over the last twenty-five years of his life. For an early treatment, see Monteil, *Esquisses sénégalaises,* or Oumar Bâ, *La pénétration française au Cayor: Du règne de Birima N'Goné Latyr à l'intronisation d Madiodo Dèguène Codou* (Dakar, 1976). An example of more recent and fuller interpretations is Mamadou Diouf, *Le Kajoor au XIXe siècle: Pouvoir ceddo et conquête coloniale* (Paris, 1990). Monteil's book also contains an essay on Albury. One of the fullest treatments of Ma Ba and his successors is Klein, *Islam and Imperialism in Senegal: Sine-Saloum, 1847–1914.* My first work on Senegal dealt with the forms of resistance organized by Abdul Bokar Kane in Futa Toro in the late nineteenth century *(Chiefs and Clerics).*

17. Barry's work has since appeared in an English-language edition, *Senegambia and the Atlantic Slave Trade,* published by Cambridge, U.K., in 1998. Subsequent references to Barry in this book are to the English edition.

18. Faidherbe continued to exercise great influence in West Africa and France until his death in 1889. He continued to publish, to maintain his library in Paris, and consult with the younger generation of Africanists, such as Louis Gaston Binger (1856–1936), who explored areas of the Soudan and Côte d'Ivoire in the late 1880s, and then was governor in Côte d'Ivoire in the 1890s before coming to the key position of director of African Affairs in the Ministry of Colonies from 1896 to 1906. See Schmitz, *Florilège,* 1:37, 40. Gaspard Devès consulted the general in 1885 about his claim to the island of Arguin (see chap. 5). Faidherbe is still the subject of great interest in French imperial and colonial history. One of the most recent biographies is Alain Coursier,

Faidherbe, 1818–1880: Du Sénégal à l'Armée du Nord (Paris, 1989). For two very thorough studies of his administration in Senegal, see Leland Barrows, "General Faidherbe, the Maurel & Prom Company, and French Expansion in Senegal," Ph.D. diss., UCLA, 1974, and Yves-Jean Saint-Martin, *Le Sénégal sous le second Empire* (Paris, 1989).

19. For Umar, see chaps. 1 and 7; also Robinson, *Holy War,* and Ly-Tall, *Islam militant.*

20. For example, see Amar Samb, "Sur El-Hadj Omar (à propos d'un article d'Yves Saint-Martin)," *BIFAN,* ser. B (1968): 803–5, which was a response to Yves Saint-Martin, "La volonté de paix d'El Hadj Omar et d'Ahmadou dans leurs relations avec la France," *BIFAN,* ser. B (1968): 785–802. A symposium on Umar, held on the bicentennary of his birth in Dakar in December 1998, symbolized the continuing importance of the Umarian tradition in Senegal.

21. For Seydu Nuru, see Harrison, *France and Islam,* 170–77. For an article that indicates the ambivalence with which African intellectuals regard this important figure, see Sékéné-Mody Cissoko and Oumar Kane, "Il y a un an disparaissait une grande figure africaine: Thierno Seydou Nourou Tall," *Afrique histoire,* 2 (1981).

22. Stanford, Calif., 1971. Johnson's work unfortunately still stands virtually alone as a study of Senegalese politics during the colonial period. Very little has been done, for example, on some quite prominent colonial chiefs and their lineages. See chap. 3, below.

23. While he deals with Moroccan and *bidan* raiding into the Senegambian zone, he does not integrate the *bidan* merchants into his African system—another indication of the impact of the divisions imposed by colonial rule.

24. Articulated especially by Barry in *Senegambia.* For a recent statement of this point of view, and complete bibliography, see Searing, *West African Slavery.*

25. Curtin's *The Atlantic Slave Trade: A Census* (Madison, Wisc., 1969) has become the authority on the former—the demography of the Atlantic slave trade.

26. One important formulation of the argument of Muslim criticism of the corrupt regimes can be found in Klein, "Social and Economic Factors."

27. Webb, *Desert Frontier,* and Searing, *West African Slavery.*

28. See, for example, Michael Marcson, "European-African Interaction in the Precolonial Period: Saint-Louis, Senegal, 1758–1854," Ph.D. diss., Princeton University, 1976; Roger Pasquier, "Le Sénégal au milieu du XIXe siècle: La crise économique et sociale," 5 vols., thèse de doctorat d'état, Paris 4, 1987.

29. Samir Amin, *Le monde des affaires sénégalais* (Paris, 1969), 19, emphasizes the British conquest of the Sudan and opening up in 1900 of Kordofan, an excellent source of gum.

30. Boubacar Barry and Léonhard Harding, eds., *Commerce et commerçants en Afrique de l'Ouest: Le Sénégal* (Paris, 1992).

31. See, for example, Klein, *Sine-Saloum,* and Robinson, *Holy War.* Stewart's work on the Sidiyya, *Islam and Social Order,* is the principal description of a Muslim community in precolonial times engaged in trade and arbitration of conflicts.

32. Harrison, *France and Islam.* See also the articles by Donal Cruise O'Brien ("Towards an 'Islamic Policy' in French West Africa," *JAH* 8 (1967), and David Robinson, "French 'Islamic' Policy and Practice in Late Nineteenth-Century Senegal," *JAH* 29 (1988).

33. Donal Cruise O'Brien has written the most useful historical accounts of the order in *The Mourides of Senegal* and *Saints and Politicians,* but these works are still oriented toward understanding more contemporary developments.

34. The best example of this literature is Samb, *Essai.* Recently, Ravane Mbaye completed a 4-vol. thesis in the same tradition on Malik Sy: "La pensée et l'action d'El Hadji Malick Sy: Un pôle d'attraction entre la Shari`a et la Tariqa: Vie et oeuvre de El Hadji Malick Sy," thèse de doctorat d'Etat en sciences humaines, Paris, 1993. Fernand Dumont wrote two important works in this vein during his years of service as a counselor at the presidency: *L'Anti-sultan, ou Al-Hajj Omar Tal du Fouta, combattant de la Foi, 1794–1864* (Dakar, 1971) and *La pensée religieuse de Amadou Bamba* (Dakar, 1975).

35. This theme is developed in Robinson and Triaud, *Le Temps des Marabouts.*

36. For a summary of this view and the sources on which it is based, see Robinson, "Beyond Resistance and Collaboration: Amadu Bamba and the Muridiyya of Senegal," *Journal of Religion in Africa,* 1991.

37. The compartmentalization has slowed the process of "nationalizing" the historiography, in comparison with the situation in Senegal.

38. Two very recent articles that set the stage of Mauritanian historiography are Timothy Cleaveland, "Islam and the Construction of Social Identity in the Nineteenth-century Sahara," and E. Ann McDougall, "Research," both in *JAH* 39 (1998).

39. But even Nouakchott was in Trarza. On the post and town, see Pitte, *Nouakchott.*

40. Both their allies at the turn of the century and earlier authors such as Muhammad al-Yadali. See Cleaveland, "Islam and the Construction of Social Identity."

41. Stewart, *Social Order* features Sidiyya al-Kabir, the grandfather of the Sidiyya Baba of chap. 9.

42. In Ould Cheikh, "Nomadisme."

43. See Bonte's doctoral thesis "L'emirat de l'Adrar," Paris, 1998, and E. Ann McDougall, "The Ijil Salt Industry: Its Role in the Precolonial Economy of the Western Sudan," Ph.D. diss., University of Birmingham, 1980. McDougall, in her review article cited in n. 38 above, cites important articles that she and Bonte have published over the last twenty years.

44. Their major works are Cleaveland, "Becoming Walati: A Study of Politics, Kinship, and Social Identity in Precolonial Walata," Ph.D. diss., Northwestern University, 1995; McLaughlin, "Sufi, Saint, Sharif: Muhammad Fadil wuld Mamin: His Spiritual Legacy and the Political Economy of the Sacred in Nineteenth-century Mauritania," Ph.D. diss., Northwestern University, 1997; Taylor, "Of Disciples and Sultans"; Webb, *Desert Frontier.*

45. In 1962, Geneviève Désiré-Vuillemin was still writing what is essentially a chronicle of the conquest in her *Contribution à l'histoire de la Mauritanie, 1900–1934* (Dakar, 1962). She was motivated by the role that her father played in the "pacification" of the country and dedicated the book to his memory. She is only one of the more recent chroniclers of the conquest.

46. For example, Cécile Frébourg, "Le Corse en Mauritanie: Xavier Coppolani, 1866–1905: L'Islam au service de la France," mémoire de maîtrise d'histoire, Paris 7, 1990.

47. See, for example, Philippe Marchesin, *Tribus, ethnies, et pouvoir en Mauritanie* (Paris, 1992). Marchesin presents a useful summary of the social scientific literature on Mauritania.

48. One striking example of this practice was noted by Yves Person, *Samori: Une revolution dyula* (Dakar, 1968), 2:440. Governor Canard, a career military officer in Senegal, was promoted to the position of governor, given his written instructions, and then criticized for obeying them when he questioned the independent initatives of the soudanais officers, who were often given oral directives by their superiors in Paris.

49. Merlin is discussed below. He escorted the young Buna to Tunis for studies in 1892, played a key role in his appointment as Burba Jolof, and relied greatly upon him thereafter.

50. See François Manchuelle, "Assimilés ou patriotes africains? Naissance du nationalisme culturel en Afrique française, 1853–1931," *CEA* 138–39 (1995). One might add Yamar Mbodj, the royal and colonial chief of Walo introduced in chap. 1, but he did not commit much work to writing.

51. Bruce Berman portrays the British administrator, especially in Kenya, as having a great deal of autonomy in relation to the central administration and passing along traditions of "wisdom" to his successors — "Bureaucracy and Incumbent Violence: Colonial Administration and the Origins of the 'Mau Mau' Emergency," in Berman and Lonsdale, *Unhappy Valley,* chap. 10. There was less autonomy within the French West African administration, although some of the dimensions of homogeneity of attitude certainly apply.

52. A crisis in law and order could force a more thorough investigation of the administrative unit and its construction in relation to the indigenous population.

53. I refer to them in some detail in chap. 3, along with Robert Arnaud, the Algerian-born Islamicist.

54. It is worth mentioning also the memoirs written by more prominent colonial officials, often with the purpose of furthering their own careers. In this category one might put the accounts that Joseph Galliéni wrote of his campaigns in the Soudan; also Henri Gouraud's versions of his experience in the Soudan and Mauritania, *Souvenirs d'un africain: Au Soudan* (Paris, 1939), and *Mauritanie Adrar: Souvenirs d'un africain* (Paris, 1945); and Ernest Noirot's rendition of his trip to Futa Jalon in 1881, *A Travers le Fouta-Diallon et le Bambouc (Soudan occidental)* (Paris, 1882). Another instance was the authorized biography; Louis Archinard, for example, made his library available to Jacques Méniaud, and the result was the 2-vol. *Les pionniers du Soudan avant, avec, et après Archinard, 1879–1894* (Paris, 1931).

55. The *fiches* for marabouts were probably drawn from Algerian formulas.

56. See, for example, Conklin, *Mission to Civilize,* 84.

57. These records have been worked in some detail by Denise Bouche, *L'Enseignement dans les territoires français de l'Afrique occidentale de 1817 à 1920* (Paris, 1975).

58. For this school and a general study of French education in Senegal, see Bouche, *Enseignement,* 321–56.

59. See Louis Brenner, "Médersas au Mali: Transformation d'une institution islamique," in B. Sanankoua et L. Brenner, eds., *L'enseignement islamique au Mali* (Bamako, 1991); François de Chassey, *Mauritanie, 1900–1975: Facteurs éconimiques, politiques, idéologiques, et educatifs dans la formation de la société sous-développée* (Paris, 1984), 154–55.

60. The Quranic school material is found in J4 and J85-90.

61. Found today in ANS 19G.

62. Abel Jeandet, the director of political affairs, was killed as he was preparing to join in military columns monitoring central Futa in September 1890. Governor Clément-Thomas and his subordinates decided to execute the alleged offenders in Podor with only the most summary appearance of a trial. I treat this in some detail in chap. 3. The basic secondary source is François Manchuelle, "*Métis* et colons: La famille Devès et l'émergence politique des Africains au Sénégal," *CEA* 96 (1984): 477-504.

63. See Roger Pasquier, "Les débuts de la presse au Sénégal," CEA 7 (1962): 477-90.

64. Contained in ANS E. See Saliou Mbaye, Histoire des institutions coloniales française en Afrique de l'Ouest, 1816-1960 (Dakar, 1991).

65. The records (in Arabic until 1913) of the Muslim Tribunal have not been extensively worked; they will undoubtedly reveal a great deal about the social history of town and colony. Formerly at City Hall, they are now located at the Centre de Recherches et Documentation in the Sud quarter of Saint-Louis. Ghislaine Lydon, of Michigan State University, surveyed these materials in 1995 and 1997.

66. I conducted interviews there in 1985, as did Kalala Ngalamulume in 1994; see his "Urban Growth and Health Problems—Saint-Louis from the Mid-Nineteenth Century to World War I," Ph.D. diss., Michigan State University, 1996. One of my most valuable interviews occurred 4 June 1985, with Umar Sarr, son of qadi Ndiaye Sarr and secretary at times to Shaikh Anta Mbacke; I make use of it in chap. 11. Several of the contributors to Barry and Harding, *Commerce,* found useful informants in Saint-Louis.

67. I have cited only examples connected with Michigan State University and my own work. Kane's sources appear in his dissertation: Mouhamed Moustapha Kane, "A History of Fuuta Tooro, 1890s-1920s: Senegal under Colonial Rule: The Protectorate," Ph.D., diss., Michigan State University, 1987. Sall's appear in his thesis: Ibrahima Abou Sall, "Mauritanie: Conquête et organisation administratives des territoires du Sud: Rôle des aristocraties politiques et religieuses, 1890-1945," doctoral thesis, Paris 7, 1998. For Babou, see "Le Mouridisme jusqu'en 1912," mémoire de maîtrise, Université Cheikh Anta Diop, Dakar, 1993. Excerpts of the latter appear in "Autour de la genèse du Mouridisme," *ISASS* 11 (1997). Lydon's interviews appear in her dissertation, "On Trans-Saharan Trails: Trading Networks and Cross-Cultural Exchange in Western Africa, 1840s-1950s," Ph. D. diss., Michigan State University, 2000.

68. The "Fonds Archinard" is located at the Bibliothèque Nationale. A thorough inventory was published in Noureddine Ghali et al., La Bibliothèque Umarienne de Segou (Paris, 1985).

69. These letters, usually in Arabic and often with French translations, were kept by the political bureaus of Senegal and the other territories. Before the 1890s they consisted of correspondence addressed to the French authorities themselves; during the conquest, the French intercepted or confiscated a number of indigenous archives. A great deal of "Umarian" material is found in the Soudan series (ANS 15G, esp. doss. 62-81). A lot of Senegal and Mauritania material is scattered through 13G and 9G, respectively.

70. See Hanson and Robinson, *After the Jihad,* which contains the original documents and translations drawn from the Umarian library of Segu, now housed at the

Bibliothèque Nationale in Paris, and some of the *correspondance indigène* contained in the ANS series for the Soudan, specficially 15G 62–81.

71. Documented in Robinson, "Emigration." For a discussion of the "exit" option in more contemporary settings, see Leonardo Villalon, *Islamic Society and State Power in Senegal* (Cambridge, U.K., 1995), 12–14, 102ff.

72. Unless one includes some of the "resistance" poetry of Amadu Bamba.

73. Samb, *Essai,* and Mbaye, "Malick Sy."

74. See Robinson, "Historien et anthropologue sénégalais: Shaykh Musa Kamara," *CEA* 109 (1988). Some African scholars, of a nationalist bent, have questioned the authenticity of Kamara's views. An annotated translation of his longest work, *Zuhur al-Basatin,* has been completed; the first of four volumes has appeared as Schmitz et al., *Florilège.*

75. This massive work, entitled the *Kitab al-Akhbar,* is contained in sixty-five school *cahiers;* it has now been indexed. On the Boutilimit library in general, see Stewart, "Colonial Justice," and for the *Akhbar,* see Ould Cheikh, "Harun wuld al-Shaikh Sidiyya, 1919–1977," both in Robinson and Triaud, *Le Temps des Marabouts.*

76. The efficacy of the declarations published at the beginning of World War I has not been examined. For the utility of the fatwa used in Algeria in the 1890s, see Ageron, *Algériens musulmans,* chap. 19. For Saad Buh's 1906 fatwa, or *nasiha* ("counsel"), see Dedoud ould Abdallah, "Guerre sainte ou sédition blâmable: Un débat entre shaikh Sald Bu et son frère shaikh Ma al-Ainin," in Robinson and Triaud, *Le Temps des Marabouts.* For Sidiyya Baba's decree of 1903 and additional commentary from a French Islamicist, see Edouard Michaux-Bellaire, "Une fetoua de Cheikh Sidia: Approuvée par Cheikh Saad Bouh ben Mohammed El Fadil ben Mamin, frère de Cheikh Ma El Ainin," *Archives Marocaines* 11, no. 1 (1907): 129–53. There are also interesting precedents found in the Algerian archives, esp. GG ALG 16H 7, and 22 H 35. For the 1903 statement of the wazir of Sokoto in Hausaland, see Remi Adeleye, "The Dilemma of the Wazir: The Place of the *Risalat al-Wazir ila Ahl al-ʿilm waʾl-Tadabbur* in the History of the Conquest of the Sokoto Caliphate," *Journal of the Historical Society of Nigeria* 4, no. 2 (1968).

77. This material is contained in the *RMM* 29 (1914), in a special issue entitled "Les musulmans français et la guerre."

78. We do not have, for example, any equivalent to Sydney Kanya-Forstner's fine study, *The Conquest of the Western Sudan,* which in effect is an analysis of conflict, manipulation, and initiative in France as well as West Africa during the period 1880–99.

79. For an extended discussion of the fatwa, see chaps. 4 and 9.

CHAPTER 3

1. For work critical of the oversimplification, see Berman and Lonsdale, *Unhappy Valley,* esp. chap. 2; Julian Cobbing, "The Absent Priesthood: Another Look at the Rhodesian Risings of 1896–97," *JAH* 18 (1977); Shula Marks, *Ambiguities of Dependence* (Baltimore, 1986); and Charles Stewart, "Islam," in Andrew Roberts, ed., *The Colonial Moment in Africa* (Cambridge, U.K., 1990), 194–202. With reference to francophone West Africa, and Senegal in particular, see Robinson, *Holy War,* 320–25.

2. *Lion Rampant* (London, 1973), chap. 1.

3. For these hesitations in the peanut basin of Senegal, see Searing, "Accommodation and Resistance," chaps. 1–2.

4. French control of the northern reaches of Mauritania would not come, however, until the 1930s.

5. For this process of centralization, see Searing, "Accommodation and Resistance," esp. chaps. 2 and 3. In chap. 1 he argues for the continuity between the precolonial and colonial periods.

6. See Kanya-Forstner, *Conquest,* chap. 1.

7. For the administration of the Colony of Senegal, see Saint-Martin, *Le Sénégal,* esp. chap. 8, 133 ff.

8. For the close relations of governors with Bordeaux interests, see Barrows, "General Faidherbe." For the administrative structure, see Saint-Martin, *Second Empire,* 133–45.

9. The exportation of slaves from the Senegalo-Mauritanian zone into the Atlantic trade was not numerically important in the nineteenth century, but the dependence on slave labor within the zone and its export into the Sahara and transsaharan trade remained very vital to the system. See Searing, *West African Slavery,* and Webb, *Desert Frontier.*

10. The Bordeaux interests, especially the Maurel family, played a significant role in the development of the plan, the augmentation of the resources, and the choice of Leon Faidherbe as the governor. See Barrows, "General Faidherbe," and Joan Casey, "The Politics of French Imperialsim in the Early Third Republic: The Case of Bordeaux," Ph.D. diss., University of Missouri, Columbia, 1973. Diouf is careful to point out that Faidherbe was not an innovator but an implementer of a plan that had been in existence for some time. *Kajoor,* 171–74. The plan included significant efforts to control the export of gum from Mauritania and the Sahara as far north as the Wadi Nun. See Lydon, "On Trans-Saharan Trails," chap. 4.

11. The Wolof of Cayor described the process as going from "merchant prince" to "great warrior." Diouf, *Kajoor,* 119–20. See my chap. 1, n. 74.

12. See Schmitz, *Florilège,* 36–37. Faidherbe was the first in a succession of *algériens* to have a significant impact on the shape of French colonial rule in West Africa. In the period between 1880 and 1920, Alfred Le Châtelier, Xavier Coppolani, Robert Arnaud, and Paul Marty played major roles. They are examined especially in chap. 4.

13. See my chapter "'French Africans': Faidherbe, Archinard, and Coppolani, the 'Creators' of Senegal, Soudan, and Mauritania," in the festschrift for Harold Marcus, *Personality and Political Culture in Modern Africa,* Boston University, African Studies Center, 1998.

14. For the Trarza campaigns, see Saint-Martin, *Second Empire,* chap. 16, and Boubacar Barry, *Le royaume du Waalo* (Paris, 1972). For Umar, see Robinson, *Holy War,* esp. chap. 5. For Cayor, see Diouf, *Kajoor,* chaps. 11–13.

15. Also called the *conseil privé.* It was the same group that took the decision to exile Amadu Bamba in 1895. The governor controlled it, and most of its members came from his administration. There were, however, two titular representatives from the commercial community, and two substitutes. These people typically came from the French and métis population. While Faidherbe worked closely with those who supported his projects, he was quite severe with anyone who stood in his way. An example is his threat to those who stood

in his way in Cayor. In 1859 he replied to the managers of the Devès & Chaumet Company, which had close ties with commercial interests in Cayor, in harsh terms: "In sending me a collective letter and protesting against my decisions, you arrogate to yourselves rights that you do not have. I will limit myself this time to a simple warning and not call you before the *conseil d'administration,* but you should know that in the future, using my powers under articles 32 and 54 of the *ordonnance organique,* I will oppose any effort on your part that would tend to weaken the respect that is required by the government." Quoted in Bâ, *Pénétration,* 202–3; taken from ANS 3B 74, letter of 14 November 1859.

16. See Myron Echenberg, *Colonial Conscripts: The Tirailleurs Senegalais in French West Africa, 1857–1960* (Portsmouth, N.H., 1991), and John Malcolm Thompson, "In Dubious Service: The Recruitment and Stabilizaiton of West African Maritime Labor by the French Colonial Military, 1659–1900," Ph.D. diss., University of Minnesota, 1989), chap. 3.

17. For these innovations, see Robinson, *Chiefs and Clerics,* 32–33, and *Holy War,* 213–14.

18. Discretionary funds controlled by the governor and director of political affairs were used to reward friends and informants and to support missions into particularly critical situations. See ANS 13G 28, for the accounting of the bureau in 1885; the successor to this institution of paid intelligence was the "Fonds secrets," which are partially documented in ANS 17G 24–28, and CAOM political affairs, 2708, 2724ff.

19. Called the Bureau des Affaires Extérieures at the time of its creation in 1845 and the Direction des Affaires Politiques for most of the late nineteenth century, this institution was obviously modeled on the *bureaux arabes* that Bugeaud and the French administration had established in Algeria. See Saint-Martin, *Second Empire,* for the descriptions of the Faidherbe "team" that operated out of this service. The Arabic translation service discussed in chap. 4 operated under this office. For impressions of the direction in the late 1870s, when Joseph Galliéni and Parfait L. Monteil were there, see Henri Labouret, *Monteil: Explorateur et soldat* (Paris, 1937), chap. 2.

20. Mbaye, *Institutions,* 33, 53–55.

21. Under Louis Archinard (1888–91, 1892–93), the most notorious of its leaders, it became independent of Saint-Louis. Kanya-Forstner, *Conquest,* passim.

22. Treated later in this chapter and in chap. 5.

23. The French also extended their presence significantly to the south, in the area called the Southern Rivers. Part of this area was the basis for the territory of Guinea, which was separated from Senegal in 1891.

24. Roume was the head of the Asian Department at the Ministry of Colonies; he was supposed to do for French West Africa what Eugene Etienne and Gaston Doumergue had done for Indochina: prepare the way for railroad construction and economic development in general. Margaret Osborne McLane, "Economic Expansionism and the Shape of Empire: French Enterprise in West Africa, 1850–1914," Ph.D. diss., University of Wisconsin, 1992, chap. 8. See also Alice Conklin, *A Mission to Civilize,* and Searing, "Accommodation and Resistance."

25. Saint-Louis did, however, remain the educational capital for a time, and it retained its reputation for political and cultural sophistication much longer still.

26. The resistance leader was Ma El Ainin; see chap. 4. Some resistance was main-

tained into the 1930s from the confines of Morocco, the Spanish colony Rio de Oro, and northern Mauritania. See Désiré-Vuillemin, *Contribution,* and Sophie Caratini, *Les Rgaybat, 1610–1934* (Paris, 1989), vol. 2.

27. The governor did control directly the Muslim Tribunal and the *indigénat* system, which consisted of rule by decree of the administrative officer; the indigénat was applied in most of the French West African Federation. See the case of Mody Mbaye discussed at the end of this chapter.

28. Indeed, as Manchuelle points out, the judiciary officials were often *antillais* who had a decidedly liberal and humanitarian orientation to certain aspects of the law. They could create serious problems for the administration, as I indicate later in this chapter. Manchuelle, *"Métis* et colons."

29. Usually areas that were annexed, or part of the colony, as distinguished from protectorates. It included the forts and immediately surrounding areas. This was the argument made by opponents of the administration in the Jeandet Affair, discussed later in this chapter.

30. See Mbaye, *Institutions,* 83 ff.; Richard Roberts, "Text and Testimony in the *Tribunal de Première Instance,* Dakar, during the Early Twentieth Century," *JAH* 31 (1990), 447–63. For the West Indian participation in the judiciary, and for the concern of these *antillais* about the application of the legislation on the slave trade and slavery, see Manchuelle, *"Métis* et colons."

31. But not, of course, over the deputyship. Blaise Diagne not only became the first African deputy in 1914, he soon created a rather modern political party structure that took control of the city halls in the four communes. At the same time, however, he served the administration by directing the intensive military recruitment of 1917–18, and after 1923 he worked closely with the Bordelese commercial interests. See G. Wesley Johnson, *The Emergence of Black Politics in Senegal* (Stanford, Calif., 1971). For a somewhat different perspective on Diagne, see Searing, "Accommodation and Resistance," chaps. 5–7.

32. The railroad from Saint-Louis to Dakar was completed in 1885, but it was the result of the initiatives of major metropolitan interests. To the east, the Commandant Supérieur operated with considerable autonomy, and he succeeded in hiving off a separate colony, the Soudan, by the end of the decade.

33. Genouille was an important and activist governor during his term, but he has been virtually expunged from the historical record. Some of the Saint-Louis community regarded him as very authoritarian and military-minded; see the 1887 letter of Hyacinthe Devès in ANS 1Z 11, #14. Genouille was brought to trial eventually for involuntary manslaughter. I have not been able to discover the final disposition of the case. For Genouille's personnel file, see CAOM EE2 647; see also the journal *Le Temps* for 1888–89. For the Cayor protest, see ANS 1D 48, "1886, Campagne du Cayor"; Diouf, *Kajoor,* 279–80; Ganier, "Lat Dyor," 253–55, 280–81; Pasquier, "Presse." For the confiscation of cattle, see CAOM SEN 4 65.

34. The principal source is Manchuelle, *"Métis* et colons." The primary archival record for the events of September 1890 and some of the controversy later in the year is contained in ANS 13G 135. For the materials sent on to Paris, see CAOM SEN 4 66a and 66b. Considerable information on the aftermath of the affair can be found in the papers of Henri de Lamothe (CAOM 4PA1). For observations derived from the oral

tradition, see Moustapha Kane, "A History of Fuuta Tooro," 86–88. For a biography of Jeandet, see B.-H. Gausseron, *Un Français au Sénégal, Abel Jeandet* (Paris, 1913). The incident has passed into the oral tradition of western Futa Toro, the region around Podor. See Fonds Johnson, session with Khaly Sall of Dodel; Fonds Robinson, sessions 4 and 5 with Ali Gaye Thiam.

35. For the general context, see Robinson, *Chiefs and Clerics,* 152–55.

36. The French used decapitation particularly to impress Muslims, who associated it with the eternal punishment inflicted on Cain (Kabel) for killing Abel. After telling the Cain story, the Quran goes on to say: "The recompense of those who combat God and His Prophet . . . will be death and the agony of crucifixion. You will cut off their feet and hands." sura 5, v. 37. Al-Hajj Umar used it for a number of his opponents (see Tyam, *Qaçida,* 46–47, 133, 142, 168). Of the popular fear of decapitation, Joseph Galliéni wrote: "Keeping their head on their shoulders is the only preoccupation of Muslims who are going to die. A decapitated man cannot cross the narrow plank leading to the gate of heaven, because he does not possess the goatee on his chin, or the 'Muhammad,' the tuft of hair that the disciples of Islam maintain so carefully on their skulls, permitting the supplicant to be seized and introduced to the Prophet." *Deux campagnes au Soudan français, 1886–88* (Paris, 1887), 86.

37. In November 1890, Devès brought the widow of Lam Toro Sidikh to Saint-Louis. She was the key to the case filed in the criminal court in the Seine jurisdiction. Devès obviously had considerable legal help in the procedures he invoked, apparently through a lawyer in Saint-Louis named André Chadelle. Manchuelle, "*Métis* et colons," 492–93; ANS 13G 135, pièce 49.

38. Couchard became deputy in Vallon's place in 1893. Devès subsequently shifted alliances several times, developed more support among the Lebu of Dakar, and finally joined forces with Descemet to gain control of the General Council in 1897 in a métis and African triumph over the interests of the Bordelese and the administration. Vallon's letter of support for the administration appeared in *Le Temps* of 10 January 1891. The Devès group did start a procedure for obstruction of justice against Clément-Thomas and de Lamothe. This was in the criminal tribunal for the Seine jurisdiction. By the time the suit was launched, in 1891, Clément-Thomas was in India as the governor of French possessions, and de Lamothe did not respond to the summons in Senegal. The French court dropped the case. Manchuelle, "*Métis* et colons," esp. 490–92.

39. In 1894 he brought fraud charges against Gaspard's son François. François was acquitted, to great acclaim by some Saint-Louisians. The trial brought to Senegal the humanitarian champion, Senator Isaac, as the lawyer for the defense. The de Lamothe papers indicate how carefully the governor handled this man of considerable metropolitan and imperial influence. This trial is discussed briefly in chap. 5.

40. Chaudié had to deal with the campaigns against Samori and was pressed by the ministry to rein in the military officers, the soudanais, who had gained such a hold in the colony of Soudan. He was given very limited authority over Guinea and Côte d'Ivoire, and had none over Dahomey. See Alice Conklin, *A Mission to Civilize: The Republican Idea of Empire in France and Africa, 1895–1930* (Stanford, Calif., 1997), chap. 1; McLane, "Economic Expansionism," esp. chap. 8. See also Kanya-Forstner, *Conquest,* chaps. 8 and 9.

41. The main archives for this affair are ANS Q 38-40, and CAOM SEN 9 56-62.

42. See CAOM SEN 4 65, and ANS 9G 14, on problems in Trarza in the 1880s and 1890s. Chaudié's successor was Noël Ballay, who presided from late 1900 until his death in January 1902. Ballay had served as lieutenant governor of Guinea in the 1890s. He left little mark on the Senegalo-Mauritanian scene.

43. Indeed, Roume's predecessors, Chaudié and Bellay, opposed the plan. The opposition and reluctance were similar to the attitudes that a number of governors of Senegal expressed toward the operations of the soudanais during the 1880s, when they were nominally subordinate to Saint-Louis. Kanya-Forstner, *Conquest*, chaps. 4-7.

44. The Coppolani campaigns are discussed in chap. 4 with reference to their impact on the "paths of accommodation." The most complete study of Coppolani's negotiations for authorization of his campaign is Frébourg, "Le Corse en Mauritanie," 1990. For an account by the daughter of a participant in the Coppolani team, see Désiré-Vuillemin, *Contribution*. Coppolani's original formulation involved occupying all of what became French Mauritania and Spanish Rio de Oro, and working from the Atlantic around the Saqiyat al-Hamra. Institut de France, Fonds Auguste Terrier, MS 5942, "L'origine de la Mauritanie," Projet d'organisation et d'occupation des pays maures, 10 March 1900. (I wish to thank Ghislaine Lydon for bringing this document to my attention.)

45. The French suspected, with possible justification, that Ma El Ainin, the older brother of Saad Buh and a distinguished scholar, Sufi, and close associate of the Moroccan court, helped to mobilize those who carried out the assassination. Ma El Ainin subsequently became, in the minds of the French, the archenemy of their conquest of Mauritania. See chap. 4 and B. G. Martin, *Muslim Brotherhoods in Nineteenth-century Africa* (Cambridge, U.K., 1976), 129-45.

46. Some incidents from Podor and the Lower Senegal valley in the early twentieth century indicate how the system worked. In 1903, an administrator in Podor stopped a boat of *bidan* traders carrying ten boys and eighteen girls and put the traders in jail. The métis merchant Théodore Pellegrin angrily intervened with the lieutenant governor in Saint-Louis: "These are traditional practices that have existed for a long time. No one has ever prevented the Moors from buying young slaves . . . and taking them wherever they wished." The prisoners were released. Désiré-Vuillemin, *Contribution*, 298-300. Slaves were also purchased by the inhabitants of Saint-Louis and used in a variety of tasks under the label of servants. See CAOM Mauritanie 4 1, 23 June 1904, Coppolani to Governor-general Roume; and Mohamed Saïd Ould Ahmedou, "Coppolani et la conquête de la Mauritanie," *Masadir*, cahier 1, 1994. Some of the slaves came from the periphery of the Senegalo-Mauritanian zone, especially the area along the Gambia River, but in the wake of the collapse of Samori's empire and other forces, a larger proportion came from the upper Senegal zone. See Bernard Moitt, "Peanut Production and Social Change in the Dakar Hinterland: Kajoor and Bawol, 1840-1940," Ph.D. diss., University of Toronto, 1984, chap. 6, and his article "Slavery and Emancipation in Senegal," *IJAHS* 22 (1989).

47. As in Senegal, colonial rule in Mauritania weakened the political and military elite relative to the marabouts, especially in terms of wealth. See Paul Dubié, *La vie matérielle des Maures*, in *Mélanges ethnologiques*, memoire 23 (Dakar, 1953), 167 ff.

48. Désiré-Vuillemin, *Contribution*, 142-43.

49. The administration remained confused and conflicted about the configuration

of the territory of Mauritania: where should the boundary be? was Mauritania a *bidan* colony? if so, what was the status of its free black inhabitants? For these debates, which persisted well into the 1920s, see Sall, "Mauritanie," pt. 4, chap. 5.

50. The French reassured the chiefs and other members of the interior elites that they would not interfere with domestic slavery and that they could even "buy slaves from foreigners in the areas where slaves continued to be sold." ANS 2G 1/122, report for March 1901. See Klein, *Slavery,* chap. 8. In fact, the administration's tolerance for the continued practice of the slave trade and slavery was important for many Saint-Louis interests as well as the ruling classes of the interior. In the 1880s, the French worried about the large-scale migration from the Walo area of cattle owners and slaveholders. These men and their families were concerned about the flight of their slaves to the "free soil" of the French colony. Hanson, "Islam, Migration, and the Political Economy of Meaning," *JAH* 35 (1994). And see my chap. 5.

51. See Bouche, *Enseignement,* 341–44; Searing, "Accommodation and Resistance," 86–102. For considerable detail on the erosion of the General Council's authority, see McLane, "Economic Expansion," esp. chaps. 6 and 8. The budget of the Colony of Senegal, over which the General Council had some jurisdiction, averaged 2.26 million francs per year in the early 1880s, but only 2.75 million per year between 1910 and 1914; the protectorate budget, which started at virtually zero in 1890, was about 5.95 million per year in the 1910–14 period. The government-general budget averaged 16.68 million per year between 1905 and 1909, and 25.7 million between 1910 and 1914. The governors (later, the governors-general) were able to transfer more and more expenses into the "obligatory" part of the budget over which the council had no control. This culminated in the Finance Law of 1900, which called for each territory to pay its own way, with the exception of armed forces; import-export duties were transferred entirely to the government-general in 1904.

52. Merlin was probably the single most influential official on French "native policy" during this whole period, and his "indirect rule" policy with the chiefs was something he always defended. He ran the bureau for most of the 1890s and returned to Senegal to serve as general secretary of Governor-general Roume in 1902–8. He gave the orders for the arrests of Amadu Bamba in 1895 and 1903, and much more. See Bâ, *Amadou Bamba,* 182: Searing, "Accommodation and Resistance," chaps. 2–3, 5–7. Merlin was governor-general of French West Africa from 1918 to 1923.

53. Bouche, *Enseignement,* 321–56.

54. *JO* of Senegal, 24 February 1894, in Bouche, *Enseignement,* 353. See also Conklin, *Mission to Civilize,* 84.

55. The names read like a roster of the aristocracy of the old regimes of Senegal. They included Fara Penda Diaw, son of Yoro Diaw; Mbakhane Diop, son of Lat Dior; Salmone Fall, son of Thieyacine, former king of Baol; Abdussalam Kane, from a prestigious patrilineage of Futa and grandson of Tamsir Hamat Ndiaye Anne of Saint-Louis; Samba Yamba Mbodj, son of Yamar Mbodj, superior chief of Western Walo; Buna Ndiaye, son of Albury, former king of Jolof; and Maissa Celle Ndiaye, son of Ibrahima, chief of Ndiambur.

56. Abdussalam Kane presided over a large section of eastern Futa Toro from 1897 until his death in 1955. Buna Ndiaye dominated the affairs of Jolof from 1895 until his voluntary retirement in 1935; he was particularly close to Martial Merlin.

Mbakhane Diop and Salmone Fall occupied a number of positions as *chefs de province,* *chefs de canton,* and agents in the colonial bureaucracy.

57. It was extremely rare, at this time or later, to find *bidan* among the pupils in the French establishments. This reflected the thinking of the French—that, in contrast to the blacks, the *bidan* had their own culture and civilization. See Ibrahima Sall, "Crise identitaire ou stratégie de positionnement politique en Mauritanie: Le cas des *Fulbe Aynaabe,*" André Bourgeot, ed., *Horizons nomades en Afrique sahélienne* (Paris, 1999), and chap. 4, below.

58. McLane, "Economic Expansionism," chap. 6.

59. D. Cruise O'Brien, "Towards an 'Islamic Policy'"; Colin Newbury, "The Formation of the Government General of French West Africa," *JAH* 1 (1960); Robinson, "French 'Islamic' Policy." The best general source on this subject is Harrison, *France and Islam.* See chap. 4, below.

60. Klein, *Slavery,* chaps. 6, 8, and 12; Moitt, "Peanut Production and Social Change," chap. 6; Searing, "Accommodation and Resistance," chaps. 3 and 4.

61. Ponty was the first of several governors-general to come out of field experience in Soudan or Côte d'Ivoire (Clozel and Angoulvant being the others). This had more effect on his declarations and rhetoric than on his policies, at least in the Senegalo-Mauritanian zone.

62. See Robinson, "'French Africans.'" For Faidherbe's team, see Saint-Martin, *Second Empire,* chap. 13. One can also discern a "Gouraud team" that originated in the campaigns against Samori in the late 1890s and included Henri Gaden.

63. A careful study of administrative and personnel files might suggest how these people appeared at crucial places at critical times. One could also look at the interest and long roles in the Senegalo-Mauritanian zone of other Frenchmen, such as Georges Adam, Ernest Noirot, and Georges Poulet. They are not as critical for this story as the ones I treat here. Two African officials who might be considered here are Yamar Mbodj, introduced in chap. 1, and Yoro Diaw, mentioned in chap. 2 (see Manchuelle, "Assimilés ou patriotes africains?"). Mbodj and Diaw were from the royal lineages of Walo, attended the school for sons of chiefs, and served for a long time in the colonial administration— and as informants and amateur historians. In chap. 6, I also consider two members of the Lô family and other Saint-Louisians who went into colonial administration.

64. See ANS 13G 153 and 154, and CAOM SEN 4, 127. Allys's personnel file is at CAOM EE 2, 721. For the suppression of the reformer Samba Diadana Ndiatch and his decapitation, see Robinson, *Chiefs and Clerics,* 152–53.

65. Klein, Islam and Imperialism, 205–6.

66. It is not clear what role Allys played in the initial French contacts with Malik Sy, who settled in Tivaouane in 1902; Malik Sy did not seek out the French administration, and the administrators did not anticipate any difficulty from his quarter. For Allys's activities at Tivaouane, see ANS 2D 14 4–5; 2G2 40–41; 2G3 42. Allys belonged to the Freemasons; in 1904 he asked for permission to attend a banquet at the lodge in Dakar (2D14 4, letter of 18 May 1904). Victor's son Leopold, born in 1886 in Saint-Louis, became a colonial administrator and served in Côte d'Ivoire, the governor-general's office in Dakar (1920–22), Djibouti, Dahomey, Niger, Guadeloupe, and Soudan. Academie des Sciences d'Outre-Mer, *Hommes et Destins,* tome 9: *Afrique Noire,* 6. See also Searing, "Accommodation and Resistance," chap. 3.

67. On Arnaud, see CAOM EE 2, 730.

68. *Un Corse d'Algérie chez les hommes bleus: Xavier Coppolani, le pacificateur* (Algiers, 1939).

69. Entitled "Précis de la politique musulmane de l'Afrique Occidentale Française." It appeared in book form in Algiers in 1906 and then as a long article in the *BCAF/RC* (1912): 3–20, 115–27, and 141–54. Arnaud interviewed Bamba's brother, Cheikh Thioro, in 1906; his observations appear in the "Précis" on 141–43. For his Moroccan mission, see CAOM AOF 3 Missions 3 (Arnaud 1906–7). For more general information, see CAOM EE 2, 730; Harrison, *France and Islam,* 43–47.

70. In 1902. The main sources on Théveniaut are *Hommes et Destins,* 8:398–405, and CAOM Missions 115, letters of 15 April 1902, note for the direction, 1er bureau, Ministry of Colonies; and 30 April 1902, Saint-Louis, Governor-general Roume to the minister of colonies.

71. Translated by Ismaël Hamet and published as *Chroniques de la Mauritanie Séné-galaise: Nacer Eddine* (Paris, 1911).

72. See chap. 11 and Searing, "Accommodation and Resistance," 253–54. He became active in Senegalese political movements and actually ran for deputy in 1914, the election that Blaise Diagne won. On his political activities, see Johnson, *Black Politics,* 151, 160–70. Théveniaut's last assignment was in Labe, a critical posting in the Futa Jalon in Guinea, in 1914. He retired in 1917, at which point he joined a private society for the exploitation of the African forests. *Hommes et Destins,* vol. 8.

73. In fact, Merlin was acting governor-general at the time, between the terms of de Lamothe and Chaudié. See CAOM SEN 1 5 127, minutes of the *conseil privé* of 16 September 1895. The document is reprinted in Oumar Bâ, ed., *Ahmadou Bamba face aux autorités coloniales, 1889–1927* (Abbeville, France, 1982). See also Robinson, "Beyond Resistance and Collaboration," 160ff.

74. Searing, "Accommodation and Resistance," 127–40.

75. For the personnel references to Merlin, see CAOM EE 2 1699 and 1726. For Merlin's work under Roume's administration, see Searing, "Accommodation," 176–80, 197–98, and passim.

76. Merlin served as governor-general of Indochina after his term in Dakar. Johnson thinks that Diagne got the "best" of Merlin, since he played a role in having Merlin replaced by Jules Carde, someone much more amenable to the deputy. G. Wesley Johnson, "The Impact of the Senegalese Elite upon the French," in Johnson, ed., *Double Impact: France and Africa in the Age of Imperialism* (Greenwich, Conn., 1985). Searing, "Accommodation and Resistance," chap. 6, is less sure.

77. Johnson, *Black Politics,* is still the standard account. For the replacement of the *conseil général* by the *conseil colonial,* see his chap. 2.

CHAPTER 4

1. An earlier version of this chapter, entitled "France as a Muslim Power in West Africa," appeared in *Africa Today* (Bloomington, Ind.) 46, nos 3/4 (1999).

2. They even translated into French the work of C. Snouck Hurgronje, the Dutch

Islamicist, about *politique musulmane* in Indonesia. Snouck Hurgronje, "Politique musulmane de la Hollande," *RMM* 5, no. 6 (1911). It was introduced with great praise by Alfred Le Châtelier, editor of the journal and a prestigious French Islamicist discussed later in this chapter. The work consisted of lectures given in Dutch to a Dutch audience and then translated and published in French. For a presentation of British policy toward Muslims in Mombasa in early colonial Kenya using a "Gramscian" framework, see Tim Carmichael, "British 'Practice' towards Islam in the East Africa Protectorate: Muslim Officials, *waqf* Administration, and Secular Education in Mombasa and Environs, 1895–1920," *Journal of Muslim Minority Affairs* 17 (1997). As late as 1955–56, a prominent Muslim soudanais, Abd al-Wahab Doukoure, was praising France as the "only great Islamic power in the West." See CAOM AFPO 2256, doss. 4.

3. On Napoleon's impact in Egypt and the impact of the Egyptian experience on France, see Jacques Fremeaux, *La France et l'Islam depuis 1789* (Paris, 1991), chaps. 1–2; J. C. B. Richmond, *Egypt, 1798–1952* (New York, 1977), chap. 2, and Edward Said, *Orientalism* (New York, 1978), 80ff. Said describes the encyclopedia *Description de l'Egypte* that Napoleon and his scientists projected; the Orientalist Silvestre de Sacy played a large role in it.

4. Charles-Andre Julien, *Histoire de l'Algérie contemporaine: La conquête et les débuts de la colonisation* (Paris, 1964), esp. chaps. 4–6, and Charles Robert Ageron, *Les Algeriens musulmans et la France, 1871–1919* (Paris, 1968), 2 vols., passim.

5. Faidherbe spent six years in Algeria during the 1840s; Coppolani lived most of his life there before going to the Soudan and Mauritania.

6. Charles Martel's victory near Poitiers in 732, over the Arab and Berber troops, "saved" the French nation in the popular understanding and textbook accounts. For a treatment of Muslims in France and French attitudes toward Islam, see Bruno Etienne, ed., *L'Islam en France: Islam, Etat et société* (Paris, 1990), esp. the chapter by Jean-François Clément, "L'Islam en France." One section of the book deals with the dimension of fear: "La 'Grande Peur' de l'Islam: Mythes et réalités."

7. The French did make an effort to establish special practices for the Kabyles of Algeria and the Berber populations of Morocco, on the relatively accurate assumption that they were not Arab and the relatively inaccurate assumption that they were not very Muslim. See Michael Brett and Elizabeth Fentress, *The Berbers* (London, 1996), esp. chap. 5; and Edmund Burke, "The Image of the Moroccan State in French Ethnological Literature: A New Look at the Origin of Lyautey's Berber Policy," in Ernest Gellner and Charles Micaud, eds., *Arabs and Berbers* (London, 1972).

8. For Cambon's important role in developing France's reputation as an Islamic power, see Frébourg, "Le Corse en Mauritanie." For the Algerian Muslims sent to sub-Saharan Africa, see Kanya-Forstner, "French Missions to the Central Sudan in the 1890s: The Role of Algerian Agents and Interpreters," *Paideuma* 40 (1994). See also CAOM GG ALG 4H, exploration et voyages, 21: indigènes faisant partie des missions, 1892–99. For the Algerians recruited to teach in the Medersas, see, for example, ANS J 93, for the school in Saint-Louis. For the Algerian Sahara and connections with French West Africa, see CAOM GG ALG 10H 30–31 and 22H 35. The Ministries of Colonies and Foreign Affairs were also interested in distributing Arabic newspapers favorable to French interests in the Muslim areas of what was becoming French equatorial Africa. They sent the

Egyptian publication *Al-Ahram* and the Paris paper devoted to Franco-Ottoman relations, *Al-Raja,* to the Oubangui colony. Governor-general Cambon was involved in these
decisions. See, for example, MAE ADP Afrique, carton 12, corresp. of 24 May and 11
October 1895.

9. The book, *Les Confréries Religieuses Musulmanes* (Algiers, 1897), became a kind of
handbook for French officials administering Muslim societies in Africa.

10. It is, however, hard to assess the credibility of these statements with the Muslim
population. In 1841, General Bugeaud, during his service in Algeria, obtained similar
documents from Mecca and Qairouan through the mission that he entrusted to Leon
Roches. CAOM GG ALG 22H 35, Algiers, 2 November 1893, draft of letter to the Ministry of Foreign Affairs. See also Edouard Michaux-Bellaire, "Une fetoua de Cheikh Sidia:
Approuvée par Cheikh Saad Bouh ben Mohammed El Fadil ben Mamin, frère de Cheikh
Ma El Ainin," *Archives Marocaines* 11, no. 1 (1907); Ageron, *Les Algériens musulmans,* 1:513.

11. See the useful summary of Moroccan identity in Henry Munson Jr, *Religion and
Power in Morocco* (New Haven, Conn., 1992), esp. chap. 2. For Morocco in relation to
French imperial thinking, see Daniel Rivet, *Lyautey et l'institution du protectorat français au
Maroc, 1912–1925* (Paris, 1988), 3 vols., esp. chaps. 1–3.

12. See, for example, the last document in John Hanson and David Robinson, *After
the Jihad: The Reign of Ahmad al-Kabir in the Western Sudan* (East Lansing, Mich., 1991),
243–48. In this letter. Amadu Sheku, the son of Al-Hajj Umar, appeals for Moroccan
intervention against the French. The community of Timbuktu made a similar appeal at
the same time, 1893. Morocco was not in any position to come to their aid.

13. In one sense this chapter is an effort to go back over the ground that Chris
Harrison trod in *France and Islam.* Harrison works from the framework created by Donal
Cruise O'Brien, in his influential article "Towards an 'Islamic Policy,'" and gives a treatment of French policy and practice vis-à-vis its Muslim subjects in West Africa, beginning in the time of Faidherbe. Unfortunately, Harrison uses only colonial archival
sources, and not all of the relevant ones, and he is thus not able to tell a continuous
story nor show the patterns of practice.

14. See my article "Ethnography and Customary Law in Senegal," *CEA* 126 (1992).

15. The most conspicuous example is Léopold Sédar Senghor, the Serer poet, phi-
losopher, and first president of Senegal (1960–80), who received his initial education in
Catholic schools on the *petite côte* of Senegal. For Roman Catholic views of the Senegalo-
Mauritanian zone in the mid nineteenth century, see Abbe D. Boilât, *Esquisses sénégalaises*
(Paris, 1855), Frédéric Carrère and Paul Holle, *De la Sénégambie française* (Paris, 1855).

16. Robinson, "French 'Islamic' Policy."

17. For an early example of French views of the Moors, prior to those articulated
by Faidherbe in the 1850s, see Lt. Col. d'Infanterie Caille, "Notes sur les peuples de la
Mauritanie et de la Nigiritie, riverains du Sénégal, recueillis en octobre 1842," *Revue
Coloniale* (September 1846). For a treatment of the evolution of European attitudes toward race and color in the nineteenth century, see Edith Sanders, "The Hamitic Hypothesis: Its Origins and Functions in Time Perspective," *JAH* 10 (1969). Sanders sees
the impact of Egypt on Napoleon's scientists as decisive in the development of "white
Hamites" as bearers of civilization to "black Africa." This thinking is applicable to all of
the dimensions of religious ethnography discussed here.

18. Abbe D. Boilât, *Esquisses sénégalaises* (Paris, 1853), 384–86; Laurent J. B. Bérenger-Féraud, *Les peuplades de la Sénégambie* (Paris, 1879), 122–52.

19. The term *Tokolor* (*toucouleur,* in French) was not used until the nineteenth century, and then specifically as a way to distinguish the sedentary, state-building Muslims from the rest of the Fulbe. On Tokolor, and specifically Umarian, images, see Moustapha Kane, Sonja Fagerberg-Diallo, and David Robinson, "Une vision iconoclaste de la guerre sainte d'Al-Hajj Umar Taal," *CEA* 133–35 (1994). For a more general treatment of Tokolor, and the term *hal-pular,* "speakers of Pular" (the name inhabitants of Futa Toro themselves use), see *Encyclopedia of Islam,* 2nd ed., 1999; s.v., Robinson, "Tokolor." For the Tokolor image in contrast to that of more tolerant and malleable Muslims, such as the Mande-speaking peoples, see Robinson, "Ethnography," 223–24.

20. Robinson, "Ethnography," 225. For Faidherbe's role in fostering the image of a parasitic Wolof court, see Diouf, *Kajoor,* pt. 3.

21. For the discussion about whether the government provided some support for the mosque, see Boilât, *Esquisses sénégalaises,* 207–8: Carrère and Holle, *Sénégambie française,* 14–15. Both of these works express a "Catholic" point of view.

22. For the strong commitment to the Muslim court, see ANS M 8, passim; CAOM SEN 8 14bis, and Fernand Carles, *La France et l'Islam en Afrique Occidentale* (Toulouse, 1915), 176–77. For a general summary of the issues of Muslim justice in colonial Senegal, see Dominique Sarr and Richard Roberts, "The Jurisdiction of Muslim Tribunals in Colonial Senegal, 1857–1932," in Richard Roberts and Kristin Mann, eds., *Law in Colonial Africa* (London, 1991), 131–45. In their colonies, the French and British followed the same broad distinction between personal law, which could come under Islamic courts, and criminal jurisdiction, which fell under the state courts. See Gabriel Warburg, *The Sudan under Wingate* (London, 1971), 124–36.

23. The lay society was the Brothers of Ploermel—a name taken from the brothers' headquarters in Brittany.

24. In Senegal, in the *Moniteur du Sénégal et Dépendances.* In France, typically in the *Revue Coloniale* and then its successor, the *Revue Coloniale et Maritime,* and in bulletins of the geographical societies of France. See Robinson, *Chiefs and Clerics,* 28–33. In all of these initiatives, Faidherbe was following Algerian precedents.

25. It was called the Bureau of External Affairs at its inception and the Direction of Indigenous Affairs at certain moments in the nineteenth century. See Saint-Martin, *Second Empire,* 139–40.

26. *Tamsir* is a Pular variant of *tafsir,* "exegesis," but refers to the exegete (in Arabic, *mufassir*). For Ndiaye and Hamat Ndiaye, I rely on my interview with Hamat's great-grandson, Buna Abdussalam Kane, in Dakar on 29 May 1985; Carrère and Holle, *Sénégambie française,* 239–43; Lucie Colvin, "Kajor," 90. Ndiaye had strong connections with refugees from Jolof who settled in Saint-Louis in the area called Jolofène. References to Tamsir Hamat are contained frequently in the newspaper that Faidherbe launched in 1856, the *Moniteur du Sénégal et Dépendances (MSD),* at times called the *Feuille Officielle du Sénégal et Dépendances (FOSD),* and eventually replaced by the *Journal Officiel (JO).* Especially useful is the obituary in the *MSD* of 20 May 1879.

27. "Journal de la Congrégation de Saint-Louis," entry for 1857.

28. CAOM SEN 1 43a, letter of 5 August 1856.

29. Hamat's salary in 1857 was 12,000 francs, a considerable sum and higher than some of the European bureaucrats. He supplemented this with property in Saint-Louis and farms outside of town. He may have been able to use indentured servants on his farms; that was certainly his request in a letter stressing the unfairness of compensation to French slaveholders and not Senegalese ones. *Moniteur du Sénégal et Dépendences* 17 November 1857.

30. For example, he wrote to the Muslim leaders in Dakar to sanction the new cemetery that the French were proposing: "Hamat is writing to the marabouts of Dakar to explain to them that what we are seeking is in no way contrary to Muslim law, which permits disinterring the dead to bury them elsewhere, whereas our intention is not to disinter but to provide for burial in the future in a new location." Contained in Governor Faidherbe to commandant of Gorée, 6 June 1860, in Jacques Charpy, ed., *La fondation de Dakar, 1845-1857-1869* (Paris, 1958), 221. In 1865, Hamat received a letter from Ma Ba Diakhu explaining that French commercial activity was acceptable, whereas political domination was not. ANS 13G 318, pièces 15-16, n.d. See Klein, *Islam and Imperialism,* 79-86.

31. *Ibnu-l-moqdad* means "son of the one who nurtures," suggesting the reputation of Abdullay within the Arabic-speaking community. For the Seck family, see Oumar Bâ, *La Pénétration française au Cayor* (1854-61) (Dakar, 1976), 1:284-86; Joseph Galliéni, *Deux campagnes au Soudan français, 1886-88* (Paris, 1891), 326-27; Vincent Monteil, *Esquisses sénégalaises* (Dakar, 1966), 107; Samb, *Essai,* 73-84; Sire-Abbas-Soh, *Chroniques du Futa sénégalais,* M. Delafosse and H. Gaden, eds. (Paris, 1913), 188-89; Paul Soleillet, *Voyage à Ségou de Paul Soleillet, 1842-86),* G. Gravier, ed. (Paris, 1887), 23-26. Many references, especially to his awards, come from the *MSD* and *FOSD.*

32. In this treatment I have relied in part on two interviews with descendants of the Seck: one of them, I conducted with Judge Aissata Rabi Almamy Wane in Dakar on 28 June 1997; the other, Ghislaine Lydon conducted with Abu Latif ibn Mohammed ibn Abdullay Seck in Saint-Louis on 5 November 1997 at the home of Sidi Mokhtar Ndiaye at Sor.

33. Paul Marty, *Etudes sur l'Islam au Sénégal,* 2 vols. (Paris, 1917), 1:18-19.

34. *MSD,* 9 April 1867.

35. This strategy was replicated in 1907-9, when Sidiyya Baba was paired as a counterforce to Ma El Ainin, the jihadist based in the Sahara desert. See below and chap. 10. For Bu El Mogdad's initiatives, see Robinson, *Holy War,* 214, where there is a translation of a poem written by Seck and published in the official journal. It is taken from Claudine Gerresch, "Jugements du *Moniteur du Sénégal* sur Al-Hajj Umar, de 1857 à 1864," *BIFAN,* ser. B, 35 (1973): 582.

36. Taken from the J. D. Hargreaves translation from the French (ostensibly that of Bu El Mogdad himself, but perhaps with the aid of someone in the Political Affairs Bureau) in his *France and West Africa* (London, 1969), 150; the selection is from ANS 1G 27, letter of Bu El Mogdad to Flize, 24 November 1860. The letter is also found in Bu El Mogdad's account of the first part of his trip, "Voyage par terre entre le Sénégal et le Maroc," *Revue Maritine et Coloniale,* vol. 1 for May 1861, 477-92. A sketch of Bu El Mogdad, with French medals displayed on his robe, was published in *Le Tour du*

Monde in 1861; see plate 2 and Saint-Martin, *Le Sénégal,* facing page 289. Almost nothing is made of the pilgrimage the following year of Hamat Ndiaye Anne; it may be that the Tamsir's journey was compensation for the support given to his younger colleague. For the notation of his pilgrimage, see *FOSD* for 25 March 1862.

37. He returned with a sword and caftans; these were gifts from the Ottoman government destined for Amadu Sheku and designed to assist in the mission that Joseph Galliéni was about to undertake, as an officer of the Direction of Political Affairs, to Segu. Galliéni, *Voyage au Soudan français: Haut-Niger et pays de Ségou, 1879–81* (Paris, 1885), 367.

38. ANS 2B 52.759, 24 October 1880, quoted in Bâ, *Pénétration,* 285. Lat Dior was equally moved: "We are in mourning, to the point where we can no longer distinguish night from day, or the elephant from the ant." From ANS 13G 260, 1880 letters, according to Vincent Monteil, *Esquisses sénégalaises* (Dakar, 1966), 107.

39. The Sarr family remained prominent in Saint-Louis through the early twentieth century, but not at the same level as the Seck. Ndiaye Sarr was a well-established merchant when he was selected for the position of qadi of the tribunal. Robinson interview with his son, Umar Ndiaye Sarr, 4 June 1985, in Saint-Louis.

40. A whole series of *traitants* who had worked for the French for many years were pressed into service in the Haut Sénégal administration, beginning in 1880. See *Annuaire,* 1880 ff.

41. See the reference to him in n. 54.

42. Dudu, like the other members of the Seck family, studied with the Ahel Lamana family of the Idabhum fraction of the Awlad Daiman. For more information on Dudu, see his "Mémoire de Bou El Mogdad (jusqu'en 1903)," Bureau politique, Colonie de la Mauritanie, (ca. 1910), Archives de la République Islamique de la Mauritanie (RIM) E/2/124; ANS 9G 14, pièce 9, and IG 70, pièce 50 (Kayes, 8 September 86); Frébourg, "Le Corse en Mauritanie," passim. Dudu was on close terms not only with Coppolani but also Merlin, Gouraud, and other important French decision makers at the turn of the century. In the near disaster that was the Blanchet mission to the Adrar in 1900, Dudu stayed behind while the black soldiers fled; he participated actively in the negotiations that saved the mission. See Hamet, *Chroniques,* "Notice de Saad Buh."

43. The best testimony comes from Governor Henri de Lamothe, who along with Merlin, director of political affairs, saw the utility of sending Dudu on the pilgrimage and using the resulting prestige. CAOM, de Lamothe papers, 4PA 1 (political affairs), 5 January 1895, de Lamothe to the Ministry of Colonies. In particular, de Lamothe wrote: "Despite being a pilgrim to Mecca, where we sent him last year, or perhaps because he is a pilgrim, he is not inclined to fanaticism. His devotion to the French cause is complete, absolute. . . . He inspires confidence among the Moors, makes them forget their assumption that we are trying to spread our beliefs in place of theirs, and dissipates their fear of seeing 'infidels' come into their land." See also Dudu's account of his mission to Tagant in 1894, not long after his return from the pilgrimage; it is obvious in his account that his *bidan* interlocutors are well aware of his hajj. Mohamedou Ould Mohameden, "Les tentatives de pénétration française dans le pays maure à travers le rapport mission de Bou El Mogdad en 1894 au Tagant," *Masadir,* cahier 1, 1994.

44. He records this in his memoir, cited in n. 42 above; see also ANS 1G 243.

45. See the interview with Abu Latif Seck cited in n. 32. Two other brothers, Ain-ina (d. 1941) and Suleymane (d. 1913), filled more routine functions in Saint-Louis with the Muslim Tribunal, the Ecole des Fils de Chefs et Interprètes, and the Medersa, or Franco-Arabic school. Marty, *Sénégal,* 1:18–19.

46. The Wane of Mbumba were quick to realize this. Amadu Samba married Mariam Buna, daughter of Bu El Mogdad, while Baila Birane, a pillar of support for Coppolani's actions in Mauritania, married Khadi, daughter of Dudu. See the interview with Judge Aissata Rabi Wane cited in n. 32 above.

47. There is no public evidence that they protested any French action. The Seck tradition says that Dudu, when asked to be present for the "trial" of Amadu Bamba in front of the *conseil privé* in 1895, absented himself ostensibly because a foot wound made it painful to walk. See the Wane interview cited in n. 32.

48. Joseph Galliéni, in his mission to negotiate a peace treaty with Ahmad al-Kabir, reported that Ahmad had dispatched envoys to the French, who were also bringing 1,000 gros of gold to Bu El Mogdad. ANS 1G 30 42, letter of 19 February 1880 from Matam.

49. It also involved strengthening the French presence in the Southern Rivers area, essentially the coast of Guinea (Conakry), and further down the coast in what would become Côte d'Ivoire.

50. All three of these reformers were Tijaniyya, and all were of Futanke origin. But Ma Ba was a Wolof speaker who grew up in the Rip, south of Salum, while the Madiyanke were Futanke on their father's side and Wolof on their mother's. Such nuances were inconsequential, of course, to the ethnic and religious stereotypes.

51. Robinson, "French 'Islamic' Policy," 427–28; Robinson, *Chiefs and Clerics,* 150. See also ANS 1G 70, pièce 92, letter of 5 August 1886; Journal de la Communauté Chrétienne de Saint-Louis, entry for 1885 on the Mahdi.

52. The key soudanais were Jean Jauréguiberry, who served a brief time as governor of Senegal, in the position of minister of the navy from 1879 to 1883, and Joseph Galliéni, Gustave Borgnis-Desbordes, and eventually Louis Archinard, who served as commandants supérieurs. Galliéni was initially director of the political affairs bureau. L. Barrows, "L'oeuvre, la carrière du Général Faidherbe, et les débuts de l'Afrique Noire Française: Une analyse critique contemporaine," *Le Mois en Afrique,* nos. 239–40 (December 1985-January 1986); A. S. Kanya-Forstner, *Conquest,* 60ff.; Person, *Samori,* 1:364–70. For the use of the Tijaniyya-Tokolor equation, see Hanson, *Migration,* 8–9.

53. The 1887 mission of Lieutenant Caron. The main archival source for Abdel Kader is ANS 1G 70. Faidherbe was an important advocate of Abdel Kader and may have secured his passage on the Caron gunboat, at a time when many French officials were becoming very suspicious about his identity (*Le Sénégal,* 398–407, 461–69; Barrows, "L'oeuvre," 144–46). For secondary sources, see Kanya-Forstner, *Conquest,* 110, 121–22; B. Oloruntimehin, "'Abd al-Qadir's Mission as a Factor in Franco-Tukulor Relations, 1885–1887," *Genève-Afrique* 7, no. 2 (1968).

54. The incident showed that the administration was woefully unprepared to evaluate the authenticity of Abdel Kader, and even to translate the Arabic letters that he brought. Colonel Combes in Kayes complained bitterly that he had had no competent translator since Abdullay, son of Bu El Mogdad, had left the Haut Fleuve administration in 1884; the "professor of Arabic" assigned to accompany Abdel Kader proved inadequate. ANS 1G 70.

55. *Les confréries musulmanes dans le Hedjaz* (Paris, 1887). For a biography, see Raymond Messal, *La genèse de notre victoire marocaine: Un précurseur Alfred Le Châtelier (1855–1929)* (Paris, 1931).

56. Le Châtelier traveled in conjunction with Joseph Galliéni, who was about to embark on his second year as commandant supérieur of the Soudan. *L'Islam dans l'Afrique Occidentale* was written primarily in 1888–89 but not published until 1899. The manuscript was in limited circulation during the 1890s. See Messal, *Le Châtelier,* chap. 4.

57. He was almost certainly wrong about that; it is unlikely that the Tijaniyya had much popularity in Saint-Louis in the late 1880s, even though Malik Sy had begun to make some impression there.

58. Le Châtelier had initially been an advocate of the Algerian interpretation. Others, including Governor-general Cambon himself, came to question the hypothesis of the "dangerous brotherhoods." Ageron, *Les Algériens musulmans,* 514–16. In the twentieth century, Le Châtelier had a great deal to do with the Marty publications. After travels in Morocco and other areas of Africa during the 1890s, Le Châtelier was appointed to a chair of "Muslim sociology" at the Collège de France, founded the Scientific Mission of Morocco and its publication, *Archives Marocaines,* and founded and became the first editor of the *Revue du Monde Musulman* in 1906. See chap. 3, pp. 72–73, and note 69, p. 266. Virtually all of Marty's volumes were published in the *Revue.* See Messal, *Le Châtelier,* 289–90; Edmund Burke, *Prelude to the Protectorate of Morocco* (Chicago, 1976), 98, 289–90.

59. The French allowed their allies to prey upon the weary travelers as they moved from east to west. In one case, in Bakel, the local commander Roux participated in the execution and decapitation of thirty-six returnees. See CAOM, De Lamothe papers, 4PA/1 (political affairs), letter 401 of 16 April 1891, "confidential and personal," governor to Ministry of Colonies. A Catholic priest took pictures of the heads of the victims, sent them to France, and forced the governor to explain, but the affair never got the publicity of the executions related to the murder of Jeandet. For the return, see Robinson, *Chiefs and Clerics,* 157–58.

60. See Ibrahima Abou Sall, "L'extension de la Tijaniyya au Futa Toro," in Robinson and Triaud, *La Tijaniyya.*

61. On Sakho, see chap. 7, and Sall, "Mukhtar Sakho." Sakho worked closely with Malik Sy and Seydu Nuru Tal in helping Futanke and Wolof Muslims adjust to colonial rule. By the time Marty published his study of Islam in Senegal *(Etudes sur l'Islam au Sénégal)* in 1917, the French were distinguishing between an Umarian and a "Wolof" Tijaniyya—the latter associated with Malik Sy.

62. This is essentially the argument I make in "French 'Islamic' Policy," 416.

63. See M. Perron, *Précis de jurisprudence musulmane, ou principes de législation musulmane civile et religieuse, selon le rite malékite, par Khalil Ibn-Ishak,* 6 vols., *Khalil b Ish'aq: Abrégé de la loi musulmane selon le rite de l'imam Malek,* 4 vols. (Algiers, 1956–62).

64. *Les confréries religieuses Musulmanes,* cited in n. 9. As part of the campaign to "domesticate" the West African Tijaniyya, the French also made some efforts to itinerate their Algerian Tijaniyya allies in West Africa in the 1890s. See CAOM SEN 4 127, Paris, 2 December 1893, letter of governor of Senegal to the Ministry of Colonies.

65. See ANS 2B 74, letter of governor to minister, April 1882; Le Châtelier, *Islam,* 329–34; Marty, "Les Fadelia," *RMM* 31 (1915–16): esp. 180–200.

66. Marty, *Sénégal,* 1:357. See ibid, 333–64, for more detail on Bu Kunta, and Faidherbe, *Le Sénégal,* 406.

67. "Le Panislamisme et la France," *Revue Franco-musulmane et Saharienne* 1, no. 4 (1902): 30–38. Coppolani expressed the same thinking in a 1900 letter to the Ministry of Colonies (10 March 1900, Institut de France, Fonds Auguste Terrier, MS 5942). This thinking was highly prevalent in certain Islamicist and French Algerian circles in the early twentieth century. See Cruise O'Brien, "Towards an 'Islamic Policy,'" 308, and CAOM Missions 115 — for example, the letter of 1 August 1902 from the Service of Muslim Affairs. In 1902, the French also printed a map of Africa in Arabic, showing the portions occupied by France. See CAOM AOF 12 3c, 22 March 1902, with note of transmission from the cabinet of the Ministry of Colonies.

68. Coppolani published his projects (almost as soon as he presented them to the ministries and the Interministeriel Commission in Paris) in his journal *La Revue Franco-Musulmane et Saharienne,* nos. 5–8, October 1902 to January 1903. The purpose of the journal was expressed in the first number of the first volume (5 May 1902): "[T]o study the Muslim world in its political and religious organization . . . and seek the means to make our Muslim subjects evolve in the direction of progress . . . and to demonstrate our deep interest in making use of religious leaders who have been won over to our cause." The patronage committee was filled by prominent exponents of French expansion, including Eugene Etienne, René Basset, Louis-Gustave Binger, Joseph Chailley-Bert, André Chautemps, François Deloncle, Charles Dupuy, Gabriel Hanotaux, and Henri Poincaré. The journal apparently discontinued publication at the end of 1903.

69. In 1900, the Blanchet scientific mission to the Adrar had almost been annihilated (see n. 42, above, also chap. 8, and "Notice de Cheikh Saad Bouh," in Hamet, *Mauritanie Sénégalaise*), and this made Coppolani's task that much more difficult. Coppolani made his arguments to a variety of officials in Paris between 1899 and 1901. He broke through the opposition, including that of Governors-general Chaudié and Bellay in Saint-Louis, thanks to the support of the president of the council and minister of the interior, Waldeck-Rousseau, who assembled an interministerial commission involving colonies, interior, and foreign affairs. He received final approval for his "pacification" campaign in October 1901, after submitting a report in which he stressed the *bidan* as the "natural link for commercial transactions between North and West Africa." But the Saqiya al-Hamra, in the process of becoming Rio de Oro, or Spanish Sahara, was excised from Coppolani's original design of 1900. CAOM Mauritanie 4.1, report of 14 October 1901, and "L'origine de la Mauritanie," MS 5942, Fonds Auguste Terrier. See also Frébourg, "Le Corse en Mauritanie," pt. 3, chap. 1.

70. Taken from the French translation provided by Michaux-Bellaire, ed. and trans., "Une fetoua de Cheikh Sidia," 137–38. It is worth noting that this journal was under the direction of Alfred Le Châtelier. In his report to Governor-general Roume on 1 July 1904, Coppolani said of Baba: "Cheikh Sidia, whose devotion to the French cause cannot be overestimated, and who is considered by everyone to be the imam of the country, launched a veritable campaign in favor of the pacification of Saharan Mauritania by the

French, the only power able to achieve this goal, and developed his arguments from religious precepts and Muslim law against the propaganda in favor of the jihad." CAOM Mauritanie 4 1. For more detail, see chap. 9.

71. The "maraboutic alliances" that were established and effective in the Senegalo-Mauritanian zone have too often been taken as desirable for, or descriptive of, French West Africa as a whole. See Triaud, intro. to Robinson and Triaud, *Le Temps des Marabouts.*

72. Many of them remained in office for considerable periods of time, despite the abuses. This suggests that the chiefs recognized some limits on abuse, and that the colonial authorities tolerated a considerable level of abuse, as long as they obtained, in return, order, reasonable loyalty, and good sources of information. See Searing, "Accommodation and Resistance," passim.

73. Klein, *Slavery,* chap. 12.

74. Arnaud and Coppolani would have supported this option on the basis of their Algerian background. For the successes and failures of "official clergy" in Algeria, see Ageron, *Les Algériens musulmans,* vol. 2, chap. 32.

75. Sidiyya Baba often functioned like a high-level administrator of accommodation and surveillance in the first two decades of the twentieth century, without sacrificing the great prestige that came from his lineage and his own credentials. He gave an early and eloquent example of this when he served as the host for Amadu Bamba during the Murid leader's second exile (1903–7).

76. See Munson, *Religion and Power,* and Geertz, *Islam Observed* (New Haven, Conn., 1968).

77. In the same sense that British prestige was enhanced by possession of India, and Queen Victoria's prestige by her title Empress of India, in the late nineteenth century. See David Cannadine, "The Context, Performance, and Meaning of Ritual: The British Monarchy and the 'Invention of Tradition,' ca. 1820–1977," in Eric Hobsbawm and Terence Ranger, eds., *The Invention of Tradition* (London, 1983), esp. 120–32.

78. The story is well told in Burke, *Prelude to the Protectorate.*

79. In the areas of the Algerian Sahara where the French were rapidly extending their control, such as the Tuat oases (see CAOM GG ALG 22H, 41, carton 89, corresp. 1893–94; GG ALG 22H 35, for 1891–14), around Timbuktu and the Niger Buckle (see Hanson and Robinson, *After the Jihad,* 243–48), and in the area that would become Mauritania (see, for example, CAOM SEN 4 128, letter of 24 June 1901, Governor-general Ballay to the Ministry of Colonies).

80. One of the most complete accounts of the conquest and Lyautey's role is Rivet, *Lyautey.* For the Pan-Islamic and Egyptian dimensions of Morocco's crisis, see Edmund Burke, "Pan-Islam and Moroccan Resistance to French Colonial Penetration, 1900–1912," *JAH* 13 (1972).

81. The emergence of Ma El Ainin diminished the standing of Saad Buh with the French. The loss of prestige was due in part to the propaganda of Baba, who missed few opportunities to "inform" the French about the "situation" in Mauritania. See Glen W. McLaughlin, "Sufi, Saint, Sharif: Muhammad Fadil Wuld Mamin: His Spiritual Legacy and the Political Economy of the Sacred in Nineteenth Century Mauritania," Ph.D. diss., Northwestern University, 1997, chaps. 5–7. McLaughlin gives a useful summary

of Ma El Ainin; the fullest English account is still the one contained in B. G. Martin, *Muslim Brotherhoods*. I have also benefited from the 1998–99 master's essay of Shannon Vance, a Michigan State University student, on Ma El Ainin.

82. In 1900, Coppolani even expressed the hope of winning the cleric over to his program of "pacification" in his presentation to the Ministries of Foreign Affairs, Colonies, and Interior. Frébourg, "Le Corse en Mauritanie," pt. 3.

83. More even than the French demonized Al-Hajj Umar and the Tijaniyya.

84. In 1909, as Gouraud led his columns into the Adrar, Ma El Ainin moved away from Smara to Tiznit in the north in an action that he defined as a hijra from the infidel. After a brief visit and tumultuous welcome of his followers in Morocco, he returned to Tiznit; he died in 1910.

85. ANS 9G, 24, pièce 22, 26 March 1907, Saint-Louis, commissaire to Governor-general Gouraud developed the same idea: "The progress of Moroccan influence in the Adrar, in the form of Ma El Ainin and because of the pompous receptions that he received in Morocco on the part of Sultans Hafid and Abd al-Aziz, [caused] the government-general to want to make the local population take note, in a striking public presentation, in what esteem it held the great marabout who had placed his religious authority in the service of the cause of civilization." "Note au sujet du voyage de Cheikh Sidia," in ANS 5D 40, pièce 20, cited in Sall, "Mauritanie," 676n.

86. For the "pairing" of Baba with Ma El Ainin and for Baba's role with the minister of colonies, see Désiré-Vuillemin, *Contribution,* 113, 125, 134, 322–23; ANS 9G 18; *Bulletin de la Société de Géographie de l'AOF,* 30 June 1908. See also Gouraud, *Souvenirs,* 31ff.

87. See n. 58. Arnaud's work was more policy-specific than that of Le Châtelier. Arnaud was officially assigned to "Muslim Affairs" in the political bureau of the secretary-general of the federation in 1905. CAOM EE2, 730, Dakar, letter of Arnaud to Ministry of Colonies, 21 November 1905. He was sent among the Ullimiden Tuareg in 1906, to Morocco in 1907, and to Guinea and Côte d'Ivoire in 1908 as an Islamic specialist under the governor-general. For his Moroccan mission, designed to assess the popularity of Ma El Ainin, see CAOM AOF 3 Missions 3, Arnaud 1906–7; Désiré-Vuillemin, *Contribution,* 348–50. It is interesting to note that Roume and Merlin sent François-Joseph Clozel, also attached to the government-general and a future governor-general himself, on a mission to Algeria in 1907 to examine the practice of colonial "higher education" for the "natives." *Hommes et Destins,* vol. 1, CLOZEL.

88. Harrison, *France and Islam,* 105–7.

89. As mentioned in chap. 2, it was at this time that a special series of the G archives, 19G for "Affaires Musulmanes," was created. The files begin with the date 1906. Information on most of the apparatus of surveillance outlined in this paragraph can be found in the 19G files.

90. Courts were created, somewhat on the Saint-Louis model, in Kayes, Jenne, Timbuktu, Boutilimit, and several other locations in the early twentieth century.

91. Published in a special number entitled "Les musulmans français et la guerre: Adresses et témoignages de fidélité des chefs musulmans et des personnages religieux de l'Afrique Occidentale," vol. 29, no. 1, published in 1915.

92. Not surprisingly, he developed a very close link to Baba, the most curious and

outgoing of the four marabouts analyzed in this book. Marty gave him the most favorable treatment, at times adopting Sidiyya positions on personalities and issues. See McLaughlin, "Sufi, Saint, Sharif," chaps. 5–7. Arnaud prepared the way for Marty's formulations of *Islam noir* and *Islam maure* in his 1906 *Précis*. See Harrison, *France and Islam*, 43–45.

93. One could argue that the French created multiple departments—Islam soudanais, Islam guinéen, and so on—corresponding to the volumes published by Marty on Islam in French West Africa between 1914 and 1921. But more typically these were grouped under *Islam noir*.

94. See Harrison, *France and Islam*, pt. 3, and Vincent Monteil, *Islam noir* (Paris, 1964).

95. The distinction was emphasized by Coppolani. In 1901, before his campaigns, he wrote: "We must never forget that the Moors have no common origin with the races of Soudan and Senegal, that their customs and social organization are completely different from those of the West African population now under our domination. It would be an irreparable mistake to apply the same administrative system [to them]." CAOM AFPO 1420, Coppolani's report to the Ministry of Colonies of 12 June 1901.

96. One could add another Maghribist to the list. Octave Houdas was a French Orientalist who taught Arabic, in Paris and Algiers. His daughter Alice married Maurice Delafosse, at the point where Delafosse was about to embark on his administrative and scholarly career in West Africa. Houdas then translated the two Arabic chronicles of Timbuktu, the *Ta'rikh al-Fettash* and the *Ta'rikh al-Soudan* (Paris, 1913), and retained a strong interest in Muslim societies in West Africa. See Louise Delafosse, *Maurice Delafosse: Le Berrichon conquis par l'Afrique* (Paris, 1976), 77 and passim.

CHAPTER 5

1. See the quote from Nicholas Dirks, in his reader *Colonialism and Culture*, 7, cited in the introduction, n. 16.

2. Its major application in Africa has been to postcolonial governments and societies, especially to the efforts of the less powerful to bring pressure to bear on the ruling classes. See Jean-François Bayart, *L'Etat en Afrique: La politique du ventre* (Paris, 1989).

3. For a classic exposition of a theory of collaboration and brokerage, with special reference to the Anglo-Egyptian Sudan, see Ronald Robinson, "Non-European Foundations of European Imperialism: Sketch for a Theory of Collaboration," in R. Owen and B. Sutcliffe, eds., *Studies in the Theory of Imperialism*, 1972. On the "Legcos," see G. Ayodele Langley, *Pan-Africanism and Nationalism in West Africa, 1900–1945: A Study in Ideology and Social Classes* (Oxford, 1973).

4. The rights of citizenship were extended in Senegal and other parts of French West Africa only during the process of decolonization after World War II.

5. Alfred Stepan uses political and civil society to refer to the public and private spheres in *Rethinking Military Politics: Brazil and the Southern Cone* (Princeton, N.J., 1988), chap. 1, but his political society is the arena of competition for the control of the state. I am not using "public sphere" in the sense of Jürgen Habermas. See Craig Calhoun, ed., *Habermas and the Public Sphere* (Cambridge, Mass., 1992).

6. The most complete sources for these institutions are Johnson, *Black Politics,* chaps. 2, 5, and 6, and François Zuccarelli, *La vie politique sénégalaise, 1789–1940* (Paris, 1987), pt. 1. Johnson gives a much better overview, but tends to overly schematize his work into successive periods of French, métis, and African dominance.

7. The right to vote, and enjoy the other aspects of citizenship, was debated continuously until it was finally resolved by legislation introduced by Blaise Diagne in 1915 to establish the rights of originaires. The government occasionally checked voting lists and barred some voters, but it was never able or willing to restrict the vote to those with clearly established French citizenship. See Johnson, *Black Politics,* 183–91.

8. Governor François-Xavier Valière (1869–76) did persuade the Ministry of the Navy to end the deputyship for three years, but it was restored in 1879. The political consequences in France of infringing upon the rights of citizens in the Senegal communes limited the options of the colonial administration.

9. The Bordeaux houses often supported retired navy officers who had served in Senegal, enjoyed a certain prestige, and were favorable to their interests. One of these men, Admiral Aristide Vallon, had served with Faidherbe in Senegal and held the position of deputy for Senegal from 1889 to 1893.

10. A concise treatment of municipal institutions in Senegal can be found in Mbaye, *Institutions,* 177 ff. Note that Hamat Ndiaye Anne was appointed third-deputy mayor of Saint-Louis by Faidherbe, in chap. 4.

11. See Lucie Colvin, "Kajor and Its Diplomatic Relations with Saint-Louis du Sénégal, 1763–1861," Ph.D. diss., Columbia University, 1972, esp. 87–88, 220, 398; Taylor, "Of Disciples and Sultans," chap. 4.

12. The decree left open the possibility for other towns in Senegal to acquire the same rights. Rufisque took advantage of this in 1880, and Dakar, which was previously associated with Gorée, obtained its own representation in 1887.

13. Until that time, the governor chose the mayors from among the councilors.

14. The electoral politics of the late nineteenth century are usually portrayed as a conflict between the Descemet and Devès clans or, by the turn of the century, between the Devès and Carpot clans. See Manchuelle, "*Métis* et colons," and Johnson, *Black Politics,* ch. 6.

15. They seemed to have a penchant for retired navy officers, such as Aristide Vallon, cited in n. 9 above.

16. Joan Casey, "The Politics of French Imperialism in the Early Third Republic: The Case of Bordeaux," Ph.D. diss., University of Missouri, Columbia, 1973, chap. 4. By and large, the Bordeaux interests were successful in getting most of the deputies to support legislation and other initiatives favorable to their interests. The deputies from Senegal were Alfred Gasconi (1879–89), Aristide Vallon (1889–93), Jules Couchard (1893–98), Hector d'Agoult (1898–1902), François Carpot (1902–14), and Blaise Diagne (1914–34). Gasconi and Carpot were métis; Diagne was black; the others were white.

17. The Ligue was a prestigious organization that monitored the situation in the colonies quite closely. Johnson, *Black Politics,* 72. One can see the extent to which the Ligue intervened in Senegalese and other imperial affairs, by looking at the files of the CAOM political affairs—for example, AFPO 512, on various kinds of litigation in the early twentieth century, including a file on Mody Mbaye, discussed in chap. 6.

18. For the council's duties and interaction with the governor, see Johnson, *Black Politics,* chap. 2, esp. 58–60, and Mbaye, *Institutions,* 151–54.

19. Later more members were added to the Rufisque and Dakar slates. The strong "republican" interests did not take effective control of the Third Republic until 1879. See Philip Nord, *The Republican Moment: Struggles for Democracy in Nineteenth-century France* (Cambridge, Mass., 1995), intro. and chap. 6.

20. Louis Descemet was the first president of the General Council and stayed in office from 1879 until 1893. He was succeeded by Léon d'Erneville, his brother Germain d'Erneville, Théodore Carpot, the older brother of deputy François Carpot, Justin Deves, and Louis Guillabert. The council was transformed into the Colonial Council in 1921. Mbaye, *Institutions,* 153. Throughout its forty-two years of existence, the presidents were all métis. One African, Bakre Waly Gueye, served as a councilor throughout the 1880s, and other Africans were members in later periods.

21. The council as a whole met only once a year, for a two-week period.

22. See Johnson, *Black Politics,* chap. 2. For a picture of the headquarters, see Alain Sinou, *Comptoirs et villes coloniales du Sénégal: Saint-Louis, Gorée, et Dakar* (Paris, 1993).

23. The independence of the General Council can be effectively seen in their minutes, contained in bound volumes, arranged by year, at the ANS. Blaise Diagne and other African politicians continued to make their presence felt in France and the communes, but their influence was confined principally to the political domain. The replacement of the General Council by the Colonial Council is a complex story, as told by Searing, "Accommodation and Resistance," chap. 6.

24. The Congregation, a combination of fathers and nuns, was created in the 1840s. The fathers, called Spiritans for short, were the leading element; the nuns ran a medical clinic and school. See Joseph Roger de Benoist, *L'Eglise et le pouvoir colonial au Soudan* (Paris, 1987), 32–34, and H. J. Koren, *The Spiritans: A History of the Congregation of the Holy Ghost* (Pittsburgh, 1958), 76–77, 91–92, 509–11.

25. The Roman Catholic missions seem to have assumed, as a condition of working with expanding French imperial interests, that they would not engage in "propaganda" in Muslim-dominated areas. See the "religious ethnography" discussed in chap. 4 and CAOM Afrique 6 122, letters of 4 July 1894, governor-general, Algeria, to Foreign Affairs, and 30 April 1894, Colonies to Foreign Affairs. Missionaries were active on the fringes of the Senegalo-Mauritanian zone: among the Serer in Sin, the Diola and other groups in Casamance, and the Malinke and Bambara in the Soudan.

26. The attitudes can be seen easily in the ACSL and JCSL.

27. See chap. 4, n. 26.

28. Tamsir Hamat Ndiaye Anne, for example, is listed as an *adjoint* to the mayor in the *Annuaires du Sénégal* in the 1850s.

29. On the Seck, see chap. 4, esp. n. 42. For Saad Buh's school, see ANS 2B 74, report of April 1882.

30. See chap. 6.

31. And perhaps the Ministry of Colonies. See the "Annales de la paroisse de Saint-Louis, 1860–1928," at the parish headquarters in Saint-Louis, entry for 1881. The Catholic community, through the Annales (ACSL) and the "Journal de la communauté de Saint-Louis, 1879–1903" (JCSL), are the best sources of reporting on Masonic

activities, if one can discount their sharp negative bias. See also Zuccarelli, *Vie politique,* 44–45.

32. The newspapers that Gaspard Devès supported in the period 1885–87 published information about Masonic lodges in Senegal. See ACSL and JCSL and Pasquier, "Presse," 477–90. Bruno, Gaspard's father, was an important member of a Masonic lodge in Saint-Louis in the early nineteenth century. Pasquier, "Le Sénégal."

33. Replaced in the 1860s by the *FOSD,* a more modest and less-expensive effort of the administration.

34. The politican who brought charges was Germain d'Erneville, claiming libel against a member of his family. See Johnson, *Black Politics,* 53; Pasquier, "Presse"; and the JCSL for 1885–87. This controversy occurred at the height of tension between the Roman Catholic Church and the Freemasons. Pope Leo XIII issued a bull condemning the Masons in 1884, encouraging church leaders to take every possible action against the "sect." Jean-André Faucher, *Les francs-maçons et le pouvoir de la Révolution à nos jours* (Paris, 1986), 138–89.

35. See CRDS, "La Presse au Sénégal"; and Pasquier, "Presse."

36. See Denise Bouche, *L'Enseignement dans les teritoires français de l'Afrique Occidentale de 1817 à 1920: Mission civilisatrice ou formation d'une élite?* 2 vols. (Paris, 1975), 1:203 ff.

37. Pasquier, "Presse," 482. After the creation of the General Council in 1879, the scholarships available for study in France increased from about two or three per year to about thirty. In the late 1880s, the colony was paying for seventy boys and thirty-nine girls in lycées and other secondary instruction in France, and for twenty-four boys in écoles preparatoires des arts et métiers. Faidherbe, *Le Sénégal,* 100–101, 184. Bouche, *L'Enseignement,* 1:261–79, describes the system of metropolitan scholarships as a very wasteful system whose resources could have been invested more profitably in secondary education in Saint-Louis. The fellowships were gradually reduced in the 1890s and completely phased out in the following decade.

38. A good example of this phenomenon is the Carpot family. Pierre Carpot, a navy bureaucrat in Senegal, married Sophie Valantin of the well-known métis family in the 1850s. They had three sons: Théodore, who became a merchant and then an employee in the electricity company; Charles, who became a doctor; and François, who became a lawyer, opened an office in Saint-Louis in 1893 and served as the deputy for Senegal from 1902–14. All three benefited from scholarships to study in France. Zuccarelli, *Vie politique,* 82.

39. Mentioned briefly in chap. 3. For this institution, see Ghislaine Lydon, "Les péripéties d'une institution financière: La Banque du Sénégal, 1844–1901," in Charles Becker, Saliou Mbaye, and Ibrahima Thioub, eds., *AOF: Réalites et héritages: Sociétes ouest-africaines et ordre coloniale, 1895–1960,* 2 vols. (Dakar, 1997), 475–91.

40. A review of the evidence in ANS Q40 shows that a very wide cross section of Saint-Louisians had accounts and borrowed from the bank.

41. See Samb, *Essai,* chapter on Saint-Louis. I have also used observations from Cheikh Diouf, "L'histoire des institutions musulmanes à Saint-Louis du Sénégal, l'ancienne capitale coloniale de l'AOF," draft of a thesis for the doctorat d'université, University of Provence, 1996.

42. A case in point is Johnson, *Black Politics;* see also Manchuelle, "*Métis* et colons," and Zuccarelli, *Vie politique.*

43. Much of this information comes from Bâ, *Pénétration,* 377–78. A study more focused on the métis community itself is Nathalie Reyss, "Saint Louis du Sénégal à l'époque précoloniale: L'émergence d'une société métisse originale, 1655–1854," thèse de 3e cycle, Paris 1, 1983. Roger, Louis's older brother, enlisted in the military and was killed fighting the Umarians at the siege of Medine in 1857; a plaque there confirms his "martyrdom" for the French cause. The children of Louis Descemet married into other prestigious families; a number of the men had administrative or military careers, such as Gabriel Omer Descemet (1879–1961), who finished his baccalaureat at the Lycée Louis le Grand in Paris, entered the Ecole Coloniale, and served as a colonial administrator and then interim governor in Soudan. He later become governor of Mauritania, with residence in the city of his birth. Personal communication to me and Hilary Jones from Sylvain Sankalé, Dakar, 3 July 1997, and from Sankalé's "Arbre généalogique des familles Descemet et Guillabert."

44. Louis Descemet probably pushed as well for the recall of Governor Genouille in 1887–88, in conjunction with Deputy Albert Gasconi. See chap. 3.

45. The main source for this section is Francine Ndiaye, "La colonie du Sénégal au temps de Brière de l'Isle (1876–81)," *BIFAN,* ser. B, 30 (1968): 463–512.

46. See the minutes of the *conseil d'administration,* 2–4 May 1878, where the shape of the General Council was being debated; contained also in AOM SEN 7, 24. The mayor was Gaspard Devès; his assistant was Jean-Jacques Crespin. Darrigrand, the head of the judiciary service, supported the position argued by Devès and Crespin that the municipal institutions of Saint-Louis had their own independent statute.

47. See Kanya-Forstner, *Conquest,* passim.

48. In 1878 Brière launched a small campaign against Sabusire in Logo Province, in the Upper Senegal. He could have achieved none of this without the support of Admiral Jean Jaureguiberry, who was minister of the navy and colonies at the time. Kanya-Forstner, *Conquest,* chap. 3.

49. Faidherbe, for example, set down the policy of selective emancipation that the French followed consistently in West Africa. One of his successors, in explaining the practice of sending back refugee slaves who belonged to allies, said: "One must always follow the spirit of the confidential circular [of Faidherbe in 1857], that is, do nothing to displease the people with whom we are friends." This is contained in an 1869 letter of the governor to the commandant of Salde, contained in ANS 13G 148, no. 81. Also cited in Robinson, *Chiefs and Clerics,* 113.

50. See Klein, *Slavery,* chap. 4; Mohamed Mbodj, "The Abolition of Slavery in Senegal, 1820–1890: Crisis or the Rise of a New Entrepreneurial Class?" in Martin Klein, ed., *Breaking the Chains; Slavery, Bondage, and Emancipation in Modern Africa and Asia* (Madison, Wisc., 1993).

51. Ndiaye, "Brière de l'Isle," 502ff. For the ways in which British authorities dealt with the difficult issues of abolition during the establishment of colonial rule in northern Nigeria, see Lovejoy and Hogendorn, *Slow Death.*

52. The following is based on the letter that Louis Descement, the president of the

General Council, wrote to the minister of the navy and colonies on 22 April 1881. AOM SEN 7, 24.

53. AOM SEN 7, 24, 22 April 1881, letter of Louis Descemet to the minister of the navy and colonies. Three years later, after a succession of weak and short-term governors, Descemet expressed regret to the explorer Parfait-Louis Monteil about the recall of Brière. Henri Labouret, *Monteil: Explorateur et soldat* (Paris, 1937), 91–92.

54. Albert Gasconi, elected deputy only in 1879, was already complaining to the ministry in December 1880 about the governor: "One has the sense that the colony is not administered but commanded." Ndiaye, "Brière de l'Isle," 497.

55. Johnson, *Black Politics,* 109–10; Zuccarelli, *Vie politique,* chap. 5.

56. Diagne also continued, for a while, the tradition of opposition to certain administration actions and attitudes. Searing, "Accommodation and Resistance," chap. 6.

57. Research into the history of the Devès and their operations in Senegal should be a high priority. Many of the family papers were deposited at the Archives Nationales in Dakar under the rubric 1Z.

58. The following information on the Devès is compiled from a wide variety of sources. See ANS 13G 135, esp. pièce 49; 13G 41, passim.; Barrows, "General Faidherbe," 120–21; Robert July, *The Origins of Modern Nationalism* (London, 1968), 142–53; Manchuelle, "*Métis* et colons"; Pasquier, "Le Sénégal," pt. 1, chap. 2; Eugène Saulnier, *Une compagnie à privilège au XIXe siècle: La Compagnie de Galam au Sénégal* (Paris, 1921), 49, 191.

59. In the nineteenth century, it was often called Devès & Chaumet, the company that Faidherbe reprimanded in 1859. See chap. 3, n. 15.

60. The Fulbe mistress also had a son Yaya who received signficant resources from Bruno, became a boat captain, conducted trade out of Dagana, and helped build the library of the Sidiyya family in Butilimit. Interview with Amadou Diagne Yaya in Saint-Louis, 19 March 1985. See also Jacques Méniaud, *Les Pionniers du Soudan,* vol. 1, 51n; Soleillet, *Voyage,* 141n.

61. Gaspard and Catherine were married in 1851. Catherine's father Guillaume was quite possibly the wealthiest métis merchant in Saint-Louis. He had married a Descemet and was closely linked to the conservative métis families. To the best of my knowledge, the 1851 wedding is the only Devès marriage that is registered at the Catholic church. On the Foy, see Pasquier, "Le Sénégal," chap. 5, esp. 437–44.

62. See the Devès archives (ANS 1Z 9) and the files on the Banque du Sénégal (esp. ANS Q40, pièce 64). Elisabeth died in 1900, a little over a year before Gaspard passed away.

63. Her picture may be found in the family archives (ANS 1Z 11). She was born Fama Daba Daguissery, or Deuira, but called Madeleine Tambe (or Tamba) Diop. The picture was taken 22 June 1889.

64. François, the youngest son, was born in 1870. Justin and Hyacinthe were already extremely active in trade and politics in the 1880s, suggesting that they were born in the late 1850s or early 1860s. Zuccarelli, *Vie politique,* 62. A Guillaume Devès, born probably in the late 1860s, also appears in the family papers (particularly ANS IZ 10–11); he may be another son of Gaspard and Tambe.

65. Consisting of his father-in-law, Guillaume Foy, Devès and Lacoste, one of the

"white" Bordeaux firms, Buhan and Rabaud, and a number of the African traders. Barrows, "General Faidherbe," 120–21. According to several administrators, searching for an explanation of his hostility to their initiatives, he had an inferiority complex and strong sense of being excluded by his Bordeaux relatives. See ANS 13G 135, pièce 49, governor to undersecretary of state, "Renseignements confidentiels sur certains personalites de SL qui ont ete les instigateurs de la reprise des poursuites dans l'affaire de Podor," November 1890.

66. Jauregiberry went on to say that Devès manipulated the black masses and then cheated them with inpunity. Maurel and Prom papers, "Negoçiants and commerçants établis à Saint-Louis," cited in Barrows, "General Faidherbe," 120. Later Brière de l'Isle echoed some of the sentiments of Jaureguiberry in a letter to one of the sons of Gaspard in 1892: "No one understood better the interests of his country in the midst of the egotistical and uninformed aspirations of those who fought against his influence." ANS 1Z 11, letter of 18 July 1892.

67. Beginning with the revocation of Gaspard Devès as mayor in 1880, on the basis of charges of fraud brought by Auguste de Bourmeister, a Frenchman allied to the Maurel interests and successor to Gaspard as mayor of Saint-Louis. Zuccarelli, *Vie politique,* chap. 3.

68. ANS 3G 3/6, letter of 24 June 1917, lieutenant governor to governor-general; Johnson, *Black Politics,* chap. 6; Zuccarelli, *Vie politique,* 62.

69. Including six mares, individually priced out at between 45 and 110 guinée cloths. Jupiter Waly, the younger brother of Bakre Waly Gueye, was a member of the commission. See ANS 13G 222, corresp. for 1883, and chap. 6. In 1885 Gaspard pursued similar claims about traders with Muntaga Tall, who commanded the Umarian garrison of Nioro. ANS 9G 39, pièce 32.

70. Brought out effectively by Manchuelle in "*Métis* et colons."

71. See ANS 13G 136, #49, governor to undersecretary of state, November 1890.

72. ANS Q40; 1Z 9; CAOM SEN 9 56–62.

73. Manchuelle, "*Métis* et colons," 501; Zuccarelli, *Vie politique,* 71.

74. Gaspard passed away in 1901. During the last years of his life he lived in Bordeaux and transferred responsibility for operations in the Senegalo-Mauritanian zone to his sons.

75. These charges are contained in a report of 2 August 1910 prepared for Governorgeneral Ponty. It and other documents about this affair are in ANS 3G 3/5.

76. Ibid.

77. Justin Deves had been raised in France; after finishing his law studies, he returned to Saint-Louis, "where he was a merchant but even more a businessman *[agent d'affaires]* living on politics." ANS 3G 3/6, letter of 24 June 1917, lieutenant governor to governor-general.

78. For what follows, I rely principally on Diouf, *Le Kajoor,* 263 ff.

79. Gasconi had initially been elected deputy over against a Bordeaux candidate, but he rapidly made peace with the major French firms. *Hommes et Destins,* 4:324–26; Zuccarelli, *Vie politique,* 53–58.

80. CAOM SEN 1 68b, letter of 8 April 1883, quoted in Diouf, *Le Kajoor,* 275, and in Ganier, "Lat Dyor," 272–73. Lat Dior's son, Mbakhane, an important colonial

chief discussed in chap. 3, wrote to Justin Devès in 1910 recalling the close relations between their two families and complained about the pressure of the administrator in Baol in the early 1900s to end his relations with the Devès. ANS 1Z 11, pièce 4, letter of 19 March 1910. See also Searing, "Accommodation and Resistance," chap. 3.

81. See Governor Genouille's letter to MC, 8 April 1883, in Ganier, "Lat Dyor," 272–73. One of Descemet's key allies was the métis merchant Raymond Martin, who played a big role also in the telegraph-line controversy in Futa Toro, discussed in chap. 6.

82. See ANS 1D 48, "1886, Campagne du Cayor"; Diouf, Kajoor, 279–80; Ganier, "Lat Dyor," 253–55, 280–81; Pasquier, "Presse." Genouille also orchestrated a campaign in the French press to present the administration case. See Le Temps, 25–26 October, 13 and 25 November, and 10 December 1886. See also Diouf, Kajoor, 279–80, 282. The same Governor Genouille was recalled for his confiscation of Trarza cattle in 1887; he was tried and convicted in 1888–89 for negligent homicide in the Southern Rivers region (see chap. 3). The Devès probably had a hand in that, as did Guadeloupan Senator Isaac. Manchuelle, "Métis et colons," 501.

83. Hanson, "Political Economy of Meaning"; Robinson, Chiefs and Clerics, 142–43. See also ANS 13G 41, pièce 58, letter of 24 May 1886.

84. The commander at Podor at the time was Aubry-Lecomte, who played a key role in the executions in Podor after the Jeandet assassination. See ANS 13G 41, pièce 58, esp. the letters of 24 May 1886, Commandant Podor to governor, and 19 and 29 June 1886, Ct. Dagana to governor; 13G 134, pièce 6, Gorée, 26 March 1886, Aubry-Lecomte to a colleague (presumably Governor Seignacs); and chap. 3.

85. The Devès claims to Arguin generated a great deal of documentation. In the family archives, see ANS 1Z 5 and 6. Gaspard had a very interesting exchange in 1885 with the former governor, Faidherbe, in which Devès presents his purchase of Arguin as a potentially rich resource in many products and presents himself as acting for French interests. See 1Z, 5, pièces 238 and 239, for 4 and 6 October 1884. For French administration reactions, see CAOM AFPO 522, esp. doss. 4; Désiré-Vuillemin, Contribution, annexes 4–6.

86. What follows comes from the report, found in ANS 1D 223, pièces 127–28. At 127 is the cover letter of Capdebosc to the governor-general; it is dated 3 April 1907.

87. Ndiago was a customs post for the emir of Trarza, who stationed a representative there in the nineteenth century to collect tolls going in and out of Saint-Louis. Lydon, "On Trans-Saharan Trails," chap. 3. It is quite conceivable, and consistent with Devès practice, that the family claimed to be collecting tolls on behalf of the emir.

88. In 1904, Coppolani complained about the arrangements of Justin Devès with the director of the interior to settle a tributary group on the south bank of the river, in return for an annual payment of 450 francs. The group was called the Kumleilen, or Idaw al-Hajj, and they had considerable herds of camels and other animals and a strong reputation in Islamic law and Sufism. See Marty, Sénégal, 1:60–65 and 78, and ANS 13G 66, 1907 ff. In the same year, Jules Couchard, former deputy and lawyer practicing in Saint-Louis, asked Coppolani to support compensation for two of his merchant clients whose boats had been pillaged by Moorish raiders, on the grounds that the government embargo on arms had prevented their agents from protecting themselves. The

merchants wanted it both ways: government protection or compensation, but also freedom to trade in weapons. Désiré-Vuillemin, *Contribution,* 298–300.

89. For an example, see Désiré-Vuillemin, *Mauritanie,* 74–78, 131–34, 154–56.

90. ANS 1D 223, pièce 134, Saint-Louis, Cheikh Sidia to Colonel Capdebosc, 9 April 1907, trans. Bu El Mogdad (Dudu Seck) 10 April 1907. The French may have suspected the Devès of having contacts with Ma El Ainin and the Moroccan court: see archives of RIM E1/37-1, Saint-Louis, telegram, n.d. (I would like to thank Ibrahima Abou Sall and Ghislaine Lydon, respectively, for drawing these sources to my attention.) For additional material on Devès efforts to block the conquest of Mauritania, see 1D 223, pièces 135–37 (Saint-Louis, Colonnel Montané-Capdebosc, letter and attachments dated 13 April 1907), and Désiré-Vuillemin, *Contribution,* passim. In a letter of 31 March 1906 to Colonel Capdebosc, Justin Devès describes Baba as the "powerful auxiliary" of the French. ANS, archives Devès, 1Z 6.

CHAPTER 6

1. See Philip Curtin, *Cross-Cultural Trade in World History* (Cambridge, U.K., 1984). He uses the term "European militarized trade diasporas" to describe the networks centered on the African coast (57), and pays little attention to the African diasporas that operated out of the same port cities. He gives a very full exposition of the Senegambian networks and the competition between the Senegal and Gambia River systems in *Economic Change in Precolonial Africa,* 1:92–152. For strategies of trading diasporas, see Abner Cohen, *Custom and Politics in Urban Africa: A Study of Hausa Migrants in Yoruba Towns* (Berkeley, Calif., 1969). For examples in the Senegambian zone, see Thomas Hunter, "The Development of an Islamic Tradition of Learning among the Jahanka of West Africa," Ph.D. diss., University of Chicago, 1977, and Lamin Sanneh, *The Jakhanke* (London, 1979).

2. It was *traite* that produced the term *traitants*—literally, "traders," but also a particular rank in the commercial hierarchy established by the French in the nineteenth century, below the ranks of négociants and marchands. See chap. 1.

3. Boilât, *Esquisses sénégalaises,* 446.

4. N. Dournaux Dupéré, "La Sénégambie française," *Bulletin de la Société de Géographie* (Paris) 2 (1871): 56–57. For additional information on the trade and the off-season in Saint-Louis, see ANS Q24; Carrère and Holle, *Sénégambie française,* 12–17, 326–32; Jules Duval, "La politique coloniale de la France," *Revue des Deux Mondes,* October 1858, 517–52, 837–79; and A. Raffenel, *Nouveau voyage dans le pays des Nègres,* 2 vols. (Paris, 1856), 2:14–75, 171–82. Most of the accounts come from the middle of the century.

5. Most of the métis entrepreneurs left the main commercial sector after the "gum fever" of the 1830s and 1840s, the emancipation of slaves, and the "free trade" system instituted under Faidherbe that gave the advantage to the more capitalized and integrated Bordeaux firms. In the *Annuaire du Sénégal* they are listed as notables and *propriétaires* in Saint-Louis. They became quite active in the colonial administration and in the electoral institutions of civil society, as the preceding chapter demonstrated. For their "eclipse," see Barry and Harding, *Commerce,* 5–58; Pasquier, "Le Sénégal," passim.

The most notable exception to this pattern is the Devès family, categorized as *négociants* and featured in the last chapter.

6. See, for example, Hamet Gora Diop later in this chapter, or Théophile Turpin, cited in n. 15 below.

7. Interviews in Saint-Louis conducted between April and June, 1985, esp. with Bra Mamoussé Gueye and his colleagues at a meeting room called the *Local,* 23 June 1985; CAOM SEN8 14 and 14bis; ANS M8 and M241. See also Lucie Colvin, "Kajor and Its Diplomatic Relations," esp. 94 ff.; Michael Marcson, "European-African Interaction in the Precolonial Period: Saint-Louis, Senegal, 1758–1854," Ph.D. diss., Princeton University, 1976); and Webb, *Desert Frontier.*

8. See chap. 6, n. 1.

9. *Jizya* was the tax levied by Muslim rulers on Christians and Jews.

10. I have used *friendship* for *muwalat,* which could also be translated association or alliance. Umar was consciously contrasting *muwalat* with the status of *dhimmi,* the protected but tribute-paying non-Muslim communities of Islamic law.

11. Hanson and Robinson, *After the Jihad,* 106–11; see, ibid., 328, for a reproduced photocopy of the original Arabic. This copy came from CAOM SEN 1 41b, a packet of materials sent by Governor Faidherbe on 11 March 1855; for at least ten years, however, the letter has not been in the file. I was fortunate to have a photocopy made in 1973. The two citations are from the Quran: sura 9, v. 29 and sura 5 v. 51, respectively. Ndiaye Sur, a prominent trader in Bakel and close associate of the administration, was probably the first recipient of this letter. See n. 91, below.

12. For the impression that the challenge made in Saint-Louis, see Carrère and Holle, *Sénégambie française,* esp. 204–7, where the letter is quoted in full.

13. Cohen, *Custom and Politics,* conclusion.

14. See Hanson, "Political Economy of Meaning."

15. A good case in point for one in the peanut basin is Théophile Turpin, a Catholic merchant who operated out of Foundiougne and engaged in peanut, millet, and tobacco trade. He was the son of a deputy mayor of Gorée. See n. 85 and Laurence Marfaing, *Evolution du commerce au Senegal, 1820–1930* (Paris, 1991), 253–55.

16. The Maurel & Prom Company, the most visible Bordeaux firm in French operations in the nineteenth and twentieth centuries, constructed and maintained the only wharf in Rufisque for the exportation of peanuts. They of course charged their competitors for use of the facility. See Marfaing, *Evolution,* chap. 6. For the close relations of the Maurel and Prom families and firms with the administration, see Barrows, "General Faidherbe," passim; and Casey, "The Politics of French Imperialism," 107 ff.

17. Le Chatelier's account was published as *Islam dans l'Afrique Occidentale* (Paris, 1899). The description of Islamic practice in Saint-Louis is found on 258–60. See chap. 4.

18. Le Chatelier, *Islam,* 258–60.

19. Individuals and families who did not accept the "terms" of operating in the Saint-Louis commercial diaspora (i.e., French overrule) do not appear in my selection and hardly appear in the record at all. It is possible to find traces of some of these people; for example, those who enlisted with Umar to wage the jihad against "paganism" and the French presence.

20. The petition can be found in ANFOM SEN 8, 14bis a, December 1843.

21. ANS 13G 212.69, for 31 March 1867. For a collection of information on Bakre Waly, see Marfaing, *Evolution*, 251–52.

22. Robinson, *Holy War*, 240.

23. Jupiter was on the conciliation commission in the early 1880s when one of the Devès debtors died (see chap. 5, n. 69). He died in Mamadu Lamine Dramé's attack in 1886, along with several other Saint-Louisians (see below and ANS 13G 240.91, statement of dead and wounded, April 1886).

24. ANS 2D 11/2, 3 February 1891; Marfaing, *Evolution*, 251–52.

25. He encountered Coppolani there in 1904, only months before the latter's death, and tried to educate him about the dangers that "pacification" posed for the commercial system — including the slave trade — of the river. See chap. 3, n. 46; Bakre was one of the interlocutors cited in Coppolani's letter of 23 June 1904.

26. In 1880, he apparently persuaded Joseph Galliéni to take a register of debts incurred by Moorish clients of his father at Bakel in 1852–53 on his mission to negotiate new arrangements in Segu. Galliéni was supposed to seek Amadu Sheku's intervention to force the payment of the debts. The register was placed in the Umarian library and archive in Segu, but with French conquest of Soudan in the 1890s it was relocated in the Bibliothèque Nationale de Paris, Manuscrits Orientaux, Fonds Arabe, vol. 5582, ff. 28–51. For the Waly Bandia property and that of other merchants cited in this section, see CAOM Depôt et Fortifications des Colonies, Supplément, Sénégal, carton 2; and for the value of the business, Curtin, *Economic Change*, 1:152.

27. *Annuaire du Sénégal et Dépendances (Annuaire)* for 1881–89; Manchuelle, "*Métis* et colons." Bakre was part of the "Descemet" clan that dominated the General Council and the city hall for most of the 1880s and early 1890s; as "dean," or oldest member, he often presided over the opening deliberations. In 1881 he was second-deputy mayor.

28. The métis elite, who considered these scholarships to be the preserve of their families, apparently persuaded Bakre Waly that the experience in France would be alienating for his sons. Based on interviews conducted by Thompson and cited in his "Dubious," 71, 87.

29. For what follows, see Manchuelle, "*Métis* et colons," esp. 496–500.

30. From the French newspaper *Le Temps* of 28 November 1897, quoted ibid., 499.

31. ANS 2D 11/2, 26 July 1893; ANS 13G 143.148–9, 28 February 1890. His sons Birame et Bassiru became merchants. Marfaing, *Evolution*, 251–52.

32. Charles Monteil, *Les Khassonkés* (Paris, 1915), 2; Lamine Gueye, *Itineraire africain* (Paris, 1966), 13.

33. For this change in commercial fortunes, see Samir Amin, *Le Monde des affaires sénégalais* (Paris, 1969), passim. For Lamine Gueye's orientation toward French education, see *Itineraire*, 13–16.

34. Specifically, he had shops in Ross-Bethio, Rosso-Sénégal, and Rosso-Mauritanie. In the Southern Rivers he worked with his brother Bucaline. See speech of his grandson El Hadj Ibrahima Mbengue, on the occasion of the inauguration of the Mbengue school in Saint-Louis, 27 April l985; Amin, *Monde*, 15, 18, 82. Other information comes from Marfaing, *Evolution*, 250–51.

35. The consumption of green tea and sugar spread rapidly in the Senegalo-

Mauritanian zone in the late nineteenth century. Much of it was imported to Morocco and shipped across the desert. Jean-Louis Miège, *Le Maroc et l'Europe, 1830–1894* (Paris, 1962) 2:538–46. Mbengue apparently began to import the same tea through Saint-Louis.

36. For Ibra Almamy, see ANS 13G 28, political affairs, registre pour 1885; for the Trarza debt, see Adama Gnokane, "La politique française sur la rive droite du Sénégal: Le pays maures, 1817–1903," thèse de troisième cycle, Paris 1, 1986–87, sec. 2.6.

37. Amin, *Monde*, 20.

38. Manchuelle, "*Métis* et colons," 483.

39. "Annales de la Congrégation de Saint-Louis" and "Journal de la Congrégation de Saint-Louis," entry for 9 September 1884.

40. See the case study later in this chapter.

41. CAOM SEN 4 67a, 24 April 1881, and 67b, n.d., but about May 1883; Robinson, *Chiefs and Clerics*, 136–38.

42. He was the political director of the journal *La Republicaine Socialiste.* Another relative, Alassane Mbengue, was born about the same time as Khayar and became an ardent disciple of Malik Sy. Alassane made the pilgrimage twice and joined Malik Sy from the time of the difficult "Ndiarnde" years. He settled in Rufisque as a prominent Tijaniyya teacher. Mbaye, "Malik Sy," chap. 6; Marty, *Sénégal*, 1:201; ANS 13G 67, *fiches de renseignement*, pièce 92.

43. Pasquier considered Fara Biram to be one of the five wealthiest African traders at the time. "*Traitants*," 152. For the petitions, see ANS M8, items 2 and 12. Mambaye's signature appears, in a very legible Arabic hand, on the first page, in the tenth position, of the 1843 petition.

44. After 1868, he disappears from the archival record. On Sidi Fara Biram, see the *Annuaire du Sénégal* for 1865–66; *Annales Sénégalaises*, 134; and ANS, 2D4 1, decree of 20 February 1862.

45. ANS 3E 46, minutes of 18 June 1881; ANS 13G 122.38, 8 May 1864.

46. ANS 13G 137.45, 29 March 1871.

47. ANS M8, items 92–93, 1885, showing his conflict with Qadi Ndiaye Sarr of the Muslim Tribunal. Mambaye married Fama Gaye, the daughter of the chief of Guet N'Dar, and she was the mother of his sons Amadu and Fara Biram. ANS 1C 760, admin. archives, Senegal, and ANS 1C 5905, from Bâ, *Ahmadou Bamba*, 176. I suspect that he was too contentious, and too overt a supporter of the administration, to have merited consideration as the replacement of Bu El Mogdad; certainly on paper he had the qualifications.

48. ANS J3, items 1 and 4.

49. See ANS, minutes of General Council meetings of 4 August 1885 and 27 December 1890, and Thompson, "Dubious," 71, 87.

50. Denise Bouche, *L'Enseignement dans les territoires français de l'Afrique occidentale de 1817 à 1920* (Paris, 1975), 268. Amadu, sometimes called Mambaye Amadu, apparently agreed to monitor Amadu Bamba during his exile in Gabon; this is often cited in Senegalese oral tradition to explain the alcoholism and administrative problems that he had later in Guinea. But Amadu is also often confused with his younger brother, Fara Biram, who had a more active role in Murid events. See Oumar Bâ, *Amadu Bamba*, 176. The Lô are remembered in Murid traditions as the main Senegalese antagonists of

Amadu Bamba. See, for example, Serigne Bachir Mbacké, *Les bienfaits de l'eternel ou la biographie de Cheikh Amadou Bamba Mbacke* (Dakar, 1995), 206 ff.

51. See ANS 9G 14, materials for 1892.

52. Bâ, *Ahmadou Bamba,* 29-88, 176; Searing, "Accommodation and Resistance," 122-24, 190.

53. ANS M8.

54. The main sources are the *Annuaire;* letter of Ibrahima Ndiaye Guthié to the director of the Centre de Recherche et Documentation du Sénégal (CRDS), 9 July 1977; Fadel Dia, "Les Noms des rues de Saint-Louis," MS at CRDS; interview with Papa Seye Charles, Saint-Louis, June 1985. The director of political affairs, Solère, accused Abdullay Mar and Abdullay Seck of using a double booking system for their commercial activities for Maurel & Prom, violating the requirements of an 1876 decree. The two men said they were following the instructions of the Bordeaux firm. There is no indication that any disciplinary action was taken; Maurel & Prom consistently played an influential role within the counsels of the administration. ANS Q24, commerce 1858-79. (My thanks to Ghislaine Lydon for this reference.)

55. His niece Rokhaya Ndiaye Aliboye married Malik Sy in about 1879. Guthié letter cited in n. 54 above.

56. Mbaye, "Malick Sy," chap. 5.

57. He was the father of the Abdullay Mar who served as mayor of Saint-Louis from 1947 to 1952.

58. Papa Mar enlisted in the army, in the rash of patriotism that many Saint-Louisians demonstrated, and probably died of wounds received during the war. Johnson, *Black Politics,* 149-50.

59. ANFOM SEN.4.127, 10 July 1895.

60. "Traitants ou negociants? Les commerçants sénégalais (2e moitié XIXe siècle, début XXe siècle): Hamet Gora Diop, 1846-1910; étude de cas," in Barry and Harding, *Commerce.* See also Amin, *Monde,* 19, 82-83.

61. For the 1913 meeting, see AFPO 512, doss. 40, entries for 1913.

62. And perhaps especially in the upper Senegal after 1908, when the capital of the Soudan was transferred to Bamako, whereupon the area of Medine and Kayes became a backwater of both Senegal and Soudan.

63. What follows is based on Robinson, *Chiefs and Clerics,* 124-38.

64. For the 1881 campaign of Pons, the administration paid for the services of barges from a number of members of the trading community, including Mambaye Fara Biram and Deputy Alfred Gasconi. ANS 3E 46, minutes of the *conseil d'administration* of 18 June 1881. The Pons column suffered some bad losses and caused considerable consternation in France.

65. Kanya-Forstner, *Conquest,* 84 ff.

66. In 1884, the French secured agreement from a group of *bidan* to build the fort, but it would have exacerbated relations with Abdul and the Bossea chiefs who surrounded him. The General Council succeeded in quashing the project by using their budgetary authority. See ANS 13G 156, pièce 3, 7 June 1886, ministry to governor, referring to the General Council meeting of 5 July 1885. For the general mobilization of the community, see ANS 13G 151. Marginal notes to pièces 97-98, letter of Abdul

Bokar to governor, received in Saint-Louis 16 November 1881, say: "Most of the leading *habitants* support that [position of Abdul Bokar] and have now won over not only G. Devès but also the most influential members of the *conseil général.*" For the ministry's and governor's frustration with the council, see ANS 13G 156.

67. This is reminiscent of the Podor information system that the Devès used in the Jeandet Affair in 1890 (described in chap. 3). For the 1881 intelligence flow, see ANS 1G 56 10, 21 August 1881, director of political affairs to governor; CAOM SEN 4 67, telegram, director of political affairs to governor, 21 August 1881. For the effects this had on the position of Abdul, see, for example, the strong position that Abdul took in the summer of 1881 after the passing of the Gababe treaties. His letter was sent on to Paris as part of the package of explanation provided by the governor to the ministry. CAOM SEN 4 67, n.d., but about August 1881, copy of Abdul Bokar to the governor. See also ANS 13G 41, pièce 58, esp. the letter of 24 May 1886, Commandant Podor to the governor.

68. These observations were made by the commandant of Salde, the métis Paul Holle, from reports on Abdul Bokar's comments in a meeting of Futanke leaders, and contained in 13G 129, pièces 134–36, November and December 1880, Commandant Salde to governor. Devès was probably the one behind the contact with lawyer Gillet. This recalls the Devès practice in the Fulbe emigration sequence described in chap. 5. CAOM SEN 4 67, telegram, director of political affairs to governor, 21 August 1881. For a letter that Abdul wrote to Devès in 1881, see ANS 13G 151, 104–5, received 30 November 1881 in Saint-Louis. See also Robinson, *Chiefs and Clerics,* 122.

69. AOM SEN 4, 68.43, letter of Deputy Gasconi to the ministry, 11 February 1886; SEN 4 67b, n.d. about May 1883, Abdul Bokar to governor.

70. CAOM SEN 4 67b, letter to Abdul Bokar of 24 April 1881, quoted in Robinsin, *Chiefs and Clerics,* 130.

71. One of the other merchants was Makhonne Seck, father of Dame Seck mentioned later in this chapter. CAOM SEN 4 68, Paris, 12 September 1885, Gasconi to undersecretary of state for the colonies. Governor Seignac acknowledged Martin's services in his letter from Kayes of 3 September 1885 in the same file. In 1886, Martin, Louis Descemet as president of the General Council and other notables from Saint-Louis met with Abdul Bokar again, mainly on the subject of emigration and his demands for recognition of his dominions. ANS 2B 75, 15 September 1886, interim governor (Ferrat) to ministry.

72. For some of the larger implications of Mamadu Lamine's movement, which I am not considering here, see Abdoulaye Bathily, "Mamadou Lamine Drame et la résistance anti-impérialiste dans le Haut-Sénétal, 1885–87," *Notes Africaines* 1970, 20–32; Humphrey Fisher, "The Early Life and Pilgrimage of Al-Hajj Muhammad Al-Amin the Soninke (d. 1887)," *JAH* 11 (1970); Kanya-Forstner, *Conquest,* 133–34, 144–46; Robinson, *Chiefs and Clerics,* 145–49.

73. Such as that supposedly presented by Amadu Bamba in 1895. Martial Merlin evoked the Tijaniyya affiliation of Bamba as one way of linking him to the "fanatic" opponents of the French presence in the past, during the preparations for Bamba's "trial" and deportation. The French actually collaborated with the Umarian Tijaniyya against the Madiyanke in the early 1870s, and again against Mamadu Lamine in 1886.

After Mamadu Lamine's "Soninke" jihad, the French began to decouple the Tijaniyya from Tokolor ethnicity. See Robinson, "French 'Islamic' Policy," 415.

74. The French claimed, after a cursory investigation, that Alpha had provided crucial information to Mamadu Lamine. On Alpha Sega, see Yves Saint-Martin, *L'Empire toucouleur et la France* (Dakar, 1967), 234–35. On the Bakel casualties, see ANS 2B 75, 12 April 1886, governor to ministry; ANS 1D 51, pièces 5 and 6, reports of the captain of Bakel of 3–4 April and 5–10 April 1886, respectively.

75. See the ACSL for a running commentary on the tribunal in the late nineteenth century. A typical entry for 1875: "The best thing would be to eliminate it [the Muslim Tribunal], since it prevents the Mohammedans from assimilating to our culture and leaves them with their own laws, customs, and habits, in a word with their own national life."

76. See, for example, the letter of 23 December 1881, from the *chef de service judiciaire* to the governor, in which he says: "French justice is not consistent with Muslim justice, which it has always considered to be unfortunate and a danger for our colonization in Senegal. French justice wishes with all its strength for the day when the French courts will have the right to apply Muslim legislation in the same way that the French courts in India apply Hindu law." ANS M8 42. This judiciary chief was probably the successor to Darrigrand, who had been transferred by this time.

77. Expressed in the letter/petition of 7 March 1904 to the minister of colonies. The letter is well phrased and was undoubtedly prepared by one of the highly literate members of the Saint-Louis community, probably someone with a judicial background. ANS M241, 26. This was the kind of function that Mody Mbaye, cited below, performed in the smaller towns of the interior.

78. Until this juncture, they were more likely to find support for their court in the administration than in the métis and French communities of Saint-Louis. In the early 1900s, the Saint-Louis community as a whole felt threatened by Dakar and a general process of marginalization, and began to draw together. See Johnson, *Black Politics,* chap. 6; Zuccarelli, *Vie politique,* chap. 5.

79. Although Hyacinthe Devès publicly urged the Muslims to accept the French system—that is, to opt for assimilation.

80. The meeting was held on 1 April; the restoration decree was 22 May. ANS 21G 1, police report of 2 April 1905; ANS M241, 26; and CAOM AOF 8 2, "Tribunal musulman, 1903–7."

81. A significant achievement at the time, and it qualified him to be an instructor in the school system. For his biography, I rely in great part on an unpublished document, prepared by Fadel Dia, former director of the CRDS in Saint-Louis, that is contained in the CRDS library. See also Johnson, *Black Politics,* 133–38, 161–63; Klein, *Islam and Imperialism,* 215; and James Searing, "Accommodation and Resistance," chaps. 2 and 3.

82. In 1904, two chiefs were convoked to Thies to answer charges of trafficking in slaves. They brought a considerable entourage with them, and a melée ensued when the administration tried to impose a sentence of prison and a fine. In the process, an administrator named Emile Chautemps, who happened also to be the son of a minister of colonies in the 1890s, was stabbed to death. The French and their agents actively pursued those involved in inciting the violence; Mbaye claimed to have played a major role in the pursuit. Searing, "Accommodation and Resistance," 199–208.

83. Although he also coveted the position of the superior chief of West Baol and waged a campaign to that effect in 1904. In 1902, he had played a significant role in bringing the tenure of Salmone Fall, the previous superior chief, to an end. Hyacinthe Devès had significant interests in Baol as well and joined in some of the same campaigns as Mbaye. Searing, "Accommodation and Resistance," 205–7.

84. The charges were subsequently dismissed. Senator Isaac, who was involved in the contestation around the Jeandet Affair and the trial of François Devès in 1894, was a prominent member of the Ligue. See AFPO 512, doss. 40, réclamations de la Ligue des Droits de l'Homme, 1913–16, on Mody Mbaye. Lamine Gueye, the most prominent Saint-Louis political leader of the twentieth century, wrote his thesis for a doctorate in law on the subject of the originaires, entitled *De la situation politique des Sénégalais originaires des communes de plein exercice* (Paris, 1921). For Mbaye's fortunes in 1913, see Johnson, *Black Politics,* 136–37.

85. Johnson, *Black Politics,* chap. 10, and Searing, "Accommodation and Resistance," chaps. 5 and 6.

86. This action was not unlike the accusation of *muwalat* ("friendship," or "association") that Umar leveled against the Saint-Louis Muslims in the 1855 letter cited above.

87. In many cases, they probably organized Quranic schools and taught the Quran. See Barry and Harding, *Commerce,* 160. In a different setting, a merchant might make comparable use of a Christian identity. This was the case with Theophile Turpin, who was probably the son of the assistant mayor of Gorée and established a thriving trade in peanuts, millet, tobacco, and other products out of Foundiogne and Kaolack in Salum at the turn of the century. He became a friend and informant of local administrators and an important pillar and contributor to the Roman Catholic Church. *Annuaire du Sénégal,* 1860; Barry and Harding, *Commerce,* 175–81; Marfaing, *Evolution,* 253–55.

88. I do not find much evidence, however, for "ethnic" specializations. Along the river, for example, most of these merchants or their agents could speak Pular and Hassaniyya as well as Wolof, and they related routinely to indigenous traders and producers of different provenance.

89. This information comes from Robinson interviews in Saint-Louis in June 1985, especially with Papa Seye Charles on 14 June 1985, at his home in Sor. Some of the information also comes from a notebook of Saly Fall, daughter-in-law of Brahim Gueye, copied on 22 June 1985.

90. In his earlier career, Al-Hajj Dame Seck represented the Bordeaux firm Ets Buhan & Teisseire, at Dagana, and acquired considerable wealth there. Barry and Harding, *Commerce,* 178, 188, 305.

91. Ndiaye Sur, a prominent trader in Bakel from the 1840s to the 1870s, was known for his close relation to the commandant of Bakel and his extensive participation in military expeditions. He was probably the first recipient of the famous letter that Umar wrote to the Bakel-based traders in early 1855. See n. 11 and Mage, *Voyage,* 148–49.

92. Massamba Cinna, a wealthy merchant in the mid nineteenth century, was a confidant of the damel of Cayor. Bâ, *Pénétration,* 287, 300, 310. Durand Magueye performed the same function for Abdul Bokar in the 1880s. See CAOM SEN 4 67b, n.d.

93. See Klein, *Slavery,* chaps. 4, 6, 8, and 12; Searing, "Accommodation and Resis-

tance," chaps. 2 and 3. For the continuation of the slave trade in twentieth-century northern Nigeria, see Lovejoy and Hogendorn, *Slow Death.*

CHAPTER 7

1. Some elements of this chapter were presented at a Tijaniyya workshop in Champaign-Urbana, Illinois, 1–5 April 1996, under the title "Between Hashimi and Agibu: The Umarian Tijaniyya in the Early Colonial Period." That paper appears in Triaud and Robinson, *La Tijaniyya.*

2. These paragraphs reflect the interpretations in my *Holy War,* chap. 9.

3. See chap. 10.

4. On multiple affiliation, see the Fadiliyya interpretation in McLaughlin, "Sufi, Saint, Sharif," chap. 3. On the Hafiziyya Tijaniyya of Mauritania, see Dedoud ould Abdellah, "Le 'passage au sud': Muhammad al-Hafiz et son héritage," Triaud and Robinson, *La Tijaniyya.* Throughout his life, Malik Sy sought multiple links to Ahmad al-Tijani. See chap. 10, and Said Bousbina, "Al-Hajj Malik Sy: Sa chaîne spirituelle dans la Tijaniyya et sa position à l'égard de la présence française au Sénégal," in Robinson and Triaud, *Le Temps des Marabouts.*

5. During the decades of the 1860s, 1870s, and even 1880s, Amadu negotiated a number of treaties with the French, received considerable supplies of weapons from them, and occasionally acted in concert—as in the case of Mamadu Lamine Dramé in 1886–87. But he always worked from a position of relative equality with the Saint-Louis authorities: he dominated his sphere, they dominated theirs. See Hanson, *Migration,* and Robinson, *Holy War,* passim.

6. Hanson and Robinson, *After the Jihad,* 247. The kidnapping and forced recruitment refer to the capture of Segu in 1890; they are dealt with below.

7. See Hanson and Robinson, *After the Jihad,* 251–63, and Robinson, "Emigration."

8. They had made the transition to chiefs, along the lines of the Futanke proverb cited in chap. 1, n. 50: "The cleric gives birth to the chief, the chief gives birth to the pagan." Gaden, *Proverbes et maximes,* 68.

9. For a discussion of the use of this term, see Hanson, *Migration,* 7–9.

10. A situation that changed dramatically with the development of strong Tijaniyya communities in Futa Toro and the emergence of Seydu Nuru Tal after World War I.

11. There is considerable confusion about the identity of this daughter. Following Madina Ly-Tall in *Un Islam militant,* 127, and Robinson, *Holy War,* 105–7, the best reconstruction is as follows: Muhammad Bello gave Umar his daughter Maryam, but she died shortly after Bello himself and before Umar left Sokoto. Ramatullahi, another daughter, was given in her place, and she was the mother of Habib, Moktar, and a certain Mamadu. She may also have been the mother of Nuru, Safur, and Wahid. She was a very strong presence in the Dingiray community.

12. Muntaga apparently blew himself up in the powder room of the palace. The French played some role in the dissidence of Muntaga. Since the early 1880s, they had been in contact with him, encouraging him to take a line independent of his brother Amadu in Segu. See Hanson, *Migration,* esp. chaps. 3 and 4.

13. This was my experience with Alfa Bougouboly Tall, son of Alfa Makki and grandson of Agibu, when I sought to interview him 18–20 August 1976. See also Louis Brenner, "Constructing Muslim Identities in Mali," in Brenner, ed., *Muslim Identity and Social Change in Sub-Saharan Africa* (Bloomington, Ind., 1993), 63–65; Hanson, *Migration,* intro.

14. See the report from Administrator Edouard Martin of Dagana in April 1890, from ANS 2D6 11, reported in Moustapha Kane, "A History of Fuuta Tooro," chap. 4. In Saint-Louis, inhabitants tore up the official notices of the victory posted in the city. See Manchuelle, *"Métis* et colons," 488–89.

15. The Umarians probably resented the distribution of the women from the Segu harem more than any other single act of their long history of relations with the French. Those who accepted the "gift" of Segu women were marked as collaborators with the colonial authorities; among their number were Mademba Sy, soon to become the "fama of Sansanding" by Archinard's appointment; Hammady Kumba Sy, an interpreter; Usman Gassi Sy, of the royal dynasty of Bundu; Ibra Almamy Wan and Shaikh Mamadu Mamudu, notables of Futa Toro; and Agibu Tal. For Agibu it was a case of getting back the wife that Amadu had detained in Segu for more than ten years. Agibu asked for and received a large share of the women and children for safekeeping; some of these people "belonged" to Agibu and had been "retained" in Segu since the 1870s. See ANS 15G 75.1: 38, 46, 48, 49, and 2: 3, 9, 11, 12, 14; 15G 76.1: 24, 50; 15G 78. 102, 105, 121; 1D 121, Agibu, 10–90. See also Hanson and Robinson, *After the Jihad,* doc. 19 B 247.

16. The Umarians initially numbered at least a thousand by my estimates. For an analysis of their movements and attitudes, see Robinson, "Emigration," 252–57.

17. See, for example, ANS 19G 1, pièce 34.

18. See Amadou Hampâté Bâ and Marcel Cardaire, *Le Sage de Bandiagara* (Paris 1957), 15; Martin, *Muslim Brotherhoods,* 72ff. Umar appointed a Tishit man, Sidi Abdallah wuld Muhammad Saghir, at Nioro. Paul Marty, *Etudes sur l'Islam et les tribus du Soudan* (Paris, 1920), 4:205.

19. At one point, when the activities of Samori cut ties between Segu and Dingiray and prevented Dingiray people from making their "pilgrimage" to Segu, Amadu wrote to Agibu and had him read the letter, which gave Tijani affiliation to all who heard it. The passage suggests that Agibu, at the very least, was a muqaddam already. Paul Marty, *L'Islam en Guinée* (Paris, 1921), 153 and annex 24.

20. Muntaga joined forces with Samori after the French capture of Segu in 1890. See below.

21. For appointments by Amadu and Agibu, see Marty, *Soudan,* 2:202 and 209, and 4:205; ANS 4E 19.

22. Makki, the oldest son of Mariatu of Bornu and the older brother of Agibu, was slightly younger than Amadu. He was an ambitious young scholar, more popular than Amadu, but he died in the Masina revolt. His legacy of distance and distrust of Amadu has been perpetuated through Agibu's actions and constructions of history. See Robinson, *Holy War,* 249–57 and passim.

23. Agibu gave these impressions to Louis Archinard as they moved against Bandiagara in 1893. Jacques Méniaud, *Les pionniers du Soudan avant, avec et après Archinard* (Paris, 1931), 2:428n.

24. See Eugène Mage, *Relation du voyage d'exploration de MM: Mage et Quintin au Soudan occidental* (Paris, 1867); Paul Soleillet, *Voyage à Ségou de Paul Soleillet (1842–86), rédigé d'après les notes et journaux de Soleillet,* Gabriel Gravier, ed. (Paris, 1887).

25. See Robinson, *Holy War,* 334–42.

26. Brief summaries of facts about some of these leaders can be found in Paul Marty, *Sénégal,* 1:161–67. Naziru actually fought for the French in the Voulet-Chanoine column.

27. Robinson, *Holy War,* chap. 8.

28. Salif's son, Cerno Bokar Salif, the "sage," was left behind and grew up in Bandiagara with other Umarian families. See Bâ and Cardaire, *Le sage de Bandiagara,* 21; Brenner, *West African Sufi,* 66–67; Robinson, "Emigration."

29. In a passage dealing with the important Sakho lineage who supported the Umarian cause to the hilt, Ibrahima Abou Sall recounts a tradition where Amadu, in the face of the loss of many disciples in battles in the middle Niger, agrees that Sakho scholars will henceforth be exempt from fighting. "Mukhtar Sakho." See also Robinson, *Holy War,* 342–50.

30. On the manufacture of the myth, see Hanson, *Migration,* intro.

31. By Umarian tradition, Hashimi is universally declared author of the hijra account, but there is no clear documentation that establishes his authorship. The material about Hashimi is summarized in Robinson, "Emigration," 258–63. Hashimi was not very prominent at the time of his departure from Bandiagara. He was young and had not yet distinguished himself in military affairs, political leadership, or scholarship. He was born in 1866 or 1867, probably in Nioro, where his father was living. He traveled around the Middle Niger for his education; his biographer concludes a brief list of teachers with the name Sa`ad Jiliya, or Seydu Jeliya Ture, the chief counselor of Amadu. This would put Hashimi in Segu in the early 1880s, before Amadu and his counselor moved to Nioro to counteract the independence of Muntaga. Hashimi may have accompanied them to Nioro or may have escaped from Segu when Archinard attacked in 1890. In any case, he arrived in Bandiagara, the last Umarian capital, some time before the 1893 emigration. John Paden, in *Religion and Political Culture in Kano* (Berkeley, Calif., 1973), 84, gives a translation of an excerpt from a chronicle about Alfa Hashim.

32. For this and what follows, see Robinson, "Emigration," 258–63.

33. According to Shaikh Musa Kamara, Hashimi recounted the story whereby Uqba ibn Nafi, the Arab conqueror of much of North Africa, married the daughter of a local chief and had four sons who became the ancestors of the basic Fulbe families. See Samb, *Essai,* 124. See also Robinson, *Holy War,* chap. 2.

34. It is not clear whether his appointment derived from Amadu, Bassiru, or some Tijani sources in the Near East, or all of the above.

35. Paden, *Religion,* 84–87. See also R. S. O'Fahey et al., *Arabic Literature of Africa,* vol. 1, *The Writings of Eastern Sudanic Africa to c. 1900* (Leiden, 1994), 300 ff.

36. ANS 19G 2.

37. G. J. F. Tomlinson and G. J. Lethem, *History of Islamic Political Propaganda in Nigeria* (London, 1927), 16–20, 28, 48, 63–65, 74, and 85. See also French intelligence information in ANS 19G 2.

38. The Umarians also had to move quickly away from French columns in the

Niamey area in 1895–97 for fear that Amadu would be captured and mistreated. Robinson, "Emigration," 255–57.

39. The principal published sources for Agibu are Yves Saint-Martin, "Un fils d'El Hadj Omar: Aguibou, roi du Dingiray et du Macina, 1843?–1907," *CEA* 29 (1968): 144–78; and A. De Loppinot, "Souvenirs d'Aguibou," *Bulletin du CEHSAOF* 2 (1919).

40. Recorded in numerous places. In ANS 15G 75, sec. 2, pièce 23 for 1890, Agibu complains that Amadu had kept Assa, sixteen other women, slaves, and gold from him.

41. In addition to the Saint-Martin article cited in n. 39 above, I have used Person's 3-vol. *Samori: Une révolution dyula* (Dakar, 1968–75). Person, who uses archival and oral material not available to Saint-Martin, presents a more nuanced picture of Agibu's leadership. See also Brenner, *West African Sufi,* 25 ff.

42. *Fama* is the Bamana word for chief, or king. Mademba was called the fama of Sansanding and had been appointed shortly before Agibu.

43. Interview with Alfa Bougouboly Makki Tal, Bandiagara, 18 August 1976. Bougouboly also indicated that Agibu said, in his letter to Amadu, that he would pardon everyone save Seydu Jeliya, whom he held responsible for poisoning Amadu's mind against him and the other brothers.

44. Letter of Henri Gaden to his father, 7 June 1895, contained in CAOM, archives privées, Fonds Gaden, 15.1.

45. See ANS 15G 75, secs. 1 and 2, passim. In his conversations with the civilian administrator in Bandiagara in the early 1900s, Agibu gave a more elaborate explanation. Most of his rationale centered around Amadu, who was the son of a slave who was herself the daughter of a slave. He was cruel and had demonstrated this in the treatment of his brothers, the hostility toward Agibu, and the detention of Agibu's wife and followers. In contrast, Umar had singled Agibu out as beloved and had said that other sons should succeed before Amadu's sons. De Loppinot, "Souvenirs," 25–27, 38–39. Some of these recollections probably relate to the great expectations that once centered around Makki, Agibu's older brother, as the Umarian leader for Masina and rival to Amadu. Makki was killed in the Masina revolt in 1863–64. Robinson, *Holy War,* 302, 310–11, 338–39.

46. Many of these qualities are undoubtedly a trope or stereotype associated with those in power who are not able to respond to all of the demands of their entourage. Agibu, for example, was known as being much more "generous" than Amadu in the Segu of the 1860s and 1870s and had some of these same qualities at Dingiray in the 1880s. See Mage, *Soudan occidental,* 234 ff.; Galliéni, *Deux campagnes,* 306–7 (observations of Lt. Oberdorf); Ibrahima Ouane, *L'Empire toucouleur d'El Hadj Omar: L'Enigme du Macina* (Monte Carlo, 1952), 45 ff.

47. See De Loppinot, "Souvenirs," and Gaden's letters written in the 1894–96 period. CAOM, archives privées, Fonds Gaden, 15.1. It is obvious that Gaden did not find much to like or respect in Agibu, who was after all not a military leader or scholar and not even an autonomous political leader but someone who complained frequently to the colonial administration and yet sought its support.

48. For example, in interviews with Lamine Bassirou Tall in Kayes and Alfa Bougouboly Tall in Bandiagara in August 1976, and with Madina Ly-Tall on 4 April 1985 in Dakar. The sample that I give here is not very broad and is Bandiagara-biased:

Alfa Bougouboly and Madina Ly-Tall are grandchildren of Agibu; Lamine Bassirou lived in Bandiagara for a time before moving to Kayes.

49. Although she and Bokar did not receive a warm welcome from Agibu. Brenner, *West African Sufi,* 65–69.

50. There is considerable confusion over what the Umarian "objects" are and where they reside. Some traditions record a passing on of objects in Masina and Bandiagara. See Robinson, *Holy War,* 316. There is also a report of objects taken from Segu at the time of the French capture; these apparently exist in some museum or archive in France today. Personal communication of Saliou Mbaye, 15 September 1995.

51. Robinson, *Holy War,* 27–30.

52. Amadou Hampâté Bâ, *Amkoullel, l'enfant peul* (Paris, 1991), 72 ff.; Brenner, *West African Sufi,* 65–69; Andrew Manley, "The Sosso and the Haidara: Two Muslim Lineages in Soudan français, 1890–1960," in Robinson and Triaud, *Le Temps des Marabouts.*

53. The most concentrated source is Marty, *Soudan,* 4:53–54. Marty calls Muntaga the "chief of the Tal family." For his influence in Segu, over the other Umarians and Tijaniyya, see Manley, "Sosso and Haidara."

54. He seems to have played a fairly prominent role with Samori, along with his uncle Lamba Tal and a small group of refugees from Segu. Marty, *Soudan,* 4:53–54; Person, *Révolution dyula,* 3:1790, 1907, 2009, 2028, 2032, 2034; and ANS 15G 131, letter of 9 June 1890. According to one tradition, from Bandiagara Amadu sent to his son a prestigious disciple, Cerno Alhassan Bâ, with a skin containing Umar's prayers for Muntaga; Amadu appointed him a muqaddam of the Tijaniyya with the authority to appoint other muqaddam. Interview with Fama Kouyaté, Segu, 13 August 1976.

55. They are good examples of the power that important women could exercise. See my interview with Fama Kouyate in Segou, 13 August 1976. There is another tradition that makes Muntaga the son of Fatimata Jawando. See ANS 15G 76.2, cited in Saint-Martin, *L'Empire toucouleur,* 422.

56. Marty, however, goes against the Tal traditions by saying that he was educated. *Soudan,* 4:53.

57. Madani, the oldest, had emigrated to the Sokoto caliphate and lived in Hadejia emirate, east of Kano. Muntaga was also long-lived; he died in 1956.

58. Marty, *Soudan,* 4:53.

59. *Onze grains* refers to one section of the prayer rosary where most Tijaniyya have twelve beads. The "Hamallists" also shortened the repetitions of prayers. Umarians and French authorities interpreted these innovations as a kind of "resistance" to colonial rule between the 1920s and 1940s. On the appointment of Hamallah, see Brenner, *West African Sufi,* 109, taken from the report of Capitaine André in 1923, in ANM 4E 18. Madani, in contrast to his cousin Hashimi, had chosen to compose with the British in 1903. Muntaga later resisted the Tal pressure to isolate Shaikh Hamallah and his disciples. While he did not support Cerno Bokar's affiliation with Hamallah, he did protest against the decision of the administration and the local Tal to exclude Bokar from the mosque in 1938, by refusing to pray there. Muntaga went instead to Mopti. Brenner, *West African Sufi,* 138.

60. Hanson, *Migration,* passim.

61. ANS 15G 76, pièce 129; Soleillet, 363, 484; Marty, *Sénégal,* 1:163–64.

62. Murtada is mentioned in the council that made the decision that Amadu should embark on the hijra, but there is no evidence that he emigrated himself. It is not clear whether the family intentionally sought to keep some members of the family in the western Sudan while encouraging others to emigrate. For Murtada, see Marty, *Soudan,* 4:228–29; ANS 19G 2, pièce 69, 13 June 1911.

63. He was buried in the cemetery of Fakha-Gadiaba, separated from the burial place of the Umarians. Constant Hamès, "Le prémier exil de Shaikh Hamallah et la mémoire hamalliste, Nioro-Mederdra, 1925," in Robinson and Triaud, *Le Temps des Marabouts.*

64. This information comes from Marty, *Guinée,* 148–76.

65. Marty, *Sénégal,* 1:161–66. Seydu Nuru's moment would come after World War I.

66. Hanson, "Political Economy of Meaning."

67. In an earlier period, the most visible practitioners of the Tijaniyya had been hostile to the Umarian enterprise. A certain Hamme Bâ from the Toro region, not far from Umar's birthplace, declared himself to by the Mahdi in the troubled times of the late 1820s. After defeat and exile, he returned to Toro and founded a new village, Wuro Madiyu. During Al-Hajj Umar's recruitment drive in Futa in 1858–59, Hamme provided critical information to the French and opposed the mission as much as possible. His sons and successors, Amadu and Ibra, led the Madiyanke movement described in chap. 1, in response to the cholera epidemic of 1867–69. They were killed, along with most of their supporters, in 1875. Their movement did as much prejudice to the French image of the Tijaniyya as the resistance of the Umarians. But in the 1850s, the French did not put the Tijaniyya label on either Umar or the "Madiyu." Nor did they distinguish clearly, in 1869–70, between their Madiyanke enemies and Amadu Sheku, with whom they were on reasonably good terms at the time. See Robinson, *Chiefs and Clerics,* chap. 4; Hanson and Robinson, *After the Jihad,* doc. cluster 13; and chap. 1.

68. See Sall, "Mukhtar Sakho," and Robinson, "Emerging Pattern."

69. The fullest existing treatment of the ferganke is Moustapha Kane, "A History of Fuuta Tooro," esp. chap. 3. See also Robinson, *Chiefs and Clerics,* 157–59.

70. For the key talibé families in the Umarian tradition, see Robinson, *Holy War,* chap. 9, esp. table 9.3 on 349.

71. He did some of the same reconfiguring of the Tijaniyya tradition that one can see in Malik Sy. See chap. 10.

72. His title was qadi supérieur and he was assigned to Regba in 1905–6, and then to Boghé for the period from 1906 until his death in 1934. For Sakho, I rely on Sall's article "Mukhtar Sakho."

73. Sall, "Mukhtar Sakho," 238–39.

74. Gaden actually was a member of the "Gouraud team" from the time of the campaigns to capture Samori in the late 1890s. He then served as a military commandant in Zinder in the early 1900s. Among his duties was watching West Africans, including a number of Futanke and Umarians, make the land pilgrimage to Sudan and Mecca. He served as Boutilimit during the conquest of Adrar in 1908–9. On his career, see CAOM EE 2 924, and archives privées, Henri Gaden.

75. Paris, 1935. For the role of Sakho and Seydu Nuru, see Gaden's introduction, viii–ix. Gaden had published *Proverbes et maximes* in 1931. For reflections on the emer-

gence of interpretations of the Umarian jihad, see Kane, Fagerberg-Diallo, and Robinson, "Une vision iconoclaste."

76. For example, in the works of Paul Marty.

77. See n. 59 above and articles by Constant Hamès, Vincent Joly, and Louis Brenner in Robinson and Triaud, *Le Temps des Marabouts.*

CHAPTER 8

1. An earlier version of this chapter appeared as "Sa`d Buh, the Fadiliyya and French colonial authorities," *ISASS* 11 (1997).

2. A representative sample of these images can be found in Lt. d'Otton Loyewski, "Coppolani et la Mauritanie," *Revue d'Histoire des Colonies* 26 (1938): 17–19. For some earlier images of Saad Buh from the French military officer Louis Frèrejean, see Désiré-Vuillemin, *Mauritanie,* 71–75, 112–15. Somewhat more muted but still negative judgments are rendered in one of the basic sources for the Fadiliyya, Paul Marty, "Les Fadelïa," 137–219.

3. In 1900, Blanchet and his colleagues were held prisoner for several months in very difficult conditions in the Adrar. See below, n. 60.

4. Albury, according to one report written after he went into exile, was even prepared to consider surrender if Saad Buh could guarantee his safety. See the notes of the commander at the new post of Kaedi in Futa Toro on 5 September 1891. ANS 2B 78.

5. See, for example, Désiré-Vuillemin, *Mauritanie,* 74–75 and passim.

6. He often styled himself "Shaikh Saad Buh of the Ahl Shaikh Muhammad Fadel." See CAOM AFPO 907, report of the *Commissaire* of Mauritania, 4th trimester 1914, dated 7 February 1915; *RMM* 24 (1915): 21.

7. Specifically to 'Ali, son-in-law and cousin of the Prophet. L. Bouvat, "Cheikh Saadibouh et son entourage d'après un manuscrit inédit," *RMM* 18 (1912): 185–99. The most complete published source on the Fadiliyya is still Marty, "Les Fadelia." The Fadiliyya were sometimes called the Al-Mamin, after Muhammad al-'Amin, the father of Fadil; ibid., 145. Useful summaries of the state of knowledge about the Fadiliyya and Saad Buh are Constant Hamès, "Shaykh Sa'ad Buh, Mauritanie, 1850–1917," *ISASS* 4 (1990): 133–37, and McLaughlin, "Sufi, Saint, Sharif."

8. See Robinson, *Holy War,* chap. 2, for instances among the Fulbe and some other West African societies. For the Kunta fabrication, see Thomas Whitcomb, "New Evidence on the Origins of the Kunta," *BSOAS* 38 (1975), 103–23, 407–17.

9. They were known as the Ahl al-Talib Mukhtar, "people of the disciple Mukhtar."

10. See Rahal Boubrik, "Processus de formation d'une confrérie saharienne," *La transmission du savoir dans l'Islam peripherique, lettre d'information* 15 (1995), 48–54.

11. McLaughlin, "Sufi, Saint, Sharif," 81–83. This tradition does not correlate with most Tijaniyya interpretations of exclusivity and superiority, and certainly not with the Umarian ones described in the preceding chapter. See Abun-Nasr, *The Tijaniyya,* chap. 3.

12. Marty, "Les Fadelia," 140. Muhammad Fadil developed the public recitation of the *dhikr* in contrast to the private one of the Kunta, and this resulted in certain charges and rumors that the Fadiliyya were not orthodox or were indeed enemies

of Islam. Hamès, "Shaykh Saʿad Buh," 133; McLaughlin, "Sufi, Saint, Sharif," esp. 88–93.

13. Dedoud in "Guerre sainte." The Quranic citations are from sura 37, v. 96, and sura 7, v. 137. I am indebted to Dedoud's translation of the *Nasiha,* written in 1906, and his commentary on it, for a number of observations in this chapter.

14. The Fadiliyya traditions contain a number of references to encounters with Umar Tal, set in the late 1850s and early 1860s when he controlled Karta and was moving against Segu and Masina. In one tradition, Umar offered a command post to Sidi Buya (also called Sidi Uthman), one of Muhammad al-Fadil's sons; Sidi refused, or refused after a brief participation. Amar Samb, ed. and trans., "La condamnation de la guerre sainte de Cheikh Moussa Kamara," *BIFAN,* ser. B, 38 (1976): 174. In another, Umar sought to impose tribute payments on the marabout, who promptly migrated further west. J Gros, ed., *Soleillet en Afrique* (Paris, 1888), 131. Saad Buh writes at some length of this in his *Nasiha,* or "counsels," to his brother Ma El Ainin in 1906. See Dedoud, "Guerre sainte," 131–33; McLaughlin, "Sufi, Saint, Sharif," 52–53.

15. There is considerable disparity about the date of Muhammad's birth, ranging from 1780 to 1798. See Boubrik, "Confrérie saharienne."

16. See, for example, Bouvat, "Cheikh Saadibouh," passim.

17. His well-known brother Ma El Ainin left the Hodh in about 1858, made the pilgrimage, and visited Morocco coming and going. It was during those visits, that he established the close relations with the Sharifian court that enhanced his prestige and frightened the French during the struggle for control of Mauritania and Morocco in the early twentieth century. See Martin, *Muslim Brotherhoods,* chap. 5.

18. Marty, *L'émirat des Trarzas,* 448–51.

19. Marty, "Les Fadelia," 186–88; Robinson interview with Farba Boudi Gaye in Matam, 13 March 1968. The governor in question was probably François-Xavier Valière (1869–76). See also Schmitz, ed., *Florilège,* 25–27.

20. A few years later, after his pilgrimage, Shaikh Mamadu married Aminata, daughter of Hamat Ndiaye Anne, who was still head of the Muslim Tribunal of Saint-Louis. She was the mother of Abdussalam Kane, the durable colonial chief of Kanel in eastern Futa. See chaps. 3 and 4. Shaikh Mamadu's credentials corresponded closely to the Fadiliyya model; he was very learned in the law, adept at working miracles, and had a kind of Futanke equivalent to Sharifian descent: a connection to Almamy Abdul. To this he added the pilgrimage and military prowess. See David Robinson, "Hedging Bets: Shaikh Mamadu Mamudu of Futa Toro," *ISASS* 9 (1995).

21. Marty, "Les Fadeliya," 181, and *Sénégal,* 1:27.

22. The Seck, or "Bu El Mogdad" family of Saint-Louis, described in chap. 4, studied with Awlad Daiman scholars in Trarza during the nineteenth century. The Awlad Daiman were one of the five branches of the Tashumsha, who constituted the Islamic learning establishment.

23. For Saad Buh's effort to settle in Trarza, I rely particularly on Rahal Boubrik, *Saints et société en Islam: La confrérie ouest-saharienne Fâdiliyya* (Paris, 1999), chaps. 7 and 9. Boubrik relies on a treatise that Saad Buh composed in 1881, entitled *Al-Asinna an-nafidha fi radd al-bayʿa al-haditha.* I found confirmation for this resistance in my interview with Al-Hajj Bokar Bâ in Kaédi on 5 April 1968; Bokar was the son of Shaikh Amadu Bâ, qadi

of Kaédi in the early colonial period, and a disciple of Saad Buh. See also Mohamed al-Mukhtar w. as-Sa ᶜd, "Emirats et espace émiral maure: Le cas du Trarza aux XVIIIe et XIXe siècles," *REMMM* 54 (1989): 53–82.

24. Bouvat, "Cheikh Saadibouh." Some themes in the Bouvat account, which is based on a commentary by a disciple of a work by Saad Buh, are reminiscent of the biblical story of Joseph: the talented younger brother who arouses resentment among the older siblings.

25. Boubrik, *Saints et société,* chap. 7.

26. His installations at Touizikht and near Saint-Louis were very close to the caravan routes and the customs collection stations that the emir of Trarza sought to maintain in the nineteenth century; they may indicate a very strategic deployment on Saad Buh's part. Lydon, "On Trans-Saharan Trails," chap. 3.

27. ANS 2B 74, report of April 1882; CAOM SEN 4 128, sec. b, governor-general to ministry, 3 June 1897; Paul Gaffarel, *Le Sénégal et le Soudan français* (Paris, 1898), 182. Marty ("Les Fadelïa," 181) shows that in the last three decades of the nineteenth century, Saad Buh occupied a number of sites, primarily in the Trarza region, along the trade routes between Saint-Louis and the Adrar.

28. Gaffarel, *Le Sénégal* (Paris, 1898), 182. Soleillet went back to Senegal later in 1880 and tried another journey into Trarza, again with the sponsorship of Saad Buh. He returned to Saint-Louis after twenty-one days in Trarza. A. Gruvel and R. Chudeau, *A Travers la Mauritanie Occidentale de Saint Louis à Port Etienne* (Paris, 1909), 31.

29. The information network was evident in the early 1900s, when Louis Frère-jean depended on Saad Buh's system, even more than Sidiyya Baba's, for information about Trarza, Brakna, Tagant, and the Adrar. See Désiré-Vuillemin, *Mauritanie,* passim.

30. One of Ma El Ainin's sons was Shaikh Hassana, a leader of the anti-French jihad in the early twentieth century. The marriages of the sons to Saad Buh's daughters seem to have survived the conflicts between the two brothers, but Saad Buh's sons repudiated their marriages to Ma El Ainin's daughters. Marty, "Les Fadelïa," 183–85. There is no good study of Ma El Ainin and his network of relations; he had a sphere of influence in the north broader than that of Saad Buh in the south; the sphere certainly extended into the court circles of the Moroccan sultan throughout the late nineteenth century. The best available account of Ma El Ainin in English is Martin, *Muslim Brotherhoods,* 125–51.

31. He provided invaluable assistance to the mission of Lt. Fabert in 1891, thanks to his ability to stay in contact with all factions in the Trarza emiral dispute. He was also on excellent terms with the emiral family of Adrar. CAOM SEN 4 65, sec. c, Fabert to governor, 30 September 1891.

32. Further research may indicate that he developed the camp at Nimjat (or nearby Khroufa) in the 1870s. In the *fiches de renseignement* for Trarza (ANS 9G 43, for 1911–13), the French give Khroufa as the birthplace and the following birth dates for several of Saad Buh's sons: The oldest, Sidi Buya in 1872; the third son, Athrana, in 1875; the fourth, Udi, in 1879; the fifth, Mahfuz (Saad Buh's "favorite"), in 1881; the sixth, Ma El Ainin, in 1882; the seventh, Taleb Buya, in 1883, and the last, Bunama, in 1887. Khroufa was the headquarters for the French district of western Trarza for several years in the early twentieth century.

33. Stewart, *Social Order*, passim.

34. Marty picked up the Sidiyya bias against Saad Buh and the Fadiliyya in "Les Fadelïa." See McLaughlin, "Sufi, Saint, Sharif," 153–57, 1894; the interview with Bokar Bâ is cited in n. 23.

35. Especially for operations in western Trarza, but also as military auxiliaries in the Tagant and Adrar missions of 1905 and 1908–9, respectively. See Désiré-Vuillemin, *Mauritanie,* passim, and Lydon, "On Trans-Saharan Trails," chap. 3.

36. Boubrik, *Saints et société,* 122. The document is *Taqrif al-ʿAsma fi adh-Dhabbi ʿan bughdi Abna' Bani as'Sibaʿ,* Institut Mauritanien de la Recherche Scientifique, MS 2141.

37. An extensive list of Saad Buh's muqaddam and disciples was provided in 1888 to the noted "Algerian" Islamicist Alfred Le Châtelier, who was surveying the "state of Islam" in West Africa at the time. See his *Islam dans l'Afrique Occidentale,* 327–32. Marty also gives a list in "Les Fadelia." I made some effort to suggest his influence in *Chiefs and Clerics,* 105, 158, and 164, n. 2. See also a brief list for Futa Toro in n. 40 below.

38. Person, *Samori,* 2:881–82.

39. Shaikh Mamadu Mamudu returned in the 1880s to Futa Toro after his pilgrimage and marriage in Saint-Louis. See Robinson, "Hedging Bets."

40. Marty, "Les Fadelia," 192–93. Many others, in Futa Toro and other regions, also affiliated with Saad Buh. A disciple named Abdu Mbodj traveled through central Futa in 1884 and evoked a positive response from the local population. The French were quite anxious about this region, where they sought to string their telegraph line. They finally came to terms in 1885 with Abdul Bokar Kane, who dominated the area. The French thought that Mbodj might be affiliated with the Sanussi, the Sufi order that they most feared. See ANS 2B 75, letter of 8 November 1884, governor to minister of colonies. Al-Hajj Bokar Bâ, son of Shaikh Amadu Bâ, an Umarian who returned from the east after the French conquest, gave me this list of followers in the area of Bossea in his interview of 5 April 1968 (see n. 23 above): Mamadu Nudoka, Alfa Sire, and Yubal Matar (all of Anyam Siwol); Amel Dia of Anyam Wuro Sire, Haimut of Dabiya, Mamadu Bineta Wane of Dumba Bossea, Amar Bela of Kaedi, Suleyman of Hore Fonde, and Bukar of Nere. The list also included some Wane from Mbumba — Mamadu Birane Almamy and Mamadu Birane Abdul — and a number of followers from the Matam area. Shaikh Musa Kamara studied with Shaikh Saad Buh in the mid 1880s, when he was twenty-two or twenty-three years old. Samb, *Essai,* 109.

41. Multiple affiliation was popular in Futa Toro in the 1870s and 1880s. Shaikh Musa Kamara studied with a variety of teachers who were masters of different texts of fiqh and had different Sufi identities during this period. He adopted the more flexible Fadiliyya option that included the knowledge of and ability to initiate into the Tijaniyya and other orders. See Schmitz, intro. to *Florilège,* vol. 1.

42. The Friday mosque — usually the main mosque in a town or quarter — is where the faithful assemble for the Friday afternoon prayer. Marty, *Soudan,* 2:6.

43. I draw on my interview cited in n. 23.

44. Ibra Almamy Wane, Abdul's arch rival, sought Saad Buh's counsel around the time he made the pilgrimage at government expense in 1893. See n. 37 above and ANS 2D 11/3 for 1894.

45. His conversion of the Tegne of Baol, Beye Bayar, was considered to be one of

his miracles. Marty, "Fadelïa," 188. Albury gave Saad Buh one hundred cattle a year. Thilmans, "Lat Dior, Cheikh Saad Bou et le chemin de fer," 19.

46. They served as one main source of supply of Coppolani's operations in western Trarza in 1903–5. See Désiré-Vuillemin, *Mauritanie,* first section. For elements of the economic activities of the Fadiliyya network, see CAOM Mauritanie 4 2bis, governor-general to Ministry of Colonies, 29 July 1907, *situation politique* for the 2nd trimester, 1907.

47. The quote comes from the commissaire-general of Mauritania in 1915, but it would be almost equally applicable to the last three decades of the nineteenth century.

48. It does not permit, however, a full delineation of the relationship and its fluctuations in a way comparable to the links between Muridiyya and the French in the early twentieth century.

49. Interview, 11 June 1985, with Serigne Moustapha Ndiaye and Ousmane Dieye, sons of Cheikh Bouya Fall Ndiaye and Amadou Sire Dieng, respectively. Dieng appears in Marty's list of Saad Buh's followers; he left at one point to work with Shaikh Mahfud, Saad Buh's nephew who had his base near Sedhiou in the Casamance. Marty, "Les Fadelia," 193–94.

50. On this bureau, see Harrison, *France and Islam,* 42–47, 105–7.

51. Some 1,250 persons in Nimzat alone.

52. See n. 49.

53. For Cayor, see Thilmans, "Lat Dior, Saad Bou et le chemin de fer," 16. For Baol and Salum, see Marty, "Les Fadelïa," 186–88. Saad Buh even intervened with his brother, Sidi l-Kheir, in the old family heartland in the Hodh, to sign a treaty with the French commander in Timbuktu in 1896. Marty, *Soudan,* 3:255–57. In 1893, his nephew Shaikh Mahfud offered his services as a possible emissary to Samori for Archinard. Marty, *Sénégal,* 1:38. It is probable that, with a more complete archival search, one would find a number of other instances in which the colonial authorities sought his help on the edges of their expanding domain.

54. In 1894, Dudu Seck told Hussein, the son of Bakar of the Idawaish, that the French gave annual presents to the marabout as a way of indicating how positive were French attitudes toward Muslims. See Mohamedou Ould Mohameden, "Les tentatives de pénétration française dans le pays maure à travers le rapport de mission de Bu El Mogdad en 1894 au Tagant," *Masadir,* cahier 1, 1994. See also the dossier of fonds secrets, esp. ANS 17G 24–25.

55. CAOM SEN 4 128, governor-general to Ministry of Colonies, 3 June 1897. For the correspondance related to Fabert's mission, see the translations of Fara Biram Lô (see chap. 6) of 23 August and 21 and 23 September 1892. The 23 August letter is from Saad Buh to the governor; in it, the cleric asks the administration to provide him with a list of books in Arabic, if they can be found at the Moroccan stores in Saint-Louis. In the 21 September letter, Si Ahmed indicates that he accepts the draft treaty that Fabert had sent, but informs the governor that he is also under the authority of the commander of the faithful, Mulay Hassan of Morocco. In the 23 September letter, Si Ahmed writes: "Saad Buh is my marabout and has done a great deal to consolidate our friendship [between me and you]." For Fabert's account, see CAOM SEN 4 65, sec. c, Fabert to governor, 30 September 1891. For a useful summary, see Commandant Gillier, *La pénétration en Mauritanie: Découverte—Explorations—Conquête—La police du désert et la pacification définitive*

(Paris, 1926), 97. Fabert made several other missions in Trarza for the governor of Senegal and brought back some good information. He died in 1896, partly as a consequence of his exhaustion. Gruvel and Chudeau, *A Travers la Mauritanie,* 31–36. Later in the 1890s, Saad Buh was host to a French mission led by Pasiade and directed at the sulfur deposits of Tafelli. I have been able to find only Saad Buh's passing reference to this in "Notice de Cheikh Saad Bouh," in Hamet, *Chroniques.* In 1897, the governor acknowledged the services that Saad Buh had rendered and how Touizikht had served as a staging area for French efforts to explore central Mauritania. CAOM SEN 4 128, letter of governor to MMC, 3 June 1897.

56. "Mémoire de Bou El Mogdad."

57. The French reported in 1899 that Ma El Ainin would not permit his daughters to join their husbands, sons of Saad Buh. ANS 1G2 43, director of indigenous affairs to governor-general, 13 January 1899.

58. For the Blanchet mission, see "Notice de Cheikh Saad Bouh"; Gruvel and Chudeau, *A Travers la Mauritanie,* 36; Désiré-Vuillemin, *Contribution,* 83; Gillier, *Pénétration,* 98–99; and her edited account of Dudu Seck's report, "A propos du rapport de l'interprète Bou El Mogdad sur sa mission dans l'Adrar en 1900," *Revue d'Histoire des Colonies* 39 (1952): 103–26.

59. The Adrar emir had asked that no armed men accompany the expedition. He later apparently relented, but the presence of black soldiers in *bidan* country, and their panic upon encountering hostile reactions, undoubtedly complicated the situation of the mission. See Désiré-Vuillemin, "A propos du rapport," 105–7.

60. I am following Saad Buh's own account in "Notice." He notes that the governor also made a request to Sidiyya Baba to intervene; by his silence, he suggests that he is a more loyal friend than his Boutilimit rival. The account is essentially confirmed by Dudu Seck, who indicates that Hassana, Ma El Ainin's son and Saad Buh's son-in-law, sought to make the negotiations fail. "Mémoire de Bou El Mogdad." For the echoes of the imprisonment and the plan to bring the survivors to Morocco, see CAOM AFPO 2711, letters from the chargé d'affaires in Tangiers to the MAE, 29 August 1900, and of the Ministry of Colonies to the MAE, 9 January 1901.

61. Personal communication from Abdel Wedoud Ould Cheikh, 14 June 1996.

62. This expression is used by Commandant Frèrejean in Désiré-Vuillemin, *Mauritanie,* 74–75. Saad Buh also notes the accusations of certain Muslims after he saved the "Christians" of the Blanchet mission toward the end of his *Nasiha.* Dedoud, "Guerre sainte."

63. In this interpretation, I am concurring with the judgment expressed by Shaikh Musa Kamara in *Al-Majmu' an-Nafis* and evoked by Dedoud, "Guerre sainte." In his *Nasiha,* Saad Buh expresses a slight hint of regret at the disappearance of the autonomous states of the western Sudan, from Cayor to Samori and the Umarians. See Dedoud, "Guerre sainte," n. 99. Saad Buh shared the *bidan* view of the Dar al-Islam: "black" Senegal and Mali lands were much less obviously Muslim than the *trab al-bidan* north of the river; French conquest was more acceptable in the former than in the latter.

64. A treatise by Al-Bashir ibn Mbarigi al-Yadmusi, quoted by Kamara in *Al-Majmu' an-Nafis* and quoted in turn by Dedoud in "Guerre sainte," 124.

65. Despite his reservations, he participated fully in the Coppolani mission, begin-

ning with the very public ceremonies of endorsement in Saint-Louis and along the river in 1902–3. See CAOM Missions 115, governor-general to Ministry of Colonies, 11 December 1903. Other correspondance in the same file indicates that the French still appreciated the assistance that Saad Buh could bring to their Mauritanian campaign.

66. The main source for the following is ANS 9G 21, chemise 14, devoted especially to the issue of Saad Buh's tours; see also 19G3 for 1906. The detailed figures for receipts come from a document provided to me by Abdoul Aidara, director of the CRDS in Saint-Louis in 1985.

67. However, this was probably without the knowledge and consent of Saad Buh, who placed a strong emphasis on the Fadiliyya tradition of rejecting weapons. Dedoud, "Guerre sainte."

68. 9G21, chemise 14, governor of Senegal to governor-general, 6 February 1905. Coppolani was assassinated in April of that year.

69. CAOM SEN 4 128, governor-general to Minstry of Colonies, report of June 1907 on first trimester, 1907.

70. CAOM Mauritanie 4 2bis, governor-general to Ministry of Colonies, 29 July 1907.

71. CAOM SEN 4 133. Marty ("Les Fadelia," 195) put the amount collected at more than 70,000 francs. He noted that forty camel loads had headed north from Saint-Louis and that the marabout's son Sidati had purchased six hundred camels (including two hundred females) at Louga.

72. Marty, *Soudan,* 3:256-58, and ANS 19G 1, pièce 34.

73. Dedoud, "Guerre sainte."

74. Edited by Ismaël Hamet, the Algerian military interpreter who later became the director of the Institut des Hautes Etudes Marocaines. See also Hamès, "Shaykh Saad Buh," 135.

75. Saad Buh was defending himself from accusations in the colonial milieu of manufacturing the letter to recoup his standing with the French. See his testimonial statement in favor of the French in the *RMM* 29 (1915): 29.

76. The letter was in fact a long treatise. For the story of its dissemination and copies of the French translation, see CAOM Mauritanie 6.1, and the *Bulletin du Comité de l'Afrique Française* (supplement no. 11 of 11 November 1909, 225-31, as "Un mandement de Saad Bouh à Ma el-Ainin"); another French translation is available in the private papers of Henri Gaden (CAOM AP 15.1, pièce 127). The letter was widely circulated in the federation in late 1909 or early 1910, and it was still being discussed as late as 1913 (ANS 19G 2, pièce 24). Shaikh Musa Kamara gives a long extract from this treatise in his commentary on holy war; see Amar Samb, "La condamnation de la guerre sainte de Cheikh Moussa Kamara," *BIFAN,* ser. B, 38 (1976). In this and in what follows, I have relied principally on Dedoud, "Guerre sainte." He has worked from two Arabic copies of the letter at the Institut Mauritanien de la Recherche Scientifique in Nouakchott. Saad Buh also gave a commentary, several years earlier, on the *fatwa* that Sidiyya Baba wrote for Coppolani's pacification in early 1903. Michaux-Bellaire, "Une fetoua de Cheikh Sidia," 140ff.

77. Sidi Buya had a brief and unsuccessful foray as chief of the Tendagha fraction of the Trarza starting in 1906; the complaints led to his revocation in 1909. Marty, "Les Fadelïa," 183-84; Désiré-Vuillemin, *Contribution,* 214.

Chapter 9

1. An earlier version of this chapter appeared in *ISASS* 13 (1999). I would like to thank Ibrahima Abou Sall and Abdel Wedoud Ould Cheikh for their help in providing sources and commentary on this chapter out of their considerable knowledge of the theme, period, and region.

2. Inferiority of weaponry was not completely obvious at the time, especially since various *bidan* groups could obtain modern weapons from competing European groups, especially the Spanish, Germans, English, and French.

3. Taken from the French translation provided by Michaux-Bellaire, ed. and trans., "Une fetoua de Cheikh Sidia," 137–38. As outlined in chap. 4, it should be recalled that the translation was published in *Archives Marocaines,* a journal under the direction of the prominent Islamicist Alfred Le Châtelier, whose *Islam dans l'Afrique occidentale* gave significant space to the Sidiyya as a branch of the Qadiriyya and especially the Kunta (324–27); his information dated from about 1888.

4. Ibid., 138. Baba gives similar arguments in a history of southwestern Mauritania that he prepared over many years. It was finally completed by one of his sons shortly after his death. See H. T. Norris, "A History of the Western Sanhaja," in his *Saharan Myth and Saga* (Oxford, 1972), 160–217. Paul Marty notes Baba's work on the manuscript in his study "Cheikh Sidia et sa 'Voie,'" in *Islam en Mauritanie et au Sénégal,* which constituted the entire issue of *RMM* 31 (1915–16); see page 38.

5. For an analysis of the content, see Yahya Wuld al-Bara, "Les théologiens mauritaniens face au colonialisme," in Robinson and Triaud, *Le Temps des Marabouts,* 108–14. For comparison with the fatwas produced by the jurists of Fez and other Maghribi schools to accommodate the growing European presence, see Khalifa Chater, "A Rereading of Islamic Texts in the Maghrib in the Nineteenth and Early Twentieth Centuries: Secular Themes or Religious Reformism?" in John Ruedy, ed., *Islamism and Secularism in North Africa* (New York, 1994).

6. Coppolani's work became the bible of French administrators of Muslim societies. See chap. 4 and Jean-Louis Triaud, *La légende noire de la Sanusiyya? Une confrérie musulmane sous les regard français, 1840–1930* (Paris, 1995), esp. chap. 21.

7. Shaikh Saad Buh endorsed Baba's ideas in a companion fatwa that appears as part of the Michaux-Bellaire article cited in n. 3. It is not clear when Saad Buh wrote his commentary. The document was communicated to Michaux-Bellaire by Robert Arnaud, who was appointed as the director of the Muslim Affairs Bureau in 1905 and traveled to Morocco in 1906. See chap. 4, and Harrison, *France and Islam,* 33 ff.

8. For the close relationships between the two men, see Gouraud, *La pacification de la Mauritanie* (Paris, 1910) and his letters to Henri Gaden contained in the Fonds Gaden (CAOM AP 15); see also n. 57 below. Saad Buh added his opinion to the statement of Sidiyya Baba and thus provided an important Fadiliyya cachet. But, as chapter 8 has shown, Saad Buh was the spokesman for the French preeminence of the late nineteenth century, not for the French control of the early twentieth. He had reason to be jealous of the young rising star in the colonial firmament.

9. The Ntishait fraction, of which the Sidiyya were part, also claimed a link to the Tendagha *zwaya* of Trarza. The classic study for this network is Stewart, *Social Order.*

Stewart relied in part on the work of a French researcher with long experience in Mauritanie, Paul Dubié *(La vie matérielle des Maures)* and on the earlier work of Marty, "Cheikh Sidia," cited in n. 4. For a recent commentary on Sidiyya al-Kabir's diplomacy in the mid nineteenth century, see Taylor, "Blood Money." For additional commentary on Stewart's study, see Abdel Wedoud Ould Cheikh, "La tribu comme volonté et comme représentation: Le facteur religieux dans l'organisation d'une tribu maure: Les Awlad Abyayri," in Pierre Bonte, et al., *Al-Ansab: La quête des origines: Anthropologie historique de la société tribale arabe* (Paris, 1991), and Ould Cheikh's article "Harun Wuld al-Shaikh Sidiyya, 1919-77," in Robinson and Triaud, *Le Temps des Marabouts.* The crucial role that the Sidiyya played in the French conquest and colonial Mauritania, as well as the prominence of the Stewart study amid the underdeveloped historiography of the *bidan,* has undoubtedly led to an overemphasis on the order at the expense of other regions and tribes. See the comments on the historiography of Mauritania in chap. 2.

10. For the Kunta "model," see Brenner, "Concepts of *Tariqa* in West Africa: The Case of the Qadiriyya," in Cruise O'Brien and Coulon, *Charisma.*

11. Sidiyya al-Kabir may also have begun the arming and training of warrior groups to protect Awlad Abyayri interests, a "violation" of the understanding of the distribution of labor and vocation between *hassan* and *zwaya* groups within *bidan* society. See the sources cited in n. 9.

12. Constant Hamès, "Pour une histoire de Boutilimit (Sahel mauritanien)," *Journal de la Société des Africanistes* 55 (1985); Stewart, *Social Order,* 79. The Awlad Abyayri tended to pasture their flocks across a vast area of eastern Trarza, adjacent to the pasturages of Brakna. The Trarza *hassan,* including the emiral family, tended to stay more in the western zones of Trarza, but they intersected with the Abyayri in their patterns of transhumance. The agricultural zone for the Abyayri was in the south, close to the river, and the *telamide* who did the farming, were slaves and harratin. See Dubié, *Vie matérielle,* esp. the map on 122, and Christian Santoir, *La région du lac Rkiz: Approche géographique et cartographique* (Dakar, 1973), 103-5.

13. For one of the earlier reports, from the commandant of Podor, see ANS 13G 120, #78, letter of 19 June 1856. For the *Moniteur,* see the issue for 17 June 1856. A summary account was then published by Faidherbe in *Annales Sénégalaises,* 68, and the image of resistance was duly reported in Alfred Le Châtelier's work published at the end of the century (*L'Islam,* 326-27); Le Châtelier does concede, however, that the Sidiyya attitude toward the French was basically "correct." The 1856 episodes have been analyzed by A. Leriche in "Deux lettres." Leriche gives excerpts of an 1856 letter of Sidiyya to Faidherbe in which the cleric invites the governor to convert to Islam. See chap. 1, n. 61.

14. Sidiyya al-Kabir's descendants, who take the name of Ahl Shaikh Sidiyya because of his importance and the large descent group that he began, emphasize the contributions of the founder rather than his grandson, Sidiyya Baba, the subject of this chapter. Baba is quite literally responsible for "saving" the Sidiyya heritage, through the creation of French colonial Mauritania, but this contribution is difficult to recognize in an independent Islamic Republic of Mauritania that has reconstructed itself as an Arab and Maghribi culture. Cf. Ould Cheikh, "Harun," 213-19.

15. According to a number of interviews and formulations in the oral tradition,

Falil lost a contest of learning and miracle working with Umar and died as a result of the beating inflicted upon him by the Tijaniyya leader. Robinson, *Holy War,* 225–27. Kamara also notes this in his *Tanqiyat,* folio 72. For further observations on the Sidiyya following in the 1880s, see Le Châtelier, *L'Islam,* 325–27.

16. See Robinson, *Chiefs and Clerics,* 70–78, and "Shaikh Muusa Kamara."

17. Included in their number were the Wane of Mbumba, chiefs of Law Province and close collaborators with the French through the late nineteenth and early twentieth centuries.

18. ANS 13G 245, letter of 17 October 1865. Fode Salum is also mentioned by Le Châtelier (*L'Islam,* 325).

19. As distinguished from the metaphor of resistance emanating from some French and contemporary Mauritanian sources. Cf. Stewart, *Social Order,* 138–42.

20. Ould Cheikh, "La tribu" and "Harun."

21. This was especially true with the Awlad Daiman, leading clerics of Trarza and the teachers of the Seck family. Shaikh Sliman was a disciple and associate of Sidiyya al-Kabir; his son Shaikh Ahmeddou succeeded him in 1862; his grandson Mohammed in turn succeeded in 1884. Mohammed (usually called Shaikh Sliman by the French) was an ally of the French during their occupation and was named shaikh supérieur of the Awlad Daiman in 1906; he retained the great influence in emiral circles that had characterized his family. Marty, "Cheikh Sidia," 82–84. On the Trarza and relations between the emiral family and the *zwaya,* see as-Sa'd, "Espace émiral," 53–82.

22. Sidna, or Sidi Muhammad. In the twentieth century, he is remembered, by some Mauritanian writers, as even more "resistance" oriented than his father. See Ould Cheikh, "Harun."

23. The same cholera epidemic that was the occasion for the emergence of the Madiyanke, the "sons of the Mahdi" mentioned in chap. 1. Baba's childhood and early adult career have not been given serious exploration in European-language publications. See Ould Cheikh, "Harun," and Le Châtelier, *L'Islam,* 325–27.

24. Le Châtelier (*L'Islam,* 326) considered the Sidiyya order to be in decline in the 1880s, several years before the crises of the 1890s drove Baba into his alliance with the French.

25. At some time in the 1880s, Baba and his contemporaries were hosts to Amadu Bamba Mbacke, who was about ten years older than Baba. Bamba was attracted to the renown of the Sidiyya in the Muslim sciences and especially within the Qadiriyya branch of Sufism. This "episode" receives very little attention in the historical record, whether that of the Sidiyya, the Muridiyya, or the French. Marty puts this episode in about 1889, after an initiation by El Hajj Kamara, the Sidiyya muqaddam in Saint-Louis. *Islam et Mauritanie et au Sénégal,* 101.

26. Faidherbe, *Le Senegal,* 444–45; Marty, "Cheikh Sidia," 81. In another work, Marty has him interceding earlier, in 1878–79, against *bidan* razzias. *Etudes: Brakna,* 81. But this would give Baba an active role at the age of sixteen.

27. The best available description is Mariella Villasante de Beauvais, "Solidarité et hierarchie au sein des Ahl Sidi Mahmud: Essai d'anthropologie historique d'une confédération tribale mauritanienne, XVIII–XXeme siècles," 4 vols., doctorat d'Etat, Paris

1995. See also Taylor, "Blood Money," and the archives of the river posts of Salde, Kaedi, Matam, and Bakel (ANS 13G); for Bakar's reaction to the suppression of the "customs" payment, see ANS 13G 64–65.

28. Indeed, Bakar was an important locus for the resistance movement until his death at the hands of the French coalition in April 1905, just one month ahead of Coppolani's own assassination. See Désiré-Vuillemin, *Mauritanie,* 225 ff.

29. The conflicts between the two *zwaya* coalitions were not resolved until World War I. To protest the favorable position that the Sidiyya and Abyayri acquired, one prominent Ijaydba leader led his followers into exile in southern Morocco. See Marty, *Etudes: Brakna,* 83–92, 154–75; Ould Cheikh, "La tribu."

30. Marty, *L'Emirat des Trarzas,* 204–22, and "Cheikh Sidia," 31, 42, 58, 71. See also Désiré-Vuillemin, *Contribution,* and *Mauritanie,* passim.

31. For Baba's pleas to the French to help him against the "reign of terror" organized by the Awlad Bu Sbaᶜ, see Désiré-Vuillemin, *Contribution,* 124 and annex 11; Désiré-Vuillemin, *Mauritanie,* 146. For the French reliance upon the resources of the Awlad Bu Sbaᶜ, see Désiré-Vuillemin, *Mauritanie,* passim. Frèrejean operated in southern Mauritania primarily thanks to mounted units from this group.

32. See Boubacar Barry, *Le royaume du Waalo;* as-Sa'd, "Espace émiral."

33. See CAOM SEN 4 127, and Guy Thilmans, "Lat Dior, Cheikh Saad Bou et le chemin de fer."

34. The "classic" portrayal in the published French record can be found in *Annales Sénégalaises,* 22–100. This work, published by the French government in 1885, represents in fact the views of Governor Faidherbe.

35. For the Trarza confederation and its troubles in the late nineteenth century, the most complete source is still Marty, *L'Emirat des Trarzas.* See also as-Sa'd, "Espace émiral," and Dubié, *Vie matérielle,* esp. 159.

36. See Robinson, "Saad Buh and the Fadiliyya and French colonial authorities," *ISASS* 11 (1997).

37. As described in chapter 3, Governor Genouille of Senegal (1886–88) may have played a role in undermining Amar's patronage. Apparently because of Amar's intervention in Jolof and Cayor, just at the time of completion of the railroad, the governor confiscated and sold a large portion of the herd of the emir, depriving him of much of his influence in Trarza. Deputy Gasconi and the Devès coalition took Genouille to task and played a large role in his removal in 1888. The Devès were extremely active in the struggles for the emirship of Trarza, and most governors in the period from the 1880s to the early 1900s criticized their role very sharply, as running generally in a direction antithetical to that of the administration. See chap. 5.

38. CAOM SEN 4 128, esp. the letter of Governor-general Chaudié to the Ministry of Colonies of 15 June 1898; Marty, "Cheikh Sidia," 74; personal observations from Ibrahima Abou Sall, June 1997, and Abdel Wedoud Ould Cheikh, September 1997.

39. Much of this material is summarized in CAOM SEN 4 128. The Bu El Mogdad family played a critical role in French commercial, political, and military relations, especially with southwestern Mauritania, across the late nineteenth and early twentieth century. In this case, Dudu Seck's ability to reassure a fellow cleric about the good intentions of the French was crucial.

40. In the words of Seck, who was Wolof and dark but ostensibly quite "cultivated" in Baba's eyes, the marabout said: "In the black countries things are very different [from North Africa]. The whites had only found little insignificant kinglets that had never known civilization. It was consequently out of kindness and generosity that they had acted in relation to the blacks." "Mémoire de Bou El Mogdad," 15.

41. Marty, "Cheikh Sidia," 58.

42. Indeed, Saad Buh suggested, in his correspondence with the French, that his rival Baba had a better rationale, from the *bidan* and Muslim standpoint: he was working with the French out of desperation, whereas Saad Buh's support was more voluntary. Notes from Ibrahima Abou Sall, from Nouakchott archives, E2 133, dated AH 1333.

43. CAOM AFPO 1420, Saint-Louis, 29 April 1902, director of indigenous affairs, Décazes, to governor-general; CAOM Missions 115; Frébourg, "Le Corse en Mauritanie."

44. Baba planned strategy with Coppolani in 1904. Coppolani told him that Morocco was now "French," thanks to the European accords of that year, and that he expected that the pacification campaign would extend to Tagant and Adrar in 1904–5. Désiré-Vuillemin, *Contribution,* chap. 3.

45. Théveniaut was an important member of the Coppolani "team." He had served in French Soudan in the late 1890s, where he undoubtedly met Coppolani. He undertook the mission of drawing a frontier between the colonies of Algeria and Soudan in 1904. He then left the military and became a civilian colonial administrator who received very choice and critical appointments. He served at Boutilimit from 1905–7 and was assigned to Diourbel in 1908. See chaps. 3 and 11.

46. Montané Capdebosc was commissaire of Mauritania between the assassination and the Adrar campaign, 1905–8. Frèrejean was a captain who played a key role during the Coppolani campaigns; his journal, published and edited by Désiré-Vuillemin, constitutes an important source for Mauritanian history in the early twentieth century. Gaden, cited in chap. 7, was a military officer, associate of Gouraud, Pular speaker, and lieutenant governor of Mauritania. It was Gaden who was stationed at Boutilimit, the northern limit of telegraph communications with Saint-Louis and Dakar, during Gouraud's attack on the Adrar in 1908–9.

47. Désiré-Vuillemin, *Mauritanie,* 197. For similar images of Sidiyya, see Louis Delafosse, *Maurice Delafosse: Le Berrichon conqus par l'Afrique* (Paris, 1976), 322 and 364; Marty, "Cheikh Sidia," esp. 36 ff.

48. Just before the assassination, the French had defeated Bakar, head of the Idawaish confederation, and he died of his wounds. Nonetheless, the tide seemed to be turning against the French in 1905–6. For Baba's letter of condolence, see Désiré-Vuillemin, *Contribution,* 145, 312–13; she reports it as a letter of 27 June 1905 addressed to Administrator Adam, who ran the Saint-Louis office (145n). This should be contrasted with the response of the Devès and other members of the General Council just after the news the assassination reached Saint-Louis. See chap. 3, n. 48.

49. See Pierre Bonte, "L'émir et les colonels, pouvoir colonial et pouvoir émiral en Adrar mauritanien," in Pierre Boilley et al., eds., *Nomades et commandants: Administration et sociétés nomades dans l'ancien AOF* (Paris, 1993). Coppolani had once hoped to enlist Ma El Ainin in his campaign of "pacification." See Frébourg, "Coppolani." In 1906, Governor-general Roume sent Robert Arnaud on a mission to Morocco to

check out the impact of Ma El Ainin (CAOM AOF 3 Missions, 3: Arnaud, 1906–7), and François-Joseph Clozel to Algeria, to investigate educational systems (*Hommes et Destins* 1, article by Jacques Serres).

50. In 1903, Coppolani found Baba at Bou Tafia because of the Ijaydba pressure. Over the next few years, French support enabled the Sidiyya to gain well sites in eastern Trarza at the expense of the Ijaydba. Marty, "Cheikh Sidia," 49, 74–75. For the consolidation of Sidiyya holdings in the Chemama, see Kane, "A History of Fuuta Tooro," 190–98, 237; Lt. Paul Cheruy, "Rapports sur le droit de propriété des Kolades dans le Chemama: Les redevances anciennement payées et les droits acquis actuellement," in *Supplément au JO de l'AOF,* 18 March, 1 and 15 April 1911, 41–58.

51. The Awlad Bu Sba͑ were quite indispensable to the conquest, and their units fought alongside those of the Abyayri, despite the tensions. See Désiré-Vuillemin, *Mauritanie,* passim; d'Otton Loyeski, "Coppolani et la Mauritanie," 1–70, passim; Marty, "Cheikh Sidia," 72–73. For Baba's continuing hostility toward the Awlad Bu Sba͑, see ANS 1D 223, #122, letter of 12 March 1907, Cheikh Sidia to Capdebosc; in this correspondence, he seeks to make sure that the French remain loyal to him and to maximize the distance between them and his archenemies.

52. See CAOM Mauritanie 4 2; ANS 1D 223, #107–8.

53. Appendix 3, 109–10, in Marty, "Cheikh Sidia." The letter is dated 15 September 1905. Another text, this time from a member of the Awlad Abyayri group that left Boutilimit and joined the entourage of Ma El Ainin early in the twentieth century. Al Adjad Wuld Al-Alem wrote Baba in the same vein in April 1906. He concluded his letter by saying: "They tell us many things about you. They even say that you remain friends with the Infidels, despite the fact that you could save yourself from them, just as the Prophet left his country and people to avoid staying among the Infidels." Marty, "Les Fadelïa," 172–73.

54. CAOM Mauritainie 4 2bis. Saad Buh was jealous of the attention given to his clerical rival and requested his own reception.

55. For the doctor, see Henri Gouraud, *Mauritanie Adrar: Souvenirs d'un africain* (Paris, 1945), 204. For the scientific mission, see Gruvel and Chudeau, *Mauritanie Occidentale.*

56. See chap. 5, n. 90. The Devès and Baba did support the same candidate for the Trarza emirship, Sidi wuld Mohamed Fall, for a long time. For additional material on Devès efforts to block the conquest of Mauritania, see 1D 223, pièces 127–28 (Saint-Louis, Colonel Montané-Capdebosc, letter and report to the governor-general dated 3 April 1907), pièces 135–37 (Saint-Louis, Colonnel Montané-Capdebosc, letter and attachments dated 13 April 1907), and Désiré-Vuillemin, *Contribution,* passim.

57. Gouraud had visited Baba in Boutilimit in December 1907, when they had long discussions about the situation and the Adrar campaign. Gouraud, *Souvenirs,* 31–33.

58. Gouraud was not an Arabist or Islamicist. Note the letters that Gouraud wrote to Henri Gaden from Morocco (CAOM AP 15, letters of 11 March and 7 April 1917) in which he extends his greetings and indicates that he is sending seven volumes in Arabic requested by Sidiyya Baba.

59. The campaign was not without some failures, and French control of the area remained fragile for some time. In addition, the minister of colonies had second thoughts

about the authorization of the campaign and at one point told Governor-general Ponty to order Gouraud to withdraw. Gouraud notes, however, that Ponty was of the "Archinard school" and authorized him in a handwritten note to continue. Gouraud, *Souvenirs,* 209–11. For the declaration of French sovereignty and installation of a young member of the emiral family, Sid Ahmed wuld Mokhtar wuld Aida, see 133–35.

60. Baba had significant interests in some palm trees and oases in the Adrar, and some animals there. ANS 1D 223, #293, 29 October 1907, commissaire of Mauritania to the governor-general. For the campaign and Sidiyya Baba's role, see Gouraud, *Souvenirs,* chaps. 7–15. See also Gouraud, *La pacification de la Mauritanie* (Paris, 1910), 137–38, 233. In February 1909, Baba received a *cadeau politique* of 800 francs from the administration, one of the largest gifts on record. ANS 17G 24.

61. *Souvenirs,* 133.

62. *Souvenirs,* 191.

63. See the files of ANS 17G for many references to cadeaux politiques for the Sidiyya in the first two decades of the twentieth century.

64. Oumar Bâ, in *Ahmadou Bamba face aux autorités coloniales* (Dakar, 1982), 93–124, has constituted the most complete archival record for the events of 1902–3. See also Bashir Mbacke, *Les bienfaits de l'eternel ou la biographie de Cheikh Amadou Bamba Mbacke,* trans. Khadim Mbacke (Dakar, 1995).

65. The single most important voice was probably that of Mbakhane Diop, son of Lat Dior and a chief in Baol, in the heart of Murid country. See Robinson, "Beyond Resistance and Collaboration."

66. Personal communication of the shaikh of the Hafiziyya, Ahmedou ould Tolba, in Bareina, Mauritania, 15 June 1996, in the company of Abdel Wedoud Ould Cheikh. See also Bâ, *Ahmadou Bamba,* 126–27.

67. See Cheikh Anta Mbacke Babou, "Le Mouridisme jusqu'en 1912," mémoire de maîtrise, Université Cheikh Anta Diop, Dakar, 1992; Robinson, "Beyond Resistance and Collaboration."

68. Constant Hames, "Le premier exil de Shaikh Hamallah."

69. Robinson, "Beyond Resistance and Collaboration," and "Emergence."

70. There was undoubtedly an element of racism in this choice: put the "black" Sufi under the care of a *bidan* master, and he will learn to behave.

71. The French also exiled Shaikh Hamallah, the symbolic leader of the *onze grains* "opposition" to the Umarian establishment to Mederdra in 1925, the year after Baba's death, before the longer exile in Côte d'Ivoire. The proximity to the Sidiyya network was part of the colonial strategy, even though Mederdra was not as obviously in the Sidiyya orbit as Souet-el-Ma. See Hamès, "Shaikh Hamallah"; Commandant Rocaboy, "L'Hamalisme," mémoire du CHEAM 938 (1947). Shaikh Lakhdar, Hamallah's teacher in Nioro, was exiled to Saint-Louis in 1907, but I have not found any trace of a period of residence in Trarza. See chap. 7 for the exile of these two men.

72. Other daughters married Shaikuna's brothers, Mawlud wuld Dadda and Muhammadun wuld Dadda, who was the father of the first president of independent Mauritania (personal communication of Abdel Wedoud Ould Cheikh, 30 September 1997). On Sidiyya strategies, see Désiré-Vuillemin, *Mauritanie,* passim; Dubié, *Vie matérielle,* 123–28; Marchesin, *Tribus, ethnies et pouvoir,* 30; Marty, "Cheikh Sidia," 47; Ould

Cheikh, "La tribu" and "Harun"; Stewart, *Social Order,* 81–82. The Awlad Daiman connection, which was very important for the Sidiyya, reinforced their linkages with the family of Bu El Mogdad in Saint-Louis.

73. For the subjects and servants, often called *telamides,* "pupils," see Santoir, *Rkiz,* 103–5. For the general results of this process of accumulation, see Dubié, *Vie matérielle,* 138 ff.; the tabulations made by Dubié have been repeated, as an example of the success of the *zwaya* groups in the colonial period, in many accounts of contemporary Mauritania. See, for example, Francis de Chassey, *Mauritanie, 1900–1975* (Paris, 1984), esp. 85 ff.

74. His Mauritanian wealth may have made him less dependent on this source of income than Saad Buh, but contributions from the south were nonetheless very significant in sustaining his clientele in the north.

75. For Futa Toro, see Kane, "A History of Fuuta Tooro."

76. "Une bibliothèque saharienne: la bibliothèque du Cheikh Sidian au Sahara," *RMM* 8 (1909).

77. Charles Stewart, "A Mauritanian Reformer: Shaikh Sidiyya Baba," *Tarikh* 7, number 25 (1971).

78. For the colonial médersa effort, see Louis Brenner's articles, "Médersas au Mali: Transformation d'une institution islamique," in B. Sanankoua and L. Brenner, eds., *L'enseignement islamique au Mali* (Bamako, 1991), and "Becoming Muslim in Soudan français," in Robinson and Triaud, *Le Temps des Marabouts.*

79. See Ould Cheikh, "Harun"; Stewart, "Mauritanian Reformer."

80. See ANS 19G 10, pièce 15, Dakar, 7 August 1916, telegram of governor-general to minister of colonies; 19G, 9 and 10, deal with the issue of supporting the secession of the Arab lands from the Ottoman Empire and the resumption of the pilgrimage. For the consultative committee see ANS 19G 1, doss. entitled "Comité consultatif des affaires musulmanes," 1916. For French reliance on Baba in general, see Marc Michel, *L'Armée de l'Afrique* (Paris, 1982), 58–60. The other "acceptable" marabout was Malik Sy of Tivaouane, but he was almost blind at the time and could not be sent. The French did nominate Malik's agent in Kaolack, Abdu Kane, but it is not clear to what extent Kane participated in the deliberations of the commission. In 1917, Sidiyya Baba gave a good reception to the leading Catholic figure of French West Africa, Bishop H. Jalabert, who was touring southern Mauritania. Baba's son Ahmed accompanied him. Jalabert was a member of the CEHSAOF described in chap. 2. CAOM, archives privées, 4PA 15, Fonds Gaden, nos. 198–203 for 1917; Louise Delafosse, *Maurice Delafosse,* 344, 399.

81. Delafosse, *Maurice Delafosse,* 322, 364.

82. See Sall, "Mauritanie," 687 and passim.

83. For Marty's relationship with Baba, see Stewart, "Mauritanian Reformer." (I wish to thank Ellen Foley of Michigan State University for reminding me of this reference.)

84. Marty, "Cheikh Sidia," 105; Stewart, "Mauritanian Reformer."

85. Ould Cheikh suggests that effective administration passed to Abdallah before Baba's death. "Harun," 204. According to French sources, Baba felt he could no longer trust his brother, and the French shared that attitude. ANM 1E 223. (I owe this reference to Ibrahima Abou Sall.)

86. In 1925, Mohamed completed Baba's compilation; Norris published it as "A History of the Western Sanhaja." See n. 4 above.

87. For the close relations that Abdallah and the Sidiyya maintained with Lamine Gueye and the elite of Saint-Louis, see CAOM AFPO 2258, doss. 5, esp. the note of Beyries of 25 July 1948, which recapitulates the history of support for the Sidiyya family.

88. Ould Cheikh, "Harun."

89. See Stewart, "Mauritanian Reformer."

90. Under President Mukhtar ould Daddah, a cousin of the Sidiyya and member of the Ntishayt fraction of the Abyayri. See n. 72 above.

CHAPTER 10

1. Portions of this chapter have appeared in different forms over several years. Some of the ideas and formulation were given as a paper at the conference on "Religion et histoire en Afrique au Sud du Sahara" at the University of Paris 1 in 1991, under the title: "Malik Sy: Intellectual dans l'ordre colonial au Sénégal." A revised version of that appeared as "Malik Sy: Un intellectuel dans l'ordre colonial," *ISASS* 7 (1993). I then presented a paper at the 1997 annual meeting of the African Studies Association under the title "Malik Sy, Teacher in the New Colonial Order," and the revised form of this paper is now in Triaud and Robinson, *La Tijaniyya.*

2. In fact, the period of active cooperation began only in the last period of Malik's life — in about 1910. Charges of "collaboration" are sometimes leveled by Murids and other Senegalese. A Tijaniyya response is articulated in my interview in Dakar with Judge Taifou Diop, a Tivaouane disciple, 24 June 1985.

3. The most complete source of information is Mbaye's 4-vol. "Malick Sy." Mbaye's thesis is a mine of information, but some of it is contradictory; in general, Mbaye is not concerned to reconstruct a careful historical account, which would be the basis for an interpretation of his actions in relation to the colonial authorities. He is principally concerned with the writing and thinking of his subject. The other principal source is Marty, *Sénégal,* 1:175ff. Both of these sources draw from Maurice de Coppet, administrator at Thiès, in his "Renseignements sur le marabout El Hadj Malick Sy: Extrait de rapport mensuel," October 1910, in ANS 2D 14,5. See also Shaikh Musa Kamara, *Zuhur ul-Basatin,* 1:165–66, and Ibrahima Marone, "Le Tidjanisme au Sénégal," *BIFAN,* ser. B, 32, no. 2 (1970).

4. The main source on the Tijaniyya is still Abun-Nasr, *The Tijaniyya;* see chap. 4 for relations with the French. Jilali al-Adnani has shown that the zawiya of Tlemcen, in contrast to those of Ain Mahdi and Temassinin, had very tense relations with the French over most of the nineteenth century. Personal communication, January 1997, and his articles, "Reflexions sur la naissance de la Tijaniyya: Emprunts et surenchères," and "Les origines de la Tijaniyya: Quand les premiers disciples se mettent à parler," in Triaud and Robinson, *La Tijaniyya.*

5. Marty, *Sénégal,* vol. 1.

6. I developed this argument in treating the origins of Saidu, the father of Shaikh Umar. Umar's own importance has motivated traditionalists to read a certain "symbolic capital" back into Saidu's life, to better explain the distinction of his son. *Holy War,* 65–71.

7. Malik's maternal uncle, according to the family tradition, was initiated by Umar during the year in which he massively recruited in Futa Toro. The encounter may have occurred in Hore-Fonde, Umar's residence for several months in 1858–59. See Robinson, *Holy War,* 220–25.

8. According to one tradition of linkage with Umar, Alfa Mayoro received a benediction from Umar for Fatimata, his sister pregnant with Malik, after presenting ten pieces of cloth. Interview at the Ecole Militaire of Thiès with Colonel Abdoulaye Tal, 16 March 1985. A somewhat similar account came from my interview in Dakar with Judge Taifou Diop, 18 June 1985. This account obviously has the effect of linking Malik Sy with Umar, but it puts the birth of Malik Sy in 1859, too late to make sense for his career. For Mayoro's ties to the Idawali and Hafiziyya tradition of the Tijaniyya, see Bousbina, "Al-Hajj Malik Sy," 183–84. Alfa Mayoro's given name was Muhammad ibn Abi Bakr ibn 'Abd al-Rahman.

9. Mbaye, "Malick Sy," chap. 2. The Sy may have come from Suyuma, a village near Podor that is also the original home of the Malik Sy who emigrated and founded the kingdom of Bundu (see Gomez, *Pragmatism*). The "maraboutic" branch of the family lived in Fanaye, not far from Gaé, while the "chiefly" branch resided in Jolof. According to one tradition, Usman died during some civil wars in Jolof, before the birth of his son. Samb, *Essai,* 332. After his education in Dimar and Jolof, Malik completed the study of the Quran in central Futa in the early 1870s.

10. Including Lat Dior, the father of Amadu Bamba and the paternal uncle of Malik Sy. For Ma Ba, see Barry, *Senegambia,* 196ff., and Klein, *Islam and Imperialism,* 63ff. According to Sy traditions, Malik's paternal uncle Amadu fought with Ma Ba in the campaigns in Jolof. See Mbaye, "El Hadji Malick Sy," chap. 3.

11. As described in chap. 1. Albury Ndiaye obtained the Jolof throne with French support after the 1875 battle, and Lat Dior was temporarily strengthened in his position in Cayor. For the Madiyanke impact, see Robinson, *Chiefs and Clerics,* 82–98. It is possible that Mayoro Wele was briefly affiliated with the Madiyanke in 1869. See ANS 13G 264, pièce 146, cited in Julian Witherell, "The Response of the Peoples of Cayor to French Penetration, 1850–1900," Ph.D. diss., University of Wisconsin, 1964, 165–66.

12. From an early age, Malik sought to distance himself from the Umarian tradition, develop multiple sources of Tijaniyya affiliation, and reduce the number of links in the initiatory chain back to Ahmad al-Tijani. He puts his first initiation into the order at the age of eighteen (ca. 1872) at the hands of Alfa Mayoro Wele, and a number of others over the course of the 1870s. These references come primarily from his main work on the Tijaniyya, *Ifham al-munkir al-jani 'ala tariqat sayyidina wa wasilatina ila rabbina Ahmad ibn Muhammad al-Tijani,* completed near the end of his life. For these observations, I have drawn principally upon Bousbina, "Al-Hajj Malik Sy," 182–91, and also his thesis, "Un siècle de savoir islamique en Afrique de l'Ouest, 1820–1920: Analyse et commentaire de la litterature de la confrerie Tijaniyya à travers les oeuvres d'Al-Hajj 'Umar, 'Ubayda ben Anbuja, Yirkoy Talfi, et Al-Hajj Malik Sy," doctorat d'université, Paris 1, 1995–96, 74. See also Mbaye, "Malick Sy," passim, and Samb, *Essai,* esp. 334.

13. See chap. 6. I am drawing also on my interview with Mamadou Lamine Diagne in Saint-Louis, 11 April 1985.

14. Shaikh Musa Kamara, in one of his writings, claimed that Malik Sy invited

him to consider jihad. This reference is not dated and is not confirmed in other sources of Kamara or elsewhere. See Amar Samb, trans., "Condamnation de la guerre sainte par Cheikh Moussa Kamara," *BIFAN*, ser. B, 38 (1976): 165.

15. This draws particularly upon Mbaye, "Malick Sy," chaps. 3–5. Another patron often cited is Makhtar Lô.

16. See Dudu Seck, "Mémoire de Bou El Mogdad," and chap. 4, n. 42. The combination of study and commerce was part of the family tradition.

17. In 1877, Abdullay Seck accompanied Governor Brière to Futa Toro to negotiate the sensitive issue of building the telegraph line. See Robinson, *Chiefs and Clerics*, 99. Abdullay was probably the chief interpreter and translator for the administration from the time of his father's death, in 1880, until he was killed at the hands of the *tène*, or king, of Baol in 1887. Just before his death, Abdullay was appointed assessor in the court that sat at Dagana, presumably in addition to his duties in Saint-Louis. It was probably in or near Dagana that he came to know Malik Sy. See chap. 4 above—for example, n. 42; ANS M9 1887, "appointment of assessors"; and Samb, *Essai*, 75. I have also relied upon Ghislaine Lydon's interview with Abdullay's grandson Abou Latif ibn Muhammad ibn Abdullay Seck in Saint-Louis, at the home of Sidi Mokhtar Ndiaye at Sor, on 5 November 1997. According to Abou Latif, his grandfather became the first Tijaniyya affiliate in the family, thanks to a commercial visit to Fez and the influence of "Hajj Malik" (there is no indication about when this affiliation took place). Finally, I have used the interviews and information contained in Cheikh Diouf, "L'histoire des institutions musulmanes à Saint-Louis du Sénégal, l'ancienne capitale coloniale de l'AOF," a manuscript being prepared as a doctoral thesis and seen by me in Saint-Louis in 1996.

18. Amadu served in World War I and was killed in 1916. Babacar succeeded his father on his death in 1922. Mbaye gives 1881 for the birth of Fatimata, the first child, and 1887 for another daughter, probably Astu, who married Amadu Ndiaye Sarr, cadi and imam in Ndar. Rokhaya subsequently had two more daughters, Khadidiatu, who married Seydu Nuru Tal and resided with him in Saint-Louis and Boghé while Malik Sy was alive; and Seynabu, who died at Ndiarndé at a young age. Mbaye, "Malick Sy," chaps. 4 and 8. In other traditions, Amadu's birth date is given as 1879, Babacar's as 1884.

19. There is a tradition by which Malik was convoked by the governor in Saint-Louis and asked if he were contemplating waging jihad. Malik's response was that his only weapon was his rosary. Interview with Taifou Diop, Dakar, 18 June 1985; Samb, *Essai*, 75 ff. This may have occurred at a somewhat later date, in the midst of a certain administration paranoia around the time of the arrest and deportation of Amadu Bamba. Umar Sarr, in my interview of 4 June 1985 in Saint-Louis, said that his father, qadi Ndiaye Sarr, advised Malik Sy to leave Saint-Louis and go to Louga because people were saying bad things about him and the administration feared any marabouts with following.

20. For some anecdotes about opposition, see Mbaye, "Malick Sy," chaps. 4 and 5. For the elegance that Malik later displayed, see his chap. 8, 228.

21. In particular, he traveled to the Idawali of Trarza and had his Tijani affiliation confirmed by a certain Muhammad Ali. See n. 12 and Marty, *Sénégal*, 1:178.

22. For Safiatu, I have used interviews that Eunice Charles conducted in Jolof with

Aliou Sakho, imam of Dahra, 26 July 1970, and with El-Hadj Moussa Dia, imam of Mbeulakhe, 18 August 1970; Mbaye, "Malick Sy," chap. 8; and Samb, *Essai,* 332–33, 374–75. Safiatu had four sons, Mohammed al-Mansur (1900–57); Abdul Aziz (1904–97); Mohammed al-Habib (1906–91); and Aliun (who died at a young age in Diaksaw). She also had five daughters: Fatimatu, who married Abdu Faty Niang, a nephew and disciple of Malik; Assiyatu, who married a disciple Yussupha Diop; Umu Kalsum, who married Momar Anta Kebe; Rokhayatu, who married Momar Bassine Ndiaye, a disciple of Malik, and later Medoune Sarr; and Nafissatu, who married Malik's disciple and cousin Momar Binta Sy, and then another cousin Momar Khudia Sy. Nafissatu lived longer than any other daughter; she died in 1993.

23. His contacts with the Jolof milieu, and particularly the Fulbe of Belhal, concerned the French, who were preoccupied by a possible coalition of their Tijani "enemies" (Albury, Saër Maty, and Mamadu Lamine Drame, who was still active in the Gambia valley). This is reminiscent of the French concern about Amadu Bamba's presence and influence in Jolof in 1895. See ANS 1D 52, pièce 21 (Noirot to the governor, 1 September 1887); to the best of my knowledge, this is the earliest archival reference to Malik Si. See also CAOM Outre-Mer, Missions 18, Le Châtelier for 1887.

24. "Malick Sy," chap. 5.

25. On the poem, see Marty, *Sénégal,* 1:212–15.

26. The other companion was probably Momar Aminata Sy. See Mbaye, "Malick Sy," chap. 5. See also Marty, *Sénégal,* 1:177.

27. Mbaye has collected the extant traditions about the pilgrimage. One correlates the birth of Safiatu's first son with the hajj. Another notes that Faidherbe died while Malik Sy was on the journey. See Mbaye, "Malick Sy," chap. 5. This resembles the traditions that linked Al-Hajj Umar and Faidherbe and may be designed to show that Malik Sy had "outlasted" the "founder" of the French colony of Senegal. Robinson, *Holy War,* 210–11.

28. The French were highly suspicious of the Moroccan Tijaniyya at this time and worried about its influence over Tijaniyya adepts in West Africa. At the turn of the century, the Tijaniyya seemed to place more emphasis on the pilgrimage than the Qadiriyya, precisely because it offered the chance to visit the zawiya in Fez. This makes the apparent absence of such a visit, in Malik's case, more puzzling. As chap. 4 revealed, the French were competing with the British, Spanish, and Germans for supremacy in the Moroccan zone. See Edmund Burke, *Prelude,* chap. 2.

29. Mbaye, "Malick Sy," chap. 5.

30. Probably in 1891. She had two surviving sons by Malik Sy, Usman and Cheikh Tidiane, and two surviving daughters, Aida, who married El Hadj Hady Ture, and Umul Khairy, who married Malik's disciple Abdullay Sow and later El-Hadj Amadu Ndoye, a Lebu notable of Dakar. See Mbaye, "Malick Sy," chap. 8.

31. And may have raised some issues for the French. The anecdote of the "convocation" of the governor, cited in n. 19, may well have occurred late in this period and encouraged Malik's next move. For this extended period in Saint-Louis, see Mbaye, "Malick Sy," chap. 5. This is also presumably the time that Lamine Gueye has in mind when he reflects on his visits to the "venerable" Al-Hajj Malik at the residence on rue André Lebon and to studying in Malik's school with his son Babacar. *Itineraire,* 16–17.

But Lamine was born in Medine in 1891 and came to Saint-Louis only in 1897 for his Islamic and French studies. He was at least six years younger than Babacar.

32. Mbaye, "Malick Sy," chap. 6.

33. On the Tijaniyya tradition, see Abun-Nasr, *The Tijaniyya,* chap. 3; Jean-Louis Triaud, *"Khalwa* and the Career of Sainthood: An Interpretative Essay," in Cruise O'Brien and Coulon, *Charisma.*

34. See Searing, "Accommodation and Resistance," chap. 2.

35. See the anecdotes cited in n. 19.

36. For commentary and some excerpts from these works, see Mbaye, "Malick Sy," and Samb, *Essai.* Samb suggests that most of his work was completed at this time; see 337-74, esp. 349.

37. What is not clear is when, how, and with what modifications the "Bu Kunta model" of insertion into the colonial economy was adopted by the Tijaniyya and Murid communities. Tivaouane is very close to the Bu Kunta capital of Ndiassane. In 1913, Bu Kunta gave one of his daughters in marriage to Mustapha, the eldest son of Bamba, and many of the Bu Kunta community moved into the Murid community on the death of their leader in 1913. See Haidara/Diagne, "La confrerie Kuntiyu de Njaasaan," and Marty, *Sénégal,* 1:333-64.

38. The French did use the Tijaniyya label in 1895 in their arrest and condemnation of Amadu Bamba. See chap. 11 and Robinson, "French 'Islamic' Policy," 415.

39. Mbaye, "Malick Sy," chap. 6, based to a substantial extent on Ibrahima Diop, *Tuhfa al-Ikhwan,* 167-84.

40. All of this can be founded in Mbaye, "Malick Sy," chap. 6, and in Marty, *Sénégal,* 1:188-210. See also the list of disciples in ANS 13G 67. One example concerns Abdu or Abdullay al-Hamid Kan, a Saint-Louisian established in Kaolack, who gave his daughter, Sokhna Astu Kane, to Malik's son Babacar. Abdu would later be recommended for the Habus Commission by Malik Sy at the end of World War I. ANS 19G 10, passim, and n. 60, below.

41. Where the old Islamic center of Pir, dear to the hearts of the reformers of Sharr Bubba and Futa Toro, was located, as well as Ndiassane, the headquarters of Bu Kunta. See Searing, "Accommodation and Resistance," chap. 1, esp. at 19.

42. There was a brief interim on Gorée, while some of the buildings and infrastructure were being readied in Dakar. See Searing, "Accommodation and Resistance"; Conklin, *A Mission to Civilize.*

43. In 1903 Allys organized the second arrest and deportation of Bamba. See chap. 11. The acting governor-general at the time was Martial Merlin, the same man who, as director of political affairs and interim governor of Senegal in 1895, engineered the first exile of Bamba. These events, and indeed a whole sequence of experiences through the 1890s and 1900s, described in chap. 4, brought the French to revise their monolithic stereotype of the West African Tijaniyya and provided more openings for cooperation with Malik Sy. Allys's long administrative career in Senegal is outlined in chap. 3.

44. Several of them were sons or relatives of Demba War. See Searing, "Accommodation and Resistance," 155-58, 212, 259-64, 309-12, 480, 511-12, 547.

45. According to Malikiyya tradition, Malik later would counsel Abdullay Niasse to move into the town of Kaolack to reassure the French that he had no negative dis-

positions toward them. Interview in Dakar with Taifou Diop 20 June 1985. Mbaye, "Malick Sy," chaps. 7 and 8, notes that Malik Sy spent some time in Dakar during the period 1900 to 1904, the year that he puts for the "definitive" installation in Tivaouane. His visits increased the influence of the Tijaniyya in Dakar quite considerably. See n. 49 below.

46. Marty, *Sénégal*, 1:179. Babacar clearly surpassed his older brother Amadu in aptitude for leadership, well before Amadu was killed in Salonica in 1916. Babacar actually worked for the PTT service for a while. It is possible that Babacar spent some of the Ndiarndé years in Saint-Louis as well. Here I use Taifou Diop, interview of 28 June 1985, and Penda Mbow, "Querelles de succession au sein de la confrérie Tidjane et Tivaouane," paper presented to the conference on Tijaniyya Traditions and Societies in West and North Africa in the Nineteenth and Twentieth Centuries, held at the University of Illinois-Champaign, 1–5 April 1996.

47. Mbaye, "Malick Sy," chaps. 4 and 8; Mbow, "Querelles de succession"; Leonardo Villalon, "The Moustarchidine of Senegal. The family politics of a contemporary Tijani movement," in Triaud and Robinson, *La Tijaniyya*.

48. The widow was Anta Sall, and the milieu was Lebu. Malik was particularly concerned about the islamization of the Lebu, in the presence of the French and some Catholilc missionaries. See Mbaye, "Malick Sy," chaps. 7 and 8. Marty gives the name of the disciple as Mbur Ndoye and the name of the wife as Sokhna Gueye. *Sénégal*, 1:178, 201–2.

49. Tivaouane traditions suggest that Malik asked Abdu Kane to exercise some guidance over Abdullay Niasse in Kaolack. See Taifou Diop interview, Dakar, 28 June 1985 and n. 54 below.

50. David Skinner, "Islam and Education in the Colony and Hinterland of Sierra Leone, 1750–1914," *Canadian Journal of African Studies* 10, no. 3 (1976): 510–18.

51. He was in Saint-Louis in 1909, according to ANS 2D 14, pièce 5, letter of 17 April 1909, and again 1911 and in 1913, to have his cataracts examined. See below, n. 55.

52. These Umarians settled particularly in Halaybe, the area around Boghé. The Sakho family carried great prestige among them. I suspect that Amadu Moktar traveled to Tivaouane, for there is no record or recollection of Malik traveling to Boghe. Sakho and Sy both played a leading role in the shaping of the career of Seydu Nuru Tal, the grandson of Umar and leading figure in the colonial Tijaniyya from about 1920. See chap. 7 and Sall, "Mukhtar Sakho."

53. See ANS 2D 14, pièce 5, and Marty, *Sénégal*, 1:208–11. On the circumstances of Saad Buh's composition and the distribution of the letter, see chap. 8, and Dedoud, "Guerre sainte." In 1910, the administrator of Tivaouane, on orders from the lieutenant governor to supply information about Malik Sy, supplied the report of October 1910 that is contained in ANS 2D 14/5. According to Marty, the French had already identified Malik as the most learned marabout of Senegal in 1908; the observation was made by Destaing, the director of the medersa of Saint-Louis, after a tour of the colony. Marty, *Sénégal*, 1:180.

54. Niasse stopped in Tivaouane on his way back from the pilgrimage and a visit to Fez, wrote the French from there, and settled on the edges of Kaolack later that year. See Klein, *Islam and Imperialism*, 224–25.

55. Marty suggests that the only tense relations of the Tivaouane branch at the time were with the Murids, whose numbers were growing rapidly in southern Cayor and western Baol, at the expense of Malikiyya loyalties. *Sénégal,* 1:206.

56. Malik Sy received medical treatment for his eyes from the French on several occasions. In 1913, the Tivaouane administrator wrote to the lieutenant governor and hospital authorities to make sure that he was treated in the French or "citizen" part and not in the *indigène* section of the local hospital. He reminded the governor that "El Hadj Malik Sy is one of the marabouts who is most devoted to our cause and has considerable influence." Letter of 12 May 1913, in ANS H11. (My thanks to Kalala Ngalamu-lume for pointing out this reference to me.)

57. For stories of succession, and discussions that the father held among Babacar, Mansur, and Seydu Nuru Tal just before his death, I use Mbow, "Querelles de succession," and Villalon, "The Moustarchidine of Senegal."

58. From the French translation of the Arabic in ANS 19G 2.10, 14 Ramadan 1330, or 29 August 1912. I have not been able to locate the Arabic original.

59. Indeed, the governor-general asked Resident-general Lyautey to publish Malik's declaration in his journal in Morocco. ANS 19G 4, pièce 148, letter of 26 June 1913.

60. The British took the lead in this initiative, but the French were deeply involved also in the support of the Meccan leader. For the French involvement, see chap. 7 and ANS 19G 10, pièces 14–25, esp. pièce 15, Dakar, 7 August 1916, governor-general to the minister of the colonies. One Tivaouane tradition claims that the outline of the mosque of Paris was traced by Abdu Kane during his trip under the influence of a dream of Malik Sy. Interview with Taifou Diop in Dakar 20 June 1985.

61. In the words of Quesnot, who studied the Tijaniyya in Senegal, Malik Sy understood the Tijaniyya as essentially a teaching order. F. Quesnot, "Influence du Mouridisme sur le Tijanisme," in *Notes sur l'Islam au Sénégal* (Paris, 1962), 124.

62. The administration claimed that Malik Sy was delighted at this gesture, and there is no reason to doubt the claim. Marty, *Sénégal,* 1:180, 183–87. See also the comments of Louise Delafosse, based on her father's journals: *Maurice Delafosse,* 322–23. Marty also noted that Malik Sy would, in case of doubt, decide on the sighting of the moon for the end of Ramadan. *Sénégal,* 1:188. But this function emanated from the general prestige that he exercised among Senegalese Muslims, not from any administrative appointment.

63. Here I draw on Mbow, "Querelles de succession," and Villalon, "The Moustarchidine of Senegal." It seems likely that Malik Sy expressed some preference for the inheritance of the oldest son, but the Malikiyya traditions are not very clear on this point. Some traditions suggest that he even considered passing leadership on to Seydu Nuru Tal, the grandson of Umar, but the Sy tradition places Seydu Nuru in a custodial role. Mbaye, "Malick Sy," chap. 8.

64. In 1910, the administrator of Tivaouane, on orders from the lieutenant governor to supply information about Malik Sy, wrote that the marabout had considerable peanut fields around the town that brought in about 4,000 francs a year, but this certainly did not exhaust their income. ANS 2D 14/5, report of October 1910. Abdoulaye Bara Diop (in *La Société wolof: Tradition et changement,* 275–85) suggests that Malik had an ideology that called for less exploitation and domination than did that of Amadu Bamba. He does

not seem to have solicited the conspicuous gifts from traditional and colonial chiefs nor to have received contributions from the colonial *fonds secrets* in the manner that one might attribute to Saad Buh and Sidiyya Baba. After Malik Sy's death, the Sy apparently followed the Murid pattern of patronage and redistribution. On the brotherhoods and their wealth, see F. Quesnot, "Influence du Mouridisme sur le Tijanisme," in *Notes,* 124 and passim.

65. For example, the Hafiziyya of Mauritania and the Niassiyya of Kaolack. See Dedoud Ould Abdellah, "La 'passage au sud': Muhammad al-Hafiz et son heritage"; Abdel Wedoud Ould Cheikh, "Les perles et le soufre: Une polémique mauritanienne autour de la Tijaniyya, 1830–1935"; and Ousmane Kane, "Muhammad Niasse, 1881–1956, et sa réplique contre le pamphlet anti-tijani d'Ibn Mayaba," in Triaud and Robinson, *La Tijaniyya.*

66. As I suggested in my paper "Malik Sy: Intellectual dans l'ordre colonial au Sénégal." See n. 1 of this chapter.

CHAPTER II

1. An earlier version of this chapter appeared as "The Murids: Surveillance *and* Accommodation," in the *JAH* 40 (1999). Some elements appeared earlier in "Beyond Resistance and Collaboration."

2. The social scientists have tended to repeat the capsule history of Marty, but no historian has yet explored or interpreted the path to accommodation in the early decades of the movement. Cheikh Anta Mbacké Babou, a doctoral student in history at Michigan State University, is doing this exploration now as the subject of his dissertation. The most important single source in English is still Cruise O'Brien, *The Mourides of Senegal.* For other treatments of the Muridiyya, see Coulon, *Marabout;* Jean Copans, *Les Marabouts de l'Arachide* (Paris, 1980); Lucy Creevey, "Ahmad Bamba, 1850–1927," in J. R. Willis, ed., *Studies on the History of Islam in West Africa,* vol. 1 (London, 1979); Cruise O'Brien, *Saints and Politicians;* Momar Coumba Diop, "La littérature mouride: Essai d'analyse thématique," *BIFAN,* ser. B, 41 (1979); Cheikh Tidiane Sy, *La Confrérie sénégalaise des Mourides* (Paris, 1969). All of these scholars go back to the work of Paul Marty, esp. "Les Mourides d'Amadou Bamba," in *Etudes sur l'Islam au Sénégal,* 2 vols. (Paris, 1917), 1:217–332. Marty came to the government-general in 1912 and stayed until 1921. For a number of documents dealing with Bamba's relations with the French, see Oumar Bâ, *Ahmadou Bamba face aux autorités coloniales* (Dakar, 1982). These documents come from a collection created by Bâ, the dossier Amadou Bamba, at ANS. They are referred to in many of the works cited above.

3. They obviously had to work with Muslim authorities of some kind over the years, and Faidherbe had put in place the learned and respected Muslims in Saint-Louis described in chapter 4. But the administration remained deeply suspicious of many Muslim leaders of the interior, sometimes with good reason, since these leaders expressed hostility to the extension of French and hence "infidel" authority over land and people who belonged to the Dar al-Islam. See Robinson, "French 'Islamic' Policy."

4. Like the generation of Muslim reformers of an earlier generation. See Klein, "Social and Economic Factors."

5. I tended to use the conventional periodization in "Beyond Resistance and Collaboration."

6. Barry, *Senegambia*, 196ff.; he relies heavily on Klein, *Islam and Imperialism*, 66ff.

7. Even less than Al Hajj Umar. See Robinson, *Holy War*, chap. 9. For Bamba's implicit criticisms of Ma Ba and his movement, see Babou, "Autour de la genèse du Mouridisme," *ISASS* 11 (1997).

8. Comparable, certainly, to the fitna among the sons and nephew of Umar, as outlined in chaps. 1 and 7. See Mbacke, *Les bienfaits de l'éternel*, esp. 28-30. Abdullay Niasse, the founder of the Niasse order based in Kaolack, apparently came to the same critique after some time spent in the entourage of Saër Maty, Ma Ba's son. See Christopher Gray, "The Rise of the Niassene Tijaniyya, 1875 to the Present," *ISASS* 2 (1988): 35-36.

9. See Diouf, *Kajoor*, chaps. 16-19. Bamba and his followers certainly played up the traditional Islamic leader's aversion to official power and his distance from the courts, but there is no reason to doubt that he developed a negative experience of the exercise of power.

10. In 1869, about the time of his move from Baol to Cayor, Momar had come to the attention of the French. In a telegram containing information from an informant named Demba, an administrator wrote the governor that "Momar Antassaly, chief of Mbake Baol, follows Lat Dior and arouses him against the ceddo. He is a dangerous marabout." See ANS 13G 264, pièce 43.

11. See chap. 1.

12. During this same period, Lat Dior handed over a dissident chief, Sidia of Walo, to the governor, signaling his willingness to work closely with the administration in Saint-Louis. Diouf, *Kajoor*, 253-54.

13. It seems Bamba did not break off relations with Ma Diakhate; the archives report his amicable contacts with the old qadi in Ndiambur in 1889. See ANS 1G 136.

14. Translated from the Arabic of an oral account in a work by Mamadou Lamine Diop Dagana and published in Samb, *Essai*, 430. Bamba was widely reputed to have said in a letter to Lat Dior, and in reference to Ma Diakhate Kala and the king, that "a learned man at the court of a king is like a fly on a pile of excrement." Samb, *Essai*, 429. He took a position in many ways similar to that of al-Kanemi in the much-better-known debate between the Sokoto leaders and Bornu about the legitimacy of jihad east of Hausaland. He esteemed that the Madiyanke had sinned but not lost their identity as Muslims. See Louis Brenner, "The *Jihad* Debate between Sokoto and Borno: An Historical Analysis of Islamic Political Discourse in Nigeria," in J. F. Ade Ajayi and J. D. Y. Peel, eds., *Peoples and Empires in African History: Essays in Memory of Michael Crowder* (London, 1992).

15. This version comes from Mbakhane's son, Amadu Bamba Diop, in his article "Lat Dior," 526.

16. A. B. Diop, "Lat Dior," 525-26; Samb, *Essai*, 429.

17. Cheikh Tidiane Sy's interview with Falilou Mbacke in June 1965, recorded in Sy, *Confrérie*, 106. See also the testimony that Bamba's maternal brother, Shaikh Thioro, gave to Robert Arnaud in 1906 ("L'Islam et la politique musulmane française," 141-43).

18. It seems likely that Bamba left Cayor in about 1884. See Babou, "Genèse," 8.

19. According to these sources, Lat Dior may have come for an endorsement that would help him rally a credible following in what would undoubtedly be his last stand;

or he may have simply sought a blessing, in thinking of the possibility of an afterlife following his "checkered" career. See, for example, A. Marokhaya Samb, *Cadior Demb* (Dakar, 1964), 54. Cruise O'Brien (*Mourides,* 11–13, 37 ff.) relies on Marokhaya Samb in his account. Marty considered Bamba to be a part of the entourage of Lat Dior. "Mourides d'Amadou Bamba," 223–24.

20. This dimension is especially stressed by Babou in "Genèse." Said Bousbina shows the same pattern in his study of Malik Sy. See his "Al-Hajj Malik Sy," and chap. 10.

21. The Sidiyya did not keep the same distance from *bidan* authorities, as chap. 9 suggests. In the 1880s, the most likely time for Bamba's travel(s) to Trarza, he undoubtedly met Sidiyya Baba, who was at the beginning of his career. Bamba would not have been able to meet Sidiyya al-Kabir (d. 1868) or his son Sidi Muhammad (d. 1869). His father, Momar, did study with Sidiyya al-Kabir and earned the nickname Sidi Dar because of his help with the construction of the Boutilimit residence. Stewart, *Social Order,* 125 and 166, n. 8.

22. Another brother, Shaikh Anta, was about three years younger than Ibra Fati; he may have begun at this time to establish the network of relationships across western Senegal that would allow him to be an effective ambassador for the new order. For Ibra Fati, Ibra Fall, and Shaikh Anta, see Cruise O'Brien, *Mourides,* 43, 52–55, 141–48, and Robinson, "Beyond Resistance," 158–59.

23. In 1890, the French invaded Jolof, drove Albury Ndiaye into exile, and ended the last viable and independent ancien régime of the Wolof region. Many of the Jolof who did not emigrate to the east with Albury moved into Bamba's circle.

24. This is suggested in Klein, *Slavery,* chap. 12, esp. 200–202.

25. As with Malik Sy's community, it is not clear when the "Bu Kunta model" of insertion into the colonial economy was adopted by the Murids. In 1913, Bu Kunta gave one of his daughters in marriage to Mamadu Mustapha, the oldest son of Bamba, and many of the Bu Kunta community moved into the Murid community on the death of their leader in 1913. See Toba Haidara/Diagne, "La confrérie Kuntiyu de Njaasaan." See also Marty, *Sénégal,* 1:333–64. (I would like to thank Mohamed Mbodj of Columbia University for drawing my attention to the Bu Kunta example.)

26. Muhammad began receiving his revelations from God in 610 CE, when he was forty years old. If Bamba was born in 1853, in the early 1890s he would have had the same age. Touba is usually correlated with the Arabic *tauba,* "repentance." Touba became the location of Bamba's tomb and the towering Murid mosque in the twentieth century. For the works created during this period, see Dumont, *Pensée,* 1–50, and Samb, *Essai,* 421–82. See also Cruise O'Brien, *Mourides,* 41.

27. I follow Cheikh Babou's description in "Genèse," 10 ff. Babou puts this in the 1880s, after Bamba's departure from Cayor for Baol.

28. The best example of this occurred in 1890–91, when Paris gave unstinting support to both governors in the Jeandet Affair, described in chap. 3.

29. In 1893, Merlin personally escorted the group of young men to Tunis for training in a Franco-Arabic school there—including the sons of Lat Dior and Albury Ndiaye. See chap. 3.

30. A political affairs officer traveled through Ndiambur in March and April and presumably expelled the "troublesome" elements at that time; included in their number

was the merchant Matar Gaye of Louga. Bamba wrote a letter (mentioned but not found) to the governor, who responded with a gentle warning to watch out for disruptive elements who might claim him as their master. ANS 3B 55, fol. 82–83, letter of 27 June 1889, governor to "Mouhamadou Bamba," reproduced in Bâ, *Ahmadou Bamba,* 28.

31. Perhaps his brother Ibra Fati. See CAOM SEN 4 127, reports of 10 July, 15 and 29 August 1895. But Marty says that Bamba did go to Saint-Louis and gave the governor a list of his most "compromised" disciples (*Sénégal,* 1:224–25), and he may have based this on the report of Leclerc, administrator of the Cercle of Saint-Louis, 15 August 1895, contained in CAOM SEN 4 127.

32. They also arrested Samba Laobe Penda, the Burba, who had been put in place of Albury in 1890. They had been preparing Albury's young son, Buna, to take over as chief of Jolof; they put him in place in 1895.

33. It is impossible to know whether Bamba thought of the exercise of French colonial power, as exemplified in the column that arrested him, in the same way that he conceived of the coercion of Ma Ba, the Madiyanke, or the court of Cayor. Bamba was certainly well known to Muslims in Saint-Louis, and they apparently felt quite uncomfortable with the arrest, "trial," and deportation. Umar Sarr, son of qadi Ndiaye Sarr, gave some interesting observations in my interview with him at his home in the Sud of Saint-Louis on 4 June 1985. According to Sarr Umar, the French consulted his father about Bamba: Ndiaye told them that he was no fanatic. The French said they were determined to deport Bamba from Senegal, whereupon Ndiaye warned Bamba of his fate. Bamba remembered the old qadi's intervention, and when he heard during his second exile that Sarr had died, he sent his brother Shaikh Anta to marry the widow, Umar's mother. According to Seck family tradition, Dudu Seck injured himself so that he would not have to be present as an interpreter at the court proceedings. I draw this from my interviews with Judge Aissata Rabi Wane in Dakar on 28 June 1997 and with Sowadou Seck and her daughter Aby Diop in Saint-Louis on 29 and 30 June 1997; all are descendants of the Seck family. See also my discussions of the Lô family and their relations with Bamba in chap. 6. Some of the reluctance to express opposition to Bamba and his vocation undoubtedly has been read back into turn-of-the-century accounts, on the basis of the great prestige of the Murids in contemporary West Africa.

34. Merlin was also interim governor for part of the interval between de Lamothe and Chaudié, who came in as the first governor-general. At this time, Mouttet was the interim governor.

35. CAOM SEN 4 127, minutes of the *conseil privé* of 16 September 1895. All of the documents in the SEN 4 127 file that are relative to Amadu Bamba and that were sent by the governor to the ministry to justify his actions can be found in Bâ, *Ahmadou Bamba,* 29–71. See also Robinson, "French 'Islamic' Policy." For Bamba's version of his arrest, see Vincent Monteil, *Esquisses sénégalaises,* 164. It is not surprising that Merlin invoked Ma Ba and the Madiyanke, as leaders of "similar" movements, to make his case against Bamba.

36. The Qadiriyya was still the "acceptable" Sufi affiliation for the French at the time, since the French had not yet dealt with the opposition of Ma El Ainin. It is not clear whether Shaikh Sidiyya at this juncture would refer to Baba; it may have been the French way of referring to the leader of the Ahl Shaikh Sidiyya.

37. 29 August 1895, letter of Merlin to the interim governor, found in CAOM SEN 4 127 (reproduced in Bâ, *Ahmadou Bamba*, 43–55).

38. For accounts of the period of exile, see Cruise O'Brien, *Mourides*, passim; and Cheikh Abdoulaye Dieye, *L'exile au Gabon, période coloniale, 1895–1902: Sur les traces de Cheikh Ahmadou Bamba* (Dakar, 1985). Bamba had a few visits during the exile in Gabon. His brother Balla visited in 1899, while Blaise Diagne, the future deputy of Senegal, attended to his needs during a stint in Gabon as customs officer in 1897–98. Bamba corresponded with Ibra Fati and other members of his family. Bâ, *Ahmadou Bamba*, 90–91; Coulon, *Marabout*, 86; Dumont, *Pensée*, 50–57; Marty, *Sénégal*, 1:227; Samb, *Essai*, 457–60. He was scheduled to depart from Dakar on 21 September 1895 and received a stipend of 50 francs per month during his internment, according to interim governor L. Mouttet. CAOM SEN 4 127, 16 September 1895, governor to MC.

39. Letter of 28 May 1903, Administrator Allys of Tivaouane to the governor-general, contained in Bâ, *Ahmadou Bamba*, 101–2.

40. For a study of the aura surrounding Bamba and his exile, see Allen Roberts and Mary Nooter Roberts, "L'aura d'Amadou Bamba: Photographie et fabulation dans le Sénégal urbain," *Anthropologie et Sociétés* 22 (1998).

41. Ibra Fati came into conflict with Shaikh Anta in 1903, when he blamed Shaikh Anta's machinations for the second arrest and deportation of Bamba. Searing, "Accommodation and Resistance," 193–97. See n. 50, below.

42. On Shaikh Anta and Shaikh Ibra Fall, see Cruise O'Brien, *Mourides*, 61, 72–73, 141–48; Marty, *Sénégal*, 1:237–39, 246–48, 258. The first archival citations that I have found for both men come from the Merlin brief of 29 August 1895 (CAOM SEN 4 127) cited above. Shaikh Anta received money from the secret funds of the French in 1910 and 1912. ANS 17G 24.

43. Coulon, *Marabout*, 194–96; Cruise O'Brien, *Mourides*, 43–44.

44. See, for example, Cruise O'Brien, *Mourides*, 43–44.

45. Baba's intervention is cited as the main cause by Marty ("Mourides d'Amadou Bamba," 227).

46. There was, however, a considerable shift away from exclusive reliance on the chiefs during this period. Demba War Sall, president of the Confederation of Cayor, died in 1902 and was not replaced; his subordinates, at the canton level, continued to function. The same was true for the Bur Sin and other "super" chiefs of considerable sway during the 1890s. This was because the French had greater knowledge and control of the situation and the chiefs, having exercised considerable authority during a time of "transition," had become less popular. But it was also because the chiefs were less able to incorporate the lower strata of pre-colonial Senegalese society than were the marabouts, who were not in the direct chain of command and who were thereby less subject to blame for the demands of the new colonial order. For reflections on this process, see Searing, "Accommodation and Resistance," esp. 549–57.

47. Bâ, *Ahmadou Bamba*, 119–22; Dumont, *Pensée*, 57–58; Mbacké, *Bienfaits*, 87–88. Marty puts great emphasis on the intercession of Baba in the return of Bamba, and of the role of Baba's son-in-law in the second arrest ("Mourides d'Amadou Bamba," 227).

48. Allys's career is briefly outlined in chap. 3.

49. In this case, Shaikh Anta was directly involved in the turmoil. He cultivated a

wide array of Senegalese chiefs, urban citizens, and French administrators. In April he had a falling out with Mbakhane Diop, the son of Lat Dior, and it was Mbakhane who pressed the administration for the removal of Bamba. Ibra Fati blamed Shaikh Anta for disturbing the fragile relationship of Bamba with the colonial authorities and moved his following to Darou-Mousty in southern Cayor after the arrest, with the permission and cover of Allys and Meissa Mbaye Sall, chef de canton and son of Demba War Sall. See ANS 2D 14 5, letters of 28 June and 6 July 1903, and Searing, "Accommodation and Resistance," 193-97. Cruise O'Brien (Mourides, 194) gives the date of founding Darou-Mousty as 1912. For Mbakhane's career, see ANS 2G 1 122 (January 1901); Bâ, Ahmadou Bamba, 188-90; Cruise O'Brien, Mourides, 67-68; Sy, Confrérie, 118-19. For the 1903 situation in general, see ANS 2D 14 5 and 2G4 49, and Bâ, Ahmadou Bamba, 97-122.

50. ANS Mauritanie 4 2bis, governor-general to Ministry of Colonies, report for first trimester 1907.

51. Allys's next sentence ("It's an indication that their marabouts demand a lot of money") reflected a widespread French assumption about marabouts and brotherhoods in general. This comes from ANS 2G 4 49, report of 4 July 1904. On attitudes toward Murid farmers in general, see Sy, Confrérie, 122-23.

52. Klein, Slavery, chap. 12.

53. I am citing the French translation of 23 June 1903, from doss. Amadou Bamba, contained in Bâ, Ahmadou Bamba, 123-24. Bâ claims that the letter never reached Bamba's brother. This may be the case, but Murid traditions suggest that Bamba communicated this counsel many times during his months in the peanut basin in 1902-3. Cruise O'Brien gives the same information but ascribes it to 23 January 1903 (Mourides, 52); this is probably a mistake. The six months that Bamba spent in Senegal demonstrated to him that his movement could survive and indeed thrive under French control, and thereby prepared him for the close surveillance that would characterize the rest of his life. Personal observation from Cheikh Babou, 28 December 1998.

54. From doss. Amadou Bamba and found in Bâ, Ahmadou Bamba, 119-22. Merlin may have incurred some criticism from Camille Guy, the new lieutenant governor of Senegal, for his defense of the colonial chiefs and arrest of Bamba. Searing, "Accommodation and Resistance," 185-98.

55. After the assassination of Coppolani in 1905, the French did not resume their advance into Mauritania until 1908-9, as described in chaps. 4 and 9.

56. For example, Mbacke, Les bienfaits, 82-89.

57. In 1906, the French actually considered relocating Bamba to distant Fort Coppolani in Tijigja, to prevent his disciples from contacting him so frequently. For this and the communications of Théveniaut and Colonel Montané-Capdebosc about Bamba's transfer, see doss. Amadou Bamba, found in Bâ, Ahmadou Bamba, 126-27.

58. For an example of the surveillance, see the selection of May 1908 from the log kept by "our secret agent of Chéyène" and communicated to the administrator in Louga. Bâ, Ahmadou Bamba, 134-38. Buna Ndiaye was a continuous and reliable source of information for the French. In June 1903, he reported on a Murid interpretation of the first exile: that Bamba had sought it in order to have solitude and that he made his own decision about when to come back; 3 June 1903, Buna to the governor,

doss. Amadou Bamba; in Coulon, *Marabout,* 86. In 1907, he sounded warnings about how the *bidan* and Futanke were interpreting the assassination of Coppolani and other signs of French weakness in Mauritania. ANS 13G 65, pièce 4, 4 January 1907, letter of Buna to the administrator in Louga. Beginning in the same year, Buna kept a close watch on Bamba's settlement. See the comments of Administrator Roux, "Notes sur le Diambour et le Djoloff," *Bulletin de la Société de Geographie de l'AOF,* 31 December 1907.

59. Ndande, 23 January 1909, "Seikhe Ibra Fall" to the (lieutenant) governor of Senegal in Saint-Louis. Shaikh Ibra called himself a "marabout proprietaire" at Medina (N'Dande), Senegal. Dossier Amadou Bamba, in Bâ, *Ahmadou Bamba,* 140–41. Deputy Carpot intervened in 1911 for Bamba's return to Diourbel, as he had for the return from Mauritania in 1907. Cruise O'Brien, *Mourides,* 44–46, 73, 144–46.

60. What follows is based on the French translation by Dudu Seck and found in doss. Amadou Bamba, treatise of 29 December 1910. Another copy can be found in CAOM AP 15 (Gaden papers), carton 1, no. 128. I have not been able to find the Arabic original. It is interesting to note that Oumar Bâ, who created the "dossier Amadou Bamba" and used it to construct his volume, *Ahmadou Bamba,* does not include this piece. I have no reason to doubt the authenticity of the document nor its representation of Bamba's *public* view. Marty, writing in 1913, gave no credence to the rumor that Bamba was assisting resistance in Morocco to the French takeover ("Mourides d'Amadou Bamba," 274–76).

61. Although Ma El Ainin died in 1910, his sons continued to resist the French intrusions into Morocco and the Sahara.

62. Théveniaut wrote a letter from Diourbel, 1 July 1908, to the lieutenant governor, in which he sought authorization for Bamba to return to Baol and live under his supervision. Bâ, *Ahmadou Bamba,* 139. On Théveniaut, see the outline in chap. 3.

63. Dakar, 13 August 1912, governor-general to the lieutenant governor, doss. Amadou Bamba, found in Bâ, *Ahmadou Bamba,* 144. The second letter of Ponty to the lieutenant governor is dated 8 November 1913. The two letters are found ibid., 144–48. See also Searing, "Accommodation and Resistance," 253–54. The administration, as this letter implies, continued to count on the influence of the Sidiyya on the Murids. Baba, his sons, and closest confidants kept in close contact with the order and supplied information to officials. Abdallah, one of Baba's sons, visited Bamba in Diourbel in 1913 and promptly reported to Saint-Louis that all was well. CAOM, archives privées 15.1, Fonds Gaden, no. 109, Arabic letter and French translation of Abdullah b Shaikh Sidiyya of 28 May 1913.

64. Ponty's comments of 1913 are very similar to those expressed by Merlin in his 1903 letter to Sidiyya Baba. Both assumed that a *bidan* Qadiriyya marabout would have great influence over a *sudan* "disciple."

65. ANS 2G 13, 7(1), in Coulon, *Marabout,* 78. See also Marty, *Sénégal,* 1:277.

66. The article "Mourides d'Amadou Bamba," referred to in n. 3. For the references to taxes, recruits, and the trip to Saint-Louis, see 279 and 294–95.

67. An episode occurred in 1914 that showed how well the links between Muridiyya and government had been consolidated. A smallpox epidemic broke out in the territory, and it affected the central peanut basin, where the Murids were so dominant. The administrator at Diourbel and the local health official recommended the standard

steps of quarantine to deal with the situation; their order was countermanded, however, by the lieutenant governor in Saint-Louis, and intervention was limited to vaccination, some isolation of particular cases, and one instance of burning an "infected" hut. The colonial authorities did not wish to intervene more sharply in an area dominated by the brotherhood. See H12, corresp. of 1914. (My thanks to Kalala Ngalamulume for calling this file to my attention.) This instance in the health domain corresponds to the reluctance of the French to intervene in the area of education. See Cruise O'Brien, *Mourides*, chap. 10, and esp. 232 ff.

68. At least fourteen hundred identifiable Murids enlisted. Bamba refused to wear the medal on the grounds that it was in the form of a Christian symbol. Cruise O'Brien, *Mourides*, 46.

69. Marc Michel, *L'Appel à l'Afrique: Contributions et réactions à l'effort de guerre en A.O.F., 1914–1919* (Paris, 1982), 380–81. See also 58–61.

70. ANS 2G 17 5, quoted in Coulon, *Marabout*, 177.

71. See Cruise O'Brien, *Mourides*, 58–61, 194–95.

72. A full account can be found ibid., 47 ff. The mosque was completed many years later, well after Murid labor had helped to complete a railway branch line to link Touba with Diourbel; ibid., 65.

73. For an account of the succession, see ibid., 48–49, 61–63. Ibra Fati and Shaikh Anta were candidates as well. Ibra Fati withdrew in favor of Mamadu Mustapha.

74. Report of Administrator Lalande of Diourbel, 10 August 1926, contained in CAOM AFPO 518, doss. 2.

75. See Cruise O'Brien, *Mourides*, 61, 72, 265. For other interesting observations on Shaikh Anta, I draw on my interview with Umar Sarr cited in n. 33; Umar became a kind of agent for Shaikh Anta in the 1920s.

76. Whereas the leaders of the Tijaniyya of Tivaouane and their interpreters have often felt a need to defend themselves and Malik Sy from accusations of collaboration. See chap. 10, n. 2, and Mbaye, "Malick Sy," 1: chaps. 15 and 16.

CONCLUSION

1. As deputy, Blaise Diagne quickly learned the political trade and was able to gain majorities in the councils of the four communes when he was reelected in 1919.

2. Baba was the first with his decree of 1903. Saad Buh wrote his counsel in 1906, although it was not circulated until 1909. Bamba made his first public declaration in 1910; Malik Sy gave a public reading to the Saad Buh document in 1910 and made his most famous statement in 1912.

3. The wealth of Murid leaders rapidly became a factor in Senegalese colonial society. Shaikh Anta, for example, became a creditor of colonial chiefs whose needs for maintaining an entourage far outran their salaries. This was one tension in his relationship to Mbakhane Diop in 1903 that led to Bamba's second arrest and exile. Searing, "Accommodation and Resistance," 185–96.

4. In the sense of the Futanke proverb cited in Gaden, *Proverbes et maximes*, 68. See chap. 1, n. 50.

5. In Robinson and Triaud, *Le Temps des Marabouts.*

6. Indeed, Baba could be considered an "organic intellectual" of the colonial regime, in the sense intended by Gramsci. See Walter Adamson, *Hegemony and Revolution: A Study of Antonio Gramsci's Political and Cultural Theory* (Berkeley, Calif., 1980).

7. I hasten to add that this autonomy was not really a form of *taqiyya* (dissimulation) until such time as European rule was ended. Muhammad Sani Umar reviews taqiyya, hijra, and jihad as traditional forms of Muslim response to adversity in his dissertation, "Muslims' Intellectual Responses to British Colonialism in Northern Nigeria, 1903–45" Ph.D. diss., Northwestern University, 1997, chaps. 2 and 3.

8. In 1862, before the Masina revolt, there is some evidence that Umar was seeking to extend the jihad throughout the western Sudan and eliminate non-Muslim regimes. Robinson, *Holy War,* 300–301, 328.

9. Following the formulation of Leonardo Villalon in *Islamic Society and State Power* (Cambridge, U.K., 1993), 258–65.

10. To some extent this is true of Harrison, *France and Islam,* because he does not make clearly the distinction among the regions of French West Africa—and does not deal with Mauritania at all. This problem is discussed in the introduction and conclusion to Robinson and Triaud, *Le Temps des Marabouts.*

Sources

ARCHIVAL MATERIALS

1. Archives Nationales du Sénégal (Building administratif, Dakar) (ANS)

a. Ancienne Série

2B. 73–8 Rapports de situation politique
1D. 51 Opérations militaires, Bakel 1886.
3E. Conseil d'administration et conseil privé du Sénégal, 46
1G. Etudes générales 27, 29, 32, 46, 50, 52, 55–6, 63, 83, 103
1G. Etudes générales 289ff, Monographies des Cercles
9G. Mauritanie, 4, 5, 9, 14, 21, 40–3
13G. Sénégal: 28–9, 33, 41–8, 57–67, 69, 76–8
13G. Sénégal: Dagana, 103–4
13G. Sénégal: Podor, 120–35
13G. Sénégal: *correspondance indigène,* 136–44, 163, 242–3, 245
13G. Sénégal: Salde and Kaédi, 147–56
13G. Sénégal: Matam, 157–61
13G. Sénégal: Bakel, 165–225, 240
15G. Soudan: *correspondance indigène,* 62–82
15G. Soudan: Medine, 108–9
15G. Soudan: Kita, 126–8, 131–2, 141, 146
15G. Soudan: Nioro, 165
17G. Affaires politiques de l'AOF, 24–28, 36, 39
19G. Affaires musulmanes de l'AOF, 1–11
21G. Police et sûreté, 1
22G. Statistiques, 6
H. Santé en AOF, 11–2, 27, 34, 36–7
J. Enseignement jusqu'en 1920, 1–7, 49–50, 59, 85–94

K. Travail, main d'oeuvre et esclavage, 11, 16, 25
M. Tribunaux judiciaires, 8–10, 79–88, 101–2, 115, 241–4
Q. Affaires économiques, 23–4, 38–40

b. Série territoriale

2D4. Rapports, Tivaouane 1

c. Archives privées

1Z. 5–18, 51 Famille Devès

2. Archives de la Republique Islamique de la Mauritanie (Nouakchott) (RIM)

E/2/124. "Mémoire de Bou El Mogdad (jusqu'en 1903)." Bureau politique, Colonie
de la Mauritanie." Ca. 1910. No longer in the archives.
1E 223.

3. Archives Nationales du Mali (Koulouba-Bamako) (ANM)

1D. Rapports, 6, 35, 42, 47–8, 51, 55, 99
4D. Successions, 82, 101, 108
5D. Recensements, 15, 18, 22, 29, 34, 36, 44–5
2E. Politique indigène, 3, 6, 12, 14
4E. Politique musulmane, 12, 16, 78–92

4. Centre d'Archives d'Outre-Mer (Aix-en-Provence, France) (CAOM)

a. Affaires Politiques (AFPO)

159, 512, 518, 522, 907–12, 914, 924–5, 1051, 1403–4, 1420, 1433, 1851, 2258,
2261, 2708, 2711, 2724–5, 2802, 3038

b. Série géographique

AFRIQUE 3, Explorations et missions, 44
AFRIQUE 4, Expansion territoriale et politique indigène, 65, 68
AOF 3. Missions, 3
AOF 4. Affaires musulmanes, 2
AOF 8. Tribunaux, 2
AOF 10. Cultes, instruction publique, et beaux-arts, 6
AOF 12. Travaux et communications, 3
MAURITANIE 4. Expansion territoriale et politique indigène, 4
MAURITANIE 6. Affaires diplomatiques, 1
SENEGAL 1. Correspondance générale, 40–4, 46–50, 56, 73
SENEGAL 2. Mémoires, 7–8, 11, 13
SENEGAL 3. Missions, 11, 15–8
SENEGAL 4. Expansion territoriale et politique indigène, 16, 44–5, 59–69, 127–8
SENEGAL 7. Administration générale et municipale, 46, 53, 68, 70–1
SENEGAL 8. Justice, 4bis, 14, 14bis, 23bis

SENEGAL 9. Questions financières, 56–60, 62
SENEGAL 10. Cultes, instruction publique, et beaux-arts, 1, 3, 20

c. Gouvernement Général de l'Algérie (GG ALG)

4H. Explorations et voyages, 4
8H. Organisation administrative, 27
9H. Surveillance politique des indigènes, 7–8
10H. Etudes et notices, 30–1, 58, 81
16H. Questions religieuses, 7, 38–9, 44–6, 49, 51–2
22H. Sud: Opérations militaires et pénétration saharienne, 35–6, 41
30H. Maroc, 8, 31–2

d. Outre-Mer

Missions 18, 66, 115

e. Archives privées

4PA. 1, papiers d'Henri de Lamothe
4PA. 15, papiers d'Henri Gaden

5. Bibliothèque Nationale (Paris) (BNP)

Manuscrits orientaux, vol. 5582, folios 28–51. Register from the Umarian library and archive of Segu. See Ghali entry in published materials

OFFICIAL PUBLICATIONS

Annales Sénégalaises
Annuaire du Sénégal et Dépendances
Moniteur du Sénégal et Dépendances
Journal officiel du Sénégal
Journal officiel de l'Afrique Occidentale Française

INTERVIEWS

1. Robinson Interviews in Senegal and Mauritania, 1968–74

Al-Hadji Bokar Bâ, Kaédi, 5 April 1968
Thierno Amadou Bokar Alfa Bâ, Hore-Fonde, 17 April 1968; 22 January 1969; 13 February 1974
Al-Hadji Mamadou Dia, Dakar, 2, 8, and 15 June; 13 and 20 July; 17 August 1968
Bani Guisse, Hore-Fonde and Anyam Siwol, 2 and 3 March 1968
Ma Diakhite Cisse Kane, Anyam Siwol, 2–3 March and 4 April 1968; 13–14 January 1969
Thierno Seydi N'Gayde and Sire Aminata Ly, Sassel Taalbe, 11 February 1974

Saada Niang, Djimbe, 21 February 1974
Ousmane Samba Sall, Mouderi, 23 February 1974
Bassirou Soumare, Waounde, 15 February 1974
Samane Sy, Bakel, 24 January 1969; 17 February 1974
Mountaga Tall, Dakar, 22 February 1968
Ali Gaye Thiam, Matam, 21–23 and 30 January; 5 March 1968; 21 and 25 January
     1969; 24 February 1974
Birane Samba Top, Gollere, 29 January 1969; 26 February 1974

2. Robinson Interviews in Senegal, 1985

Mame Latir Diagne, Saint-Louis, 11 April 1985
Demba Matalibé Dièye, Saint-Louis, 12 June 1985
Al-Hadji Amadou Diop, 11 June 1986
Judge Taifou Diop, Dakar, 18–28 June 1985.
Bouna Abdoussalam Kane (with Mohamed Moustapha Kane), Dakar, 29 May 1985
"Local": Al-Hadji Brahima Mamoussé Gueye and other members of the "groupement."
     2 June 1985
Nouroudini Mbaye and Madou Alioune Mbaye, Saint-Louis, 12 April 1985
Al-Hadji Abdoulaye Alassane Ndiaye, Saint-Louis, 5 June 1985
Serigne Moustapha Ndiaye and Ousmane Dièye, Saint-Louis, 11 June 1985
Umar Ndiaye Sarr, Saint-Louis, 4 June 1985
Papa Seye Charles, Saint-Louis, 14 June 1985
Colonel Abdoulaye Tal, Ecole Militaire, Thiès, 16 March 1985

3. Interviews Conducted by Eunice Charles in Jolof

Al-Hadji Moussa Dia, imam, Mbeulakhe, 18 August 1970
Aliou Sakho, imam, Dahra, 26 July 1970

4. Interviews Conducted by Ghislaine Lydon in Senegal

Abou Latif ibn Mohammed ibn Abdullay Seck, Saint-Louis, 5 November 1997
Modike Wade, Saint-Louis, 31 October and 5 November 1997

5. Miscellaneous Interviews

Robinson interview with Director Abdoul Aïdara, CRDI, Saint-Louis, 1 June 1996
Robinson interview with Maître André Guillabert, Dakar, 8 June 1996
Robinson interview with Ibrahima Abou Sall, Paris, 12 July 1991
Hilary Jones and Robinson interview with Sylvain Sankale, Dakar, 3 July 1997
Robinson interview with Sowadou Seck and her daughter Aby Diop, Saint-Louis, 29
     and 30 June 1997
Robinson interview with Judge Aissata Rabi Wane, Dakar, 28 June 1997

Unpublished Materials

Babou, Cheikh. "Le Mouridisme jusqu'en 1912." Mémoire de maîtrise, Université Cheikh Anta Diop, Dakar, 1993.

Barrows, Leland. "General Faidherbe, the Maurel & Prom Company, and French Expansion in Senegal." Ph.D. diss., UCLA, 1974.

Bonte, Pierre. "L'emirat de l'Adrar." Thesis, doctorat d'Etat, Paris, 1998.

Bousbina, Saïd. "Un siècle de savoir islamique en Afrique de l'Ouest (1820-1920): Analyse et commentaire de la littérature de la confrérie Tijaniyya à travers les oeuvres d'Al-Hajj `Umar, `Ubayda ben Anbuja, Yirkoy Talfi et Al-Hajj Malik Sy." Thesis, doctorat d'université, Université de Paris 1, 1995-96.

Casey, Joan. "The Politics of French Imperialism in the Early Third Republic: The Case of Bordeaux." Ph.D. diss., University of Missouri, Columbia, 1973.

Cleaveland, Timothy. "Becoming Walati: A Study of Politics, Kinship, and Social Identity in Pre-colonial Walata." Ph.D. diss., Northwestern University, 1995.

Colvin, Lucie. "Kajor and Its Diplomatic Relations with Saint-Louis du Sénégal, 1763-1861." Ph.D. diss., Columbia University, 1972.

Devisse, Jean. "La crise de 1968." Paper distributed in 1968.

Dia, Fadel. "Les Noms des rues de Saint-Louis." MS at CRDS, Saint-Louis.

Diouf, Cheikh. "L'histoire des institutions musulmanes à Saint-Louis du Sénégal, l'ancienne capitale coloniale de l'AOF." MS being prepared as a doctoral thesis in Saint-Louis, 1996, for presentation at the Université de Paris 7.

Fall, Saly, daughter-in-law of Brahim Gueye. Notebook copied by Robinson on 22 June 1985.

Frébourg, Cécile. "Le Corse en Mauritanie: Xavier Coppolani (1866-1905): L'Islam au service de la France." Mémoire de maîtrise d'histoire, Paris 7, 1990.

Gnokane, Adama. "La politique française sur la rive droite du Sénégal: Le pays maures, 1817-1903." Thesis, de troisième cycle, Paris 1, 1986-87.

Guthié, Ibrahima Ndiaye. Letter to the director, Centre de Recherche et Documentation du Sénégal (CRDS), 9 July 1977.

Haidara/Diagne, Toba. "Contribution a l'etude de l'Islam au Senegal: La confrérie Kuntiyu de Njaasaan, 1884-1914." Mémoire de maitrise, University of Dakar, 1984-85.

Hunter, Thomas. "The Development of an Islamic Tradition of Learning among the Jahanka of West Africa." Ph.D. diss., University of Chicago, 1977.

Kane, Mouhamed Moustapha. "A History of Fuuta Tooro, 1890s-1920s: Senegal under Colonial Rule: The Protectorate." Ph.D. diss., Michigan State University, 1987.

Ly, Boubacar. "L'honneur et les valeurs morales dans les sociétés oulof et toucouleur du Sénégal: Etude de sociologie." Thesis, doctorat de troisième cycle, Sorbonne, 1966.

Lydon, Ghislaine. "On the Trans-Saharan Trails: Trading Networks and Cross-cultural Exchange in Western Africa, 1840s-1950s." Ph.D. diss., Michigan State University, 2000.

Marcson, Michael. "European-African Interaction in the Precolonial Period: Saint-Louis, Senegal, 1758-1854." Ph.D. diss., Princeton University, 1976.

Mbaye, Ravane. "La Pensee et l'action d'El Hadji Malick Sy: Un pôle d'attraction entre la Shari`a et la Tariqa: Vie et oeuvre de El Hadji Malick Sy." Thesis, doctorat d'Etat en sciences humaines, Paris 4, 1993.

Mbow, Penda. "Querelles de succession au sein de la confrérie Tidjane et Tivaouane." Paper presented to the conference on Tijaniyya Traditions and Societies in West and North Africa in the Nineteenth and Twentieth Centuries, held at the University of Illinois-Champaign, 1–5 April 1996.

McDougall, E Ann. "The Ijil Salt Industry: Its Role in the Precolonial Economy of the Western Sudan." Ph.D. diss., University of Birmingham, U.K., 1980.

McLane, Margaret Osborne. "Economic Expansionism and the Shape of Empire: French Enterprise in West Africa, 1850–1914." Ph.D. diss., University of Wisconsin, 1992.

McLaughlin, Glen. "Sufi, Saint, Sharif: Muhammad Fadil wuld Mamin: His Spiritual Legacy and the Political Economy of the Sacred in Nineteenth-Century Mauritania." Ph.D. diss., Northwestern University, 1997.

Moitt, Bernard. "Peanut Production and Social Change in the Dakar Hinterland: Kajoor and Bawol, 1840–1940." Ph.D. diss., University of Toronto, 1984.

Ngalamulume, Kalala. "Urban Growth and Health Problems, Saint-Louis from the Mid Nineteenth Century to World War I." Ph.D. diss., Michigan State University, 1996.

Ould Cheikh, Abdel Wedoud. "Nomadisme, Islam, et pouvoir politique dans la société maure précoloniale (XI–XIX siècles)." Thesis, doctorat d'Etat, Paris 5, 1985.

———. "La société Maure: Contribution à l'étude anthropologique et historique d'une identité culturelle ouest-saharienne." Dossier d'habilitation présenté devant l'Ecole des Hautes Études en Sciences Sociales, 1999.

Pasquier, Roger. "Le Sénégal au milieu du XIXe siècle: La crise économique et sociale." Thesis, doctorat d'état, Paris 4, 1987.

Pheffer, Paul. "Railroads and Aspects of Social Change in Senegal, 1878–1933." Ph.D. diss., University of Pennsylvania, 1975.

Reyss, Nathalie. "Saint Louis du Sénégal à l'époque précoloniale: L'émergence d'une société métisse originale, 1655–1854." Thesis, troisième cycle en histoire, Paris 1, 1983.

Saidu, Lukumanu Muhammad. "The Fall of the Segu Caliphate and the Tukolor Exodus, 1891–1903." M.A. thesis, Bayero University, Kano, 1989.

Sall, Ibrahima Abou. "Mauritanie: Conquête et organisation administratives des territoires du Sud: Rôle des aristocraties politiques et religieuses, 1890–1945." Thesis, doctorat nouveau regime, Paris 7, 1998.

Sani Umar, Muhammad. "Muslims' Intellectual Responses to British Colonialism in Northern Nigeria, 1903–45." Ph.D. diss., Northwestern University, 1997.

Searing, James. "Accommodation and Resistance: Chiefs, Muslim Leaders, and Politicians in Colonial Senegal, 1890–1934." Ph.D. diss., Princeton University, 1985.

Taylor, Raymond. "Of Disciples and Sultans: Power, Authority, and Society in the Nineteenth-century Mauritanian Gebla." Ph.D. diss., University of Illinois, 1996.

Thompson, J. Malcolm. "In Dubious Service: The Recruitment and Stabilization of West African Maritime Labor by the French Colonial Military, 1659–1900." Ph.D. diss., University of Minnesota, 1989.

Villasante-de Beauvais, Mariella. "Solidarité et hierarchie au sein des Ahl Sidi Mahmud:

Essai d'anthropologie historique d'une confédération tribale mauritanienne, XVIII–XXeme siècles." Thesis, doctorat d'Etat, Paris, 1995.

Witherell, Julian. "The Response of the Peoples of Cayor to French Penetration, 1850–1900." Ph.D. diss., University of Wisconsin, 1964.

PUBLISHED SOURCES

Abun-Nasr, Jamil. *The Tijaniyya: A Sufi Order in the Modern World.* Oxford, 1965.

Adamson, Walter. *Hegemony and Revolution: A Study of Antinio Gramsci's Political and Cultural Theory.* Berkeley, Calif., 1980.

Adeleye, Remi. "The Dilemma of the Wazir: The Place of the Risalat al-Wazir ila Ahl al-ʿilm wa'l-Tadabbur in the History of the Conquest of the Sokoto Caliphate." *Journal of the Historical Society of Nigeria* 4, no. 2 (1968).

———. *Power and Diplomacy in Northern Nigeria, 1804–1906.* London, 1971.

Ageron, Charles Robert. *Les Algériens musulmans et la France (1871–1919).* 2 vols. Paris, 1968.

Ajayi, J. F. Ade, and J. D. Y. Peel, eds. *Peoples and Empires in African History: Essays in Memory of Michael Crowder.* London, 1992.

al-Adnani, Jilali. "Reflexions sur la naissance de la Tijaniyya: Emprunts et surenchères." In *La Tijaniyya,* ed. Triaud and Robinson.

———. "Les origines de la Tijaniyya: Quand les premiers disciples se mettent à parler." In *La Tijaniyya,* ed. Triaud and Robinson.

Al-Azmeh, Aziz. "Barbarians in Arab Eyes." *Past and Present* (1992).

Amin, Samir. *Le monde des affaires sénégalais.* Paris, 1969.

Arnaud, Robert. *Précis de la politique musulmane: 1: Pays Maures de la rive droite du Sénégal.* Algiers, 1906.

———. "L'Islam et la politique musulmane de l'Afrique Occidentale Française." *BCAF/RC* (1912): 3–20, 115–27, 141–54.

Bâ, Amadou Hampâté. *Amkoullel, l'enfant peul.* Paris, 1991.

———. *Oui, mon commandant.* Paris, 1994.

Bâ, Amadou Hampâté, and Marcel Cardaire. *Le sage de Bandiagara.* Paris, 1957.

Bâ, Mahmadou. "Notice sur Maghama." *BIFAN,* ser. B, 1, no. 4 (1939): 743–6l.

Bâ, Oumar. *La pénétration française au Cayor: Du règne de Birima N'Goné Latyr à l'intronisation de Madiodo Dèguène Codou.* Dakar, 1976.

Bâ, Oumar, ed. *Ahmadou Bamba face aux autorités coloniales (1889–1927).* Abbeville, France, 1982.

Bâ, Tamsir Ousmane. "Essai historique sur le Rip." *BIFAN,* ser. B, 19, 1957.

Babou, Cheikh. "Autour de la genèse du Mouridisme.' *ISASS* 11 (1997).

Barry, Boubacar. *Le royaume du Waalo: Le Sénégal avant la conquête.* Paris, 1972.

———. *Senegambia and the Atlantic Slave Trade.* Cambridge, U.K., 1998.

Barry, Boubacar, and Léonhard Harding, eds. *Commerce et commerçants en Afrique de l'Ouest: Le Sénégal.* Paris, 1992.

Bayart, Jean-François. *L'Etat en Afrique: La politique du ventre.* Paris, 1989.

Becker, Charles, Saliou Mbaye, and Ibrahima Thioub, eds. *AOF: Réalites et héritages: Sociétes ouest-africaines et ordre coloniale, 1895–1960.* 2 vols. Dakar, 1997.

Bérenger-Féraud, Laurent J. B. *Les peuplades de la Sénégambie.* Paris, 1879.

Berman, Bruce, and John Lonsdale. *Unhappy Valley: Conflict in Kenya and Africa.* Book 1, *State and Class.* Book 2, *Violence and Ethnicity.* London, 1992.

Binger, Louis. *Du Niger au Golfe de Guinée.* Paris, 1892.

Blanchard, Marcel. "Administrateurs d'Afrique Noire." *Revue d'Histoire des Colonies* 41 (1953).

Boilat, Abbé P. D. *Esquisses sénégalaises.* Paris, 1853.

Boilley, Pierre, et al, eds. *Nomades et commandants: Administration et sociétés nomades dans l'ancien AOF.* Paris, 1993.

Bonardel, Rogine. *Saint-Louis du Sénégal: Mort ou Naissance?* Paris, 1992.

Bonte, Pierre, et al. *Al-Ansab: La quête des origines: Anthropologie historique de la société tribale arabe.* Paris, 1991.

Boubrik, Rahal. "Processus de formation d'une confrérie saharienne." *La transmission du savoir dans l'Islam peripherique, lettre d'information* 15 (1995).

———. *Saints et societé en Islam: La confrérie ouest-saharienne Fâdiliyya.* Paris, 1999.

Bouche, Denise. *L'Enseignement dans les teritoires français de l'Afrique Occidentale de 1817 à 1920. Mission civilisatrice ou formation d'une elite?* 2 vols. Paris, 1975.

Boulègue, Jean. "La participation possible des centres de Pir et de Ndogal à la revolution islamique sénégambienne de 1673." In *Contributions à l'histoire du Sénégal,* ed. Boulègue. Paris, 1987.

Bourdieu, Pierre. *The Logic of Practice.* Stanford, Calif., 1990.

Bourgeot, André, ed. *Horizons nomades en Afrique sahélienne.* Paris, 1999.

Bousbina, Saïd. "Al-Hajj Malik Sy: Sa chaîne spirituelle dans la Tijaniyya et sa position à l'égard de la présence française au Sénégal." In *Le Temps des Marabouts,* ed. Robinson and Triaud, 1997.

Bousquet, G. H., trans. and ed. "Khalil b Ishᶜaq." In *Abrégé de la loi musulmane selon le rite de l'imam Malek.* 4 vols. Algiers, 1956–62.

Bouvat, L. "Cheikh Saadibouh et son entourage d'après un manuscrit inédit." *RMM* 18 (1912).

Brenner, Louis. *West African Sufi: The Religious Heritage and Spiritual Search of Cerno Bokar Saalif Taal.* London, 1984.

———. "Concepts of Tariqa in West Africa: The Case of the Qadiriyya." In *Charisma and Brotherhood in African Islam,* ed. Cruise O'Brien and Christian Coulon, 1988.

———. "Médersas au Mali: Transformation d'une institution islamique." In *L'enseignement islamique au Mali,* ed. B. Sanankoua and L. Brenner. Bamako, 1991.

———. "The Jihad Debate between Sokoto and Borno: An Historical Analysis of Islamic Political Discourse in Nigeria" In *Peoples and Empires in African History,* ed. J. F. Ade Ajayi and J. D. Y. Peel, 1992.

———. "Constructing Muslim Identities in Mali." In *Muslim Identity and Social Change in Sub-Saharan Africa,* ed. L. Brenner, 1993.

———. "Becoming Muslim in Soudan français." In *Le Temps des Marabouts,* ed. Robinson and Triaud, 1997.

Brenner, Louis, ed., *Muslim Identity and Social Change in Sub-Saharan Africa.* Bloomington, Ind., 1993.

Brett, Michael, and Elizabeth Fentress. *The Berbers.* London, 1996.

Brooks, George. "Peanuts and Colonialism: Consequences of the Commercialization of Peanuts in West Africa." *JAH* 16 (1975).

Burke, Edmund. "The Image of the Moroccan State in French Ethnological Literature: A New Look at the Origin of Lyautey's Berber Policy." In *Arabs and Berbers,* ed. Ernest Gellner and Charles Micaud. London, 1972.

———. "Pan-Islam and Moroccan Resistance to French Colonial Penetration, 1900–1912." *JAH* 13, no. 1 (1972).

Calhoun, Craig, ed. *Habermas and the Public Sphere.* Boston, 1992.

———. *Bourdieu: Critical Perspectives.* Chicago 1993.

Cannadine, David. "The Context, Performance, and Meaning of Ritual: The British Monarchy and the 'Invention of Tradition', ca. 1820–1977." In *The Invention of Tradition,* ed. Eric Hobsbawm and Terence Ranger. 2 vols. London, 1983.

Caratini, Sophie. *Les Rgaybat, 1610–1934.* Paris, 1989.

Carles, Fernand. *La France et l'Islam en Afrique Occidentale.* Toulouse, 1915.

Carmichael, Tim. "British 'Practice' towards Islam in the East Africa Protectorate: Muslim Officials, waqf Administration and Secular Education in Mombasa and Environs, 1895–1920." *Journal of Muslim Minority Affairs* 17 (1997).

Carrère, Frédéric, and Paul Holle. *De la Sénégambie française.* Paris, 1855.

Chandône, Paul. "Mademba, Fama de Sansanding." *Revue Indigène* 1, no. 7 (1906).

Charles, Eunice. "Shaikh Amadou Ba and Jihad in Jolof." *African Historical Studies* 8 (1975).

Charpy, Jacques, ed., *La fondation de Dakar, 1845–1857–1869.* Paris, 1958.

Chater, Khalifa. "A Rereading of Islamic Texts in the Maghrib in the Nineteenth and Early Twentieth Centuries: Secular Themes or Religious Reformism?" In *Islamism and Secularism in North Africa,* ed. John Ruedy. New York, 1994.

Cheruy, Lt. Paul. "Rapports sur le droit de propriété des Kolades dans le Chemama: Les redevances anciennement payées et les droits acquis actuellement." In *Supplément au JO de l'AOF,* nos. 52–4 (1911).

Cissoko, Sékéné-Mody, and Oumar Kane. "Il y a un an disparaissait une grande figure africaine: Thierno Seydou Nourou Tall." *Afrique histoire* 2 (1981).

Clancy-Smith, Julia. *Rebel and Saint: Muslim Notables, Populist Protest, Colonial Encounters (Algeria and Tunisia, 1800–1914).* California, 1994.

Clark, Terry Nichols. *Prophets and Patrons: The French Univrsity and the Emergence of the Social Sciences.* Cambridge, Mass., 1973.

Cleaveland, Timothy. "Islam and the Construction of Social Identity in the Nineteenth-century Sahara." *JAH* 39, no. 3 (1998).

Clément, Jean-François. "L'Islam en France." In Bruno Etienne, ed., *L'Islam en France: Islam, Etat et société.* Paris, 1990.

Clifford, James. *The Predicament of Culture: Twentieth-Century Ethnography, Literature, and Art.* Cambridge, Mass., 1988.

Cobbing, Julian. "The Absent Priesthood: Another Look at the Rhodesian Risings of 1896–97." *JAH* 18 (1977).

Cohen, Abner. *Custom and Politics in Urban Africa: A Study of Hausa Migrants in Yoruba Towns.* Berkeley, Calif., 1969.

Cohen, William. *Rulers of Empire: The French Colonial Service in Africa.* Stanford, Calif., 1971.

———. *French Encounter with Africans.* Bloomington, Ind., 1980.

Colombani, Olivier. *Mémoires coloniales: La fin de l'Empire français d'Afrique vue par les admistrateurs coloniaux.* Paris, 1991.

Colvin, Lucie. "Islam and the State of Kajoor: A Case of Successful Resistance to Jihad." *Journal of African History* 15, (1974).

Conklin, Alice. *A Mission to Civilize: The Republican Idea of Empire in France and West Africa, 1895–1930.* Stanford, Calif., 1997.

Copans, Jean. *Les Marabouts de l'Arachide.* Paris, 1980.

Coulon, Christian. *Le Marabout et le Prince.* Paris, 1981.

Coursier, Alain. *Faidherbe, 1818–1880: Du Sénégal à l'Armée du Nord.* Paris, 1989.

Creevey, Lucy. "Ahmad Bamba, 1850–1927." In *Studies on the History of Islam in West Africa,* ed. J. R. Willis. Vol. 1. London, 1979.

Cruise O'Brien, Donal. "Towards an 'Islamic Policy' in French West Africa." *JAH* 8 (1967).

———. *The Mourides of Senegal.* Oxford, 1971.

———. *Saints and Politicians.* Cambridge, U.K., 1975.

Cruise O'Brien, Donal, and Christian Coulon, eds. *Charisma and Brotherhood in African Islam.* Oxford, 1988.

Curtin, Philip. *The Atlantic Slave Trade: A Census.* Madison, Wisc., 1969.

———. *Economic Change in Precolonial Africa: Senegambia in the Era of the Slave-Trade.* 2 vols. Wisconsin, 1975.

———. *Cross-Cultural Trade in World History.* Cambridge, 1984.

de Benoist, Joseph Roger. *L'Eglise et le pouvoir colonial au Soudan.* Paris, 1987.

de Chassey, François. *Mauritanie 1900–1975: Facteurs économiques, politiques, idéologiques, et éducatifs dans la formation de la société sous-developpée.* Paris, 1984.

Dedoud ould Abdallah. "Guerre sainte ou sédition blâmable: Un débat entre shaikh Saʿd Bu et son frère shaikh Ma al-Ainin." In *Le Temps des Marabouts,* ed. Robinson and Triaud, 1997.

———. "La 'passage au sud': Muhammad al-Hafiz et son heritage." In *La Tijaniyya,* ed. Triaud and Robinson, 2000.

Delafosse, Louise. *Maurice Delafosse: Le Berrichon conquis par l'Afrique.* Paris, 1976.

Delafosse, Maurice. "Traditions historiques et légendaires du Soudan occidental." *BCAF/RC* 8 (1913).

de la Tourrasse, Joseph du Sorbier. *Au pays des Woloffs: Souvenirs d'un traitant du Senegal.* Paris, n.d. but between 1886 and 1900.

Delavignette, Robert, and Charles-Andre Julien. *Les constructeurs de la France d'Outre-Mer.* Paris, 1946.

de Loppinot, A. "Souvenirs d'Aguibou." *Bulletin du CEHSAOF* 2 (1919).

Depont, Octave, and Xavier Coppolani. *Les Confréries Religieuses Musulmanes.* Algiers, 1897.

Deschamps, Hubert, and Paul Chauvet. *Galliéni pacificateur: Ecrits coloniaux de Galliéni: Choix de textes et notes.* Paris, 1949.

Désiré-Vuillemin, Geneviève. "La fondation de Nouakchott (souvenirs de Frerejean)." *Mélanges et Documents: Archives et Souvenirs, RHCF* 38 (1951).

———. "Autour du Capitaine Mangin." *Mélanges et Documents: Archives et Souvenirs, RHCF* 38 (1951).

————. *Contribution à l'histoire de la Mauritanie, 1900–1934.* Dakar, 1962.

Désiré-Vuillemin, Geneviève, ed. "A propos du rapport de l'Interprete Bou El Mogdad sur sa mission dans l'Adrar en 1900," by Dudu Seck. *Mélanges et Documents, RHCF* 39 (1952).

————. *Commandant Frèrejean: Mauritanie, 1903–1911: Mémoires de randonnées et de guerres au pays des Beidanes.* Paris, 1995.

Diallo, Thierno, Mame Bara M'Backe, Miriana Trifkovic, and Boubacar Barry. *Catalogue des Manuscrits de l'IFAN.* Dakar, 1966.

Dièye, Cheikh Abdoulaye. *L'exile au Gabon, période coloniale, 1895–1902: Sur les traces de Cheikh Ahmadou Bamba.* Dakar, 1985.

Diop, Abdoulaye Bara. *La Société wolof: Tradition et changement.* Paris, 1981.

Diop, Amadou Bamba. "Lat Dyor et le problème musulman." *BIFAN*, ser. B, 28 (1966).

Diop, Momar Coumba. "La littérature mouride: Essai d'analyse thématique." *BIFAN*, ser. B, 41 (1979).

Diouf, Mamadou. *Le Kajoor au XIXe siècle: Pouvoir ceddo et conquête coloniale.* Paris, 1990.

————. "Intellectuals and the State in Senegal: The Search for a Paradigm." In *Academic Freedom in Africa*, ed. Diouf and Mahmood Mamdani. Dakar, 1994.

Dirks, Nicholas, ed. *Colonialism and Culture.* Ann Arbor, Mich., 1992.

d'Otton Loyewski. "Coppolani et la Mauritanie." *RHCF* 26 (1938).

Dournaux Dupéré, N. "La Sénégambie française." *Bulletin de la Société de Géographie* (Paris) 2 (1871).

Du Puigaudeau, Odette. *Pieds nus à travers la Mauritanie.* Paris, 1936.

Dubié, Paul. *La vie matérielle des Maures.* Dakar, 1953.

Dumont, Fernand. *La pensée religieuse de Amadou Bamba.* Dakar, 1975.

————. *L'Anti-sultan, ou Al-Hajj Omar Tal du Fouta, combattant de la Foi, 1794–1864.* Dakar, 1971.

Duval, Jules. "La politique coloniale de la France." *Revue des Deux Mondes* (October 1858).

Echenberg, Myron. *Colonial Conscripts: The Tirailleurs Senegalais in French West Africa, 1857–1960.* Portsmouth, N.H., 1991.

Faidherbe, Louis Léon César. *Le Sénégal: La France dans l'Afrique Occidentale.* Paris, 1889.

Faucher, Jean-André. *Les francs-maçons et le pouvoir de la Révolution à nos jours.* Paris, 1986.

Faye, Ousseynou. "Mythe et histoire dans la vie de Kaan Fay du Cangin (Senegal)." *CEA* 136 (1994).

Forêt, Auguste. *Un voyage dans le Haut Sénégal: Description du fleuve.* Paris, 1888.

Fremeaux, Jacques. *La France et l'Islam depuis 1789.* Paris, 1991.

Frey, Henri. *Campagne dans le Haut Sénégal et dans le Haut Niger, 1885–86.* Paris, 1888.

Gaden, Henri. *Proverbes et maximes Peuls et Toucouleurs.* Paris, 1931.

Gaden, Henri, ed. and trans. *La Vie d'El Hadj Omar: Qaçida en poular,* by Mohammadou Aliou Tyam. Paris, 1935.

Gaffarel, Paul. *Le Sénégal et le Soudan français.* Paris, 1898.

Galliéni, Joseph. *Deux campagnes au Soudan français, 1886–88.* Paris, 1887.

Ganier, G. "Maures et toucouleurs sur les deux rives du Senegal: La Mission de Victor Ballot auprès de Sidi Ely roi des Maures Braknas, février-juin 1884." *BIFAN*, ser. B, 30 (1968).

Garcia, Sylvianne. "Al-Hajj Seydou Nourou Tall, 'grand marabout' tijani: L'histoire d'une carrière (v. 1880–1980). In *Le Temps des Marabouts,* ed. Robinson and Triaud.

Gausseron, B. H. *Un Français au Sénégal, Abel Jeandet.* Paris, 1913.

Gellner, Ernest. *Conditions of Liberty: Civil Society and Its Rivals.* London, 1994.

Gellner, Ernest, and Charles Micaud, eds. *Arabs and Berbers.* London, 1972.

Gerresch, Claudine. "Jugements du Moniteur du Sénégal sur Al-Hajj Oumar, de 1857 à 1864." *BIFAN,* ser. B, 35 (1973).

Ghali, Noureddine, et al. *La Bibliothèque Umarienne de Segou.* Paris, 1985.

Gillier, Commandant. *La pénétration en Mauritanie: Découverte—Explorations—Conquête— La police du désert et la pacification définitive.* Paris, 1926.

Gomez, Michael. *Pragmatism in the Age of Jihad.* Cambridge, U.K., 1992.

Gouraud, Henri. *La pacification de la Mauritanie.* Paris, 1910.

———. *Souvenirs d'un africain: Au Soudan.* Paris, 1939.

———. *Mauritanie Adrar. Souvenirs d'un africain.* Paris, 1945.

Gramsci, Antonio. *Selections from the Prison Notebooks of Antonio Gramsci,* trans. and ed. Q. Hoare and G. Nowell Smith. New York, 1971.

Gray, Christopher. "The Rise of the Niassène Tijaniyya, 1875 to the Present." *ISASS* 2 (1988).

Grosz-Ngate, Maria. "Power and Knowledge: The Representation of the Mande World in the Works of Park, Caillié, Monteil, and Delafosse." *CEA* 111–12 (1988).

Groves, C. P. *The Planting of Christianity in Africa.* 4 vols. London, 1948–55.

Gruvel, A., and R. Chudeau. *A Travers la Mauritanie Occidentale de Saint Louis à Port Etienne.* Paris, 1909.

Gueye, Lamine. *De la situation politique des Sénégalais originaires des communes de plein exercise.* Thesis, doctorat en droit. Paris, 1921.

———. *Itineraire africain.* Paris, 1966.

Hailey, Lord. *An African Survey: Revised 1956.* Oxford, 1957.

Hamès, Constant. "Cheikh Hamallah ou qu'est-ce qu'une confrérie islamique (Tariqa)?" *ASSR* 55, no. 1 (1983).

———. "Pour une histoire de Boutilimit (Sahel mauritanien)." *Journal de la Société des Africanistes* 55 (1985).

———. "Shaykh Sa`ad Buh Mauritanie, 1850–1917." *ISASS* 4 (1990).

———. "Le prémier exil de Shaikh Hamallah et la mémoire hamalliste (Nioro-Mederdra, 1925)." In *Le Temps des Marabouts,* ed. Robinson and Triaud.

Hamet, Ismaël, trans. and ed. *Chroniques de la Mauritanie Sénégalaise: Nacer Eddine.* Paris, 1911.

Hanson, John. "Generational Conflict in the Umarian Movement after the Jihad: Perspectives from the Futanke Grain Trade at Medine." *JAH* 31 (1990).

———. "Islam, Migration, and the Political Economy of Meaning: *Fergo Nioro* from the Senegal River Valley, 1862–1890." *JAH* 35 (1994).

———. *Migration, Jihad and Muslim Authority in West Africa.* Bloomington, Ind., 1996.

Hanson, John, and David Robinson. *After the Jihad: The Reign of Ahmad al-Kabir in the Western Sudan.* East Lansing, Mich., 1991.

Hardy, Georges. *L'Enseignement au Sénégal de 1817 à 1854.* Paris, 1920.

———. *La mise en valeur du Sénégal de 1817 à 1854.* Paris, 1921.

————. *Une conquête morale: L'enseignement en Afrique Occidentale Française.* Paris, 1921.

Hargreaves, John, ed. *France and West Africa: An Anthology of Historical Documents.* London, 1969.

Harrison, Chris. *France and Islam in West Africa, 1860–1960.* Cambridge, U.K., 1988.

Hobsbawm, Eric, and Terence Ranger, eds. *The Invention of Tradition.* London, 1983.

Hommes et Destins. Publications de l'Academie des Sciences d'Outre-Mer: Travaux et Memoires, tome 9: Afrique Noire. Paris, 1989.

Houdas, Octave, ed. and trans. *Ta'rikh al-Soudan.* Paris, 1900.

————. *Ta'rikh al-Fettash.* Paris, 1913.

Human Rights Watch/Africa. *Mauritania's Campaigns of Terror: State-Sponsored Repression of Black Africans.* New York, 1994.

Idowu, H. O. "The Establishment of Elective Institutions in Senegal, 1869–80." *JAH* 9 (1968).

Introduction à la Mauritanie. Centre de Recherches et d'Etudes sur les Sociétés Mediterraneannes, Paris, 1979.

Joffe, George, ed. *North Africa: Nation, State, and Region.* London, 1993.

Joffre, General J. J. C. *My March to Timbuctoo.* New York, 1915.

Johnson, G. Wesley. *The Emergence of Black Politics in Senegal: The Struggle for Power in the Four Communes.* Stanford, Calif., 1971.

Johnson, G. Wesley, ed. *Double Impact: France and Africa in the Age of Imperialism.* Greenwich, Conn., 1985.

Julien, Charles-Andre. *Histoire de l'Algérie contemporaine: La conquête et les débuts de la colonisation.* Paris, 1964.

July, Robert. *The Origins of Modern Nationalism.* London, 1968.

Kamara, Shaikh Musa. *Florilège au jardin de l'histoire des noirs: Zuhur al-Basatin.* Trans. and ed. Jean Schmitz et al. Vol. 1 of 4. Paris, 1998.

Kane, Mohammed Moustapha, Sonja Fagerberg-Diallo, and David Robinson. "Une vision iconoclaste de la guerre sainte d'Al-Hajj Umar Taal." *CEA* 133–35 (1994).

Kane, Mohammed Moustapha, and David Robinson. *The Islamic Regime of Fuuta Tooro: An Anthology of Oral Tradition Transcribed in Pulaar and Translated into English.* East Lansing, Mich. 1984.

Kane, Ousmane. "Muhammad Niasse (1881–1956) et sa réplique contre le pamphlet anti-tijani d'Ibn Mayaba." In *La Tijaniyya,* ed. Triaud and Robinson, 2000.

Kanya-Forstner, Sydney. *The Conquest of the Western Sudan.* Cambridge, U.K. 1969.

————. "French Missions to the Central Sudan in the 1890s: The Role of Algerian Agents and Interpreters." *Paideuma* 40 (1994).

Khalil ibn Ishaq. See works by Bousquet and Perron.

Klein, Martin. *Islam and Imperialism in Senegal: Sine-Saloum, 1847–1914.* Stanford, Calif., 1968.

————. "Social and Economic Factors in the Muslim Revolution in Senegambia." *JAH* 13 (1972).

————. *Slavery and Colonial Rule in French West Africa.* Cambridge, U.K., 1998.

Klein, Martin, ed. *Breaking the Chains: Slavery, Bondage, and Emancipation in Modern Africa and Asia.* Madison, Wisc., 1993.

Koren, H. J. *The Spiritans: A History of the Congregation of the Holy Ghost.* Pittsburgh, 1958.

Labouret, Henri. *Monteil. Explorateur et soldat.* Paris, 1937.

Langley, G. Ayodele. *Pan-Africanism and Nationalism in West Africa, 1900–1945: A Study in Ideology and Social Classes.* Oxford, 1973.

Lautour, Gaston. *Journal d'un spahi au Soudan, 1897–99.* Paris, 1909.

Le Châtelier, Alfred. *Les confréries musulmanes dans le Hedjaz.* Paris, 1887.

———. *L'Islam dans l'Afrique occidentale.* Paris, 1899.

Leriche, A. "Deux lettres du temps de la pacification (Mauritanie)." *BIFAN,* ser. B, 14 (1952).

Leservoisier, Olivier. *La question foncière en Mauritanie.* Paris, 1994.

Levtzion, Nehemia, and Randall Pouwels, eds. *A History of Islam in Africa.* Athens, Ohio, 2000.

Lovejoy, Paul, and Jan Hogendorn. *Slow Death for Slavery.* Cambridge, U.K., 1993.

Low, D. Anthony. *Lion Rampant.* London, 1973.

Ly-Tall, Madina, and David Robinson. "The Western Sudan and the Coming of the French." In *History of West Africa,* ed. J. F. A. Ajayi and M. Crowder. Vol. 2. London, 1987.

———. *Un Islam militant en Afrique de l'Ouest au XIX siècle.* Paris, 1991.

Lydon, Ghislaine. "Les péripéties d'une institution financière: La Banque du Sénégal, 1844–1901." In *AOF: Réalites et héritages,* ed. Becker, Mbaye, and Thioub.

Mage, Eugène. *Relation du voyage d'exploration de MM. Mage et Quintin au Soudan occidental.* Paris, 1867 and 1868.

Mahibou, Sidi Mohamed, and Jean-Louis Triaud, eds. *Voilà Ce Qui Est Arrivé: The Bayan Ma Waqaᶜa d'Al-Hajj Umar al-Futi.* Paris, 1984.

Manchuelle, François. *"Métis* et colons: La famille Devès et l'émergence politique des Africains au Sénégal." *CEA* 96 (1984).

———. "Assimilés ou patriotes africains? Naissance du nationalisme culturel en Afrique française, 1853–1931." *CEA* nos. 138–39 (1995).

Mangin, Charles. *Lettres du Soudan.* Paris, 1930.

Manley, Andrew. "The Sosso and the Haidara: Two Muslim Lineages in Soudan français, 1890–1960." In *Le Temps des Marabouts,* ed. Robinson and Triaud.

Marchesin, Philippe. *Tribus, ethnie, et pouvoir en Mauritanie.* Paris, 1992.

Marfaing, Laurence. *L'evolution du commerce au Sénégal, 1820–1930.* Paris, 1991.

Marks, Shula. *Ambiguities of Dependence.* Baltimore, 1986.

Marône, Ibrahima. "Le Tidjanisme au Sénégal." *Bulletin de l'Institut Fondemental d'Afrique Noire,* ser. B, 32 (1970).

Martin, B. G. *Muslim Brotherhoods in Nineteenth-century Africa.* Cambridge, U.K., 1976.

Marty, Paul. *Etudes sur l'Islam maure: Cheikh Sidia, les Fadelia, les Ida ou Ali.* Paris, 1916.

———. *L'Islam en Mauritanie et au Sénégal.* Published in *RMM* 31 (1915–16).

———. *Etudes sur l'Islam au Sénégal.* 2 vols. Paris, 1917.

———. *L'Emirat des Trarzas.* Entire work published in *RMM* 36 (1917–18).

———. *Etudes sur l'Islam et les tribus du Soudan.* 4 vols. Paris, 1920.

———. *L'Islam en Guinée.* Paris, 1921.

Massignon, Louis. "Une bibliothèque saharienne: La bibliiothèque du Cheikh Sidia au Sahara." *RMM* 8 (1909).

Mbacké, Serigne Bachir. *Les bienfaits de l'eternel ou la biographie de Cheikh Amadou Bamba Mbacke.* Trans. from Arabic by Khadim Mbacke. Dakar, 1995.

Mbaye, Saliou. *Guide des Archives de l'Afrique Occidentale Française.* Dakar, 1990.

————. *Histoire des institutions coloniales françaises en Afrique de l'Ouest, 1816–1960.* Dakar, 1991.

McDougall, E. Ann. "Research in Saharan History." *JAH* 39 (1998).

Méniaud, Jacques. *Les pionniers du Soudan avant, avec et après Archinard, 1879–1894.* 2 vols. Paris, 1931.

Messal, Raymond. *La genèse de notre victoire marocaine: Un précurseur Alfred Le Châtelier, 1855–1929.* Paris, 1931.

Michaux-Bellaire, Edouard. "Une fetoua de Cheikh Sidia: Approuvée par Cheikh Saad Bouh ben Mohammed El Fadil ben Mamin, frère de Cheikh Ma El Ainin." *Archives Marocaines* 11 (1907).

Michel, Marc. *L'appel à l'Afrique.* Paris, 1982.

Miège, Jean-Louis. *Le Maroc et l'Europe (1830–1894).* 4 vols. Paris, 1962.

————. *Histoire d'Outre-Mer: Mélanges en l'honneur de Jean-Louis Miège.* 2 vols. Aix-en-Provence, 1992.

Miers, Suzanne, and Richard Roberts, eds. *The End of Slavery in Africa.* Madison, Wisc., 1988.

Mohamed al-Mukhtar w. as-Sa ᶜd. "Emirats et espace émiral maure: Le cas du Trarza aux XVIIIe et XIXe siècles." *REMMM* 54 (1989).

Mohamedou Ould Mohameden. "Les tentatives de pénétration française dans le pays maure à travers le rapport de mission de Bu El Mogdad en 1894 au Tagant." *Masadir* 1 (1994).

Moitt, Bernard. "Slavery and Emancipation in Senegal." *IJAHS* 22 (1989).

Mollien, Gaspard. *Travels in the Interior of Africa.* London, 1820.

Monod, Théodore. "Un poème mystique soudanais." *Le Monde non-chrétien,* no. 2 (1947).

Monod, Théodore. "Un homme de Dieu: Tierno Bokar." *Présence Africaine,* 8–9 (1950).

Monteil, Charles. *Les Khassonkés.* Paris, 1915.

Monteil, Parfait-Louis. *Souvenirs Vecus: Quelques feuillets de l'histoire coloniale: Les rivalités internationales.* Paris, 1924.

Monteil, Vincent. *Islam noir.* Paris, 1964.

————. *Esquisses sénégalaises.* Dakar, 1966.

Ndiaye, Francine. "La colonie du Senegal au temps de Brière de l'Isle, 1876–1881." *BIFAN,* ser. B, 30 (1968).

Newbury, Colin. "The Formation of the Government General of French West Africa." *JAH* 1 (1960).

Noirot, Ernest. *A Travers le Fouta-Diallon et le Bambouc (Soudan occidental).* Paris, 1882.

Nord, Philip. *The Republican Moment: Struggles for Democracy in 19th c. France.* Cambridge, Mass., 1995.

Norris, H. T. *Saharan Myth and Saga.* Oxford, 1972.

Oloruntimehin, B. Olatunji. "Abd al-Qadir's Mission as a Factor in Franco-Tukulor Relations, 1885–1887." *Genève-Afrique* 7 (1968).

Ouane, Ibrahima, *L'Empire toucouleur d'El Hadj Omar: L'Enigme du Macina.* Monte Carlo, 1952.

Ould Ahmedou, Mohamed Saïd. "La Mauritanie, Saint-Louis, et la gomme aux XIXe siecle." *Annales de la Faculté des Lettres et Sciences Humaines* (Nouakchott) no. 2 (1990).

———. "Coppolani et la conquête de la Mauritanie." *Masadir* 1 (1994).

Ould Cheikh, Abdel Wedoud. "La tribu comme volonté et comme répresentation: Le facteur religieux dans l'organisation d'une tribu maure: Les Awlad Abyayri." In *Al-Ansab: La quête des origines,* ed. Bonte et al.

———. "Les fantômes de l'amir: Note sur la terminologie politique dans la société maure précoloniale." *Maghreb Review* 22 (1997).

———. "Harun Wuld al-Shaikh Sidiyya, 1919-1977." In *Le Temps des Marabouts,* ed. Robinson and Triaud.

———. "Les perles et le soufre: Une polémique mauritanienne autour de la Tijaniyya, 1830-1935." In *La Tijaniyya,* ed. Triaud and Robinson, 2000.

Paden, John. *Religion and Political Culture in Kano.* Berkeley, Calif., 1973.

Pasquier, Roger. "Les débuts de la presse au Sénégal." *CEA* 7 (1962).

———. "Les traitants des comptoirs du Sénégal au milieu du XIXe siècle." In *Actes de Colloque Entreprises et Entrepreneurs en Afrique (XIXe et XXe siècles),* ed. Catherine Coquery-Vidrovitch. 2 vols. Paris, 1983.

Perron, M. *Précis de jurisprudence musulmane, ou principes de législation musulmane civile et religieuse, selon le rite malékite, par Khalil Ibn-Ishak.* 6 vols. in 4. (Paris, 1848-52).

Person, Yves. *Samori: Une revolution dyula.* 3 vols. (Dakar, 1968-75).

Pitte, Jean-Robert. *Nouakchott: Capitale de la Mauritanie.* Paris, 1977.

Poulet, Georges. *Les Maures de l'Afrique Occidentale Française.* Paris, 1902.

Quesnot, F. "Influence du Mouridisme sur le Tijanisme." In *Notes sur l'Islam au Sénégal.* Paris, 1962.

Raffenel, Anne. *Nouveau voyage dans le pays des Nègres.* 2 vols. Paris, 1856.

Rancon, André. *Dans la Haute Gambie: Voyage d'exploration scientifique.* Paris, 1894.

Ranger, Terence O. "Taking Hold of the Land: Holy Places and Pilgrimages in Twentieth-century Zimbabwe." *Past and Present* (1987).

Revue Franco-Musulmane et Saharienne, nos. 5-8 (1902-3).

Richmond, J. C. B. *Egypt, 1798-1952.* New York, 1977.

Rinn, Louis. *Marabouts et Khouans.* Algiers, 1884.

Ritchie, Carson. "Deux textes sur le Sénégal, 1673-1677." *BIFAN,* ser. B, 30 (1968).

Rivet, Daniel. *Lyautey et l'institution du protectorat français au Maroc, 1912-1925.* 3 vols. Paris, 1988.

Roberts, Allen, and Mary Nooter Roberts. "L'aura d'Amadou Bamba: Photographie et fabulation dans le Sénégal urbain." *Anthropologie et Sociétés* 22 (1998).

Roberts, Andrew, ed. *The Colonial Moment in Africa.* Cambridge, U.K., 1990.

Roberts, Richard. "Text and Testimony in the Tribunal de Première Instance, Dakar, during the Early Twentieth Century." *JAH* 31 (1990).

Robinson, David. *Chiefs and Clerics: Abdul Bokar Kane and the History of Futa Toro, 1853-1891.* Oxford, 1975.

———. *The Holy War of Umar Tal: The Western Sudan in the Mid-Nineteenth Century.* Oxford, 1985.

———. "The Umarian Emigration of the Late Nineteenth Century." *IJAHS* 20 (1987).

———. "Historien et anthropologue sénégalais: Shaykh Musa Kamara." *CEA* 109 (1988).

————. "French 'Islamic' Policy and Practice in Late Nineteenth-Century Senegal." *JAH* 29 (1988).

————. "Beyond Resistance and Collaboration: Amadu Bamba and the Murids of Senegal." *Journal of Religion in Africa* 21, (1991).

————. "Ethnography and Customary Law in Senegal." CEA 126 (1992).

————. "Hedging Bets: Shaikh Mamadu Mamudu of Futa Toro." *ISASS* 9 (1995).

————. "Sa`d Buh, the Fadiliyyya, and French Colonial Authorities." *ISASS* 11 (1997).

————. "An Emerging Pattern of Cooperation between Colonial Authorities and Muslim Societies in Senegal and Mauritania." In *Le Temps des Marabouts,* ed. Robinson and Triaud, 2000.

————. "Tokolor." In *Encyclopedia of Islam,* 2nd ed., 1999.

————. "The Murids: Surveillance *and* Accommodation." *JAH* 40 (1999).

————. "Malik Sy, Teacher in the New Colonial Order." In *La Tijaniyya,* ed. Triaud and Robinson, 2000.

Robinson, David, and Jean-Louis Triaud, eds. *Le Temps des Marabouts: Itinéraires et stratégies islamiques en Afrique occidentale française, v. 1880–1960.* Paris, 1997.

Robinson, Ronald. "Non-European Foundations of European Imperialism: Sketch for a Theory of Collaboration." In *Studies in the Theory of Imperialism,* ed. R. Owen and B. Sutcliffe. New York, 1972.

Rocaboy, Commandant Joseph. "L'Hamalisme." *Mémoire du CHEAM* 938 (1947).

Roger, Baron. *Kélédor, histoire africaine.* Paris, 1829.

Roux, Administrator. "Notes sur le Diambour et le Djoloff." *Bulletin de la Société de Géographie de l'AOF* (31 December 1907).

Roy, Olivier. *The Failure of Political Islam.* Cambridge, Mass., 1994.

Saad Buh. "Un mandement de Saad Bouh à Ma el-Ainin." *BCAF/RC,* supp. 11 (11 November 1909).

Said, Edward. *Orientalism.* New York, 1978.

Saint-Martin, Yves. *L'Empire toucouleur de la France: Un demi siècle de relations diplomatiques, 1846–93.* Dakar, 1966.

————. "La volonté de paix d'El Hadj Omar et d'Ahmadou dans leurs relations avec la France." *BIFAN,* ser. B, 30 (1968).

————. "Un fils d'El Hadj Omar: Aguibou, roi du Dingiray et du Macina, 1843?–1907." *CEA* 29 (1968).

————. *Le Sénégal sous le Second Empire.* Paris, 1989.

Sall, Ibrahima Abou. "Cerno Amadu Moktar Sakho, Cadi Supérieur de Boghé, Futa Toro, Mauritanie, 1905–1934." In *Le Temps des Marabouts,* ed. Robinson and Triaud.

————. "Crise identitaire ou stratégie de positionnement politique en Mauritanie: Le cas des Fulbe Aynaabe." In *Horizons nomades en Afrique sahélienne,* ed. André Bourgeot. Paris, 1999.

Samb, A. Marokhaya. *Cadior Demb.* Dakar, 1964.

Samb, Amar. "Sur El-Hadj Omar (à propos d'un article d'Yves Saint-Martin)." *BIFAN,* ser. B, 30 (1968).

————. *Essai sur la contribution sénégalaise à la littérature d'expression arabe.* Dakar, 1972.

————. ed. and trans. "La vie d'El Hadj Omar par Cheikh Moussa Kamara." *BIFAN,* ser. B, 32 (1970).

————. ed. and trans. "L'Islam et le Christianisme par Cheikh Moussa Kamara." *BIFAN,* ser. B, 35 (1973).

————. ed and trans. "La condamnation de la guerre sainte de Cheikh Moussa Kamara." *BIFAN,* ser. B, 38 (1976).

Sanankoua, Bintou, and Louis Brenner, eds. *L'enseignement islamique au Mali.* Bamako, 1991.

Sanders, Edith. "The Hamitic hypothesis: Its Origins and Functions in Time Perspective." *JAH* 10 (1969).

Sanneh, Lamin. *The Jahanke.* London, 1979.

————. *Translating the Message: The Missionary Impact on Culture.* Maryknoll, N.Y., 1989.

Santoir, Christian. *La région du lac Rkiz: Approache géographique et cartographique.* Dakar, 1973.

Saulnier, Eugène. *Une compagnie à privilège au XIXe siècle: La Compagnie de Galam au Sénégal.* Paris, 1921.

Savishinsky, Neil. "The Baye Faal of Senegambia: Muslim Rastas in the Promised Land." *Africa* 64, no. 2 (1994).

Schmitz, Jean, et al., trans. and ed. *Florilège au jardin de l'histoire des noirs: Zuhur al-Basatin,* by Shaikh Musa Kamara. Vol. 1. Paris: 1998.

Schneider, William. *The Image of Africa in the Popular Press.* Chapel Hill, N.C., 1980.

Searing, James. *West African Slavery and Atlantic Commerce: The Senegal River Valley, 1700–1860.* Cambridge, U.K., 1993.

Seck, Bou-El-Moghdad. "Voyage par terre entre le Sénégal et le Maroc." *Revue Maritime et Coloniale* 1 (1861).

Seck, Dudu. See Désiré-Vuillemin.

Seed, Patricia. *Ceremonies of Possession in Europe's Conquest of the New World, 1492–1640.* Cambridge, U.K., 1995.

Sibeud, Emmanuelle. "La naissance de l'ethnographie africaniste en France avant 1914." *CEA* 136 (1994).

Sinou, Alain. *Comptoirs et villes coloniales au Senegal.* Paris, 1993.

Skinner, David. "Islam and Education in the Colony and Hinterland of Sierra Leone, 1750–1914." *Canadian Journal of African Studies* 10, (1976).

Snouck Hurgronje, C. "Politique musulmane de la Hollande." *RMM* 5, (1911).

Soh, Sire Abbas. *Chroniques du Fouta sénégalais.* Ed. and trans. M. Delafosse and H. Gaden. Paris, 1913.

Soleillet, Paul. *Voyage à Ségou de Paul Soleillet, 1842–86, rédigé d'après les notes et journaux de Soleillet.* Ed. Gabriel Gravier. Paris, 1887.

Stepan, Alfred. *Rethinking Military Politics: Brazil and the Southern Cone.* Princeton, N.J., 1988.

Stewart, Charles. "A Mauritanian Reformer: Shaikh Sidiyya Baba." *Tarikh* 7, no. 25 (1971).

————. "Colonial Justice and the Spread of Islam in the Early Twentieth Century." In *Le Temps des Marabouts,* ed. Robinson and Triaud.

Stewart, Charles, with Elizabeth Stewart. *Islam and Social Order in Mauritania.* Oxford, 1973.

Sy, Cheikh Tidiane. *La Confrérie sénégalaise des Mourides.* Paris, 1969.

Terrier, Auguste, and Charles Mourey. *L'expansion française et la formation teritoriale: Gouvernement Général de l'AOF.* Paris, 1910.

Thilmans, Guy. "Lat Dior, Cheikh Saad Bou, et le chemin de fer." *Saint-Louis-Lille-Liège,* no. 1 (1992).

Tomlinson, G. J. F., and G. J. Lethem. *History of Islamic Political Propaganda in Nigeria.* London, 1927.

Triaud, Jean-Louis. "Khalwa and the Career of Sainthood: An Interpretative Essay." In *Charisma and Brotherhood in African Islam,* ed. Cruise O'Brien and Christian Coulon.

———. *La légende noire de la Sanusiyya? Une confrérie musulmane sous les regard français, 1840–1930.* Paris, 1995.

Triaud, Jean-Louis, and David Robinson, eds. *La Tijaniyya: Une confrérie musalmane à la conquête de l'Afrique.* Paris, 2000.

Tyam, Mohammadou Aliou. *La Vie d'El Hadj Omar: Qaçida en poular.* Ed. and trans. Henri Gaden. Paris, 1935.

Umar Tal. *Kitab Rimah Hizb al-Rahim ʿala Nuhur Hizb al-Rajim.* Published in the margins of Ali Harazim, *Kitab Jawahir al-Maʿani wa Bulugh al-Amani.* Cairo, 1383AH/ 1963–64.

Verite, Monique. *Odette du Puigaudeau: Une bretonne au desert.* Paris, 1993.

Villalon, Léonardo. *Islamic Society and State Power in Senegal.* Cambridge, U.K., 1993.

———. "The Moustarchidine of Senegal: The Family Politics of a Contemporary Tijan Movement." In *La Tijaniyya,* ed. Triaud and Robinson, 2000.

Wane, Yaya. "Ceerno Muhammadu Sayid Baa ou le soufisme intégral à Madina Gunaas." *CEA* 14 (1974).

Webb, James, Jr. *Desert Frontier: Ecological and Economic Change along the Western Sahel, 1600–1850.* Madison, Wisc., 1994.

Whitcomb, Thomas. "New Evidence on the Origins of the Kunta." *BSOAS* 38 (1975).

Willis, J. R., ed. *Studies on the History of Islam in West Africa.* Vol. 1. London, 1979.

Wooten, Stephen. "Colonial Administration and the Ethnography of the Family in the French Soudan." *CEA* 131 (1993).

Wuld al-Bara, Yahya. "Les théologiens mauritaniens face au colonialisme." In *Le Temps des Marabouts,* ed. Robinson and Triaud, 1997.

Zuccarelli, François. "Les maires de Saint-Louis et de Gorée de 1816 à 1873." *BIFAN,* ser. B, 35 (1973).

———. "De la chefferie traditionnelle au canton: Evolution du canton colonial au Sénégal, 1855–1960." *CEA* 13 (1973).

———. *La vie politique sénégalaise, 1789–1940.* Paris, 1987.

Index

Page references in **bold** indicate main treatment of important subject.